Humans and Machines

Delaware Symposia on Language Studies

Series Editor

Robert J. Di Pietro

1 *First Delaware Symposium on Language Studies,* Robert J. Di Pietro, William Frawley, and Alfred Wedel, Editors (University of Delaware Press)

2 *Linguistics and the Professions,* Robert J. Di Pietro, Editor

3 *Linguistics and Literacy,* William Frawley, Editor (Plenum Press)

4 *Humans and Machines,* Stephanie Williams, Editor

5 *Languages in the International Perspective,* Nancy Schweda-Nicholson, Editor

6 *Second Language Research in the Classroom,* James P. Lantolf and Angela Labarca, Editors

HUMANS AND MACHINES

Stephanie Williams, Editor

Delaware Symposium 4

Proceedings of the 4th Delaware Symposium on Language Studies
October 1982
The University of Delaware

ABLEX PUBLISHING CORPORATION
NORWOOD, NEW JERSEY 07648

Printed in the United States of America.

Library of Congress Cataloging in Publication Data

Delaware Symposium on Language Studies (4th : 1982 :
University of Delaware)
Humans and machines.

(Delaware symposia on language studies ; 4)
Includes bibliographies and index.
1. Linguistics—Data processing—Congresses.
2. Language and languages—Computer-assisted instruction
—Congresses. I. Williams, Stephanie. II. Title.
III. Series: Delaware Symposium on Language Studies.
Delaware symposia on language studies ; 4.
P98.D39 1982 410'.28'54 84-20359
ISBN 0-89391-272-7

Ablex Publishing Corporation
355 Chestnut Street
Norwood, New Jersey 07648

CONTENTS

Preface to the Series Delaware Symposia on Language Studies

Robert J. Di Pietro
Series Editor

The volumes in this series are intended to bring to larger audiences select papers from the annual symposia on language studies held at the University of Delaware. These symposia are sponsored by the Program in Linguistics at the University. Each year, a general theme is chosen in the application of linguistics and a call is sent out for papers dealing with that theme in some way. The abstracts received as a result of this call are evaluated anonymously by a committee of linguists. The program for each symposium is made up of the papers chosen through this evaluation process. In addition to the refereed papers, several plenary lectures are arranged, and invitations to present them are sent out to leading scholars in the field. A second evaluation takes place after each symposium, and results in the papers which we publish here.

The present volume, edited by Stephanie Williams, is the first of the series. It comprises the proceedings of the fourth symposium, held in October, 1982. The first symposium took place in the Fall of 1979 and dealt with linguistic studies of language contact, second-language acquisition, and bilingualism. Papers from that symposium have been published by the University of Delaware Press under the editorship of Robert J. Di Pietro, William Frawley, and Alfred Wedel. The second symposium addressed the application of linguistics to law, medicine, business, and governmental bureaucracy. The proceedings of the second symposium were edited by Robert J. Di Pietro under the title *Linguistics and the Professions* and are available as Volume VIII in the Ablex series Advances in Discourse Processes. The papers of the third symposium have been edited by William Frawley and are being published by the Plenum company under the title *Linguistics and Literacy*.

Henceforth, all proceedings volumes will follow the present one as part of this special series. Thanks to a close collaboration between Ablex and the Program in Linguistics at Delaware, a broad range of interested readers will have accessibility to these significant and timely papers.

Introduction

At a time when information technologies are undergoing rapid development, computer usage likewise has expanded to include not only areas of business and government, but also such fields as medicine, agriculture, and even education. This modern technology has increased the speed at which information can be collected, sorted, analyzed, and stored, thus making available to the teacher and manufacturer alike greater amounts and a greater variety of knowledge from which to draw in the development of new ideas and the reinvestigation of old.

This volume combines research conducted in the area of computers and programmed language with current issues in linguistics and second language teaching. The fundamental connection between language education and information processing has emerged in recent years, as numerous prominent linguists have turned their attention to the computer. Its ability to constitute a permanent archive for use in linguistic research of all kinds, above all in projects where a scholar would find data gathering, indexing, and retrieval to be too tedious to attempt by traditional means, has been its primary attraction.

Interest in the computing field, however, has not all been unidirectional, for the information analyst has likewise needed to turn to linguistics and language education for models, techniques, and explanations required in language programming. Thus, the pressing theoretical and practical problems encountered by scholars in both fields have produced the type of cross-disciplinary research that this volume discusses.

The essays contained herein were originally scheduled for presentation and/or presented at the fourth annual Delaware Symposium on Language Studies, held in October, 1982 at the University of Delaware. They are divided into three principal sections: 'The Technology of Computers', 'Computer Assisted Instruction', and 'Delaware Summer Institute in Computer Assisted Instruction for Foreign Languages'. The latter presents an overview and reports the results of the University of Delaware's summer language institute, held from June to July, 1982, in which 30 secondary school foreign language teachers participated.

Linda Garcia's 'Computer Literacy in an Information Age' paints a historical portrait of the related development of technology and literacy in the United States, and offers new images of the effects of the new computer technology and computer literacy upon our society. The United States is fast becoming an information-oriented society—a society in which socioeconomic status and political power depends on the individual's ability to gain access to information for evaluation and manipulation purposes. And if this trend is to serve as an indication of the future of our nation, then the individual must embark now upon the road to acquiring knowledge of computers and of their capabilities and limitations. As the new computer technology has increased our access to information, so must we enhance our ability to use information to account for past actions and predict future events through the fostering of a public understanding of the use of the new computer technology.

As the information industry is awakening to the social implications of problems in the use of computers, researchers in both psychology and computer science are actively investigating the area of human-computer interaction. This interaction is treated by Galambos et al. in 'A Diagrammatic Language for Instruction of a Menu-Based Word Processing System'. The paper, a description of a Learning and Using Systems Project conducted at Yale University, applies some of the relevant principles of cognitive psychology to the designing of instructional materials. The authors view, as the major goal of the LUSP study, increasing computer literacy by developing training techniques that can be used to teach computer use more effectively, and by devising ways to design systems that are easier to learn and use.

The computer as an aid to military, government, to the businessman, the designer, the manufacturer, and to the educator has met with comparatively more success than its function as an aid to the language translator. The reasons for its lack of success, explains Alan K. Melby ('Machine Translation Vs. Translator Aids: A False Dichotomy'), lie in the widely held belief that computer translation must produce a fully-automatic, high-quality translation. A new and opposing viewpoint has proposed that the computer, in its function as an AID to translation, be utilized strictly as a tool at the discretion of the human translator. If this more modified view of machine translation is adopted and incorporated into a system of translator aids, the author contends, then the dichotomy existing between machine translation and translator aids will become unnecessary. Melby describes in brief a successful system (based upon the aid approach) which is presently being used by the Canadian government to translate weather forecasts from English into French. He also describes in detail the Brigham Young University translator aid system, still in development, that integrates word processing, terminology access, and machine translation to produce a design which takes pains to insure that the human translator is not eliminated from the task, but rather becomes more productive and effective as he or she retains control of the computer at every level.

The computer, in its many gathering, storing, and retrieving functions, may become the linguist's primary aid in understanding how language is processed, as it is the only entity other than humans (and to some extent, animals) that can relate symbols to the real world they represent. The semantics of a language then, suggests Daniel Chester ('Towards a Natural Language Semantics Formalized in Terms of Physical Symbol Systems') can be specified in a language-free fashion by the employment of the computer as a physical symbol system capable of receiving data through its sensor fields and acting upon that data to the outside world through motor devices. The manner in which the computer accomplishes this semantic bond is through programming, which will reproduce, by digital computer acting upon sensor data, the processes performed by the brain in receiving and decoding incoming signals through neurological sense data.

Computer simulation of the interpretative processes of the brain within the limited framework of ungrammatical but meaningful sentences is accomplished in

'Two Strategies of Robustness for Natural Language Understanding Systems'. The Augmented Transition Network, the tool by which brain functions are simulated by the author, is seen to be of great value in parsing grammatical sentences, as it possesses transformational capabilities which can produce deep structures of the same sort as those of a transformational grammar. Amir M. Razi makes use of the edges and nodes of the Network to process ungrammatical inputs within a computational system through meta-rules. These rules can, by means of parsing, identify grammatical errors and relax the constraints of the grammar, so that a partial interpretation may be assigned, despite errors, to ungrammatical sentences in a manner analogous to that of the human brain.

Use of computers in analyzing the semantics of a language is treated, in addition, by Evens et al. According to these authors, lexical-semantic relations may be useful in the retrieval of both syntactic and semantic information. These relations, identified from a machine-readable form of *Webster's Seventh Collegiate Dictionary* in 'Lexical-semantic Relations for Information Retrieval' and grouped semantically for the purpose of discovering new relations in the defining formulae of the dictionary, have shown a machine-readable dictionary to be the most valuable tool for the automatic extraction of relational information. Furthermore, the relational thesaurus obtained from this extraction can substantially improve recall for a controlled group of queries.

A machine-readable version of Webster's dictionary also serves as the database from which Thomas E. Ahlswede builds a similar relational thesaurus for adjective definitions. The relational lexicon generated by him is the result of the parsing and extracting of semantic information by means of a linguistics string grammar developed by the author, and is intended to ultimately extend the power of an automatic information retrieval system by enabling the system to search for words related to specific adjective entries of a dictionary, the problem of creating programmed languages through the progressive linking of units of text in sequences characteristic of the logic of human discourse. The creation of any artificial semantic metalanguage, then, must ultimately draw on the principles of episodic textual organization if it is to simulate, in any significant way, human language and the human brain. Such work in artificial intelligence, together with recent research in applied linguistics, serves as the point of departure in John W. Oller's treatment of the nature of episodic organization as it relates to second language instruction in 'Episodic Organization and Language Acquisition'. The author discusses four interrelated hypotheses about second language acquisition—input, textuality, expectancy, and episode—in relation to the manner in which they link the event sequences of ordinary experience with the utterances of discourse, or texts. Implications of these hypotheses upon second language materials preparation and instruction are also provided. Comprehension can be facilitated, Oller concludes, 'by capitalizing on the textuality of ordinary experience, respecting its logic, harnessing the cognitive momentum that this logic creates, and in general by employing good story-telling techniques in preparing, packaging, and presenting language teaching materials.'

The computer's function as a valuable tool to the linguist in the collecting, indexing, storage, and retrieval of massive amounts of data is again emphasized in 'Patterns of Textual Cohesion in Genre-Specific Discourse' (Frawley and Smith). The authors, using APL, examine 16,000 word samples of fiction, religion, science, and journalism in order to determine whether texts from these four genres can be so classified because they possess patterns of cohesion peculiar to other texts in the same genres, and different from patterns in other genres. Through frequency and distribution studies of the cohesive function of pronouns in English text, the relative importance of endophoric and exophoric pronominalization, as well as the most dominant syntactic functions of pronouns throughout these four genre, is determined. All findings are discussed in terms of the genres in question and the function of cohesion in texts in general.

The computer is an intelligent entity, as it is capable of 'understanding' language. It manipulates and reacts to symbols and may, therefore, be said to understand language, since language itself is a symbol system. 'Computers and Their frame of Mind—The Linguistics Component' discusses the epistemological and ethical impact of automatic linguistic data processing upon man's view of the computer as an understanding system. It also investigates and rejects the contention that computer programs are not minds by themselves due to their lack of intentionality, and offers in support natural language understanding programs which are indeed capable of understanding, as they analyze meaning linguistically and not biologically. The author, Klaus K. Obermeier then suggests that, by describing language understanding programs of the computer, as accomplished in his work, we may be able to go beyond the structural aspect of language to psychological and philosophical insights into the human mind.

As computers are fast becoming an integral part of the educational system, it is becoming increasingly necessary to develop effective courseware that will exploit the computer to its fullest potential. To assure that economically-feasible and educationally-sound CAI lessons are developed, courseware designers must be guided by the established principles that are procedures of the instructional design process. For it is only by adopting this systematic process, with its emphasis on learner needs, performance objectives, instructional strategies, and evaluation (both formative and summative), that the low quality commercial courseware on the market today will be eliminated. Stephanie Paulauskas and Susanne Holunga, in 'Designing Effective Computer-Assisted Courseware,' develop these objectives by outlining the design process that will guarantee development of effective instructional materials, and by applying this process to the development of writing materials for computer-assisted instruction. Finally, the authors incorporate their ideas into three modes of CAI instruction: drill and practice, tutorial and simulation, and gaming.

'The MENTOR System: An Answer to Problems of Computer-Aided Language Teaching' traces the development, progress and success of the MENTOR system—a computer-based teaching system developed at the University of Melbourne, Australia for the creation, running, and reporting of lesson programs for use at the elementary and intermediate levels of language instruction. The system is not designed as a self-contained teaching system, but rather as a support system for existing courses and structures. Among the advantages of MENTOR, as reported by the author, Roland Sussex, are its suitability for the teaching of other disciplines (due to its initial development on a large, more powerful computer installation), its adaptability for use on microcomputers of the type that are increasingly being found in secondary schools, and its ease of manipulation for teachers and students alike.

'Cohesion in EFL Programs: An Automated Approach to Text Analysis' focuses upon the constraints imposed on Egyptian learners of English by the nature of present EFL programs and pedagogy in Egypt, and on the impact of these constraints upon English proficiency. Thabet investigates these issues through the analysis by computer of three major EFL textbooks utilized in the Egyptian public education system and, in addition, by the machine cataloguing of specific grammatical and cohesive constructs utilized in compositions written by Egyptian students. Conclusions made by the author evaluate the following key issues in Egyptian EFL instruction: (a) the degree of pedagogical cohesion in existing elementary and preintermediate programs; (b) their effects upon aiding students in adopting more than sentential proficiency, i.e., that level of proficiency necessary for the acquiring of a cohesive grammar of composition, and (c) the effects of machine analysis in providing a satisfactory database which yields a conclusive statistical analysis useful in selecting, grading, sequencing, and presenting EFL materials.

'Les Quatre cents Mots: A French Vocabulary Computer Lesson' describes the preliminary results of a triple-format pilot computer program at the University of Delaware. The program, designed to aid students in acquiring a specific vocabulary list, combined classroom instruction with an original-script language-laboratory program and computer lesson. The language-laboratory portion of the program stressed oral comprehension and sound discrimination, and the computer lessons the written form of the language through review of vocabulary lists. The final portion of the program, which utilizes random-access tape recorders in conjunction with computer terminals, is still in the programming stages and remains to be tested. Braun and Mulford review the preliminary results of the first two formats of the program and provide, as well, student reactions to a French vocabulary computer lesson.

The future of the computer as a valuable tool for the teaching of language in its present form, is seen in 'On the Role of the Computer in Foreign Language Instruction' as a dubious one. This assessment is based upon the fact that computer language instruction programs until now have been unable, in any significant way, to engage the learner in language use as it was intended to be used: to communicate real meaning. Instead, a survey of computer-assisted language instruction programs conducted by the author, James P. Lantolf, has revealed that the majority of the earlier-developed programs in use today have incorporated into their format in some form or other drills, error correcting, and analysis, and have utilized these as the major tools in language instruction. The difficulty with this approach is that it destroys the integrity of language by segmenting it into bits and pieces which are isolated from pragmatic contexts. Lantolf concludes then that potentially successful computer-assisted language programs are those which focus on content in a manner that is intensely interesting to the learner. He then reviews a few programs currently in development or use which aim at achieving this communicative interaction between learner and computer.

The current crisis in literacy facing the nation's colleges may be resolved, as suggested in 'Computers, Linguistics, and Basic Writing', by the advent of relatively-inexpensive microcomputers fitted with word processing programs. These programs are especially well adapted to techniques of sentence combining and paraphrasing for teaching writing; and computer assisted instruction allows for an intensity of instruction not achievable by conventional methods. Chaika further explains that, by visually presenting changes in text almost as fast as the brain can produce and comprehend them, and by involving every student in the class in every bit of creating and analyzing, the computer can aid students in working towards the formulation of rules of written discourse on their own.

The role of microcomputers in teaching writing is further investigated by Helen J. Schwartz ('Microcomputers in the Composing Process'). The author reviews various programs which can help students think creatively about their topics, others that can make it easy to create and revise, and special program features which allow students to share their work with other students. Programs reviewed by Schwartz include Burns' program on 'invention'—a program to help students with a systematic search of memory, analysis, and research; a program written by the author, entitled 'Seeing Eye Elephant Network', which asks series of questions that are considered to be conventional in a discipline; and word processing, grammatical correctness, and spelling programs which aid in writing and revision, and in assessing coherence and readibility of written work.

Part 3 of this volume discusses the results of the 1983 University of Delaware Summer Institute in Computer-Assisted Instruction for Foreign Languages. The first essay, by Gerald R. Culley, examines in detail the goals, methods, and structure of the institute as well as the daily and weekly activities in which participants took part. Reactions and implications of computer-assisted instruction for foreign language teaching on the high school level are discussed by three program participants: Richard C. Ten Eyck, from New Jersey; Helen St. Louis, from New York; and Danea A. Caskey, from Maryland. The final essay in this section, entitled 'Developing "Smart" Lessons', (again by Culley), treats the quality of programs presently available for foreign language instruction, and outlines some of the requisites for the development of 'smarter' language lessons—i.e., ones that in some sense are capable of generating their own exercises and of understanding a student's typed responses, even if these responses are not technically correct.

Stephanie Williams

PART I

THE TECHNOLOGY OF COMPUTERS

ONE

Computer Literacy in an Information Age*

Linda Garcia
Office of Technology Assessment
United States Congress

COMPUTER LITERACY: A SOCIALLY MEANINGFUL DEFINITION

Most of the recent discussions about computer literacy have been concerned with trying to reach a consensus about what computer literacy is and what it entails (see, for example, Johnson et al. 1980, Ball & Charp 1977, Billings and Morsund 1979, Molnar 1978). Writing from the perspectives of different groups and different disciplines, authors addressing the subject have arrived at a widely varying list of things one must know, or be familiar with, in order to be computer literate. On such a list there might be included, for example: knowledge of computer science, programming experience, hands on experience as an end-user, an understanding of computer capabilities and limitations, an understanding of algorithmic thinking, and an understanding of the ethical and societal issues raised by the large scale demployment of computers.

This effort to characterize computer literacy as a set of computer-related skills may help educators to develop a curriculum to foster public understanding, familiarity, and appreciation of the use of the computer. It fails, however, to provide a basis for assessing the social and individual value of computer literacy. It fails, moreover, to provide a basis for understanding 'who' needs 'how much' and 'what kind' of literacy in order to effectively carry out 'which' tasks in present day American society. Before we, as a society, can make intelligent policy decisions about the use of and access to computer technology, we will need to have such an understanding.

Literacy is a relative term, which can only be meaningfully defined in terms of the socioeconomic context in which people must work and live (Heath 1980). The level and kinds of skills that constitute literacy, and the degree of access to these

* This paper relies heavily on information generated during the recent OTA assessment, *Information Technology and its Impact on American Education*. However, the views, as they are expressed here, reflect the author's personal opinions, and do not represent the perspective of the Office of Technology Assessment.

skills, has varied in different times and places. How societies have viewed literacy has reflected their underlying values and the structure of their political and socioeconomic orders.[1] Definitions of literacy have become more rigorous and the need for literacy more widespread as the role of the individual in society has been enhanced, and as the tasks that individuals perform have become more intellectually demanding.

LITERACY IN AMERICA

Americans have traditionally supported the goal of universal literacy. By providing for universal literacy, Americans hoped to achieve a number of goals. Literacy was seen, first of all, as a prerequisite of democracy. Remarking upon the importance that Americans attached to the role of education, Alexis de Tocqueville, the well-known commentator on American society, noted in 1831:

> Everyone I have met up to now, to whatever rank of society they belong, has seemed incapable of imagining that one could doubt the value of education. They never fail to smile when told that this view is not universally accepted in Europe. They agree in thinking that the diffusion of knowledge, useful for all peoples, is absolutely necessary for a free people like their own, where there is no property qualification for voting or for standing for election. That seemed to be an idea taking root in every head. (de Tocqueville 1971)

The American commitment to education grew in the wake of the Civil War. Concerned about the problems of reconstruction in the South, the influx of Catholic immigrants, and the advent of industrialization in the North, Americans saw in education a way of providing access to a common, and therefore a unifying, culture (Tyack and Hansot 1981). Moreover, in the period of urbanization and rapid industrialization that followed the Civil War, literacy came to be viewed as essential to industrial growth and economic development. By educating the public, Americans hoped to prepare a growing number of people from increasingly different social, economic, and ethnic backgrounds for an increasingly differentiated set of economic rules.

As the institutional means for universal public literacy, Americans established a wide range of public educational institutions—schools, institutions of higher education, libraries, and museums. This commitment to public education is, as de Toc-

---

[1] Decisions that society takes to affect literacy can serve a variety of ends and have a variety of consequences. To impose political unity on their empire, the Romans, for example, made Latin the official language and the use of it a necessary requirement for literacy. The Catholic Church restricted access to literacy skills in order to preserve both its institutional authority and Christian dogma. In opposition to the Church's authority, literacy was redefined during the Reformation to be essential for those middle class individuals who were considered to be responsible for carrying out the economic affairs of society. Philosophers of the Enlightenment extended the scope of this definition, believing universal literacy to be necessary to the dignity of man and to the effective functioning of a democratic society. (Wick 1980)

queville noted, quite unique. While the governments of most modern industrial societies have provided public support for educational institutions, in no other country have these institutions been conceived of as such an integral part of the political, social, and economic order. In no other country have they been established with such deliberate purpose and public expectation.[2]

While Americans have always supported the goals of universal literacy, the idea of what constituted literacy has changed significantly over time. In the earliest period of American history, for example, a person would have been considered literate if he could write his name and read his catechisms or familiar passages from the scriptures. Today, in contrast, just to be able to fill out an income tax form an individual needs to read at between the 10th and the 12th grade levels (Graham 1981).

The increasing skill levels needed to operate effectively in society helps to explain how it can be that, while Americans in general have had more education than ever before (measured in terms of years of schooling), many of them are considered in today's world to be illiterate. It has been estimated, for example, that 23,000,000 Americans—that is to say, 1 in 5 adults—are unable to read and write well enough to handle the minimal requirements of daily life. Thirty million more people are only marginally qualified to be productive workers. Demographers predict that this number will continue to grow reflecting the increase in the number of high school dropouts and immigrants from Latin America and Asia (U.S. News and World Report 1982).

Figures such as these have led many educators, parents, and public officials to become increasingly concerned about what appears to them to be a national literacy crisis (Berg 1979, Copperman 1980, Williams 1981). It is in this context that the question of computer literacy can, from a policy perspective, be most usefully framed. Developments in the area of computer technology may not only be partly responsible for increased skill requirements; they may also provide some new kinds of solutions to our more general literacy problem.

---

[2] The American commitment to public education grew in the wake of the Civil War. This commitment was so intense, it gave rise to a national crusade to establish public schools. Americans saw public schooling as a way of preserving the social, economic, and political system. By educating American youth in common, public schools, they hoped to inculcate them with a common set of patriotic, protestant, and republican values. (Tyack and Hansot 1981, Welter 1962)

With the passage of the Morrill Act of 1962, institutions of higher education also received public support. Under this act, land grant colleges open to children of all backgrounds were established to provide education in fields such as agriculture, engineering, home economics, and business administration. Unlike the traditional colleges, the land grant colleges were not isolated communities. Their activities were designed to serve the state. (Kerr 1972).

Libraries, too, benefited from this upsurge of public support. Travelling libraries were founded to bring news and reading materials to rural areas. Book deposit stations were set up in grange halls, neighborhood stores, fire stations, and women's clubs. In the cities, libraries were established not only to provide access to books, but also—like the settlement houses—to provide a haven with adult education programs for a growing number of working-class immigrants. (Mathews 1976)

TECHNOLOGY AND LITERACY

The nature of literacy in any society is affected not only by the policies and actions of its decision-makers, but also by technological developments. Technology can have an effect on literacy in a number of ways. It can, for instance, increase the importance of some skills, while reducing that of others. The invention of letters and the development of a written language had such an effect by increasing the need for analytic skills and diminishing the need for some of the poetic skills that facilitate memorization (Gouldner 1976, Havelock 1980).[3] Moreover, technologies can broaden individuals' access to the skills and information required to be literate. It was in this manner that the invention of the printing press and the development of processes for duplicating books, at the time of the Reformation, provided members of the middle classes with the information and channels of communication necessary to challenge the authority of the traditional literati.

On the other hand, technologies can also, and at the same time, increase the number and level of skills required to be literate, and the number and classes of people who need to have such skills. Thus, while the provision of printed materials to the general public made mass literacy possible, in the long run it also made it necessary. It created a world in which, in order to fully participate, individuals were required to be able to read. It created a world in which societies needed to have a literate citizenry in order to experience social cohesion, political community, and economic growth.

THE NEW INFORMATION TECHNOLOGIES

The last hundred years has witnessed a rush of new information technologies including the telegraph and telephone, broadcast communication, photocopier and facsimile transmission, computers, and related software, each considered to be an equally important technology in its own right. These inventions have increased the speed at which information can be communicated, increased the quantity of information that can be collected, stored, manipulated, and transmitted, increased access to information, and enhanced our ability to use information to account for past actions and to predict future events.

In the next few decades, information technologies will continue to undergo rapid development, and will be applied to an ever expanding number of activities and tasks. The microprocessor, an inexpensive, mass-produced computer on a chip, will become ubiquitous in the home, the office, and in industry—not only in the easily identifiable form of the personal computer, but also as a component of numerous other consumer products and services. Highspeed, low-cost communication links will be available in such forms as two-way interactive cables, direct broadcast satellites, and in further evolution of computer-enhanced telecommunication ser-

[3] Even at the time when letters were first introduced, Plato anticipated that their widespread use might have just such an effect. He feared that by allowing people to rely on external aids for their memories, writing might foster forgetfulness. (Plato 1928)

vices. New video technologies such as video disks and high resolution television will also be available. These technologies will be integrated to form new and unexpected types of information processing, retrieval, and storage products and services that can be provided over telephone or cable or be broadcasted directly into the home.

THE INFORMATION SOCIETY

The development and widescale deployment of the new information technologies have helped to give rise to what some social observers have characterized as a "post-industrial," or "information," society (Bell 1973, Molitor 1981). In this society, the creation, use, and communication of information will play a central role. Not only will there be more information; there will also be a greater reliance placed upon it.[4]

In the economy, information will serve as the primary economic resource—the most important factor of production. It will become, moreover, a prerequisite to the development and allocation of other resources (Artandi 1979). Given its economic importance, information will be treated less and less as a free good, and more and more as commodity, to be bought and sold in the market place.[5] As the economic value of information and knowledge increases, so too will the economic rewards for those who have the greatest access to it.[6]

---

[4] Already we can see how many businesses and governmental institutions have become dependent upon information and on the information technologies that are needed to manage and process it. Airlines, for example, use computer networks to control passenger reservations, schedule equipment usage and maintenance, and to prepare flight plans. Banks and other financial institutions rely completely on computers and world-wide communications networks for managing accounts, clearing checks, exchanging funds, and for providing a wide variety of new financial services. The Internal Revenue Service and the Social Security Administration require the aid of large automated information systems to handle the accounts of hundreds of millions of clients. And the operation of national defense depends on the use of complex computer-communications systems, both for day to day management of the military establishment and for the command and control of modern sophisticated weaponry.

[5] This trend can already be seen by the rapid growth of the information market place. The information industry, which comprises those enterprises that produce the machines that handle information, runs the communication networks, and employs this technology to provide information products and services, is now the fastest growing sector of the economy. Even in the present depressed economy, this industry has experienced an annual growth rate of over 20%.

[6] The shift in the United States from a manufacturing and agricultural economy to an information and service economy is creating more jobs with information handling requirements. Furthermore, traditional jobs will increasingly require the handling of automated equipment, a trend that is already visible in the office. With the advent of automated information systems, the skills of a secretary in the wired office of the future will be substantially different from what they are today. In fact, the concept of 'secretary' may entirely disappear.

A similar trend will also occur in the factory where robotics and other forms of computer-aided manufacturing are beginning to transform the way that goods are produced. Automation will require that the worker learn new skills oriented toward the operation and control of computerized equipment. Some experts predict, in fact, that within two decades only a few of the present 20,000,000 manufacturing jobs will still exist.

Information will also come to play a central role in the political process. It will increasingly be brought to bear to make decisions about the complex problems of an advanced industrial society. As the value of information to decision-making increases, information and the ability to store, manage, retrieve, and manipulate it will become more important as a source of political power.

Individuals, too, will have to deal with greater amounts and a greater variety of information. Moreover, they will be subject not only to the information that they generate for themselves, but they will also be increasingly subjected to efforts by others to use the same information resources in an attempt to influence their economic and political choices. As the amount of information people receive increases, they may have less time and fewer resources available to process and evaluate it.

An increase in public literacy will be essential to the well being of an information society. Gains in productivity and economic growth will be limited if workers are unable to adopt new techniques, to fill new types of jobs created by innovation, or to conduct basic research and development in promising new fields (OTA 1982). Moreover, no society can remain free and democratic if the public's skills and knowledge fail to keep pace with the growing complexity of the problems that it faces.

THE COMPUTER AS A TOOL FOR LITERACY IN AN INFORMATION AGE

Increased literacy and information skills will also be essential to an individual living in an information society as information will become the primary means by which he can gain access to income, status, and authority (Artandi 1979). To fully participate in the economic, political, social, and cultural life of such a society, the ability to read and write, or even to receive and transmit information with new technologies will not be sufficient. Individuals will have to know how to critically evaluate information and to manipulate it to make it relevant for their own particular needs.

Furthermore, in an information age, people will have to continually update their knowledge. Lifelong education will become the norm, and much more of it will occur outside of traditional educational processes. As information rapidly changes, the emphasis in education will be on process, or how we learn, rather than on content, or what we learn (Mead 1978).

The computer and other related information technologies can play a major role in helping people to develop skills, and to gain access to the information necessary to operate effectively. The computer can, moreover, be used to extend education beyond the boundaries of traditional educational institutions to provide educational services to people who, because of age, location, or physical condition, may have previously been deprived (OTA 1982). Computer technology may even be able to go beyond some of the pedagogical boundaries of traditional educational technologies and to provide new intellectual tools and frames of references (Papert 1980).

Using the computer in this fashion will require knowing more than how computers work, how they are used, and their impact on society (Watt n.d.). To use the computer to one's own, and to its own, advantage will require the kind of familiarity that comes from growing up together. To use the computer as a problem solving tool and to analyze information generated by the computer, an individual will need to be able to program software, to make judgments about the suitability of particular software for particular purposes, and to understand the assumptions, values, and limitations inherent in any software program (Watt n.d.).

LITERACY FOR WHOM?

To be familiar enough with the computer to be able to take advantage of all its benefits will require having access to it on a fairly regular basis. It will also require having access to others who are already skilled in its use. At present only a limited number, and select group, of people have such access—those who already rank high on literacy skills and who can afford and be inclined to purchase computers and other related information technologies for their homes. Hardware manufacturers and software developers continue to gear their products for the home market while, in most cases, schools and other educational institutions lack the financial, human, and institutional resources necessary to incorporate computers into their programs in a meaningful way.

The circumstances in this country today are not so different from those that existed in the period that followed the Civil War when we sought, with education, to reunite and reconstruct our nation. Moving towards a new economic base, we face problems of economic dislocation and readjustment. Confronted with an increase in the amount and diversity of informational stimuli, we lack social cohesion and political community. As in the past when we looked to public institutions to provide literacy on a universal basis, so too we now may need to support our public institutions to assure that the new computer technologies, and the skills that derive from them, are equally accessible to, and provide a common cultural context for, all.

REFERENCES

ABBOTT, WILLIAM. 1977. Work in the year 2001. The Futurist, February.

______. May 17, 1982. Ahead: A nation of illiterates? U.S. News and World Report.

ARTANDI, SUSAN. 1979. Man, information, and society: New patterns of interaction. Journal of the American Society of Information Science, January.

BALL, MARION, and SYLVIA CHARP. 1977. Be a computer literate. Morristown, NJ: Creative Computing Press.

BELL, DANIEL. 1973. The coming of post industrial society. New York: Basic Books.

BERG, PAUL C. 1979. Who is literate? Compact, Summer 11–13.

BILLINGS, KAREN, and DAVID MOURSUND. 1979. Are you computer literate? Dilithium Press.

COHEN; DAVID K., and BARBARA NEUFIELD. 1981. The failure of high school and the progress of education. America's schools: Public and private. Daedalus, Summer.

COPPERMAN, PAUL. 1980. The decline of literacy. Journal of Communication, Winter 113–120.

CORNISH, EDWARD. 1981. The coming of an information society. The Futurist, April.

DRUCKER, PETER. 1970. Technology, management, and society. New York: Harper & Row.

EISENSTEIN, ELIZABETH L. 1980. The emergence of print culture in the west. Journal of Communication, Winter 95–105.

GOODY, J., and L. P. WATT. 1963. The consequences of literacy. Comparative Studies in the History of Society 5.304–345.

GOULDNER, ALVIN. 1976. The dialectic of technological change.

GRAFF, HARVEY J. 1979. The literacy myth. New York: Academic Press.

GRAHAM, PATRICIA ALBJERG. 1981. Literacy: A goal for secondary schools. America's schools: Public and private. Daedalus, Summer.

HALD, ALAN. 1981. Towards the information-rich society. The Futurist, February.

HAMRIN, ROBERT. 1981. The information economy: Exploiting an infinite resource. The Futurist, August.

HANSON, THOMAS P., DANIEL L. KLASSEN, RONALD E. ANDERSON, and DAVID C. JOHNSON. 1981. What teachers think every high school graduate should know about computers. Schools Science and Mathematics, October 462–467.

HAVELOCK, ERIC A. 1980. The coming of literate communication to western culture. Journal of Communication, Winter 80–98.

HEATH, SHIRLEY BRICE. 1980. The functions and use of literacy. Journal of Communication, Winter 123–132.

JOHNSON, DAVID C., C. ANERSONE, RONALD E. HANSON, and DANIEL L. KLASSEN. 1980. Computer literacy—what is it? Mathematics Teacher 73.91–96.

JOHNSON, MILDRED FITZGERALD. 1980. Computer literacy: What is it? Business Educational Forum 35.18–22.

KERR, CLARK. 1972. The uses of the university. Cambridge, A: Harvard University Press.

MATHEWS, U. H. 1976. Libraries for today and tomorrow. New York: Doubleday.

MEAD, MARGARET. 1978. Culture and commitment, the new relationships between the generations in the 1970s. New York: Anchor Books.

MOLITOR, GRAHAM. 1981. The information society: The path to post-industrial growth. The Futurist, April.

MOLNAR, ANDREW R. 1978. The next great crisis in American education: Computer literacy. Technological Horizons in Education.

———. 1981. The coming of computer literacy: Are we prepared for it? Education Technology, January 26–28.

PAPERT, SEYMOUR. 1980. Mindstorms, children, computers, and powerful ideas. New York: Basic Books.

PLATO. 1928. Phaedrus. The works of Plato, ed. by I. Edman. New York: Modern Library.

ROLAND, JOHN. 1979. The microelectronic revolution: How intelligence on a chip will change our lives. The Futurist, April.

OFFICE OF TECHNOLOGY ASSESSMENT. 1982. Informational technology and its impact on American education. Washington, DC: U.S. Congress.

SERLING, ALBERT M. 1979–1980. The measurement of public literacy. College Board Review 114.26–29.

TOCQUEVILLE, ALEXIS DE. 1831/1971. Journey to America (George Lawrence, trans.). New York: Anchor Books.

TYACK, DAVID, and ELIZABETH HANSOT. 1981. Conflict and consensus in American public education. America's schools: Public and private. Daedalus, Summer.

WATT, DANIEL. n.d. Education for citizenship in a computer based society.

WELTER, RUSH. 1962. Popular education and democratic thought in America. New York: Columbia University Press.

WESTON, ALAN F. 1982. Information abuse and the personal computer. Popular Computing, August 112–116.

WILLIAMS, J. D. 1981. The literacy crisis: A time for reevaluation. The College Board Review 19.20–21, 28–29.

TWO

A Diagrammatic Language for Instruction of a Menu-Based Word Processing System*

James A. Galambos
Yale University

Marc Sebrechts
Wesleyan University

Eloise Wikler
Yale University

John Black
Yale University

The use of computers is fast becoming a basic requirement for dealing with everyday life. Many people use computers when going to a bank, using a telephone, driving a car, operating a TV or stereo, or setting a digital watch. The use of all these devices (and more) now, or in the near future, will involve operating computers that are built into them. If everyone will need to use computers, it will be necessary to teach how to use them. However, computers can be difficult to operate and there are important questions concerning how best to instruct people in their use. In this paper, we will discuss the instruction of a common type of computer system, the word processor. In so doing, we hope to address the more general issue of how to teach people of varying abilities how to use computers.

There are, moreover, some very important social issues involved. For example, there is the real danger of a stratification of society into computer literates, who can deal with this new world, and computer illiterates, who cannot. The problem extends into the workplace. One of the major economic and social difficulties facing American society in the next few years will be how to retrain workers who have lost their jobs in production-line, labor-intensive, heavy industry. The clear trend is that a worker with computer skills is an employed worker, while the worker without such skills finds it harder to stay employed.

It is thus important to increase the amount of COMPUTER LITERACY in our society. Computer literacy is a buzz-word for understanding how a computer works,

* The writing of this paper and the research described was funded by a grant from IBM Corporation. We would like to thank Jack Carroll and Bob Mack of IBM Thomas J. Watson Research Center, Yorktown Heights, New York, for their valuable suggestions and discussions concerning this work. We are also grateful for the efforts of Joe Deck of Wesleyan University, and Rick Wagner of Yale University, both important contributing members of the Learning and Using Systems Project.

what it can do, and how to make it do what you want. We are trying to increase computer literacy by developing training techniques that can be used to teach computer use more effectively, and by devising ways to design systems that are easier to learn and use. We hope that the results of our studies will help ease the transition from a fundamentally computer-naive population to a more computer-literate society.

The Role of Psychology in Computer Science

The social implications of the problems in computer use are quite far reaching. An important part of the solution involves investigating the ways in which the human and the computer interact with each other. The computer industry is awakening to this problem, and researchers in psychology and computer science are actively investigating the area of human-computer interaction. However, this interest in making computers easier to use is new.

It was not so many years ago that computers were operated solely by self-appointed wizards. If one wanted to interact with the computer, it was through the intervention of these mystics (and often with punched paper tape or decks of Hollerith 80 column cards). The notion that people could interact with the computer without this intervention took a while to catch on. There was a default solution to the problem of human-computer interaction: just don't let humans interact with computers at all.

This solution did not hold up. With the development and increasing use of CRT terminals and interactive computer operating systems, the number of computer USERS increased dramatically. With the advent of mini computers in offices too small to support fulltime computer operators, and with the introduction of micro computers into the home, finally some serious attention was paid to the question of how to make the computer more approachable by people who do not need to know all the technical details about computers. These office workers or home computer users typically want to use the computer casually to solve small sets of recurring problems. Such uses include managing accounts receivable, playing games, balancing the checkbook, and word processing. These tasks do not require that the users have degrees in computer science. Computer-literate people, using well designed systems, should be able to perform these tasks with relative ease. There is still much to be done to make this goal a reality.

Defining the Problem. There are two general strategies to the problem of making the computer easier to use. The first is the systems design strategy. This involves the development of systems that are more consistent, rational, and understandable from the user's point of view. The second strategy (and the one on which this paper focuses) is the attempt to develop instructional and documentation materials that facilitate the use of the computer and promote computer literacy. This second strategy (i.e., helping people use an existing system) involves designing better instruction (and documentation) of the programs and systems devised by the system designers. Both of these strategies can benefit from the insight, research, and expertise of disciplines concerned with human behavior. Furthermore, these strategies are not independent. The system design will almost always impact on the way in which it is learned. Similarly, the difficulties that people have with a particular system design should inform the system designers of areas needing improvement.

At Yale University, the Human-Computer Communications Research Group is working on both of these strategies. The emphasis of the Cognition and Programming Project, lead by Elliot Soloway and Kate Ehrlich, is on the systems design strategy. They are investigating a number of issues concerned with designing programming language constructs to accord with the mental models that users bring to the task of programming. The Learning and Using Systems Project (LUSP), lead by John Black, James Galambos, and Marc Sebrechts, emphasizes the second strategy. LUSP is investigating instructional techniques and materials for novice users of stand-alone systems such as word processors. In this paper we will discuss this work in detail.

Documentation. While we will be dealing primarily with instructional materials, there is a second, related, type of supporting documentation which should be discussed briefly (i.e., the reference manual). The lack of availability of useful reference manuals is a problem for new users and also for those who have some familiarity with the system. Anyone who has attempted to work with a large mainframe computer has probably had occasion to grapple with pages and pages of reference documentation. There are often shelves full of supporting information near any medium to large scale computer installation, such as those found in computing centers at universities. As if the mere mass of this information were not enough, the materials always seem to be written BY engineers FOR engineers, and pity the poor mere mortal who attempts to find out how to fix a little error in his first program (or even his twentieth). It is a case of both too much, and yet not enough. There is so much information, but one cannot find the specific bit needed in the present instance.

This is the DOCUMENTATION problem: that is, the problem of finding information about a particular aspect of the functioning of the computer after one has gained some familiarity with the system. The documentation problem concerns how to develop supplementary informational materials (whether in the form of written manuals or on-line help systems) which help the user perform specific tasks using the system. Much of the problem is a result of poor writing, inconsistency, bad organization, unclear descriptions, and so forth. However, it is not likely to be solved merely by clearing up stylistic problems. There are a number of important psychological issues that must be resolved either by empirical means or by psychologically informed choices. The problem is made particularly acute by the trend towards systems that consumers purchase at retail outlets, take home (or to the office), set up themselves, and use. The demands of the marketplace dictate that supporting materials be made understandable by unsophisticated computer users. There are two psychological questions involved: what does it mean for a manual to be understandable, and how can we determine what are the knowledge needs of the user. As this market develops, there will be a sales advantage for those systems that are well documented with documentation that is easy to use and fills the needs of the user.

Instruction. These demands of the marketplace should also lead to concern for the INSTRUCTIONAL problem. A number of the same psychological issues are applicable to this problem as well. However, the instructional materials are aimed at NOVICE users. There are many hurdles that a novice faces on the track to computer literacy. Novices must learn both how to communicate with a computer and something about how the computer understands what the user tells it. There is a good deal of OVERHEAD, in the sense of expenditure of time, involved in beginning to use computers. There is much that novices must learn before they can start to use the particular computer systems to perform specific tasks. Typically, these systems then require additional learning before the users can make the computer do what they want it to do. How can one teach the novice who is confronted with all of this apparent complexity? The underlying psychological questions in this case are how does the learning process take place and how can it be facilitated. These issues are two of the primary questions of psychology and have engaged many scholars in this discipline for their entire careers. Thus, there is a large pool of knowledge that can be evaluated for applicability to the problems of instructing computer use.

The rest of this paper describes our work on the instructional problem, but it is important to note that instruction and reference are not independent. Specifically, the way in which new material is organized during learning will influence how the learner tries to increase his understanding when consulting the reference manuals. For instance, it might be helpful to have the instructional text that one uses to learn a system also serve as the initial reference source when one has a question sometime later. In practice, when a user of the system either forgets how to accomplish some function or needs to know how to perform some new function, the instructional manual is the first source consulted. One solution (which has been adopted in various forms by some manual writers) is to provide information in the instructional manual (e.g., footnotes, or page numbers to refer to in other manuals) which allows the user to index the reference materials for more extensive discussions. There is, however, a trade-off between how much information the experienced user needs to have at his fingertips, and how much material the novice user can wade through when learning the system. This is only one of a number of psychological questions concerning the integration of the two types of information materials which would benefit from further investigation.

THE INSTRUCTIONAL RESEARCH PROJECT

One of the more widespread uses of computer systems is in the creating, editing, and printing of textual documents. Word processing is a fairly complex use of the computer and it requires a good deal of instruction. This paper is a description of a

LUSP study concerned with developing informational materials used to instruct users of word processors. Before getting into the details of the experiment, we give an overview of the research project. Our procedure is to take the existing manual of a word processing system and rewrite it according to a set of principles. These principles have been adapted from a variety of findings in cognitive psychology. We attempt to apply these principles in such a way as to rewrite the existing manual, without making changes in the amount or kind of information provided in the original manual, or in the topic structure of the original. We then teach use of the word processor to a number of naive computer users. Half of the subjects receive their instruction from the original manual, and half from the rewritten manual. Finally, we compare their performance on the system at the end of the 1 week training regimen. Both manuals are tutorial; the user follows instructions as he actually performs the functions on example materials. Thus, the users in both conditions are actually learning by doing. In general, learning by doing aids the recall of information as compared with merely reading about the word processor (see Jacoby 1978 for such a comparison in rote memory for words).

An important additional aspect of this research is that we are examining three DIFFERENT word processing systems in the same way. In so doing, we hope to isolate issues which have more general applications and are not restricted to the idiosyncrasies of a single system. While we will be dealing primarily with the IBM Displaywriter, we have also applied the instructional principles in the rewriting of manuals for the Wordstar word processor (running on a Northstar personal computer and most others with a CP/M operating system), and the UCSD Pascal word processor (running on a Terak micro computer). These three systems (all of which are generally available) share the characteristic of being MENU based word processing systems, although they differ in the ways the menus are organized. It is our hope that applying the principles to three different systems will allow us to examine the generality of the instructional techniques we've developed.

Menu Systems

The MENU SYSTEM is one of the most successful and widely used system design techniques to make the computer easier to use. Any complex program will have a large number of possible operations or functions. It is difficult for the new user to know what can be done when using the program. Menu systems help novices by presenting them with a list of choices (like the list of meals presented to people at a restaurant). For example, Figure 1 shows an example of a menu concerning the selection of the format for a document. This menu list provides users with some information concerning what sorts of things the software can do and occasionally information on how to do them. The items in the list are brief descriptions of the tasks that can be done. In Figure 1, these items include changing the margins and changing the tabs. These descriptions are associated with letters (ID letters) or numbers that can be entered into the computer (e.g., *b* for changing the margins). The tasks can be chosen in a fashion analogous to choosing the answer to a multiple choice test question. Typically, upon entering a selection from the first menu, the

```
FORMAT SELECTION

a     Change Line Format
b     Change Margins
c     Change Tabs
d     Change Page Format
e     Change Header


Type ID letter for choice:_
```

Figure 1. Example Menu.

system displays another menu with the subtasks of the item selected from the first menu. Again referring to Figure 1, if the user selects the item Changing the Margins by entering the ID letter *b,* the system will respond with another menu giving choices related to the ways the margins can be changed. The user can then select one of these more specific items to further define the task he wants to perform. Depending on the complexity of the program, there can be many levels of menus and a user actually accomplishes the task in mind only after making a series of choices from the menus.

The menu system, as a general system design solution, has a number of advantages. It allows the user to become acquainted with the range of possibilities that the system offers. The menus tell the user what operations can be performed, often including descriptions of what those operations do. The menu system helps decrease the information load on users, since they need not keep too much in mind at any one time. It also helps users take advantage of operations which they might not have known how (or when) to use. In short, menu based programs are one type of solution to the problems of making the computer easier to use. Their success is manifest in the number of systems that employ them. The word processing system that we are examining, the IBM Displaywriter, is an example of a system designed to include a fairly extensive menu organization. Menu systems, however, may be used in a wide range of applications (not limited to word processors) where the user can interact with the computer to perform some function (searching for information in a data base, or selecting some particular statistical routine from a statistical package are two examples).

Difficulties in Learning Menu Systems. Menu systems can be arranged hierarchically, in a structure similar to a decision tree. The user moves through a series of menus by making choices from superordinate menus. Contingent upon these choices, the system presents subordinate menus with more detailed items. If the users select the correct item from each menu, they will be able to perform their particular task. Notwithstanding the advantage of menu systems, a number of their shortcomings have surfaced. One problem is making the wrong choice. This can arise from a lack of understanding of what the choices mean, and, in turn, can lead to a wide variety of other difficulties. One of these is that the user can perform some function on a file which changes it in a way that the user did not intend. Carroll and Mack (1982) describe an example of a user who accidentally issued a command which changed the file and stored it away. Not only was it difficult to get back to the file to continue to work on it, but when the file was restored, the change caused other instructions (which the user was in the process of learning from a manual) to work differently. The user was confused when the instructions in the manual did not do the things they were supposed to do.

A second difficulty with making the wrong choice is that novice users can find themselves lost in the menu system. Given the contingent nature of the arrangement of the menus, when an inappropriate choice is made on one menu, the next menu to appear may be irrelevant to the user's needs. As an example, let us say that a novice user sits down to type a letter using a word processor. Assuming that the person can get into the system, he will see the initial, top-level menu which describes, at a very general level, what can be done with the system. This might include printing, creating, editing, formating, filing, and directory listing. It is often unclear which of these items is the appropriate choice. To someone who knows about computer editors the obvious choice is creating, but to the naive user this is far from clear. Let us say that the user picks what seems like a reasonable choice—printing, since clearly what he wants is a letter printed on paper to be able to send off. After the user enters this choice, the system will display a menu that gives a number of functions that are specific to printing (e.g., how many copies are desired, what size paper, etc.). So far the initial error might go unnoticed and the user might ask for three copies. At this point the computer would ask for the name of the document to be printed. At this point it should dawn on the user that something is amiss; but the question is how to get out, how to recover from the mistake made two steps back in the menu path. The user experiences a sense of loss of control.

There are many other ways in which the user can become lost in the system (see Bott 1979, and Carroll & Mack 1982, for a variety of other examples). There are really two problems here; the first is how to make the right choices at each choice point, and the second is how to recover from errors. To make the right choices, the user must understand what the choices mean. Since this cannot be expected of the novice user, the manual must be fairly explicit in the way that it guides the user through the system. Furthermore, some provision for recovery from errors is needed. The poor person in the example above not only made the wrong choice, but probably would not know how to extricate himself from the printing area. At the same time, since the menus guide the user through the system, there is little motivation to understand the organization of the hierarchy or the differences between the different regions in the decision space. It is important that the manual be integrated with the displays on the CRT in such a way as to make clear the reasons for the choices. It is the case quite frequently that the organization of the menus is not understood at all by the casual or novice user.

The Menu Geography Metaphor

You may have noticed that, in describing this problem, we have slid into a metaphor that will play an important role in the instructional technique we are examining. The metaphor of the word processing system is like a geographical entity (albeit a TERRA INCOGNITA at least initially) which has PATHS from one PLACE or REGION to another, and (most importantly) in which someone can become lost. Carroll (1982) has compared learning such menu based systems to playing the adventure computer game in which the players try to find their way around in a maze of caves. Our basic motivation when rewriting the existing manuals was to make the geography of the system more explicit by showing the relationships among the different menus and the regions in the system that they define. We expect that the geography metaphor will aid learning. Part of the reason why it should help is that it allows the development of an image of the organization of the system. There is much evidence from studies of imagery (e.g., Bower 1972) showing that people are particularly good at using spatial images to organize material for better memory at a later time. Further, research on problem solving (Carroll, Thomas, and Malhotra 1980) shows that people are more facile at using spatial, rather than temporal, metaphors when solving problems.

We attempted to develop manuals which would teach the word processor in the way in which one would teach the geography of Central America—by giving the user a set of MAPS to guide his explorations of the system. The maps, or DIAGRAMS, which we developed preserve the sense of which regions are adjacent to which others, and which routes to take to get from one place to another. One of our major assumptions is that we can help the novice learn the word processing system by presenting it as a region with different parts or locations. To do this we need to provide information concerning how to move between locations, including how to leave one area, and how to get to and enter another. The reader should note that a menu system is particularly conducive to this sort of treatment since the menus specify the major areas and their component parts. We have designed a simplified diagrammatic language to describe the relationships between parts of the system.

Survey Diagrams. We developed two different types of diagrams. The first is called a SURVEY diagram and provides an overview of all the relevant regions in the word processing system and how they are related. The survey diagram (Figure 2) was presented in the first topic of the instruction manual. (The original text manual was broken down into 10 chapters which were called TOPICS. We maintained consistency with this manual and called our chapters, topics, as well.)

The purpose of the survey diagram is to provide the learners with a general framework of what parts there are to the system they are learning. The survey diagram contains all the menus that are going to be covered in the following tutorial topics. As seen in Figure 2, the menus are given in boxes (boldface rectangles) with the list of choices available. These boxes represent the information that would appear on the CRT screen when the user is viewing a menu. To continue the analogy with learning the geography of Central America, a survey map gives the large overall picture of the arrangement of countries. Such a large scale map gives the general orientation and relationships of the countries with respect to each other. From such a map one would discover that Mexico is north of Guatemala, that El Salvador is north and west of Panama, and that Nicaragua has both a Pacific coast and a coast on the Gulf of Mexico. In the survey diagram for the Displaywriter, it can be seen, for example, that the Task Selection Menu is the most superordinate and that printing and displaying an index have special status as Request Tasks.

The boxes are connected to each other by directed lines indicating major paths or relationships between the different menus. Thus, the survey diagram provides the novices with a general framework which can serve to organize the tutorials they will receive in the course of their instruction. These tutorials can be thought of as more detailed explorations of the major components of the survey diagram. The survey diagram gives the context for the individual paths in the route diagrams. A secondary advantage of the survey diagram is that it gives the learners an estimate of the amount of material they are to learn. This provides the users with a sense that the system (or, at least, that part of it which they will learn from the manual) is bounded. The training is to proceed by systematically exploring each part of the survey diagram.

The Route Diagrams. The bulk of the manual is devoted to the second type of diagram, called the ROUTE diagram (see Figure 3). There are about 60 route diagrams in our instructional manual; almost every major concept or idea to be learned has its own diagram. (There is an important issue here concerning the unitization or CHUNKING of the information to be learned into meaningful units. We will return to this issue in the next section.) The route diagrams are designed to perform the tutorial function of showing the user how to perform the basic operations in the system. They guide the user through the menus, indicating which choices to make and how to get to the correct place to perform particular operations. The route diagram is similar to the 'triptik' that automobile clubs give out to their members to help them drive to a faraway place. The route diagram specifies which particular actions to take, and at which points, to accomplish the main goal of the tutorial. On each route diagram there is a red line starting at the top of the page and going down through the actions and menus that need to be traversed. (In the figures in this chapter red lines are replaced by dotted lines, but we will continue to refer to them as red lines since that is the way the learners encounter them.) The basic work of the tutorial involves following the red line and doing the actions indicated.

The distinction between a route and a survey map was made by Hart and Moore (1973) in their studies of how children develop an understanding of the relationships among places in their communities. The route maps specify the particular path from one place to another (e.g., from home to school). If that path is blocked, a pure

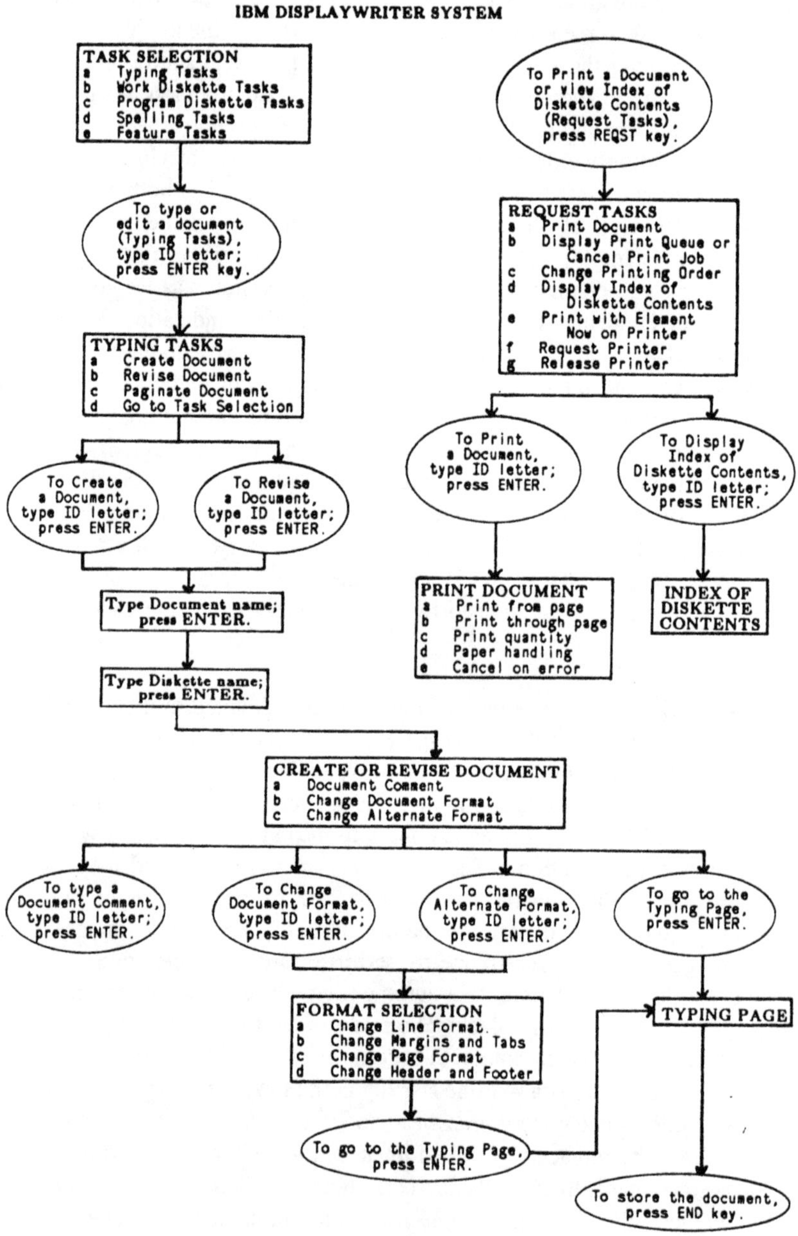

Figure 2. Survey diagram for the IBM Displaywriter Menu System.

CHANGING THE STARTING FORMAT FOR A DOCUMENT (CONT.)

Changing Margins

When you choose the item in the Format Selection menu to change the Margins and Tabs, the instructions for how to make these changes are always in the menu on the display. When this menu is displayed, the scale line cursor is positioned under the current left margin setting. The setting, indicated by << , is highlighted.

Remember, when the highlighted choices in the menu are what you want, you are finished with the menu. As always, when you are finished with a menu, you press ENTER to continue.

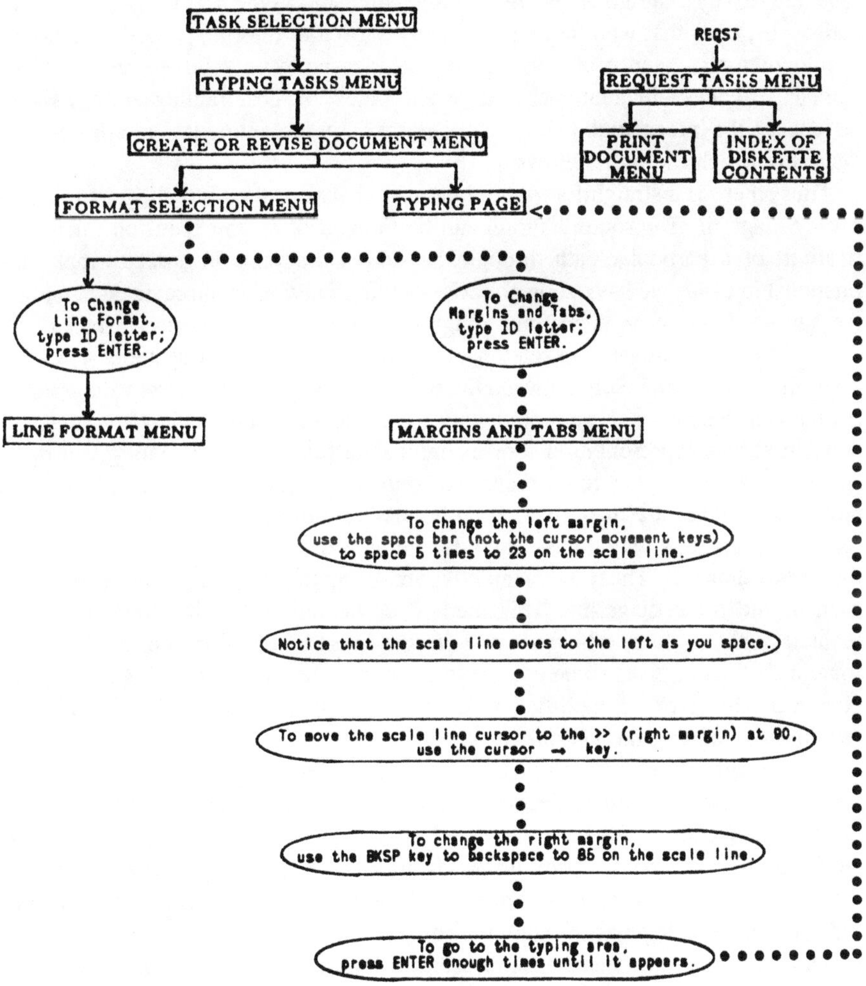

Figure 3. Example page with diagram from the revised manual (dotted lines are used here in place of the red lines and arrows in the actual manual given to subjects).

form of the route map does not provide sufficient information. Route maps are often quite procedural, in the sense that they are learned from actual navigation from starting points to destinations and include landmarks as well as information about what to do when reaching one of these landmarks (e.g., turn left when you come to the MacDonald's). As people increase their experience with some area, their cognitive maps come to resemble surveys (Thorndyke and Hayes-Roth, 1982, Seigel and White 1975). This kind of map represents information about an area, and the places within it, in terms of a fixed set of coordinates. It thus provides the context which can be used to determine paths between two arbitrarily chosen points. In our case, the survey diagram gives information which allows the user to figure out novel paths (i.e., ones that were not taught in any particular tutorial). Since the standard developmental sequence in learning an area is to build up a survey representation from experiences with a number of different routes, the best training strategy should be to teach the information in the survey diagram by presenting it in a series of route diagrams which the user follows.

Thus, there is a straightforward relationship between the route diagrams and the survey diagram. The route diagram can be thought of as an expansion (or magnification) of a particular path through the survey diagram. In order to make this relationship clear, we have adopted the principle of giving an abbreviated version of the survey diagram on each route diagram. We called this the SKELETON of the survey. Figure 4 shows the skeleton of the IBM Displaywriter system. As can be seen, the main relationship between the principle regions on the survey diagram are maintained. However, there is obviously a good deal of condensation from the more detailed survey representation. For example, the full menus are only given in the survey diagram. In the route diagrams, only the menu NAMES are given in the boxes. The boxes are made with slightly heavier outlines and are arranged on the route diagrams in a way that is as consistent as possible with their arrangement on the survey diagram. Thus, the menu boxes make up the skeleton, or framework, for each of the route diagrams. This method of including the skeleton (as well as including other options which we will discuss later) involves an addition to a PURE route map since it gives some context to the particular path involved in the tutorial. However, this type of modified route map should underscore the geographical relationships among the various menus.

In any enterprise such as this, there is the danger that the instructional aid introduces its own complexities in addition to the complexities already inherent in the computer system. We have attempted to avoid this by using a very simple set of conventions in the construction of the diagrams. As shown in Figure 3, there are three basic components: lines, boxes, and circles (more like ellipses). The lines indicate permissible paths through the word processing terrain. The boxes represent system information (either menus or prompts for choices) that appears on the CRT screen at various points. The circles specify actions that the user takes to get from one box (and its associated region) to another.

The basic way in which the users accomplish the task in a given tutorial is to perform the actions specified in the circles, that is, to move from one box to

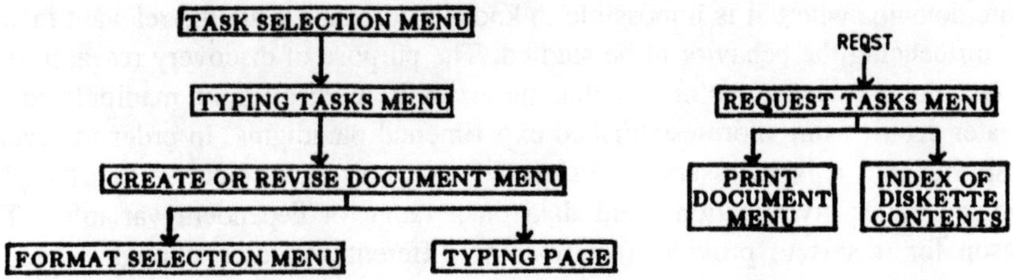

Figure 4. The skeleton of the Displaywriter menu system.

another. They can check the display on the screen to see if they are doing the right things. When they perform an action in a circle, they can compare the information that appears on the screen with the box below that action in the route diagram. If they match, the users can confidently move on to the next action, secure in the knowledge that they are still on the right track. Furthermore, since the place they will ultimately get to (if they follow the directions) is also on the diagram, we remove a certain amount of anxiety concerning whether or not the set of actions that they are performing will take them to their ultimate goal. This can be particularly useful when a long string of actions is needed and, perhaps, some of the earlier ones do not seem to bear a strong resemblance or relationship to the desired end.

Theoretical Issues

Discovery Methodology in Applied Research. As we indicated earlier, the design of the diagram manuals was guided by a number of principles arising from recent work in cognitive psychology. The applications of results from the highly refined and controlled experiments in these fields are typically not direct and obvious. The application domain is sufficiently multifaceted that specific techniques developed in the laboratory may have little success in directly influencing solutions to these problems. Unfortunately, this attitude has taken on the character of a dogma, and this dogma has influenced many researchers against attempting the applications of their findings. It is considerably easier to apply well-established analytic methodologies to the examination of increasingly subtle laboratory phenomena than to explore the applied problems in all their muddiness. In this sense, applied problems should be viewed as challenges for cognitive psychology. Black and Sebrechts (1981) argue that it is to the benefit of both the applied domain and the discipline of cognitive psychology to attempt a reconciliation of the two fields. The authors discuss a number of psychological results that are important to applied concerns. On the other hand, the issues that arise when one attempts to construct systems that are easily learned and used can also lead to important new insights concerning cognitive processes.

The approach that we espouse requires a synthetic attitude. This view is described in Black, Galambos, and Reiser (1984), where some examples of the DISCOVERY methodology are discussed. Discovery methodologies attempt to explore domains where it is impossible to know beforehand what the relevant factors are influencing the behavior to be studied. The purpose of discovery research is to isolate these relevant factors so that they can be controlled or manipulated, in greater detail, using more established experimental paradigms. In order to accomplish this end, it is necessary to design the discovery experiment so that the phenomena under investigation yield data on a range of dependent variables. The reason for this is to provide a number of different windows through which to observe the phenomena of interest. As will become clear when we discuss the variety of measurement techniques we employed in examining the phenomena of learning to use a word processor, this project shares many of the attributes of a discovery experiment.

Mental Models. The primary motivation for this project developed out of concern with the role of COGNITIVE MODELS in the learning of a computer system. The models that are in the minds of the users influence both how they will understand the instructional materials and the system itself. Before starting to learn the word processor, the user has a good deal of knowledge which can be used to make this new skill comprehensible. This might include the knowledge of the skill of typing or filing. The user may try to bring knowledge of this sort to bear on the problem of understanding what this new task is all about. The instructional materials may encourage this use of former knowledge by providing ANALOGIES between the new material and the other tasks. We have tried to encourage the use of a mental model in the form of a SPATIAL IMAGE of the system and its components. The implementation of the geographical metaphor will, hopefully, help the user organize new information into a spatial model of the relationships among the menus in the word processor. Finally, we are interested in the nature of the mental model that the user has of the system at the end of his training, as well as the way in which the user develops that model.

Our investigation of the first of these issues involves the assumption that the user attempts to learn the system by applying his pre-existing knowledge structures. It is important that, wherever possible, the learning situation be structured in such a way as to fit new information into knowledge structures which are well learned, and which have usefully served the users in understanding other aspects of their world. Work in artificial intelligence on frames (Minsky 1975) and scripts (Shank and Abelson 1977) has provided some useful characterizations of this type of knowledge structure. Scripts are configurations of information in memory concerning stereotyped sequences of actions involving the performance of mundane activities. Soloway, Bonar, and Ehrlich (1983) have examined how the learning of programming constructs is facilitated by how well those constructs accord with natural representations of the functions served by those constructs. NATURALNESS is roughly defined as the existence of script-like planning structures which the programmers bring to the task of learning the programming construct. In psychology, Bower, Black, and Turner (1979) have examined the ways in which people use these types of knowledge structures to comprehend new information contained in text. Thus, the knowledge structures that the user brings to the comprehension of the instructional materials and the learning of the system have an important influence on the way in which the system is understood and on the ease with which it is mastered.

The knowledge the user applies to the learning of a computer system can take the form of analogies (like those discussed by Carroll and Thomas 1982, and Gentner and Stevens 1983). These analogies can be misleading in that the lack of fit between the analogy and the target (to-be-learned) domain can result in mistaken inferences or incorrect understanding. For example, common analogies in the word processing domain are to typewriters or filing cabinets. Carroll and Mack (1982) and Halasz and Moran (1982) have examined a number of ways in which this analogy misleads novice users. The problem is that while some of the characteristics of typewriters and filing cabinets are analogous to aspects of word processing, many other characteristics do not apply. It is difficult for the user to know which characteristics are, and which are not, analogous.

The instructional materials should structure learning in such a way that the mental model of the system (as developed by the user in the course of his training) appropriately captures the components of the system and their interrelationships. The present experiment examines the extent to which the geographical metaphor provides a natural structure for the menu system without eliciting misleading inferences.

In our reliance on the spatial characteristics of the geographical metaphor, the instructional materials encourage users to develop a spatial image of the system. Specifically, we intend that the users develop an interacting set of images for the various regions of the system. The survey diagram provides a bird's eye view of the system and the route diagrams spatially represent the details of parts of that system. This arrangement implements some aspects of the Kosslyn and Shwartz (1977) model of mental imagery. Specifically, those researchers found that mental imagery appears to be organized hierarchically with specific details of the image represented at lower levels in the hierarchy. The hierarchy specifies the relationship of the detailed images to the more general overview. In our instructional materials, the use of the skeleton representation on the route diagrams provides a basis for the linking of the particular chunk of information with the overall image of the system.

Finally, we want to determine the nature of the model that the user has of the system at the end of his training and how the model developed during the course of the training. Insofar as it is possible to determine the extent of match between the user's representation of the system and its actual characteristics, it may be possible to determine where improvements in the instructional materials can be made. Thus, we have designed a number of post-tests to attempt to examine how users conceptualize the system they have just learned. One issue here is to what extent the user understands the differences between the different REGIONS of the system in terms of which commands belong in which region.

We want to examine whether the user's knowledge of word processing activities comes to show the characteristics of other well-learned activities, such as those represented by scripts. In order to do this, it is necessary to adapt research techniques used in the examination of script-like knowledge structures. In studies of the knowledge structures for a number of common activities (such as changing a flat tire or writing a letter), Galambos and Rips (1982) and Galambos (1982) demonstrated a number of salient features of the organization of the components (e.g., taking off the hubcap and unscrewing the lugs when changing a flat) of the activities. For example, differences in the CENTRALITY (or importance) of the components to the performance of the activity appear to be represented as differences in strength of association of those actions in the knowledge structures for the activities. Another factor examined in these studies in the representation of SEQUENTIAL ORDER of the actions in the accomplishment of the task. This ordering seems to depend on the causal relations between the actions involved in performing the subgoals of activity.

The materials we developed attempt to make these causal relations explicit by presenting each action the learner performs with the goal for performing that action. This should facilitate the incorporation of the commands and functions into a script-like representation. This representation, if indeed script-like, should provide a representation which organizes the components of the word processing tasks in their correct sequential order. The more general point here is that, insofar as the representations of the activities involved in word processing come to be represented in the same way as other activities, they should show similar patterns. By using some of the reaction time methodology developed by Galambos and Rips (1982), it is possible to examine the representations for information about word processing activities for the presence of script-like characteristics.

Furthermore, it is important to examine the developmental course of the representation of these activities as they become increasingly routine. It is difficult to come up with ways to do this for activities like changing a flat tire. Nonetheless, the ways in which the representations are learned is an important theoretical issue, the answer to which would have a great impact on theories of mental organization. Here, however, is a case where the development of an activity can be observed in reasonably well-controlled conditions. We are using subjects that are quite uncontaminated in terms of their prior knowledge of the target activity. We can observe them as they become increasingly skilled in the activity and can test their knowledge at the end of the training. This is a good example of where experiments in the applied domain can influence theory in cognitive psychology and vice versa.

Diagrams and Flowcharts. The diagrams that comprised the bulk of our manual are superficially similar to the FLOWCHARTS (Goldstein and von Neumann 1947) that textbooks on computer programming used to insist that programmers draw before starting to write the program code (e.g., Aron 1974, Bohl 1971, Farina 1970). There has been something of a controversy among computer scientists as to the utility of drawing flowcharts (see Brooks 1975, Fitter and Green 1979, Shneiderman, Mayer, McKay, and Heller 1977). Although most of the results are somewhat equivocal, it seems there is at least the suspicion that flowcharts don't live up to their reputation as fundamental aids to clear thinking in computer programming. There are important differences between program flowcharts and the diagrams we've developed as instructional aids. For one thing, the diagrams are simpler in the sense that there are only three fundamental components rather than the many different types of state representations in program flowcharts. This may make it easier to use the diagrams since learning the graphical LANGUAGE does not in itself present a hurdle for the user attempting to comprehend the informational content of the representation.

More importantly, the function of our diagrams is quite different from that of flowcharts. We are using the diagrams to structure a tutorial session for novice users. Flowcharts fundamentally are used by programmers to organize their thinking so they can write an efficient program. The research on flowcharts has emphasized the extent to which they serve this planning function. Thus, the research does not directly address whether flowchart-like representations are didactic aids for new users of a pre-existing system. The didactic function of a diagrammatic representation is an important issue that has been insufficiently examined in the flowchart reserach.

Our research examines some of the issues surrounding this controversy in terms of the utility of flowchart-like representations in the initial instruction of a software system. Some of the results of research on flowcharts as planning aids may be relevant to our concerns. Specifically, some of this research (Kammann 1975, Sheppard and Kruesi 1981, Sheppard, Kruesi, and Curtis 1981, Wright and Reid 1973) has advanced the claim that complex procedural information is ill-expressed in a prose format. Other representations (such as our diagrams) may be better suited to the communication of this sort of information, particularly for novice users of a system. The tutorials in the standard instruction manual are indeed quite procedural; they specify a series of steps the user is to take to carry out some function or to do some task. Some of our pilot work indicates that, when reading procedural instructions in the midst of paragraphs that are declarative descriptions of functions, users can become confused as to where the description stops and the instruction to perform the function begins. It is easy to miss an action that was actually to be performed. Later on when the next action is performed, the system is often not in the correct state for that subsequent action to succeed. The diagrams should remedy this by explicitly separating descriptions of functions from the instructions to actually enter the functions into the computer.

Our research examines this issue by comparing the results of two groups of novices learning to use a word processing system. In order that the comparison informs us on this issue, we have gone to a great deal of effort to insure that the two manuals differ only in the mode in which the information is presented (i.e., text vs. diagrams) and not in the information itself. Therefore, we tried to design the materials so that the amount of material, its organization into topics, and the tasks and tutorial aspects of the information was the same in both manuals. Thus, differences in performance of the subjects in the two groups can be understood as due to the difference between the diagrammatic and the prose representation of how to carry out the actions in each tutorial.

Advance Organizers. Another issue is how learners organize the material presented to them in an instructional text. One of the important findings in the educational psychology literature concerns the advantages of ADVANCE ORGANIZERS. When someone is to read a chapter in a textbook it helps considerably to have a brief summary of what the chapter contains presented before beginning the chapter itself. This brief description can point out some of the key concepts or provide a summary of the main points to be made. The advance organizer need not contain specific content from the passage, but it does need to provide a general framework within which to understand the ideas presented. Cognitive psychologists interested in reading comprehension have conducted a number of studies to determine what are good advance organizers and under which conditions advance organizers have their strongest effects. Some of the original research was done by Ausubel in the early 1960's (discussed in Ausubel 1968). Interestingly some of the effects of advance organizers were rather weak. However, when used for technical material, like that involved in describing computer systems, the effects became more clearcut. Recent research by Mayer (1979) has shown that advance organizers seem to have their greatest effect for unfamiliar technical material. Furthermore, the reason for their advantage seems to be that they provide a concrete model into which the unfamiliar information can be fit.

The instruction manual for the IBM Displaywriter is actually quite good in this regard. For one thing, it is TASK ORIENTED in that the commands are taught in relation to particular tasks (such as editing or printing) which the user might want to accomplish. The task to be done serves as the organizer for the commands that are involved in its performance. This organization helps because users need their information in this way, rather than in terms of a list of possible commands (i.e., in manuals for the Wordstar and the Terak there is such a COMMAND ORIENTATION). Furthermore, in the IBM manual each topic is introduced with a brief summary outline of what major function is to be learned and the definition of key commands that will be discussed in the topic. This alone should help users comprehend the new material they are about to learn. The diagrammatic version that we designed maintained this characteristic (we included the same introductory outline for each topic). There is, however, another type of advance organization provided by the manual with diagrammatic representations. The diagrams make the framework of the system quite explicit. Thus, having the survey diagram (as well as route diagrams from previous topics, which themselves may be understood in the context of the survey diagrams) may help the user integrate the new information to be learned in a given topic. Similarly, the route diagram for a given concept provides the skeleton which also helps to organize the new material into the framework. Finally, the general framework is kept consistent throughout the diagrammatic manual which should also help the learner. This consistency allows users to employ the same general organization used in the last topic to aid them in understanding the concepts in the next topic.

The Principles of Text-to-Diagram Translation

As we have said, our experiments with menu based systems involved a comparison of the standard instruction manuals with the diagrammatic manuals we developed. In this section we want to go over some of the principles that guided our development of these new manuals. We have mentioned some of the principles in the last section. We developed a simple and consistent diagrammatic language which is easily learned. There are only three major components to the diagrammatic language with a single syntactic rule (to move from an earlier box to the subsequent box, do the action in between them). The major features of the diagrammatic representation, as well as how to perform the tutorials, were explained to the subject as the beginning of the diagram manual. There was a similar section in the original manual with instructions appropriate to the text presentation.

Undiagrammed Information. It was not always simple to translate the material in the textual manual to the diagrammatic form. Some of the material was not appropriate to a diagrammatic representation. For example, most definitions of important terms and locations of special function keys (e.g., the REQST key) were included in brief paragraphs preceding the route diagram where that information was needed. For example, a key concept in the use of a word processor is the notion of a cursor (the flashing symbol on the CRT indicating the location where the information typed on the keyboard will appear). We described the cursor in the introductory material preceding an early diagram. When a diagram involved the learning of a new KEY FUNCTION (a function which is performed by pressing a specially marked key on the keyboard), we described the general reason for using the new function, as well as where to find the key on the keyboard. Similarly, we often introduced general concepts and warnings in these introductory paragraphs. This information was almost always copied verbatim from the textual instruction manual, although some editing was done when the resulting introduction did not seem to be sufficiently contextualized.

Another sort of information that was not integrated into the diagrams were the topic introductions and concluding summaries in the text manual. These were merely copied in full and placed before and after (respectively) the set of route diagrams developed for each topic. Finally, we used all the figures and examples from the text manual in the diagram manual and, of course, the examples to be typed in or edited were the same in both manuals.

A Typical Topic. In order to convey the general nature of the instructional materials we developed, let us work through the major components of a single topic. A typical topic in the diagram manual began with a introductory page (taken from the text manual) which specified which commands were to be learned and the main purpose of the topic. The first route diagram in the topic (Figure 5) often prepared the system (or set up the menus) for the specific tasks to be learned by guiding the user through the menus to the place where the task could be performed. For example, in the Displaywriter system, the DELETE command applies when users are in an area called The Typing Page where the document they are working on is displayed. One can use the DELETE command to remove part of a document (a single letter, a word, etc.), however, to use the command one must be in The Typing Page. The first route diagram guides the user from the initial menu (Task Selection) through a series of other menus to get to where the DELETE command can be performed. In this instance, the user needs to go through the Typing Tasks and the Revise Document menus, enter the diskette, and document names, before getting to The Typing Page. On this first route diagram we show the actions that are done in order to move through these menus.

To continue the example, the next route diagrams in the topic specify in detail how to use the DELETE command on an example document. In these diagrams it is assumed that the user has worked his way through the higher level menus to arrive at The Typing Page region. This assumption is incorporated into the diagram by showing only the skeleton of the system at the top of the diagram and starting the red line at The Typing Page box. Figure 6 shows the skeleton of the system where the actions are deleted from the upper portion of the diagram (i.e., those involved in getting to The Typing Page). The skeleton appears at the top of route diagrams which follow the one specifying how to get to the appropriate place in the system to learn the new command. The user follows the instructions in the first diagram to work his way through the menus in the skeleton to get to The Typing Page. The subsequent diagrams then show these menus in skeleton form, and the user follows the path indicated by the red line beginning at The Typing Page. Thus, the main structural organization of the system is present on each route diagram, either in a skeleton (as in Figure 6) or in a more fully articulated fashion showing the actions that provide the paths through the menus in the skeleton (as in Figure 5). Thus, this organization is constantly reinforced and, in the diagrams with a skeleton, the new commands are understood in the context of, and in their proper relation to, the rest of the system.

The remainder of a typical topic will include other route diagrams instructing the user in other applications of, for example, the DELETE command, as well as the use of other related operations (e.g., adding new material at the place where deletions took place). In the next section we will describe the construction of the route diagrams in greater detail. For the moment, however, let us return to a point mentioned earlier; the chunking (or unitization) of the learning process.

The route diagrams impose a certain organization on the way in which information about the system is learned. Specifically, they contain only a limited amount of information (often only the two or three main actions necessary to perform a command). This not only eases the comprehension load by dividing the learning into small manageable parts, but also it encourages the learner to treat the particular command as a unit. Having the detailed steps for a given command organized into a

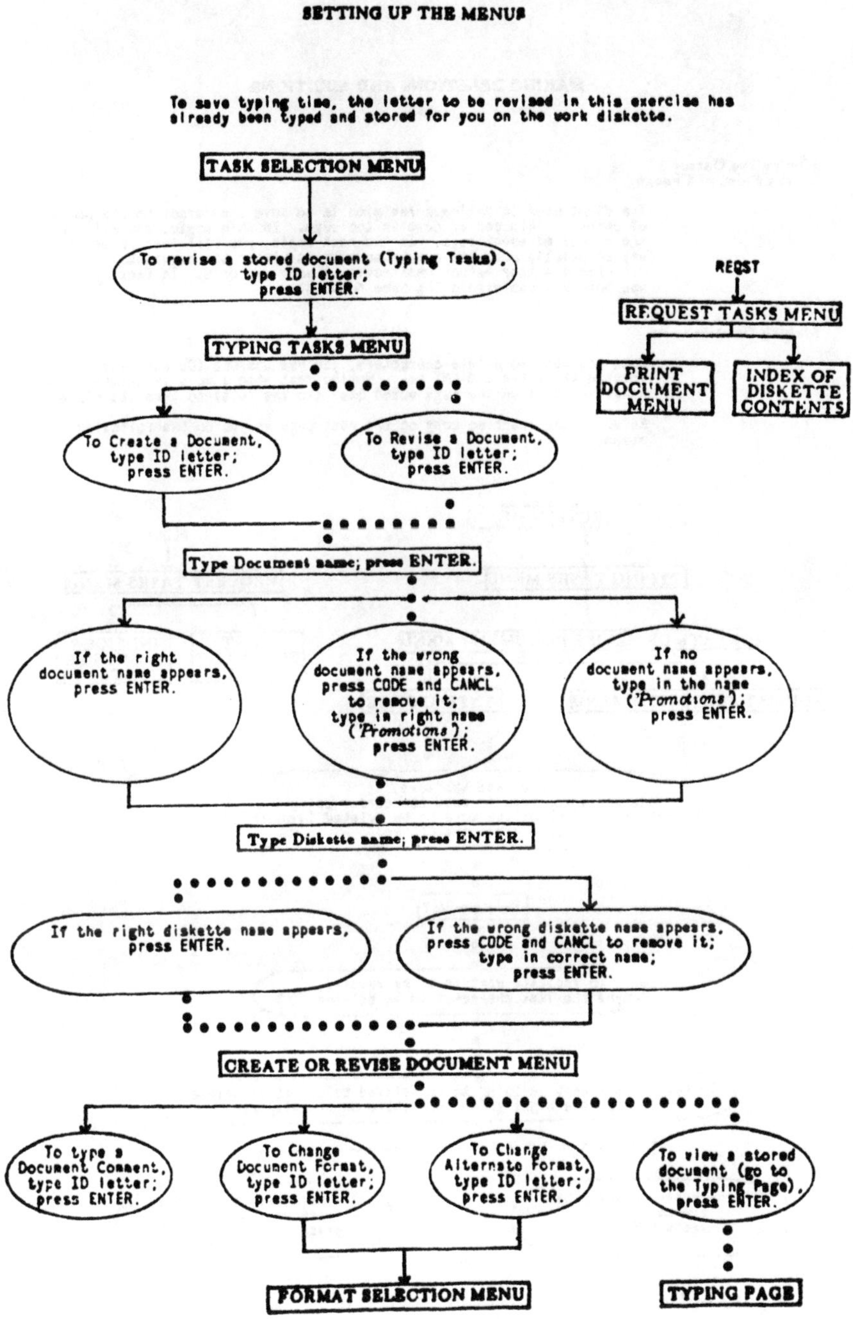

Figure 5. Example of a diagram that would begin a new topic.

MAKING DELETIONS AND ADDITIONS

Moving the Cursor To the Point of Change

The first step in making a revision is to move the cursor to the point of change. This can be done in two ways. In this topic, you will use the cursor movement keys. In the next topic, you will learn a second way to quickly move the cursor to a point within the document. You can choose either method when revising your own work. In fact, you can use both methods within the same document.

Making Deletions

When you want to delete characters, you use the DEL (Delete) key located above the CHG FMT key. Notice that when a word is deleted, the remaining text on the page moves over (to the left) to take its place.

Refer to the exercise copy on the next page as you do the following steps.

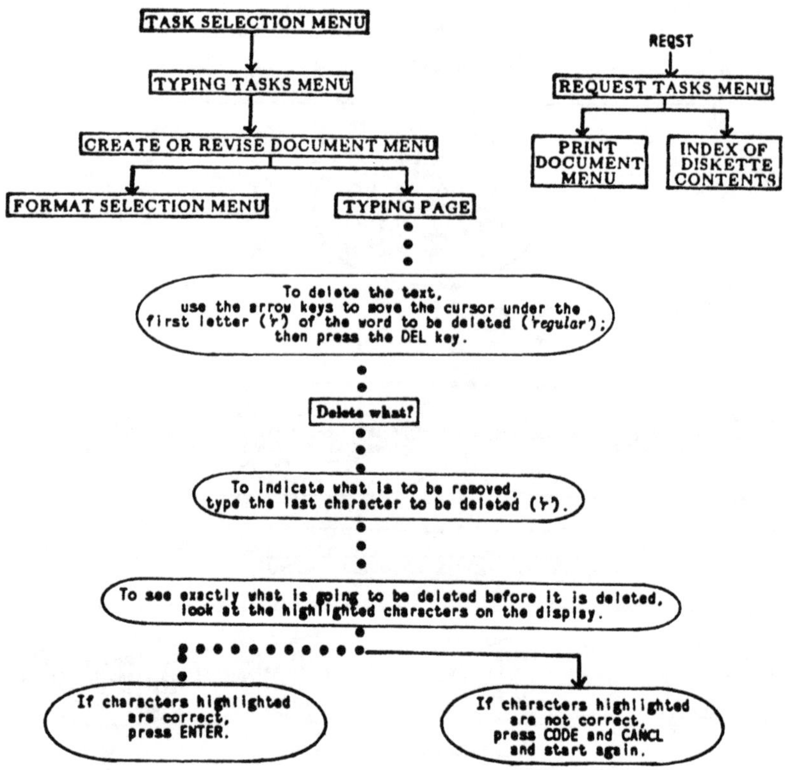

Figure 6. Diagram for instructing the use of the DELETE command.

unit makes it easier to remember those details. Cognitive psychologists including Hayes-Roth (1977), Smith, Adams, and Schorr (1978), Black and Bower (1979), and Reder (1982) have found that the integration of information into meaningful units is one way to get around the so-called PARADOX OF THE EXPERT. The paradox is that the more information you know about some topic, the harder it should be to use or retrieve any particular piece of information since there is so much that must be searched through. For example, consider the problem of retrieving some bit of information from a disorganized desk. There may be many important papers on this desk and as new ones are added it makes it more difficult to find any particular one. If, however, the papers are organized into piles for each different topic, then the retrieval of a given item may be simplified considerably. Similarly, when the many different steps that are required to accomplish word processing tasks are organized into meaningful units, it is easier to remember how to do those steps. This is because one can access the unit directly thus, the recovery of the details is not subject to confusion with the details of other units.

This unitization is important in that commands often require multiple steps (e.g., the DELETE command requires moving the cursor to the point of the deletion, pressing the DEL key, moving the cursor again—this time to the end of the portion to be deleted, and finally pressing the ENTER key). It is, therefore, possible to be confused about which of these steps are part of the operation to be learned and which are not. The potential for confusion is increased insofar as there is too much other information (including steps that are actually part of some other command) being taught at the same time. Once again, the original text manual seemed to do an adequate job of chunking the learning process and we attempted to keep the units the same in the diagram manual. Nonetheless, having a separate diagram for each new concept may amplify the advantage due to chunking when compared with the text manual in which the chunking was done by treating different commands in different paragraphs (which sometimes occurred on the same page).

Finally, the unitization yields an additional, somewhat derivative, advantage. The organization of the manual into small units facilitates its use as a reference source. The reader will recall that it was not our intention in this study to investigate the documentation problem. Nonetheless, it is inescapable that a good instruction manual will be treated by users as the initial reference source when they are trying to recall how to use a difficult command. If the information in that manual is organized so that most commands are on a single page (usually with the necessary definitions and warnings in the introductory paragraph), it is very simple to refresh one's memory on how to use that function. This can be done without wading through extraneous material. Furthermore, the presence of the skeleton indicates the context in which the command can be performed. The skeleton also provides a brief summary, if necessary, of how to get into the right region for the command to function correctly.

The final route diagram in many of the topics involved printing a hardcopy of the document that was used in the editing tutorials (e.g., the letter which was used in demonstrating the DELETE command). The printing stage is important for anyone using a word processor, therefore the writers of the original text manual decided to give the learner repeated practice with it. We agree, and also included a diagram representing the steps involved in printing a document wherever the text manual instructed the user to print the exercise. In this way the user can assure himself that the editing actually took place and the document was changed. In the case of our example, the user can see whether or not the material that was to have been deleted actually was.

At the very end of each topic was included a summary of the main points that were covered. These summaries were taken directly from the text manual. Occasionally there was some additional information about the commands learned in the topic. This information amplified the concepts learned and often gave more general principles for their use. Once again, we included this material wherever it had been in the original manual.

The Construction of the Route Diagrams. As we said above, the diagrams contained three different primitive elements: boxes, circles, and lines. The boxes represent information that is presented on the CRT screen, and the lines specify the relationships between the boxes. The circles represent the actions that the user is to perform when doing a tutorial. We adopted a simple strategy for translating the actions given in the text manual into the diagrammatic representation. Whenever the original manual required the learner to enter a command, we added a circle to the relevant diagram. Thus, all actions that a user was instructed to make in the original manual were also included in the diagram manual.

In the original manual, the actions the user was to take were generally set off from the rest of the text (using a different typeset and written in all capital letters). The original manual was somewhat inconsistent in whether or not the subject was informed about the reason for doing the particular action. In the diagram version, we prefaced the action to be taken with a phrase describing the GOAL governing the performance of the action. For example, there were many cases in which the manual described the items that could be chosen from a menu in the middle of a paragraph about that menu. Then at some other point on the page, the manual instructed the learner to enter a specific letter. We would attempt to make the connection between action taken (in this case entering the ID letter for a particular item in a menu) with the GOAL that the action serves (to move to the next menu for information about the selected item). For example, in Figure 5, the action of choosing the Typing Tasks item from the Task Selection Menu (at the top of this diagram) is preceded by the goal of that action:

To revise a stored document (Typing Tasks).

The reason for this is to make the learner conscious of not only the sequence of actions needed to accomplish his task, but also of the link between the action and the purpose for doing it. Wherever possible, the goal phrase and the action phrase are on separate lines within the circle, separated by a comma at the end of the goal phrase. When there is more than one action in a circle (usually when the command requires that the user press the ENTER key to record the primary action), the two actions are separated by a semi-colon. While concern with these details might appear overly compulsive, it is important that the representation be consistent so that it does not potentially add an element of confusion to the already difficult task of learning the system.

In very explicit diagrams such as these, there is the danger that the users merely perform the actions in the right order without processing what they are doing to any deep extent (and thus, perhaps, not fully understanding why they are performing the action). We were concerned that the learner might be able to work through the tutorial diagrams without comprehending the reasons for the actions and thus, perhaps, without really learning the way to perform the various functions. This rote behavior is unlikely to lead to learning which is transferable to situations that are somewhat different from those in which the learning originally took place.

Part of the reason for providing goals with the actions is to give the user a specific context for the action. One of the psychological issues involved concerns the transferability of learning from the context in which material is first encountered, to other contexts in which the material might be used. The result from cognitive psychology that is relevant here is the encoding specificity principle (Tulving and Thompson 1973, and Watkins and Tulving, 1975) which states that the likelihood of recalling an item (at some point after it is learned) is related to the degree of similarity between the context of recall, and the context in which the item was originally learned. Thus, it is important to provide a context for the learning of an item which matches the context in which the item is to be used. The goals for the actions specify, in a fairly general way, the context in which the actions are appropriately performed. At least this aspect of the context in which the actions are learned is likely to recur when the actions are needed later. Thus, the goal phrase should aid the recall of the actions at the appropriate time.

Another reason for providing goals, linked with the actions performed, is to encourage the learners to represent the relations between the actions done and the purpose for doing them in memory. This is one way to increase the processing done by the learners on the actions that they perform. Research in cognitive psychology (Craik and Lockhart 1972, Craik and Tulving 1975) indicates that when a to-be-remembered item is only superficially processed, it is less likely to be registered in memory. However, if to-be-learned material is elaborated by processing it in connection with other information, recall of the material is aided. This is because the elaboration leads to the representation of more paths in memory which may be searched in order to recover the material. The presentation of goals with the actions provides one sort of elaboration of the action concepts.

For the same reason (to increase elaborative processing), we typically specified the action part of the circle in terms that encouraged the user to look at the screen. For instance, the manual often told the learners which specific letter from a menu should be entered. As an example, a common instruction in the original manual was:

Type a, press ENTER.

In contrast, our action statement told the subjects to choose (for themselves) the appropriate item from the menu:

Type the ID letter for Typing Tasks, press ENTER.

The subject then would be forced to read through the choices in the menu in order to find the correct letter to enter. It was always clear from the statement of the goal which action should be chosen, but the subject had to look to the screen to find out which letter signified this choice. This, of course, is what users must do when they use the system on their own and they should be encouraged to do this as early as possible in their training. Furthermore, it may be that the additional processing that is done on the action may increase its memorability.

As we described, another principle is to always have at least one circle between each box (except for the skeleton menus on those diagrams which do not involve moving through the skeleton). The actions in these circles specify how one moves from one state to another in the system or how to perform the operations in the tutorial. The boxes represent the system states, since those states are equivalent to changes in the information on the display (at least when moving through the menus and prompts). However, it would not only be redundant, but also graphically undesirable, to present all the information that is contained in the menus each time the learner goes through them. Fortunately the system is designed so that each menu has a name at the top of the menu display. (The menu boxes in Figures 3, 5, and 6 present these names.) This allows the learner to check that the preceding action on his part did in fact lead him to the correct menu.

System prompts (single line messages from the system indicating that the user is to type in a command, a menu item letter, or a name for a document) are treated a little differently. Prompts are included verbatim in boxes since they are typically short and difficult to abbreviate in any consistent fashion. An example of a prompt box is:

Type Document name, press ENTER.

in the middle of Figure 5, or the prompt:

Delete What?

in Figure 6. Like the menu boxes, the prompt boxes in the diagrams are places where the user can check to see if the result of his action (as displayed on the screen) accords with the result indicated in the diagram.

The diagrams also were designed to allow for a certain amount of error recovery. Whenever there were multiple choices of actions that could be taken from a given box, the diagram specified these choices and the boxes that would be present if the actions were taken. For example, at the bottom of the diagram in Figure 5, there are four different actions that the learner could take when viewing the Create and Revise Document menu. These four actions are the ones that are actually used at some point in the manual. The correct choice for the purpose of the tutorial is specified by the red colored lines. The other possible actions and their resulting states are indicated in black (the Document Comment item is a special case where the user merely types in a phrase describing the document). This feature of the diagrams allows users to localize errors they might make. In this case, if the users erroneously end up at the Format Selection menu, instead of the Typing Page, they can not only see that they are in the wrong place, but they can see how they got there. Furthermore, having the four actions present in this diagram may serve the geographical function of acquainting the user with the paths not taken. It is as though one were driving a car and upon coming to a fork in the road was told to turn right. Knowledge of where the left fork leads, although not necessary in following the instruction to turn right, might, nonetheless, provide some confidence in the reason for following the instruction. Moreover, having this knowledge may prove to be useful the next time one is driving down that road. Thus, the inclusion of these alternative actions and where they lead may provide reinforcement of the learner's sense of knowing the geography of the system.

Another error recovery device that is integrated into the diagrammatic representations is also illustrated in Figure 5. Some of the system prompts request that the name of some document or diskette (the storage medium on which the documents created in the word processor are written) be entered into the computer. Depending on what actions have been done up to the point where one of these prompts appears, the system may already have the correct name, or an incorrect name, or in the case of the document name prompt, no name at all. All of these options are present in the diagram. Although the users are guided (by the red lines) to the action that is appropriate given the history of the tutorial session, there still is the possibility that they can recover, if they have entered a wrong name, in order to get back on the right track.

Experimental Design

We taught the IBM Displaywriter system to 12 people; 6 used the original manual, and 6 used the diagrammatic manual. The subjects in this experiment spent about 10–12 hours in our laboratory; approximately 2 hours a day for 5 consecutive days. Subjects were recruited from the New Haven area, and not all of them were students. They were paid $40–$50 dollars for their participation.

The Training Days. Two of the five days (the second and third) were spent working through the tutorials in the manuals. Subjects took between 3 and 6 hours to cover the instructional materials. Subjects worked through the first seven of the topics in the manuals on the first of the two training days and the last three topics on the second training day. These training sessions were videotaped using two cameras, one recording the subject's behavior and the other recording changes on the CRT screen. The signal from the cameras ran through a time generator which superimposed a clock image on the videotape. This permitted fairly accurate timing of the details of the subject's training; including how long it took to do each page in the manual and how long for each topic. Audio recordings were also made from lapel microphones worn by the subject and the experimenter.

The experimenter sat next to the subject through the training and took notes on the subject's performance. It might be argued that the presence of the experimenter could be considered an intrusive factor that is not matched in many real training situations. However, the experimenter was quite nonintrusive and did serve as a person to whom questions could be addressed. Typically, these questions were carefully turned away by encouraging the subject to search for the answers in the manual. Nonetheless, there were occasions when the subject put the system into states which only the experimenter could set aright. Furthermore, the presence of the experimenter encouraged the subject to concentrate on the task of working through the tutorials in the manual. If the subjects were left on their own, the comparisons of their times to do the tutorials would be less informative. Thus, the presence of the experimenter assured a certain amount of consistency across subjects in these data. Finally, there are probably many training situations in which someone is looking over the shoulder of the learner (e.g., a supervisor or a tutor).

In the remainder of this section we will briefly describe the battery of tests and exercises that our subjects performed before and after their training. We used a fairly wide variety of measures of the subjects' abilities and word processing knowledge. Each of these measures yields data that will help us determine what the subjects learned during their training, as well as what differences in their word processing skills arose from the two different training conditions. In subsequent reports of this project we intend to describe in much greater detail these tests and exercises, our motivation for using them, and the data they provide.

Testing on the First Day. On the first day, and the last two days, the subjects took a variety of tests. Some of the tests on the first day were for screening purposes. We were interested in the training of people who had no previous experience using computers or word processors. In a questionnaire, we asked a number of questions about their experience with computers, how they felt about computers (i.e., whether they liked them, were afraid of them, etc.), and what their ideas were about how computers and word processors worked. The same questionnaire was given to subjects on the first and last days of the experiment, as we were interested in the extent to which their responses to the questions changed as a result of the training. Another pretest was given to measure the typing speed and accuracy of the subjects. Word processing involves a considerable amount of typing and it is important to know whether differences in performance between the two groups of subjects are explainable in terms of differences in their mean typing speed. We also administered a commercially available aptitude test for computer skills called the Computer Operators Aptitude Battery (available from Science Research Associates). This Battery is comprised of a set of short tests measuring different aspects of the skills used in working with a computer. In addition, we administered some brief intelligence tests concerned with spatial abilities, such as the ones used by Egan, Bowers, and Gomez (1982) in their study of the Unix line editor. We also obtained other pertinent information concerning the subject's age, educational background, work history, and so forth. Much of this information is used to examine questions concerning possible individual differences among the subjects.

Another important test which was given on both the first and last days of the experiment was a similarity ratings task. In this test we presented subjects with pairs of words and asked them to rate how similar they were on a seven point rating scale. Their responses were timed from the onset of the presentation of the word pairs to the making of the rating for that pair. In constructing the stimuli for this experiment 15 words are chosen that represent concepts that are used in the training manuals (e.g., Delete, Find, and Move) as well as 5 other words that sound as though they might have been used in the system as commands, but were not (e.g., Replace). Using multidimensional scaling techniques, it is possible to represent the subject's ratings in terms of a number of dimensions in a semantic relatedness space. The results of the same test given at the end of the experiment can be given a similar treatment and the two sets of results can then be compared. The hypothesis is that those words that represent commands which are performed in the same region in the word processing system (e.g., words which are involved with printing, as opposed to revising, a document) will tend to be rated as more similar to each other after the training than before. This result would be manifest in a greater amount of clustering in the semantic space defined for the results of the second test as compared with that for the first test. The five words that are not part of the system may serve as reference points in interpreting the movements in the semantic space since the ratings of similarity of these words with the others should not show large differences in the before and after tests. These tests should provide a way of determining the characteristics of the mental models that subjects have of the system at the end of their training.

Testing Word Processing Skills. A critical question is whether the people in the two experimental conditions differ in their word processing skills at the end of the training. Thus, although we are evaluating how quickly the two groups can work through the manual, it would be useless to show that the subjects in the diagram condition are faster, if these subjects do not learn the system as well.

In order to evaluate the ability of the users after their training, we had them perform a number of exercises that were typical word processing tasks. On the fourth day of the experiment, subjects were given four different word processing exercises. Subjects were videotaped as they did the exercises and they were under a certain amount of time pressure to complete them. There were overall time limits for each exercise. Within each exercise (especially the fourth exercise) subjects were encouraged to move to the next part of an exercise if they spent too much unproductive time on a prior part. However, subjects were asked to at least attempt to do all parts of the exercises as well as possible.

The first exercise involved the creation of a short document (a simple office memo). Subjects were given a copy of the memo and asked to reproduce it. The memo had a number of moderately difficult parts including a centered heading, and changing margins and spacing. The subjects had to type the memo into the computer so that they could print out a copy which matched the example. We measured how long this took and how close the subject's copy came to the original. We also examined how the subjects performed the task, and when and where they had trouble. Subjects were fairly unconstrained in this task in the sense that they could use whatever commands they wanted, in whatever order, as long as they produced a faithful copy of the original.

The second exercise involved making corrections in a long memorandum. In this case there was a file in the system which contained the uncorrected memo. Subjects were given a copy of the memo with notations of the things to be changed. This is very similar to the situation that normally occurs when one is asked to revise a document. This exercise was designed to test the subjects' ability to make specific types of changes. For example, in this exercise subjects had to change all occurrences of one word to another, correct typographical errors, rearrange paragraphs, and make insertions.

The third exercise was similar to the second in that an uncorrected document was in the computer and the subject had to make a set of specific corrections. As with the second exercise, the corrections were specified on a copy of the document. This exercise, however, was more difficult and contained tabular material interspersed with text. This exercise involved a considerable amount of spatial reconfiguration of the information in tables. Certain entries in the tables were to be moved to other columns and new columns were to be formed. The purpose of this exercise was to test the transferability of the subjects' skill to a task that differed from the material in the tutorials (which mostly involved typing and editing straightforward prose). Although everything that was needed to accomplish the exercise had been covered in the tutorials, we incorporated some of the more complex functions used in novel ways.

The final exercise was the most constrained test of the subjects' knowledge of the various commands covered in the tutorial. Here again we had the subjects make corrections on a file already stored in the computer, using a copy showing what was to be changed. For this exercise, we told subjects exactly which commands we wanted them to use to make the corrections, as well as the exact order in which the corrections were to be made. For example, at one point, after a certain correction had been made, the subjects were asked to use the FIND command to move to the next place of correction in the document. Clearly, an alternative to using the FIND command would be to use cursor movement keys to move the cursor to the next point in the text. However, by specifically instructing the subjects to use the FIND command, we could evaluate whether or not they knew how to perform this task. Given these constraints, it was also possible to time the performance of each command and to compare the times and knowledge of the different functions across subjects at a fairly detailed level.

On the fourth day all of these exercises were to be performed without consulting the instructional materials. Here again the experimental situation may depart somewhat from normal learning conditions in which the manual is presumed to be nearby as the users do their first tasks after their training. For our purposes, it was important that the manual not be used because we wanted to find out what the subjects learned during the training, and how well different commands were understood.

The last thing subjects did on the fourth day was to take the Nelson-Denny

Reading test which measured vocabulary skills, as well as reading speed and comprehension. The purpose of this test was to check the extent to which differences among subjects' performances might be due to factors other than the organization of the instructional materials.

On the fifth and last day of testing, subjects were given four new word processing exercises which were very similar (in form, not content) to the four exercises given on the fourth day. Again, these exercises were timed and subjects were asked to do them as quickly and accurately as possible. The major difference was that the subjects were permitted to use the instructional manuals to look up the commands about which they might be unsure. This provided the subject with the opportunity to check on the specifics of particular commands. Incidentally, this aspect of the testing gave us some information on the utility of the manuals as reference materials. That is, we could evaluate the ease with which subjects used the manuals to find information relevant to a specific need.

The other tasks for the subject on the last day were to make similarity judgments on the pairs of computer words for a second time, in order to compare them with the ratings made before the training sessions. Also, subjects were given a paired associate test to examine how well they memorized relationships between pairs of concepts. This ability may also influence the ease with which subjects can learn the relationships among word processing concepts.

This wide variety of measures will yield a considerable amount of data for analysis. Our analysis strategy will begin with some overall comparisons of the subjects in the two experimental groups. At this stage, it will be useful to examine the ease of learning using the two different manuals (in terms of the time required to go through the topics). We will also compare the performance of the two groups of subjects in the exercises that followed the training sessions. We want to determine whether there are differences in how well the two groups can do standard word processing functions. We will examine the extent to which these differences (in performance times and word processing skills) can be explained by individual subject ability differences (as measured by the tests of spatial abilities, paired-associate learning, typing speed, and so forth). The next step will be to look at the skills of the subjects in greater detail to determine whether certain commands are better learned by subjects in one group, while the other group is superior on another set of commands. (There are probably commands which neither group understand.) It will be necessary to examine the individual tasks and their component commands in some detail in order to uncover the reasons for the overall results. In addition, the videotapes of the training sessions will allow us to go back to the points where problematic commands are first encountered in order to attempt to isolate the specific problems. Subjects' errors and misunderstandings (if systematic) can be an important source of data, as well as of hypotheses, for future experiments. The data we collected also sheds light on a number of other issues discussed in this paper (e.g., the nature of the mental models the users have of the system). Finally, we will compare the results of the parallel studies of the IBM Displaywriter, Wordstar, and Terak word processors. This will tell us something about the generalizability of our findings, as well as help us isolate the source of difficulties users have in learning word processing systems.

At this point in the LUSP project, we are just beginning these analyses, and we estimate that they will take a considerable amount of time and effort. We hope to show that, overall, the revised manuals lead to better and more rapid learning. The preliminary indications are in that direction—subjects seemed to finish the training sessions more quickly in the diagram condition (even though they had more material to cover—both text and diagrams) and also seemed better at the exercises. However, one of our main goals is to develop more specific hypotheses concerning the reasons for the differences between the groups, and to test these hypotheses in subsequent experiments. This is one of the major functions of discovery methodology; the generation of empirical hypotheses that can be tested in situations in which the appropriate controls are understood and implemented.

CONCLUSIONS

In this paper we have attempted to outline one part of the research program of the Learning and Using Systems Project. The purpose was to lay out the theoretical motivations for the project as well as for the more specific details of the design of the instructional materials. Subsequent papers will expand upon issues raised in this paper and will report the results of our analyses. In the description of our project on instructional materials, we hope that some of the relevant issues that have can be applied from cognitive psychology were covered. For example, cognitive map research guided our overall design of the revised manual. Concerns with encoding specificity, elaborative processing, and chunking influenced the details of the construction of the tutorial diagrams. We feel that this sort of research may lead to the development of better instructional materials and, thereby, promote computer literacy. Furthermore, we hope to meet a challenge for cognitive psychology—the examination of theoretical issues of human cognition in an applied context.

REFERENCES

AUSUBEL, D. P. 1968. Educational psychology: A cognitive view. New York: Holt, Rinehart, and Winston.

BLACK, J. B., and G. H. BOWER. 1979. Episodes as chunks in narrative memory. Journal of Verbal Learning and Verbal Behavior 18.309–318.

———, and M. M. SEBRECHTS. 1981. Facilitating human-computer communication. Applied Psycholinguistics 2.149–178.

———, J. A. GALAMBOS, and B. J. REISER. 1984 (in press). Coordinating discovery and verification research. New methods in the study of immediate processes in comprehension, ed. by D. Kieras & M. Just. Hillsdale, NJ: Erlbaum.

BOHL, M. 1971. Flowcharting techniques. Palo Alto, CA: Science Research Associates.

BOTT, R. 1979. A study of complex learning: Theory and methodologies. Center for Human Information Processing Technical Report No. 82, University of California, San Diego.

BOWER, G. H. 1972. Mental imagery and associative learning. Cognition in learning and memory, ed. by L. Gregg. New York: Wiley.

______, J. B. BLACK, and T. J. TURNER. 1979. Scripts in memory for text. Cognitive Psychology 11.717–726.

BROOKS, F. P. 1975. The mythical man-month. Reading, Ma: Addison-Wesley.

CARROLL, J. 1982. The adventure of getting to know a computer. Computer 15.49–58.

______, and R. MACK. 1982. Actively learning to use a word processor. Proceedings of the Fourth Annual Conference of the Cognitive Science Society. Ann Arbor, Michigan.

______, and J. C. THOMAS. 1982. Metaphor and the cognitive representation of computing systems. IEEE Transactions on Systems, Man and Cybernetics 12.107–116.

______, J. C. THOMAS, and A MALHOTRA. 1980. Presentation and representation in design problem solving. British Journal of Psychology 71. 143–153.

CRAIK, F. I. M., and R. S. LOCKHART. 1972. Levels of processing: A framework for memory research. Journal of Verbal Learning and Verbal Behavior 11.671–684.

______, and E. TULVING. 1975. Depth of processing and the retention of words in episodic memory. Journal of Verbal Learning and Verbal Behavior 11.671–84.

EGAN, D. E., C. BOWERS, and L. M. GOMEZ. 1982. Learner characteristics that predict success in using a text-editor tutorial. Proceedings of the Conference on Human Factors in Computers Systems, Gaithersburg, Maryland.

FARINA, F. 1970. Flowcharting. Englewood Cliffs, NJ: Prentice Hall.

FITTER, M. and T. R. G. GREEN. 1979. When do diagrams make good computer languages? International Journal of Man-Machine Studies 11.235–261.

GALAMBOS, J. A. 1982. Normative studies of six characteristics of our knowledge of common activities. Cognitive Science Technical Report 14, Yale University.

______, and L. J. RIPS. 1982. Memory for routines. Journal of Verbal Learning and Verbal Behavior 21.260–281.

GENTNER, D., and A. L. STEVENS. 1983. Mental models. Hillsdale, NJ: Erlbaum.

GOLDSTEIN, H. H., and J. VON NEUMANN. 1947. Planning and coding problems for an electronic computing instrument, Part II, Vol. I. Report prepared for U.S. Army Ordinance Dept. Reprinted in J. von Neumann, Collected Works, Vol. A, ed. by A. H. Taub, 80–151, New York: MacMillan.

HALASZ, F., and T. P. MORAN. 1982. Analogy considered harmful. Proceedings of the Conference on Human Factors in Computer Systems, Gaithersburg, Maryland.

HART, R. A. and G. I. MOORE. 1973. The development of spatial cognition: A review. Image and environment ed. by R. M. Downs & D. Stea. Chicago: Aldine.

HAYES-ROTH, B. 1977. Evolution of cognitive structures and processes. Psychological Review 84.260–278.

JACOBY, L. L. 1978. On interpreting the effects of repetition: Solving a problem versus remembering a solution. Journal of Verbal Learning and Verbal Behavior 17.649–667.

KAMMANN, R. 1975. The comprehensibility of printed instructions and the flowchart alternative. Human Factors 59.183–191.

KOSSLYN, S. M., and S. P. SHWARTZ. 1977. A simulation of visual imagery. Cognitive Science 1.265–298.

MAYER, R. E. 1981. The psychology of how novices learn computer programming. Computing Surveys 13.121–141.

MINSKY, M. 1975. A framework for representing knowledge. The psychology of computer vision, ed. by P. H. Winston, 211–277. New York: McGraw-Hill.

REDER, L. M. 1982. Plausibility judgments versus fact retrieval: Alternative strategies for sentence verification. Psychological Review 89.250–280.

SCHANK, R. C., and R. ABELSON. 1977. Scripts, plans, goals and understanding. Hillsdale, NJ: Erlbaum.

SHEPPARD, S., and E. KRUESI. The effects of the symbology and spatial arrangement of software specifications in a coding task. Trends and applications 1981: Advances in software technology. The Institute of Electrical and Electronics Engineers, 7–13.

______, E. KRUESI, and B. CURTIS. 1981. The effects of symbology and spatial arrangement on the comprehension of software specifications. Proceedings of the Fifth International Conference on Software Engineering. The Institute of Electrical and Electronics Engineers, 207–214.

SHNEIDERMAN, B., R. E. MAYER, D. MCKAY, and P. HELLER. 1977. Experimental investigations of the utility of detailed flowcharts in programming. Communications of the Association for Computing Machinery 20.373–381.

SIEGEL, A. W., and S. H. WHITE. 1975. The development of spatial representations of large-scale environments. Advances in child development and behavior, ed. by H. W. Reese. New York: Academic Press.

SMITH, E. E., N. ADAMS, and D. SCHORR. 1978. Fact retrieval and the paradox of interference. Cognitive Psychology 10.438–464.

SOLOWAY, E., J. BONAR, and K. EHRLICH. 1983. Cognitive factors in programming: An empirical study of looping constructs. Communications of the Association for Computing Machinery 26.853–860.

THORNDYKE, P. W., and B. HAYES-ROTH. 1982. Differences in spatial knowledge acquired from maps and navigation. Cognitive Psychology 14.560–589.

TULVING, E., and D. M. THOMPSON. 1973. Encoding specificity and retrieval processes in episodic memory. Psychological Review 80.352–373.

WATKINS, M. J., and E. TULVING. 1975. Episodic memory: When recognition fails. Journal of Experimental Psychology: General 104.5–29.

WRIGHT, P., and F. REID. 1973. Written information: Some alternatives to prose for expressing the outcome of complex contingencies. Journal of Applied Psychology 57.160–166.

THREE

Machine Translation vs. Translator Aids: A False Dichotomy

Alan K. Melby
Brigham Young University

BACKGROUND ON COMPUTERS AND TRANSLATION

Advances in Computers

The past 30 years have been a period of rapid development for computers and their uses. In computer hardware, we have seen a progression from vacuum tubes to transistors to integrated circuits to microprocessors. In computer uses, we have seen an expansion beyond military and business applications that includes computer-aided design and manufacturing, bibliographic data retrieval, concordance making, education, and, of course, games. Where does translation fit into this picture?

Machine Translation: An Old and Unsuccessful Effort

Actually, the use of computers for translation is one of the oldest and least successful computer applications. It is one of the oldest because it was suggested by Warren Weaver over 30 years ago in a well-known memo (see reprint of memo in Weaver 1955). The reasons for its lack of success are complex, but I suggest that at least some of the failures are a result of unfortunate assumptions. Early work in computers and translation assumed that the only acceptable goal was fully automatic high-quality translation and, with equal misfortune, assumed that any interaction between the computer and the human translator was temporary and undesirable. These assumptions are a part of the machine translation tradition which continues today.

Translator Aids: An Opposing Approach

The translator aid tradition arose in reaction to these assumptions. This new tradition has seen considerably more success. Translator aids include terminology access, document access, and word processing, and they are in daily use, particularly in Canada and Europe. An important factor in their success is, of course, the fact that translator aids do not translate. They are strictly tools to be used at the discretion of human translators.

Until recently, there was no middle ground between machine translation and translator aids. Translator aid projects have been designed to help human translators become more productive and effective, while machine translation projects have been designed to eliminate human translators. Designs so diametrically opposed in goals are, surprisingly, not incompatible. But is this dichotomy necessary?

Recent Motions Toward Integration

In this paper I will argue that the dichotomy is unnecessary and that it can be dissolved if one adopts a modified viewpoint of machine translation and incorporates it into a system of translator aids.

In the past few years, some machine translation systems have been marketed as machine-assisted translation systems. The computer does the translation, perhaps asking questions of the human along the way, and then presents a rough translation to the human translator for revision. For nearly a decade, I was a member of a team working on one of these machine-assisted translation systems. These systems do not replace human translators, but rather increase their productivity. So are they really translator aids? Not yet. This is because of the way the translator perceives the machine. The translator is told to postedit and, perhaps, to answer questions. The human translator often feels like a tool for the machine. Happily, however, the scene is changing. Some commercial teams which market machine translation systems are now also offering new tools for translators. It is important to translators whether they are the tool or the machine is the tool. When machine translation is viewed as one of many tools for a human translator to choose from, the dichotomy between machine translation and translator aids disappears.

INTEGRATING TRANSLATOR AIDS AND MACHINE TRANSLATION

A Success Story: The METEO System

An example of a translation system involving machine translation yet breaking out of the old tradition is the METEO system developed by the University of Montreal. This system daily translates many thousands of words of Canadian weather forecasts from English to French (Chandioux 1978). Until it was installed, the Canadian government had considerable difficulty retaining weather forecast translators because of the boring nature of their work. Now, a computer program identifies the straightforward sentences (about 80%) and translates them automatically. In the remaining sentences, the computer system detected some problem, such as an unknown word or grammatical construction which would probably cause a flaw in the machine output. These sentences are presented to the human for translation. Note that the human is not asked to postedit the machine translation of these sentences. The human does not even see the French translation, but rather translates the original English. From the translator's point of view, the machine is a tool for filtering out the boring sentences. The translators are relieved of much drudgery and are significantly happier in their work.

In contrast, consider a traditional machine translation system in which the translator is asked to postedit the raw machine translation of an entire text, compared with the METEO system, in which the human translates those sentences which the computer cannot handle. To the translator, the difference is dramatic. In the traditional system, the translator is a 'garbage collector', removing the botched up words along the sentences of the machine translation. In the METEO system, however, the translator is an executive, handling the difficult cases that are beyond the capacity of the limited intellect of the computer. The success of the METEO system shows that machine translation can be effective when used in the proper environment.

The BYU Translator Aid System

The remainder of this paper will describe a system design which integrates word processing, terminology access, and machine translation. The system is a tool for the translator, yet includes a machine translation component which, hopefully, extends some principles found in the METEO system to a more general environment. The system is being developed at Brigham Young University (BYU) as an academic research project. It is called the BYU Translator Aid System. The design is the result of years of discussion with colleagues. Special credit for inspiration should be given to Martin Kay (see Kay 1980).

The system provides three integrated levels of aid to the translator. The software is being implemented on a single-user microcomputer consisting of a processor, video screen with 24 lines of 80 characters, keyboard, two diskette drives, and printer. To go beyond a demonstration version to a practical system, it is necessary to add a hard disk with a storage capacity of at least 5,000,000 characters. At level one, the translator can sit down with a text in the source language and begin translating immediately. To use level two, the source text must be available in a segmented form on diskette or over a network. A segment is a piece of text of up to about 100 words. It may be one long sentence or several short sentences. The source text may be available in machine readable form, as a by-product of publication in the source language, or it may be obtained using optical scanners. To use level three, the source text must be processed off-line by a machine translation system which keeps track of problems encountered. The machine translation must be segmented to correspond to the segments of the source text and each problem encountered must be associated with some segment.

If several translators are working together, they should share disk files by means of a network. They should not be multiple users of a single processor, as processors are inexpensive while people are not. Multiple processors in a network provide consistent response time to each user for local tasks, such as word processing, regardless of what other users are doing.

The Operation of the System

We will explore the operation of the system at the various levels. At each point in the translation process, the screen is divided into windows. For example, the first line on the screen might be a title, lines 3 through 11 might form the upper window, and lines 12 through 24 might form the lower window. At another point the screen may be divided up into three windows. A special case is the final revision step.

After the translator aid system has been used to produce a draft translation and the translator is satisfied with the content of the translation, the text file is converted to a standard word processing file and the translator uses a standard word processor to make final revisions and to adjust the format as desired. In the final revision step, the whole screen consists of a single window and the text is no longer segmented. Thus, the translator produces a translation in two steps: first, the draft translation step, using one or more levels of aid and switching freely among available levels, and second, the final revision step, using a standard word processor. We will now look at the three levels of aid in the draft translation step.

Level One Word Processing. At level one, the system can look much like a word processor. The screen consists of two major windows. The bottom window (consisting of 10 lines) is the translator's work area. Nothing goes into the bottom window except what the translator puts there. At some point, the translator decides to move on to a new segment by pressing the appropriate function key. The segment moves into the upper window and the bottom window is filled with the next segment or, if there are no more segments, the window is blank and ready for a new segment of translation. The translator can freely move forwards and backwards through the text by segment, or move to the top or bottom of the file or to a specific segment. Editing can always be done on the segment of text which is in the bottom window. To edit something in the upper window, the translator simply scrolls down a segment at a time until the text in question is in the bottom window, thus becoming the current or active segment. A standard word processor scrolls by line or by screen. The one being discussed scrolls by segment. While a standard word processor allows changes to be made to the text anywhere on the screen, this one allows changes to be made in the current segment, which is in a window consisting of approximately the bottom half of the screen. I have worked with standard word processors and with this unconventional one and do not find it difficult to adjust from one to the other. The reason for this segment orientation in the draft translation step is to make the three levels of aid look very much the same to the translator. At level one, the source text is on paper and the translator places it next the computer display. At levels two and three, the source text appears on the screen one segment at a time, and the screen is divided into three major windows: the current segment of source text, aids corresponding to that segment, and the current segment of target text. Inside the computer, each segment of target text is linked back to its corresponding source segment. This means that as the translator scrolls back and forth through his or her translation, the appropriate source segment can be automatically displayed in the upper window. If the text were not segmented, the translator would have to scroll separately through the source and target texts. At level one, since the source text is not on disk, the system would not have to work with segments, but this would be at the cost of decreasing the similarity among the three levels. I have attached a very high priority to making the three levels look very much alike to the translator. It may take years of experimentation before it becomes clear whether this was a good decision.

Level One Terminology Access. A terminology access option is still available at level one. At the touch of a function key, the upper portion of the screen becomes a window into a bilingual terminology file. The translator enters the term to be looked up and a bilingual dictionary entry for that term is retrieved from disk and placed in the upper window. If there is more than one window of information on the term, the translator can move forward or backward through the information associated with that term. If the term is not found, the term can be added. Existing entries can also be modified. A number of terminology banks already exist, such as those of the Canadian government and the European Community, and these term files can be accessed on video terminals. The translator aid system would provide the ability to access these remote files, but the primary access would be to its own local term files. These local term files could be built up item by item by the translator as new translations are identified, or they could be purchased from or traded with other translators or from term banks. The local storage option provides much faster lookup and avoids long distance telephone charges. Local storage also provides the possibility of local printouts of glossaries or subsets of glossaries.

An important feature of this terminology access is that the translator need not leave the word processor to access the terms. In fact, the current segment of translation is visible during the entire terminology access procedure, and a simple keystroke returns the system to word processing mode with the cursor exactly where it was before the term was looked up. Upon returning to word processing mode, the dictionary entry is still visible in the upper window and the translator can pull down the desired translation and insert it into the current segment of translation with two or three keystrokes.

A special format, monolingual term file is also available at level one. This file, called the expansion code file, allows the translator to define abbreviations which are automatically expanded at the touch of a special function key. This feature is useful whenever there are words or phrases which occur repeatedly, such as names of parts in a machine or titles of organizations. The translator decides which terms occur frequently enough to warrant an expansion code and devises a short code for those terms. For example, the code UI might be defined by the translator to be expanded as USER INTERFACE. The term is inserted into the translation by typing UI and then pressing the expansion key. This feature is already available in a number of word processing systems and has been shown to be useful. However, two cautions are in order. The first is that the access must be very fast to be useful. The delay between the instant the translator presses the expansion key and the point where the system has expanded the code so that the translator can go on typing text should be well under a second. The second caution is against eliminating the expansion key. Some systems automatically check for expansion codes every time the space bar is pressed, potentially causing surprises for the translator. As a rule, nothing should happen in the current segment window unless the translator specifically requests it. This policy is consistent with the effort to design a system in which the translator feels in control, is treated with respect, and is provided with an array of tools from which to choose.

Other Options at Level One. Other options which should be available at level one are communication with other translators and retrieval of relevant documents. Communication with other translators may be accomplished via electronic mail or electronic bulletin boards. Retrieval of relevant documents could be provided by access to data bases of translated materials or target language publications. If a new term is not in the printed dictionaries and not yet in the term banks, the translator may have to do some basic research. One approach is to find a recently translated document containing the term in question. Another approach is to find a recent article in the target language dealing with the topic at hand. By studying such articles, the translator may determine by context that a certain term is the translation for which it is looking.

Level Two Suggested Terms. At level two, the source text to be translated is available in segmented, machine readable form, which adds a new type of screen to the word processing, terminology access, and communications screens already available at level one. This new screen consists of three windows. The top window contains a segment of source text to be translated. The middle window contains suggested translations for highlighted terms in the segment. The bottom window is the translator's work area for the current segment, as in the other level. The system finds suggested translations of terms (words or phrases) simply by splitting the current source segment into words, finding the root of each, and looking them up in the local term file. When several entries are found to begin with the same word, the system chooses the term which matches the longest stretch of words in the source segment. For example, if the source segment contains the phrase *fountain pen* and there are two entries in the term file, one for *fountain* and another for *fountain pen,* the system will choose *fountain pen* because it is a longer match. Those terms in the source segment which are found in the term file are highlighted and numbered. The translations found in the term file are placed in the middle window with numbers corresponding to the numbers in the source text. The translator is free to use the suggestions or to ignore them. To use a suggestion the translator simply types the number of the suggestion and presses a function key which pulls down the suggestion and inserts it into the current segment.

Suppose that the current segment of source text contains the French expressions *grand public* and *démarcheurs à domicile* and that the system correctly suggests the translations *general public* and *door-to-door salesmen.* The translator might type in something such as: *Sales to the 1$ may be done through 2$ or by mail.* The dollar signs indicate that some special key was pressed at that point. Pressing that key tells the computer to use the preceding number as a suggestion number. The suggestion with that number is instantly retrieved from the suggestion window and inserted into the text at the cursor position. Thus, two or three keystrokes suffice to use a suggestion, no matter how long the suggestion might be. As the translator marks additional entries in the term files, the number of suggestions that appear per segment increase. Its usefulness is also influenced by the system's effectiveness at finding root forms and reconstructing appropriate inflected forms. Of course, if a suggestion is often found to be unusable, it can be modified or the entry can be marked so that it does not appear automatically. It is important to note here that nothing is imposed on the translator. Suggested translations of terms will never appear in the target text unless the translator explicitly requests that they be inserted. The translator may also choose to switch back to a level one screen at the touch of a function key.

Level two is intended to be more convenient to the translator than level one. At level two, the translator has the current segment of source text on the screen along with suggested translations of terms, and as the translator scrolls back and forth through the translation, the appropriate segment of source text automatically appears in the upper window. As mentioned previously, this avoids having to scroll separately through the source and target texts and is the main motivation for using segments throughout the system. Another benefit of level two is that it can facilitate communication among several translators working on the same project. Given that a term file with suggestions is shared by several translators, they will automatically be made aware of standard translations that have been established for technical terms. This could help the team produce translations with more consistency in terminology. Consistency of usage in technical documents is important as lack of it can lead to confused readers. Moreover, another benefit of level two is that having the source text in machine readable form allows preprocessing of the source text, including a spelling check and a check for repeated phrases that may need standard translations.

Level Three Suggestion Translations of Larger Units. Level three does not take anything away from levels one and two, rather it does make one huge addition: it includes a modified machine translation system. Eventually, the machine translation component may be completely incorporated into a high-powered translator work station. But for the moment, I anticipate a link with an existing off-line machine translation system. I have a tentative agreement with the University of Grenoble (France) to integrate their machine translation system, so I will use it as an example. Their system runs on an IBM mainframe, accepts a source text, divides it into segments in approximately the way prescribed for level two, and translates the text a segment at a time. To be used in the BYU Translator Aid System, the Grenoble system will have to be modified to keep track of problems encountered during translation, such as missing words in the dictionary, unknown syntactic constructions, and questionable translation choices. The output of the system must be a series of segment clusters. In each cluster will be the source segment, the machine translation of it, and the problem record for it. This information is presented to the translator work station on diskette or over a network, along with the segmented source text. At level two, only the segmented source text is presented to the work station. At level three, each segment of source text is accompanied by a problem record and perhaps a machine translation of the segment. The translator work station is always set to a particular tolerance level. When a given source segment is displayed, the translator work station checks the problem record in the segment cluster against the translator's tolerance level. If the problem severity does not exceed the tolerance level, then the machine translation for the segment will be displayed in the middle window of the screen. The translator can examine it and, if it is acceptable as is or with minor changes, can pull it down into the bottom window (the work area) and edit it. Or, if the machine translation is not acceptable, the translator can ignore it or switch back to a level two suggested term screen or to a level one screen. If a number of translated segments are unacceptable, the translator may choose to lower the tolerance level, thus blocking more segments. On some documents, the machine translation may be so poor that the translator finds it more efficient to turn off level three entirely. The translator can even turn off level two and proceed at level one with word processing and only those dictionary entries explicitly requested.

It should be obvious at this point that the design takes pains to ensure that the translator is in control, even at level three. The role of the translator is neither temporary nor undesirable. The translator is viewed as a competent professional who can be trusted to use the level of aids most appropriate for a given text and segment within a text. No piece of machine translation is ever forced upon the translator and cannot appear in the target text unless the translator requests it to be there. It should also be clear that to the translator there is little difference between the levels, despite the radical underlying differences. The translator can freely switch among various windows in the upper portion of the screen: previous text, terminology access, communications, suggested terms, and suggested segment translations. To the translator, all the screens are part of one integrated system. It just happens that on some documents, level two and level three aids are not available, and on other documents, level two aids are available and level three aids are available only on some segments. This integration of levels, retaining respect for the translator, resolves the conflict between machine translation and translator aids. Stripped of the assumption that every segment must be translated by machine, machine translation becomes more friendly and more *useable*. The idea may be simple, but it has come into being only recently after nearly 30 years of hitting heads against fully automatic walls.

A possible objection to the approach proposed in this paper is that it limits work in machine translation by assuming that it will not work. Actually, it should encourage work in machine translation by allowing it to be useful, even if it is not of consistently high quality. If the machine translation component produces a perfectly acceptable translation for each segment of a text, the translator can simply pull down each segment of machine translation and pass it through as fast as the machine translation can be read. On the other hand, if the machine translation is somewhat less than perfect, the good segments can be pulled down and the translation process still proceeds smoothly. No limit is imposed on the sophistication of the machine translation component.

A final note is in order to explain the status of the BYU Translator Aid System. Last year we implemented a limited version of level two. We also have a separate version of a portion of level one. We will soon begin writing a new version on a 16-

bit microcomputer. This new version will include level one and two and at least a simulation of level three. True implementation of level three depends on the progress of negotiations to obtain access to a machine translation component. Undoubtedly, there will be surprises and design changes during the implementation and testing of the system. Our hope is to produce a *useable* demonstration system in the next few years or to spread ideas to the right people so that someone else will develop the system. In either case, I am very hopeful that the dignity and professional status of translators will be increased by treating machine translation as a tool, rather than as a replacement for translators, thus dissolving a dichotomy which is false because it is unnecessary and unproductive.

REFERENCES

ANDREYEWSKI, ALEXANDER. 1981. Translation: Aids, robots, and automation. META Translators' Journal 26:1.57–66.

CHANDIOUX, JOHN. 1978. METEO. TAUM: The University of Montreal.

KAY, MARTIN. 1980. The proper place of men and machines in language translation. Palo Alto, CA: Xerox Corporation.

MELBY, ALAN K. 1982. Multi-level translation aids in a distributed system. COLING82, ed. by Ján Horecký, 215–220. Amsterdam: North Holland.

WEAVER, WARREN. 1955. Translation. Machine translation of languages, ed. by W. N. Locke and A. D. Booth, 15–23. New York: Wiley.

FOUR

Towards a Natural Language Semantics Formalized in Terms of Physical Symbol Systems

Daniel Chester
University of Delaware

INTRODUCTION

An important part of the study of a language is a study of its semantics. In the past, the semantics of a language was described in another language or in a subset of the same language. For example, the meaning of an English sentence might be explained by translating it into an expression in a formal language or by explaining it in simpler terms in English. If the formal method is chosen, it has a semantics of its own that is ultimately explained in English. In either case, the explanation of the meaning of a sentence depends, in the last analysis, on a prior understanding of a part of natural language. That part may be small, but it is necessary as long as the semantics of a language is explained in a language.

Just as a dictionary is not a complete specification of vocabulary (words are defined in terms of other words) without some way of knowing what particular words mean, a specification of the semantics of a language is not complete without the help of something outside the language. Words and phrases have to be related to the world in some manner that depends on the physical nature of the people who understand them. However, people aren't born with an understanding of any particular language; they learn it initially from observations of language in use. Thus, it is possible to come to an understanding of the semantics of a language without prior knowledge of that language. Therefore, it should be possible to specify the semantics of a language in a way that is totally independent of any language. A methodology for specifying semantics in such language-free fashion would be an advance in linguistics as it would allow complete and objective semantics to be given for the first time. In this paper we propose an approach for the development of such a methodology.

Our proposed approach to language-free semantics specification stems from considering the task of programming a computer to verify sentences by examination of its environment through various optical, audio, and tactile sensors. The computer is the only entity besides man (and to some extent, animals) that can relate symbols to the real world; it therefore can play the role of the human who has not yet learned a language. By proper programming, it can embody the semantics of a language in that it can verify or deny sentences by virtue of its physical construction, without prior knowledge of the language being built into the hardware.

COMPUTABILITY OF SEMANTICS

The critical task in developing a language-free specification is to determine how the semantics of a natural language can be reduced to computable algorithms. Whether this is possible is an open question; but people learn their first language although born without a knowledge of any part of it, and there is reason to believe that what people do when they understand language utterances is computable. The brain appears to operate like a computer; what it does appears to be completely determined by its chemical and physical construction, and by the patterns of sensory stimuli that it receives, both past and present. Furthermore, what the brain does with the signals from its sensory neurons should be computable on a digital computer. There are a finite number of sensory neurons, each sensing the value of some property in some small volume integrated over a short interval of time. There are limits to the spatial and temporal resolution of neurons, suggesting that the sense data can be approximated to a high degree of accuracy by discrete sensing devices with digitized output and similar resolution. If brain behavior is determined by sense data, that behavior can be reproduced by a digital computer acting on sensor data approximating the brain's sense data.

A language is more than a symbol system with a grammar for combining symbols into expressions and an inference mechanism for generating new expressions from old ones; the symbols and expressions have to be interpreted in the world, which is what we mean by the semantics of that language. Some expressions in the language refer to objects in the world, others refer to events, and still others refer to abstractions of various sorts. But the brain (or, rather, the entire nervous system) does not perceive objects and events directly; it constructs them mentally out of sense data—the ultimate source of all its knowledge of the world. Sense data are the (neurological) signals produced by light, pressure, chemical, and temperature sensitive neurons in the sense organs, which are the points of contact between the nervous system and the world. Thus, the semantics of a language need to be described in terms of properties that can be measured by physical devices (sensors) at specific locations at specific times. This is a lower level of description than has been used in the past; generally, the meanings of sentences have been given in terms of objects, events, and their relations and properties. But since those entities (or rather our perceptions of them) derive from sense data, a complete description of how a language relates to the world must go down to the sense data level.

FORMALIZATION OF THE PROBLEM

In order to formally describe semantics in terms of computable algorithms, we propose to model the speaker/hearer of language utterances as a PHYSICAL SYMBOL

SYSTEM (a term borrowed from Newell 1980), that is, as a computer with input devices sensing its environment (e.g., video cameras, probes, microphones) and output devices affecting its environment (e.g., motor-powered arms, wheels). In other words, a physical symbol system (PSS) is a robot, but we emphasize the symbolic computations within it, rather than the workings of its physical body. The PSS emits utterances by broadcasting them (perhaps via radio teletype) so that other PSSs can receive them.

A PSS has a finite number of sensor types (e.g., detectors for light, color, heat, smoke, physical contact). We therefore represent the environment as a finite set of fields, one for each sensor type. We shall call them SENSOR FIELDS, or S-fields. The value of an S-field at each place and time represents what a sensor of the appropriate type would detect for that place and time. By representing the world in terms of sensor data, we do not make any commitments as to what objects there are in the world. Thus we do not take notions such as 'physical object' or 'event' as given; we must account for them in our model of language interpretation.

Similarly, a PSS has a finite number of output devices. Each of these devices has a location at any given time and is controlled by a signal from the computer. This signal causes a physical process to occur that may result in a change in the computer's environment. For example, on receiving a signal from the computer, an output device might move to a new location, carrying an attached sensor along with it, pushing some object out of the way, or releasing a chemical from a reservoir.

We assume that the computer in a PSS is interfaced to many input and output devices. Additionally, we assume that each input and output device has a unique name and that its location, relative to a fixed coordinate system, can be known at all times. Each device has a known type and produces or accepts a value of some simple data type (e.g., an integer or an element from a finite set of alternative values). There is a correlation between the signals sent to the output devices and the data received from the sensors because the output devices cause physical changes in the world and these changes are in turn detected by the sensors.

The semantic description problem can now be stated formally in terms of a language, a physical symbol system as speaker/hearer of the language, and a finite number of S-fields representing the directly knowable world. In the case of statements, the problem is to describe how to compute their truth on the basis of data obtained from the fields. In the case of commands, the problem is to describe how to recognize when a PSS carries them out by activating output devices in appropriate sequences. In the case of questions, the problem is to describe how to recognize that certain expressions are the answers (but not necessarily how to find them).

A SIMPLIFIED VERSION

If we try immediately to describe the meanings of everyday statements, we will be overwhelmed by the complexity of recognizing people and other objects in terms of ocular sense data, and of recognizing actions such as dancing, running, and deceiving. We therefore have to simplify the problem, making it tractable by eliminating features that are less relevant to linguistic issues. Such features include the shapes and sizes of objects and their biological or mineral composition.

We propose that formal studies of computable natural language semantics begin by considering a simple world in which the objects are particles. These particles might be spots on a television screen, insects crawling on a wall viewed from such a distance that their legs and wings can not be distinguished, or specks of dust floating on a pond. These particles are capable of moving about, of suddenly coming into view, of disappearing, and of splitting into two or more particles. These particles reside in a two-dimensional space that is devoid of features other than the particles.

Only a small subset of English vocabulary will be applicable in this world, but if we can devise how to program the computer to verify statements, execute commands, and answer questions in this world, we will have laid a foundation for understanding how language is understood in the real world.

Representation of the World

Although it is customary to think of the world as composed of objects that interact, that view already assumes that a considerable amount of sense data processing has taken place in the brain. In a PSS, the corresponding sensor data processing is part of the symbolic computations we want to understand, thus we model the world at the level of uninterpreted sensor data. Specifically, we model the world as a collection of S-fields. For simplicity let us assume that both time and space are discretized into uniform pieces. In our frame of reference, *t* is an integer parameter denoting time. The parameters *x* and *y* are integer quantities denoting coordinates in a rectilinear coordinate system. An S-field is a pair <Stype,Sf> where Stype is the sensor type of the field and Sf is a function mapping <*x*,*y*,*t*> triples into values of a kind appropriate for sensor type Stype. The S-field <Stype,Sf> denotes the potential values that can be measured by a sensor type Stype when it is located at position <*x*,*y*> at time *t*. We assume perfect operation of sensors; there is only one value that can be measured at a given place and time regardless of which sensor (of the given type) makes the measurement. (We allow more than one sensor to occupy a given place and time.) Ours is thus an idealized representation of the world as experienced through sensors.

It is important to realize that an S-field function of Sf represents a physical function and not a mathematical one. It associates a unique value with each combination of place and time, but this association is made by virtue of the nature of the world. The only way to know what the associated value is is to measure it with a sensor. The mathematician may construct a set of n-tuples that happens to correlate with this association (because it pairs the same values with the places and times as Sf does), but that is just one of many functions in the world of mathematics and there is no mathematical reason to prefer it over any other. An appropriate set of n-tuples may be stored in a computer to represent an S-field, but that set is distinct from the physical function that it represents.

At any time *t* and for any sensor *s* of type Stype, if *s* is located at position <*x*,*y*>, the PSS to which *s* belongs can call a subroutine that returns the value (Sf(x,y,t) of the Stype S-field. The PSS can then store the fact

(OBSERVATION Oname Stype Sf(x,y,t) x y t)

for later use. (Oname is a unique symbol created to serve as a name for the observation.) In this paper we will assume that sensor measurements have already been done and the observations have been stored. Since computations extend over relatively long periods of time and observations are over in an instant, the language processing programs of a PSS will have to handle such stored data, and it simplifies our model further if we assume that all observations are stored in this way before the programs access them. (They could be stored by a concurrent process that continually updates the observation data base while the language processing programs are running.) This assumption also makes it irrelevant whether the observation data came from actual sensors or whether they came from a simulation; as long as exactly the same data becomes accessible in exactly the same order, it doesn't matter where they came from to the computer programs.

Object Recognition

The sensor data on which all PSS computations are based are similar to the data that image processing researchers input into their programs. Object recognition is a major task in the image processing field and it is an essential part of our proposal, but in order to focus on the linguistic issues that arise in discourse about objects after they have been recognized, we have proposed to limit the objects to point objects. These particles occupy only one $\langle x,y \rangle$ location at any one time; thus they have unique x-coordinates and y-coordinates that vary with time. For simplicity let us assume that there is only one type of sensor such that the world is modelled by a single S-field $\langle p,f \rangle$. In this model the value $f(x,y,t)$ is always equal to zero except in the small number of places where particles are located. The property p is analogous to luminosity; distinct levels of brightness are denoted by a range of values, with zero as the default value (the value measured by a sensor in the absence of a stimulus). The object recognition task consists of identifying the observations that correspond to the particles as they endure over a period of time.

Recognizing particles requires at least a two-stage process. First, observations of a particle in continuous view are grouped together to make PARTICLE SEGMENTS; then particle segments corresponding to multiple appearances of the same particle are grouped together to make a PARTICLE. The first grouping might be done on the basis of a simple proximity rule like:

01 continues as 02 iff
 01 occurred at a time *t*,
 and 02 occurred at a time *t* + 1,
 and of all the observations at time *t*,
  01 is the nearest to 02,
 and of all the observations at time *t* + 1,
  02 is the nearest to 01.

Note that this rule does not mention the luminosity observed at times t and $t + 1$; particles can change brightness during a period of continuous observation. Observations are partitioned into particle segments according to the equivalence relation

01 is particle-segment-equivalent to 02 iff
 01 = 02,
 or 01 continues as 02,
 or 02 continues as 01,
 or there is an observation 03 such that
  01 is particle-segment-equivalent to 03,
  and 03 is particle-segment-equivalent to 02.

All of the observations that belong to the same equivalence class are observations of one particle segment. In simple cases, these are just the observations of a single particle from the time that it comes into view to the time that it vanishes from view. If a particle splits in two, however, there will be three particle segments: one is the particle up to the split and the other two are the two particles seen leaving the split. Whether one of the latter is identified with the former as observations of the same particle depends on the second grouping stage.

The second grouping is based on some property other than proximity, such as similarity of brightness or behavior exhibited by the particle segments. There is no objective way to be certain of the identity of an object that goes out of view and then comes back, but people make assumptions about such identities all the time. (Is that really your cousin whom you haven't seen for 10 years?) A simple criterion based on similarity of brightness or behavior should be satisfactory for preliminary efforts to work out the relation between objects and sentences about them.

CONNECTIONS WITH LANGUAGE

Representation of Events

The solutions to many linguistic problems are expressed in terms of events. According to a proposal of Davidson (1967), for example, the sentence *John walked to the store* should be represented by

(FOR SOME x) (WALK(John,x) & TO(the-store,x)).

This can be read as "there is an event which is a walking of John and which is to the store." But Davidson does not explain what an event is. Lemmon (1967) proposed that an event is the volume of space-time occupied by the objects participating in the event. We view events differently: an event, at least in simple cases, is a collection of physical functions that are defined on a particular region of space-time, namely, the region of space-time where the event occurs. Within this region, the functions coincide with some (or possibly all) of the S-fields, as there are functions for only some (or possibly all) sensor types. The possibility of restricting the type of sensor data involved allows for several events to occupy the same space, as when a particle flickers at the same time that it moves from one place to another.

The partial functions composing an event can be defined by restricting the proximity grouping relation that determined the segments of particles in various ways. A motion segment, for example, might be defined as the equivalence class for the relation RM(x,y), where

> RM(x,y) holds iff
> x continues as y,
> and the location of x does not equal the location of y.

This relation divides up particle segments into subsegments in which particles are in motion, separated by subsegments in which they are at rest.

Other events might be defined by monadic predicates restricted by the grouping relation. Thus, if a particle were to be said to glow when it had a particular brightness c, glowing events would be the observation equivalence classes determined by the relation

> x continues as y,
> and x has brightness c,
> and y has brightness c.

Conceptual Objects

Events defined by forming equivalence classes from relations and properties that have been restricted by the proximity grouping relation are elementary in that it is easy to see how they can be computed, either on a digital computer or in the brain with the aid of feature detectors such as those believed to exist in the eye. More complex and abstract events, however, may be constructed by applying various operations comparable to the higher level grouping principle for forming particles out of particle segments, plus some mathematical operations. The objects so created are more conceptual in nature and are, in some sense, less real than physical objects (the classes determined by the grouping operations given earlier).

Imagine that the notions of objects and events elaborated for particles were extended to people and their locomotions. A walking event would be formed by grouping together particular types of motion events involving the same person and these simpler motion events would be grouped in a particular order. When John walks to the store his torso moves more or less evenly through space while his legs go through a complex motion in which one end (the foot) makes contact with the ground and remains relatively motionless at regular intervals. The walking event is thus a complex object having a hierarchical structure owing to its decomposition into simpler motions. Together these simpler motions coincide with the S-fields restricted to the volume of space occupied by John's body during the time that he was walking to the store. This walking event is the one that was said to exist by the existential statement given earlier.

Now imagine a particle moving from location A to location B while glowing at the same time, and assume that the world is modelled by only one S-field. According to the simple notion of event given earlier, the moving event and the glowing event would be the same event because they consist of the same S-field restricted to the same space-time region. It is natural, however, to think of them as two separate events, as when we say 'the particle glowed as it moved from A to B.' The separation is also evident in the clear nonequivalence of 'the particle's glowing resulted in its arrival at B' to 'the particle's moving resulted in its arrival at B.' These distinct glowing and moving events can be explained by allowing the notion of event to include new conceptual objects formed by abstraction, generalization, and projection operations. The moving event can then be thought of as a projection of the particle made by deleting some of its properties; in this case the brightness of the particle is removed so that only the position as a function of time remains. The glowing event is just the opposite; it is an association of brightness with time but without location.

POSSIBLE SCOPE OF PSS PROGRAMS

Although the version of the semantics specification problem proposed here is simple, it has a wide scope of possibilities for computational and linguistic investigations. A computer could be programmed to respond to sentences in a subset of English. This subset would have a vocabulary of function and generic words appropriate to the description of moving particles. The grammar of the subset could be a simple portion of English grammar; large enough to include major features common to many languages, but small enough to omit idioms and complex constructions peculiar to English.

The computer could be programmed to act as a PSS, that is, it could verify declarative sentences in the English subset as to their truth concerning a set of observations. A simple display program could show the observations as particles moving about on a CRT screen. The meanings of specific words as they apply to the display could be studied by making the PSS program determine correctly the truth of sentences such as

1. Particle A suddenly moved part particle B.
2. The particle that changes brightness pushed particle C next to the stationary particle.
3. Particle A circled particle B three times before it split into two particles.
4. Particle A collided with particle B, causing it to change brightness and start to behave erratically.
5. Two particles suddenly appeared from nowhere.

The sentence-verification program could consist of a parser and semantic routines that translate the sentences into representations for concepts constructed by the abstraction, generalization, and projection operations mentioned earlier. These representations could then be interpreted as recognition programs that determine whether the sentence describes the PSS's sensor data. They should agree with human judgments based on observing the graphic display of that data.

Studies in communication could be carried out by letting some of the moving particles act as PSSs. Each would have its own set of sensor data and computational processes for responding to its environment. Each could be programmed to obey commands and answer questions. Each could be made to respond appropriately to sentences such as

1. What is your brightness level?
2. Where is the zig-zag particle?
3. Push particle A next to particle B.
4. Drag particle A around with you from now on.
5. Don't let particle C pass you when it charges.

The several PSSs could be programmed to broadcast messages to each other in the subset of English. They could inform each other of observations that are not accessible to all, ask questions of each other when they need additional information, and give commands to each other in order to solve problems together, such as rounding up all of the non-PSS particles that may be wandering about.

DIRECTIONS FOR RESEARCH

There are many engineering, linguistic, psychological, and philosophical issues that can be studied in the context of PSSs and S-fields. Research concerned with the computational problem of representing the meanings of language expressions, however, can focus on issues pertaining to concept representation, particularly of events, communication of concepts between PSSs, and knowledge representation. The following is a discussion of some of the issues that can be explored.

1. Imprecise concepts. How can concepts be defined in terms of S-fields and retain the imprecision of natural language concepts? One possible explanation is that most concepts are not defined explicitly. Most concepts are formed by generalization from examples. These generalizations can be described as rules for recognizing instances of a concept. Thus, a concept C might be defined by a set of rules of the form

If X has property P then X is a C.

These rules do not give a closed definition of C, however, because they do not rule out the possibility that there are Cs that satisfy properties not covered by the rules. Nevertheless, it is useful for a PSS to behave as if the rules cover all possible cases. The PSS may someday come upon a new instance of C that is not covered by its rules (identified by some trusted source, such as another PSS), so it must be prepared to change them from time to time.

2. Indirect knowledge. The semantics of a language may be described in terms of direct computation of the truth of statements from the S-fields. However, suppose that a PSS broadcasts a true statement S to another PSS that is not in a situation where it can verify S for itself. How does the second PSS represent the meaning of S? How does it draw inferences from it and other statements? Generally, how does the way that a PSS handles knowledge learned from other PSSs differ from the way that it handles knowledge discovered firsthand?

3. Representation of events. How can a PSS recognize events? Events to be considered include objects that have gradually changing properties but endure over a long period of time, events involving motion, events of creation and destruction, including objects that split or merge in collisions, and events involving arrangements of many objects (e.g., a party). How are events represented, particularly when the PSS can observe only a part of them? How are events described and referred to in English? How do sentences asserting that an event has occurred relate to a noun phrase referring to the event, to a question about the event, or to a command to cause the event to happen?

4. Nonsentences. How can a PSS handle ungrammatical sentences and sentence fragments? Can meaning be ascribed to them by applying some general problem-solving technique? How are the meanings of multiword phrases built up from the separate meanings of the words? How are these meanings and operations on meanings described in terms of the S-fields?

5. Hypothetical entities. How does a PSS represent hypothetical entities such as electrons and the computations taking place in another PSS? These objects and events are not directly observable in the S-fields; they are postulated at an abstract conceptual level to explain observed phenomena. How are the meanings of sentences about these entities to be represented? How does the semantics of a language extend to these sentences?

6. Episodic memory. A PSS will store some sensor data in its memory for future use. These data make a finite number of values in the S-fields available from the past for verification of statements about events extending over time. How can these data be best organized to facilitate future recognition of various events? How can that organization help the PSS to process sentences broadcast by other PSSs?

RELATION TO OTHER WORK

Many researchers have combined vision with their language processing systems, but most have not addressed the issues with which we are concerned. Winograd (1972), Simmons and Bennett-Novak (1975), and Novak (1976) generated pictures to illustrate the understanding of English exhibited by their systems, but no pictures were analyzed and no events were recognized from low-level data. Harris (1972) programmed a robot that learned to map a lexicon into its sensory/motor concepts, and a grammar for a language in which statements, questions, and commands appropriate to its world could be made, but that world was a 8 by 4 grid in which tables and chairs, existing as unstructured entities, were located. Coles (1972) and Kawaguchi et al. (1979) wrote programs that analyzed pictures, but these pictures were symbolic diagrams—drawings of electrical circuits, chemical structures, geometric figures, or weather maps. In all cases the pictures were static, so no notion of event was needed.

Tsuji et al. (1979), Okada (1979), and Abe et al. (1981) wrote programs that analyze sequences of pictures, but these pictures were cartoon-like and the sequences resembled slide shows rather than movies. Some researchers have analyzed movie sequences of pictures. Badler (1975) generated descriptions from line drawings. Tsotsos (1981) recognized events occuring in an x-ray movie of a beating heart, and Marburger et al. (1981) analyzed television images of traffic. All of these researchers were concerned with recognizing the most basic events in their respective domains without concern for linguistic issues or for higher-level perceptions such as causality and purpose.

Waltz (1978) argued that 'without a connection to the real world via perception, a language system cannot know what it is talking about' (p. 149). He supported the view that there is an innate internal language. Waltz and Boggess (1979) wrote a program that builds analog models from input sentences and then answers questions about the modeled scene. Linguistically, the program was concerned primarily with prepositions of relative location. Later, Waltz (1980, 1981) began to investigate dynamic scenes, but still from a generative point of view. His objective was to understand text with the help of event simulations to determine which interpretations of the text are plausible. But he did not make clear what an event is.

Some researchers, such as Talmy (1978), Herskovits (1980), and Jackendoff (1975), discussed the meanings of words in terms of relationships between objects. These treatments sometimes did so formally by giving axiomatic definitions, but the predicates in these axioms still require interpretation. Most discussions gave the semantics of the primitive concepts by means of pictures instead of formally, as we are attempting to do.

Sondheimer (1977, 1978) came closer to defining words in terms of measurable properties in time and space. He proposed to treat objects and events as extending in both spatial and temporal dimensions, and analyzed some cases of case grammar in terms of the spatio-temporal properties of objects, but his research in this area is just a beginning in the direction of an objective semantics.

Allen (1981a, 1981b) formalized some higher-level concepts concerning events, but did not explain what events are. Similarly, Barwise (1981a, 1981b) and Barwise and Perry (1981) developed situational semantics for language without formally relating situations to data concerning measurable properties of events and objects.

The questions raised by this paper involve some deep philosophical issues that have been debated for some time. Recently Carnap (1967) and Goodman (1977) attempted to give formal treatments of objects and properties in terms of sense data. Both, however, started with the assumption that the data were unstructured and had to be analyzed with a few topological relationships. We do not make the same assumption because we view the data as that collectible by present-day computers and sensing devices. We allow ourselves any relationship that can be defined in terms of the types and values of measurable properties (the S-fields) and the spatio-temporal coordinates of where those properties are measured. This gives us a richer environment in which to construct (a perception of) the world.

CONCLUSION

As a beginning step towards a methodology for specifying the semantics of a language without appealing to human interpretation, we have proposed that the semantics of a portion of English be specified in terms of computer programs that process data gathered from sensors. For simplicity, the world is assumed to be composed of animate particles whose location and brightness are detectable via sensors. A computer program would parse English sentences and verify or deny whether they are true of the world as perceived through the sensor data. The experience and techniques that go into such a program should be generalizable to techniques that apply to a larger portion of English and to natural languages in general.

This line of research might form the basis of a constructive theory of concepts. This theory would show how new concepts can be formed from old ones by operations such as partitioning and projection. Some of the constructible concepts would be identified with basic notions such as objects and events. This theory might help in the solution of some linguistic problems, including the impreciseness of natural concepts, the representation of information obtained through language instead of from direct sensing of the environment, the representation of events, the semantics of sentence fragments and ungrammatical expressions, the need for hypothesized entities, and the organization of episodic memory for efficient language processing.

REFERENCES

ABE, NORIHIRO, ITSUYA SOGA, and SABURO TSUJI. (1981). A plot understanding system on reference to both image and language. Proceedings of the Seventh International Joint Conference on Artificial Intelligence, 77–84. University of British Columbia, Vancouver, Canada, August 24–28.

ALLEN, JAMES F. 1981a. A general model of action and time. Technical Report TR 97, Computer Science Department, University of Rochester, Rochester, NY.

______. 1981b. What's necessary to hide?: Modeling action verbs. Proceedings of the 19th Annual Meeting of the Association for Computational Linguistics, 77–81. Stanford University, Stanford, California, June 29–July 1.

BADLER, NORMAN. 1975. The conceptual description of physical activities. American Journal of Computational Linguistics, Microfiche 35.

BARWISE, JON. 1981a. Scenes and other situations. The Journal of Philosophy 78.369–397.

______. 1981b. Some computational aspects of situation semantics. Proceedings of the 19th Annual Meeting of the Association for Computational Linguistics, 109–111. Stanford University, Stanford, California, June 29–July 1.

BARWISE, JON, and JOHN PERRY. 1981. Situations and attitudes. The Journal of Philosophy 78.668–691.

CARNAP, RUDOLF. 1967. The logical structure of the world and pseudoproblems in philosophy, translated by Rolf A. George. Berkeley, CA: University of California Press.

COLES, L. STEVEN. 1972. Syntax directed interpretation of natural language. Representation and meaning, ed. by Herbert A. Simon and Laurant Siklossy, 211–287. Englewood Cliffs, NJ: Prentice-Hall.

DAVIDSON, DONALD. 1967. The logical form of action sentences. The logic of decision and action, ed. by Nicholas Rescher, 81–95. Pittsburgh, PA: University of Pittsburgh Press.

GOODMAN, NELSON. 1977. The structure of appearance, 3rd ed. Dordrecht, Holland: D. Reidel Publishing Company.

HARRIS, LARRY RONALD. 1972. A model for adaptive problem solving applied to natural language acquisition. Technical Report TR 72–133, Department of Computer Science, Cornell University, Ithaca, NY.

HERSKOVITS, ANNETTE. 1980. On the spatial uses of prepositions. Proceedings of the 18th Annual Meeting of the Association for Computational Linguistics, 1–5. University of Pennsylvania, Philadelphia, Pennsylvania, June 19–22.

JACKENDOFF, RAY. 1975. A system of semantic primitives. Theoretical issues in natural language processing, ed. by R. Schank and B. L. Nash-Webber, 24–29. Cambridge, Massachusetts, June 10–13.

KAWAGUCHI, EIJI, MASAO YOKOTA, TSUTOMU ENDO, and TUNEO TAMATI. 1979. An understanding system of natural language and pictorial pattern in world of weather report. Proceedings of the Sixth International Joint Conference on Artificial Intelligence, 469–474. Tokyo, August 20–23.

LEMMON, E. J. 1967. Comments on D. Davidson's 'The logical form of action sentences'. The logic of decision and action, ed. by Nicholas Rescher, 96–103. Pittsburgh, PA: University of Pittsburgh Press.

MARBURGER, HEINZ, BERND NEUMANN, and HANS-JOACHIM NOVAK. 1981. Natural language dialogue about moving objects in an automatically analyzed traffic scene. Proceedings of the Seventh International Joint Conference on Artificial Intelligence, 49–51. University of British Columbia, Vancouver, Canada, August 24–28.

NEWELL, ALLEN. 1980. Physical symbol systems. Cognitive Science 4.135–183.

NOVAK, GORDON S., JR. 1976. Computer understanding of physics problems stated in natural language. Technical Report NL–30, Department of Computer Science, University of Texas at Austin.

OKADA, NAOYUKI. 1979. SUPP: Understanding moving picture patterns based on linguistic knowledge. Proceedings of the Sixth International Joint Conference on Artificial Intelligence, 690–692. Tokyo, August 20–23.

SIMMONS, ROBERT F., and GORDON BENNETT-NOVAK. 1975. Semantically analyzing an English subset for the clowns microworld. American Journal of Computational Linguistics, Microfiche 18.

SONDHEIMER, NORMAN K. 1977. Spatial reference and semantic nets. American Journal of Computational Linguistics, Microfiche 71.

———. 1978. A semantic analysis of reference to spatial properties. Linguistics and Philosophy 2.235–280.

TALMY, LEONARD. 1978. The relation of grammar to cognition—a synopsis. Theoretical issues in natural language processing–2, 149–156. University of Illinois at Urbana-Champaign, July 25–27.

TSOTSOS, JOHN, K. 1981. Temporal event recognition: An application to left ventricular performance. Proceedings of the Seventh International Joint Conference on Artificial Intelligence, 900–907. University of British Columbia, Vancouver, Canada, August 24–28.

TSUJI, SABURO, MICHIHARU OSADA, and MASAHIKO YACHIDA. 1979. Three dimensional movement analysis of dynamic line images. Proceedings of Sixth International Joint Conference on Artificial Intelligence, 896–901. Tokyo, August 20–23.

WALTZ, DAVID L. 1978. On the interdependence of language and perception. Theoretical issues in natural language processing—2, 149–156. University of Illinois at Urbana-Champaign, July 25–27.

———. 1980. Understanding scene descriptions as event simulations. Proceedings of the 18th Annual Meeting of the Association for Computational Linguistics, 7–11. University of Pennsylvania, Philadelphia, June 19–22.

———. 1981. Toward a detailed model of processing for language describing the physical world. Proceedings of the Seventh International Joint Conference on Artificial Intelligence, 1–6. University of British Columbia, Vancouver, Canada, August 24–28.

———, and LOIS BOGGESS. 1979. Visual analog representations for natural language understanding. Proceedings of the Sixth International Joint Conference on Artificial Intelligence, 926–934. Tokyo, August 20–23.

WINOGRAD, TERRY. 1972. Understanding natural language. New York: Academic Press.

FIVE

Two Strategies of Robustness for Natural Language Understanding Systems*

Amir M. Razi
University of Delaware

Augmented Transition Networks, ATN (Bates 1978), have been used successfully in representing a language's grammar. They have proved to be flexible, easy to write and debug, able to handle a wide variety of syntactic constructions, and easy to interface to other components of a total system. They provide a useful way to give an account of linguistic structures, can be easily communicated to humans and computers, and may be presented by easily visualized diagrams.

An ATN is a network of nodes and edges. Nodes correspond to the computational state of the parse, and edges (arcs) correspond to the legal grammatical items. There is a start state and a set of final states. Transitions from state to state consume input words, perform tests, and set registers. An input sequence is said to be accepted by the network if, beginning in the start state, some path can be followed which terminates at a final state and accounts for the whole input.

Each arc includes a test and a sequence of actions. The test associated with an arc must be satisfied for an arc to be taken, and the actions are executed as the arc is traversed. The actions construct pieces of structure and keep them in registers. Registers and their contents are available on subsequent arcs, and can be changed or added to as more of the input is processed.

The arrangement of states and arcs reflects the surface structure of acceptable input sequences, and the actions permit rearrangement and embeddings to create a structure which may be different from the surface structure. This very general mechanism provides transformational capabilities which can produce deep structures of the sort employed by a transformational grammar, and it makes the ATN formalism equivalent in power to a turing machine.

There are several types of arcs: a CAT arc may be taken if the current input word is of the syntactic category specified by the arc. A JUMP arc specifies the state to which a transition is to be made without consuming a word. A PUSH arc initiates a new, perhaps recursive, call to the network which begins in the state indicated by

* This is based upon work supported in part by the National Science Foundation under Grant No. IST-8009673.

the arc and which looks for a constituent. A POP arc signals finding a complete constituent, and causes control to return to the PUSH arc which requested the constituent. Together, these allow definitions of complex constituents, such as English noun phrases. A WORD arc specifies the exact word of input which is required. A VIR arc checks to see whether a constituent of the named type has been placed on the HOLD list by a HOLD action of some previous arc. This accounts for phrases that have been moved from their normal position, e.g., the relativized noun phrase of English relative clauses. Figure 1 illustrates a simple ATN grammar which could be used in parsing example sentences in this paper.

Spoken or written language does not always follow the grammar rules strictly. There are utterances which are ungrammatical but meaningful (e.g., *He works good*). A theoretical linguist who studies the human facility of language must answer the question that Chomsky (1961, p. 386) asks:

> by what mechanism can a grammar assign to an arbitrary phone sequence a structural description that indicates its degree of grammaticalness, the degree of its deviation from grammatical regularities, and the manners of its deviation.

A computational linguist who builds a natural language interface to a computer system must consider how to identify an error, and assign at least a partial analysis to an improperly formed utterance. In response to this need, Weischedel and Sondheimer (1980) have developed a framework for processing ungrammatical

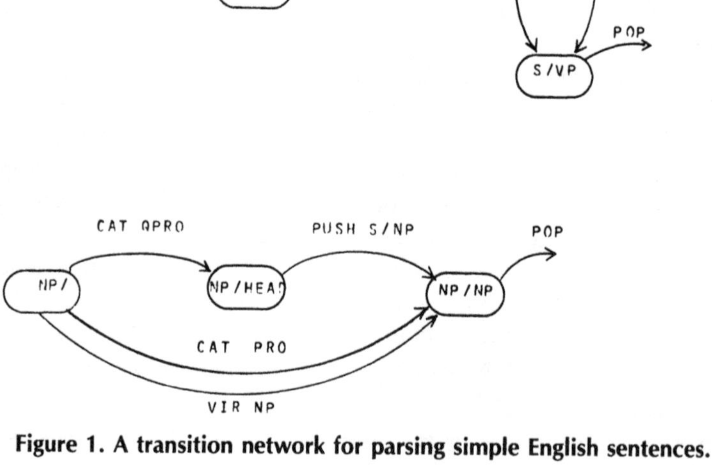

Figure 1. A transition network for parsing simple English sentences.

inputs within a computational system. They have used meta-rules to relate ungrammaticality explicitly to the rules of grammaticality.

The general approach is based on the separation of grammatical and ungrammatical forms. When a grammar fails to analyze an input, ungrammaticality processing begins. First, a heuristic identifies the cause of the failure, based on the partial interpretations produced by the grammar. Then the constraints imposed by the grammar around the suspected point of the error are relaxed and parsing continues.

Meta-rules capture the heuristic necessary to identify errors, and show how to relax the constraints of the grammar so that a partial interpretation may be assigned despite errors. Meta-rules are, roughly, functions from grammars to grammars. They map ATN grammars to ATN grammars that accept ungrammatical utterances.

Meta-rules have the form of simple rewrite rules:

```
C1 C2 . . . Cn ===> A1 A2 . . . Am
```

The left hand side (LHS) of the rule is a set of conditions in the form of predicates all of which must be true for the meta-rule to be applied. The conditions in the LHS look at the computational state of a failed path. The right hand side (RHS) of a meta-rule is a set of actions to be carried out when the LHS matches. These actions change the ATN configuration of a blocked path. The application of the meta-rule, therefore, gets us past the point of the blockage.

We have been experimenting with the RUS English grammar produced by Robert Bobrow at Bolt, Beranek, and Newman (Bobrow 1978). Presented with the ungrammatical utterance *where did you wanted to go,* the grammar is incapable of parsing it. The parser attempts 64 paths through the grammar; each path ends at an arc that does not allow continuation. Which one of these 64 paths is a reasonable candidate for relaxation? Weischedel and Sondheimer (1980) limit the consideration of blocked paths to those that have accounted for the largest part of the input. This reduces the set of paths to 12, all of which failed when trying to interpret the verb *wanted.* Applying the meta-rules would restrict the set further. A meta-rule to allow for the type of error represented by our example has one condition: (FAILED-TEST? (CHECKF V UNTENSED)). This is true if the blocked arc has a test that failed and if that test included a predicate (CHECKF V UNTENSED) that was false. In our grammar, this predicate is true if the word under consideration is an infinitive. Only one of the 12 paths satisfies this condition.

The RHS of a meta-rule is a set of actions to be carried out when the LHS matches. In order to relax the constraints on the grammar, the actions change the ATN configuration of a blocked path. In addition, the structure being produced by the parse is modified to record the application of the meta-rule. For our example the RHS is:

```
(NEW-CONFIGURATION
  (SUBSTITUTE-IN-ARC (CHECKF V UNTENSED) T)
  (FAILED-CONSTRAINT (INFINITIVE FORM ASSUMED)))
```

This action replaces the test for infinitive with "TRUE" and adds a deviance note to the parse tree to mark the use of the meta-rule.

The application of the meta-rule gets us past the point of the blockage, and the parser then produces a complete interpretation with the same structure as "where did you want to go."

As mentioned earlier, the heuristic suggested by Weischedel and Sondheimer (1980) limits the consideration of blocked paths to those that have got furthest in the input. Intuitively, this is a good heuristic to apply. If there are two blocked paths, one of which consumed more input than the other, it is more likely that the longer path will lead to a complete parse after relaxation of a failed constraint. But what if the true failure is associated with a shorter path? In that case, the true problem would be missed and parsing would fail.

As an example, consider the utterance *what did you wanted to say* from natural discourse (Fay 1980). The grammar is incapable of parsing it. The parser attempts 177 paths through the grammar. The furthest-in-the-input heuristic reduces the set of paths to 17, all of which failed after the verb *say* was consumed. The parser, considering a declarative interpretation using the phrase *what did you* as subject of the utterance, consumed all of the words in the input, but failed because no object was found for the transitive verb *say*. This is analogous to *what did it,* which is the subject of *what did it, wanted flowers* when uttered after *my flowers were trampled.* This interpretation could be avoided by using appropriate semantics.

The meta-rule for relaxing the tense of the verb *wanted* was not applicable to any one of the 17 paths in the test; hence the true problem was missed.

This heuristic could be altered slightly, to consider blocked paths that have accounted for the second largest part of the input, if consideration of blocked paths which have got furthest in the input does not yield any complete parse. This process can continue by considering paths which consumed one less word than previously considered, till a possible parse is found.

The problem with the altered heuristic is efficiency. It might hypothesize many inappropriate arcs.

A promising alternative to the above heuristics is to parse the utterance from right to left (RL) after the blockage of the left to right (LR) parse. When the RL parse blocks, the two partial parses of LR and RL will be compared. If they join except for one ATN arc, then the corresponding arc could be a strong candidate for relaxation. This arc is supported by both of the contexts to the left and right of the failure point, as opposed to only the left context used in previous heuristics.

This heuristic can pinpoint errors more accurately, and could be used to identify the type of errors. Identifying the type of errors could even suggest new meta-rules.

There are many ways to implement right to left parsing. The grammar could be inverted through indexing by determining, for each state, which arcs can enter it and, for each arc, which state it comes from.

The inverted grammar could be used by a context-free parser. The parser starts at the right end of the utterance, and goes from right to left. After a context free path has been found, one must traverse that path left to right to handle context-sensitive tests.

Alternatively, RL parsing could be simulated by LR parsing. Basically, we want to find a partial parse for the last part of the utterance which is one gap away from the potential parse corresponding to the first part of the utterance. This could be done by computing configurations that are one gap away from a blocked configuration, parsing from left to right, and then trying to complete those using a context-free version of the grammar. We have to use a context-free parse because of the lack of left context. This scheme would come up with a considerable number of context-free parses, each representing a potential path for a complete parse. Context sensitive tests must be carried out on the candidate path after relaxation, to get a complete parse.

A minor variation of the last strategy is to compute the configurations that are one gap away from a blocked configuration, and then trying to complete those going context-free, from left to right, at the level where blockage occurred, as before, but using the original context-sensitive grammar when pushes (i.e., requests for parsing new constituents) occur. This assumes that the grammar does not need any left context information for parsing new constituents (i.e., pushes). This would save the parser from trying to parse those constituents for the second time. It seems that this method is the most efficient of all. We call this ISLAND-LIKE parsing.

The decision to choose a right to left parsing has not been made yet, but island-like parsing is the most promising one.

To compare the performance of the heuristic proposed here with the heuristic proposed by Weischedel and Sondheimer (1980), experiments have to be conducted on a large corpus of ungrammatical utterances exhibiting the variety of problems which must be faced by practical systems.

Utterances can be classified with respect to the constructs which are troublesome in parsing. These include: (a) co-occurrence violations, which result from a problem such as lack of agreement; (b) ellipsis, which is omission of some of the words required for a complete sentence; (c) quantifiers; (d) conjunction; and a combination of (a) through (d). The last two classes are not ungrammatical, but special techniques are needed to handle them. Several experiments have been performed to analyze classes of sentences which break the rules of language. Malhotra (1975) performed an experiment on live subjects in designing a system to support decision making activities. Thompson (1980) and Eastman and Mcleen (1981) have performed similar experiments and classified sources of problems with their frequencies of occurrences in an utterance. These statistics illustrate the magnitude of the problem and indicate how important they are. Studies of this sort provide insight into the range of errors that can occur in the use of language.

The relevant parameters for performance comparison are the time and space usage of each heuristic, the frequency of cases where the true problem is missed (reliability), and the frequency of hypothesizing inappropriate arcs (efficiency) in each class of sentences.

ACKNOWLEDGMENTS

I would like to thank my advisor, Ralph M. Weischedel, and Norm K. Sondheimer for their support and patient instruction.

REFERENCES

BATES M. 1978. The theory and practice of augmented transition network grammars. Natural language communication with computers, ed. by L. Bolc, 191–259. Berlin: Springer-Verlag.

BOBROW, R. J. 1978. The RUS system. Research in natural language understanding, ed. by B. L. Weber and R. Bobrow. BBN Report No. 3878. Cambridge, MA: Bolt, Beranek and Newman.

CHOMSKY, N. 1964. Degrees of grammaticalness. The structure of language: Readings in the philosophy of language, ed. by J. A. Fodor and J. J. Katz, 384–389. Englewood Cliffs, NJ: Prentice-Hall.

EASTMAN, C. M., and D. S. MCLEEN. 1981. On the need for parsing ill-formed input, American Journal of Computational Linguistics 7.257.

FAY, D. 1980. Transformational errors, errors in linguistic performance: Slips of the tongue, ear, pen, and hand, ed. by V. A. Fromkin, 111–122. New York: Academic Press.

MALHOTRA, A. 1975. Design criteria for a knowledge-based English language system for management: An experimental analysis. MAC TR 146. Cambridge, MA: M.I.T.

SONDHEIMER, N. K., and R. M. WEISCHEDEL. 1980. A rule-based approach to ill-formed input. Proceedings of the Eighth International Conference on Computational Linguistics, 46–53, 46–53. Tokyo.

THOMPSON, B. H. 1980. Linguistic analysis of natural language communication with computers. Proceedings of the Eighth International Conference on Computational Linguistics, 190–201. Tokyo, September 30–October 4.

SIX

Lexical-Semantic Relations in Information Retrieval*

Martha Evens
Illinois Institute of Technology

James Vandendorpe
Bell Telephone Laboratories
Naperville, Illinois

Yih-Chen Wang
Illinois Institute of Technology

1. INTRODUCTION

Lexical-semantic relations provide a compact and powerful structure for both syntactic and semantic information. A number of new relations have been identified from definitions in the machine-readable form of *Webster's Seventh New Collegiate Dictionary* (hereafter W7). Experiments in information retrieval show that a thesaurus constructed from these relations can increase the recall of relevant information for poorly constructed queries.

A lexical-semantic relation is a rule that associates one English word with another. The synonymy and antonymy relations are the most familiar. *Speedy* is a synonym for *fast,* and *hot* is an antonym for *cold.* The taxonomy or ISA relation is often explicitly expressed in definitions: a beagle is a kind of dog.

Defining formulae are phrases like 'of or relating to' which reoccur in many definitions. The defining formulae in W7 often signal lexical-semantic relations. By counting recurring phrases we identified defining formulae and constructed sets of relations for different parts of speech. Definitions were parsed using Sager's (1981) Linguistic String Parser to extract relationships.

These sets of relations were grouped together into five semantically defined categories for the purpose of an extensive information retrieval experiment. Results showed a significant increase in the recall of relevant material for poorly defined

* We gratefully acknowledge the support received from the National Science Foundation under grant IST 79-18467. We wish to thank the G & C Merriam Company for allowing us to use the computer tapes of *Webster's Seventh New Collegiate Dictionary* prepared by John Olney. Dr. Vandendorpe's share of the work was completed while he was at IIT. He is now working for Bell Telephone Laboratories. This paper was not reviewed by Bell Telephone Laboratories.

queries with a less than normal degradation in the precision of the material retrieved. The best results seem to occur, as in Fox's (1981) work, with a combination of relations that exclude antonymy. We predict that individual relations will be most useful in interactive experiments where the user can guide the search.

In order of presentation, this paper:

- discusses the lexical-semantic relations used in our experiments.
- defines a partially automated procedure for discovering new lexical-semantic relations and recovering relationships from dictionary definitions using defining formulae.
- displays definitions produced by a computer using defining formulae.
- describes the experimental apparatus, an information retrieval system known as IRS, and presents the results of the IRS experiments.
- suggests further research in this area.

When we proposed this research (Evens 1979) we began with two questions: Can lexical-semantic relations be identified automatically? Can they provide a basis for a useful thesaurus for an information retrieval system? This paper reports our findings.

2. LEXICAL-SEMANTIC RELATIONS

Uses for Lexical-Semantic Relations

Lexical-semantic relations allow us to express both syntactic and semantic information in a form that is compact and easy to retrieve. Relational information is of immediate use in making inferences. Suppose a system is processing a story that begins:

> Alice was crossing the clearing when she heard a mew. She turned and saw a small black kitten. It crawled up to her and started to lick her toes.

In order to answer the question, 'What did the cat do?' the system must use the information that a kitten is a young cat. This fact could be stored as an axiom in a predicate calculus formulae, for example, but the same kind of information would have to be repeated in lexical entries for *calf, puppy,* and *lamb*. Instead this information can be expressed by using the lexical relation CHILD. The lexical entry for *kitten* need contain only CHILD *cat,* while the lexical entry for *puppy* contains CHILD *dog*.

Lexical relations such as CAUSE (causation), TAX (taxonomy, the is-a-kind-of relation), and TLOC (typical location of action) can also be used in making inferences about verbs. The verb *bake* has an intransitive sense *bake1* and a transitive sense *bake2*, which means CAUSE *bake1*. Since *bake2* TAX *make*, if the story says, 'Mother baked a cake,' the system can infer that she made one. The fact that *bake2* CAUSE *bake1* permits the deduction that the cake has baked. Since the lexical entry for *bake2* includes kitchen TLOC bake2

we have the additional information about where this cake was probably baked and can answer the question 'Where is Mother?'

Relational Models

Raphael (1968) pioneered in the use of relations in a question-answering system. Further work has been done by Simmons (1973) and more recently by Schwind (1975) in Munich, Fahlman (1979) at MIT, and Hendrix (1975, 1979) at SRI.

Anthropologists have used relations in ethnographic studies of a number of cultures. The work of Casagrande and Hale (1967) and Werner (1969, 1974) is particularly significant. Several psychologists have used relational models of long-term memory (Kintsch 1972, Litowitz 1981, Miller 1978, Norman and Rumelhart 1975).

Relational models have played a very important part in Soviet linguistics. Žolkovsky and Mel'čuk (1970) developed a theory of lexical functions for Russian which they used as a basis for constructing paraphrases automatically. They joined with Apresyan (1970) to define a large set of lexical functions for use in the Explanatory-Combinatory Dictionary of Russian. This monumental project has now been completed. It contains a tremendous amount of syntactic and semantic information expressed in relational terms. Mel'čuk, now at the University of Montreal, is working on a similar dictionary for French, as well as carrying on further theoretical work with relations. His comments have been of very great assistance in our work. A survey of relational models can be found in Evens et al. (1980).

Computer Analysis of Definitions

Raoul Smith has done several thought-provoking studies of the definitions in W7 (e.g., 1978, 1981) and used these data to study semantic primitives (MS).

Schwind (1975) has worked on the automatic parsing of definitions in Bourbaki's *General Topology*, so that she is dealing with a more restricted vocabulary. She has also applied some of her results to information retrieval (Schwind and Janas 1977).

Amsler started from Simmons' relational model (Simmons and Amsler 1975) and did a large-scale study of verb definitions in the *Merriam-Webster Pocket Dictionary* using a model with two relations IS-A (taxonomy) and IS-PART (part-whole). He has now completed an even more comprehensive study of taxonomy in both noun and verb definitions in the *Pocket Dictionary* (1981). Recently (1982), he has proposed a multifaceted attack on dictionary problems.

Fox's Experiments with Relations in Information Retrieval

Fox (1981), working with Salton at Cornell, assembled a long list of relations from the linguistics literature and used them in a relational thesaurus. In a series of experiments with Salton's (1971) SMART system he found that use of this relational thesaurus made a significant improvement in recall. He divided his relations into 11 different groups. All groups contributed to the improvement in recall except antonymy. The best results came when all relations except antonymy were combined together. These experiments were done on a collection of only 82 document abstracts. He is now working on a much larger experiment, but the results have not yet been published.

Relations for Information Retrieval

Table 2.1 shows the groups of relations that were used in our information retrieval experiments. The first group contains relations which connect parts with wholes, elements with sets, and objects with their substances. The second group contains collocation relations; these are relations between words that frequently co-occur in the same phrase or sentence. These include the typical fillers of case slots and a number of other relations that associate nouns with the verbs that accompany them. Other collocation relations match nouns with the prepositions that commonly govern them and items that occur next to each other on lists.

Paradigmatic relations relate different forms which share the same semantic core, like *sun* and *solar, kitten* and *cat,* and *went* and *go*. The fourth group contains the classical relations, taxonomy and synonymy. Some scholars, like Werner (1974), treat synonymy as a limiting case of taxonomy, not as a separate relation, and it is with this justification that we have grouped them together.

The last group, antonymy, was dissected into three components by Lyons (1977). We have added a fourth, reciprocal kinship, on the basis of work with a question-answering system (Evens and Smith 1978).

Table 2.1 is by no means complete. Indeed it is deliberately open-ended. Whenever a new lexical regularity is seen in the data, a new relation is added. In the next section we describe our work with dictionary tapes which led us to develop separate relation lists for different parts of speech, containing many further relations.

3. FINDING RELATIONS

Our information retrieval experiment, like Fox's (1981), was performed with a controlled vocabulary. The thesaurus was built by hand with great effort. Practical application of relational thesauri will require complete relational information for many thousands of words. Less expensive thesaurus construction techniques must be found.

These practical problems motivated us to study the definitions in the machine-readable form of W7 in the hope of discovering more relations, and finding methods for extracting relational information automatically.

We determined to use W7 as a source of definition data because it was the best available (Olney 1968) and because Raoul Smith, then at Northwestern University, offered us the use of data-sets drawn from Olney's machine-readable version of the dictionary. The G & C Merriam Company generously gave us permission to use these tapes.

Our premise was that the defining formulae in W7 definitions contained clues to the needed relational information. Unfortunately, the same relation may be signaled

Table 2.1. Groups of Lexical Semantic Relation Used In Information Retrieval Experiments.

Parts and Wholes

PART	part-whole	horn	PART	cow
CAP	head-organization	chief	CAP	tribe
EQUIP	personnel-object	crew	EQUIP	gun
PIECE	count-mass	lump	PIECE	sugar
SET	set-element	flock	SET	sheep
MADEOF	substance	ski	MADEOF	wood
COMEFROM	provenience	milk	COMEFROM	cow

Collocation Relations

TAGENT	typical agent	conqueror	TAGENT	to conquer
TOBJECT	typical object	loser	TOBJECT	to beat
TRESULT	typical result	hole	TRESULT	to dig
TINST	typical instrument	needle	TINST	to sew
TEXPER	typical experiencer	lover	TEXPER	to love
TSOURCE	typical source	earth	TSOURCE	to sprout
TLOC	typical location	kitchen	TLOC	to bake
HOME	habitat-object	Africa	HOME	hyena
SON	characteristic sound	bark	SON	dog
PREP	preposition-object	on	PREP	list
Q	queuing	Monday	Q	Tuesday
COPUL	special copula verb	to fall	COPUL	victim
LIQU	destroying verb	to correct	LIQU	mistake
PREPAR	verb which means prepare for use	to lay	PREPAR	table
DEGRAD	deterioration verb	to decay	DEGRAD	tooth
INC	increase verb	to mount	INC	tension
DEC	decrease verb	to shrink	DEC	cloth

Paradigmatic Relations

MALE	male-unmarked term	drake	MALE	duck
FEMALE	female-unmarked term	lioness	FEMALE	lion
CHILD	offspring-parent	kitten	CHILD	cat
CAUSE	cause-action effected	to send	CAUSE	to go
BECOME	verb-adjective	to redden	BECOME	red
NOMV	process noun-verb	death	NOMV	die
ADJN	adjective-noun	solar	ADJN	sun
ABLE	adjective-verb	combustible	ABLE	to burn
BE	verb-adjective	to neighbor	BE	near
IMPER	irregular imperative	fire!	IMPER	to shoot
PAST	perfect-infinitive	went	PAST	to go
PP	past participle-infinitive	gone	PP	to go
PLURAL	plural-singular	men	PLURAL	man

Taxonomy and Synonymy

TAX	taxonomy	lion	TAX	animal
SYN	synonymy	speedy	SYN	fast

Antonymy Relations

COMP	complementarity	single	COMP	married
ANTI	antonymy	hot	ANTI	cold
CONV	converseness	to buy	CONV	to sell
RECK	reciprocal kinship	husband	RECK	wife

by a number of defining formulae. For example, the concept of causation appears in at least two different verb formulae, 'to cause' and 'to make':

to send—'to cause to go'
to clear—'to make clear'
to heat—'to make or grow hot'

Typically, relations are signaled by different formulae for definitions involving different parts of speech. Causation looks like this in adjective definitions:

doleful—causing grief or affliction
dread—causing great fear or anxiety
fatal—causing death
giddy—causing dizziness

Our first goal was to use the W7 database to identify new lexical-semantic relations. To do this, we divided Smith's data into separate files, one file for each part of speech: adjectives, adverbs, nouns, and verbs. A KWIC index was made of each file using the Northwestern University TRIAL system developed by Dillaman and Chalice. Table 3.1 is a portion of one such table. Slaviero (1981) at Illinois Institute of Technology analyzed the KWIC index files by collecting and counting the recurring phrases. Table 3.2 shows a portion of her program output.

The recurring phrases were sorted in order of frequency and then manually scanned to develop sets of relations and corresponding defining formulae. This process yielded a rich list of noun relations (see Table 3.3) and tentative lists of adjectives and adverb relations. The adjective list became the basis of Ahlswede's work (1982).

Once we had a list of relations that we were satisfied with, the next step was to try to extract word1-relation-word2 triples automatically from the W7 definition of word1. For the CHILD relation this is quite simple, as these examples show:

chick—'a young chicken; also a young bird'
duckling—'a young or little duck'

Table 3.1. KWIC Index Output for Adjective Definitions.

OF OR RELATING TO ADMINISTRATION OR AN ADMINISTRAT	ADMINISTRATIVE	0
OF OR RELATING TO AMERICA.	AMERICAN	1
OF OR RELATING TO ANALYSIS OR ANALYTICS; ESP SEPAR	ANALYTIC	1
OF OR RELATING TO ANIONS.	ANIONIC	1
OF OR RELATING TO AN ECONOMY.	ECONOMIC	3C
OF OR RELATING TO AN EDITOR: AN ~ OFFICE.	EDITORIAL	1
OF OR RELATING TO AN ELECTOR: THE ~ VOTE.	ELECTORAL	1
OF OR RELATING TO AN EXECUTIVE.	EXECUTIVE	3
OF OR RELATING TO AN ENEMY.	HOSTILE	1
OF OR RELATING TO AN ADVANCED STAGE IN POINT OF TH	LATE	1B
OF OR RELATING TO AN ANIMATE BEING.	LIFE	1
OF OR RELATING TO AN ACADEMIC SUBJECT REQUIRING FE	MINOR	5
OF OR RELATING TO AN OBJECT OF ACTION OR FEELING	OBJECTIVE	1A
OF OR RELATING TO AN OFFICE, POSITION, OR TRUST.	OFFICIAL	1
OF OR RELATING TO ARTISANS OR MACHINISTS.	MECHANICAL	2
OF OR RELATING TO ATHLETES OR ATHLETICS.	ATHLETIC	1
OF OR RELATING TO BALLISTICS OR A BODY IN MOTION.	BALLISTIC	0
OF OR RELATING TO BEATNIKS.	BEAT	2

Table 3.2. The Search for Defining Formulae—Phrase Counts from W7 (Slaviero)

FREQUENCY	PHRASE
12	BY , OR
17	BY ,
51	BY A
12	BY AN
32	BY OR
48	BY THE
487	BY
20	CAPABLE OF BEING
48	CAPABLE OF
51	CAPABLE
10	CARE
19	CAUSING
12	CENTER
10	CENTRAL
10	CERTAIN
15	CHANGE
34	CHARACTER
13	CHARACTERISTIC OF A
40	CHARACTERISTIC OF
42	CHARACTERISTIC
11	CHARACTERISTICS OF
14	CHARACTERISTICS
77	CHARACTERIZED BY
78	CHARACTERIZED

kitten—'a young cat; also sometimes the young of other animals'
lamb—'a young sheep'

Here, word2 is the first noun after *young*. The SET relation is much harder to manage (and much more typical):

herd—'a number of beasts, esp. of large animals, assembled together'
flock—'a company of people, hence pl. multitudes; also an aggregate, collection, or group'

Ross (1982) wrote a program that reads in a W7 definition, finds the defining formula, if one is present, and isolates the part of the definition containing word2. A segment of the output of this program is shown in Table 3.4. While this process works for some relations most of the time and for others some of the time, it is not nearly reliable enough to use in the automatic construction of a lexical network. The relations are correctly identified from the defining formula, but to identify word2 requires parsing.

Sager very kindly gave us a copy of her Linguistic String Parser (LSP) for use in parsing. Several members of her research group—Ralph Grishman, in particular—have given us invaluable help in using it. The major parsing effort has been carried out for adjective definitions by Ahlswede (1984).

Table 3.3. Noun Relations and Defining Formulae.

	RELATION	FORMULA
1	TAXONOMY	A COMMON
2	TINSTR	A DEVICE
3	TAXONOMY	A FORMAL
4	SET	A GROUP OF
5	METHOD	A MEANS OF
6	ELEMENT	A MEMBER OF
7	SET	A NUMBER OF
8	PART	PART OF
9	TAGENT	A PERSON WHO
10	PIECE	A PIECE OF
11	SERIES	A SERIES OF
12	SET	A SET OF
13	SMALL	A SMALL
14	NOUNMAGN	A SPECIAL
15	NOMADJ	A STATE OF BEING
16	STATE	A STATE OF
17	NVABLE	ABILITY TO
18	ACT	ACT OF
19	ACT	ACTION OF
20	ACT	INSTANCE OF
21	PROCESS	PROCESS OF
22	TAXONOMY	ANY OF
23	AMOUNT	AMOUNT OF
24	RANK	BELOW A
25	PART	A BRANCH OF
26	NVABLE	CAPACITY
27	CENTER	CENTER OF
28	SET	CLASS OF
29	SET	COLLECTION OF
30	WHOLE	COMBINATION OF
31	NOMADJ	CONDITION OF BEING
32	STATE	CONDITION OF
33	MADEOF	CONSISTING OF
34	PART	CONSTITUTENT OF
35	AMOUNT	DEGREE OF
36	TINSTR	DESIGNED TO
37	ANTI	AS DISTINGUISHED FROM
38	PART	DIVISION OF
39	ELEMENT	ELEMENT OF
40	NOUNMAGN	EXCESSIVE
41	NOMADJ	FACT OF BEING
42	STATE	FACT OF
43	FEMALE	A FEMALE
44	FUNCTION	FUNCTION
45	NOUNBON	GOOD
46	NOUNMAGN	GREAT
47	NHAVE	HAVING
48	CAP	HEAD OF
49	COMPARISON	LIKE
50	MADEOF	MADE OF

Table 3.3 (*Continued*)

51	NHAVE	MARKED BY
52	ANTI	NOT
53	TAXONOMY	ONE OF
54	NOMADJ	ONE THAT IS
55	TAGENT	ONE THAT
56	TAGENT	ONE WHO
57	ORGAN	ORGAN OF
58	PART	THE PART OF
59	PART	A PART OF
60	PIECE	A PORTION OF
61	NVABLE	THE POWER OF
62	NVABLE	THE POWER TO
63	PRACTICE	PRACTICE OF
64	TEXPER	SOMETHING THAT
65	NOMADJ	THE QUALITY OR STATE OF BEING
66	NOMADJ	THE STATE OF BEING
67	WHOLE	THE WHOLE
68	AMOUNT	A UNIT OF
69	TINSTR	USED TO
70	MALE	A MALE
71	CHILD	A YOUNG
72	HOME	LIVING IN
73	SON	SOUND

Klick has developed the simple LSP grammar for adverb definitions shown in Table 3.5. Most adverb definitions are preposition phrases, and Klick's grammar was designed to handle a part of this subset. It does not parse citation or usage directions.

Noun definitions are in the form of noun phrases, and Sager's noun phrase grammar (LNR) works well for those examples that we have tried. The noun identified by her parser as the core of the noun phrase after stripping off the defining formula is usually the word2 that we are searching for. We have not tried to work with verb definitions, since Amsler (1980) handles them so well.

Table 3.4. Identifying Formulae in Definitions (Ross).

Main Entry		Relation	Formula	Remainder of Definition
ACE	6	TAGENT	ONE THAT	EXCELS AT SOMETHING
ACHIEVEMENT	1	ACT	ACT OF	ACHIEVING
ACHIEVEMENT	2B	NOUNMAGN	GREAT	OR HEROIC DEED
ACQUAINTANCE	1B	NOMADJ	THE STATE OF BEING	ACQUAINTED
ACQUAINTANCE	2B	NJANTI	NOT	A PARTICULARLY CLOSE FRIEND
ACRE	2	TAXONOMY	ANY OF	VARIOUS UNITS OF AREA

Table 3.5. LSP Grammar for Adverb Definitions (Klick).

```
*BNF
   <SENTENCE>   ::= <CENTER>  '.'   .
   <CENTER>     ::= 'ADVERB'  ':'   <ADVDEF>  .
   <ADVDEF>     ::= <PN>   .
   <PN>         ::= <PP>   <NSTG>   .
   <PP>         ::= <*P>   |  <*P>   'OR'   <*P>   |   <PP1>  .
   <PP1>        ::= <*P>   'OR'   <*P>   |   <PP1>   .
   <NSTG>       ::= <LNR>   .
   <LNR>        ::= <LN>   <*N>   <RN>   .
   <LN>         ::= <TPOS>   <QPOS>   <APOS>   .
   <TPOS>       ::= <*T>   |   <*NULL>   .
   <QPOS>       ::= <*Q>   |   <*NULL>   .
   <APOS>       ::= <AJ>   |   <AD>   <AJ>   |   <*NULL>   .
   <AD>         ::= <*ADV>   |   <*ADV>   <AD>   .
   <AJ>         ::= <*ADJ>   |   <*ADJ>   <AJ>   .
   <RN>         ::= <PN>   |   <*NULL>   .

*LISTS
   ATTRIBUTE=SINGULAR,PLURAL,NCOUNT.
   TYPE STRING=PN.
   TYPE ADJSET=LN,RN.
   TYPE LADJSET=LN.
   TYPE RADJSET=RN.
   TYPE LXR=LNR.
```

4. CREATING DICTIONARY DEFINITIONS

Once we had collected a number of defining formulae we turned our attention to analyzing W7 dictionary definitions, with the plan of extracting relationships automatically. One step in the analysis was an experiment with the automatic construction of definitions.

One serious problem for scholars using the W7 dictionary tapes as a source of semantic information is that many common English words do not possess W7 entries of their own. Instead they are listed in other entries as derived words or they appear in one of the large prefix groups. Advers in -LY, in particular, almost never have separate entries. Instead they appear at the foot of the definition for the corresponding adjective. The RE- prefix group contains such frequent words as *reappear, refinish,* and *reload.* Peterson (1982) has found that abou 21% of the total W7 vocabulary is listed without definitions. The Merriam Company editors presumably felt that readers of the dictionary could compute the meanings of these words with relative ease.

We decided to try producing definitions automatically. As a first step, Ernest Grove (1981) did a small study of nouns ending in some common suffixes, -ER, -OR, -MENT, -NESS, and -ION. He compiled a list of nouns ending in these suffixes that have main entries of their own, and another list of those that do not. A large proportion of the nouns with main entries of their own have at least two definitions.

The first definition is typically very predictable; the most common formula for -ER nouns derived from verbs is ONE THAT <verb>S. For example, *bailer* is 'one that bails.' We hypothesize that the W7 editors chose to insert a main entry for a derived word only when it has other common meanings beside the typical pattern. We searched our lists of defining formulae to see which ones corresponded to particular derivational suffixes. These are the source of patterns used in constructing definitions. We did a similar study for words with UN- and RE- prefixes.

When an -LY adverb appears in an adjective definition, then it is almost always an adverb of manner. Main entries for adverbs in -LY derived from adjectives are rather rare, but they do exist, and in these entries manner definitions seem to come first, as in these examples:

DIRECTLY—'in a direct manner; without delay'
EXACTLY—'in an exact manner; quite so'
HEAVILY—'in a heavy manner; slowly and laboriously; to a great degree'
ORDINARILY—'in an ordinary manner; to an ordinary degree'

As a result we decided to use the formula: IN AN <adjective> MANNER. Sometimes, even when the main entry is a noun, there is a derived adjective also mentioned in the entry. In that case the adverb can be treated as derived from the adjective, and the same formula can be used.

If the main entry is a noun and the adverb is derived directly from the noun, we use the formula: IN THE MANNER OF A <noun>. The time adverbs in -LY derived from nouns—such as MONTHLY, WEEKLY, DAILY—have main entries of their own, fortunately, since this rule would not make sense for them.

If the main entry is a verb and the adverb ends in -INGLY, then we use the formula: IN A <verb>ING MANNER. This gives, among other examples:

DELUDINGLY—'in a deluding manner'
DEPRESSINGLY—'in a depressing manner'

Our -LY adverb algorithm is shown in Table 4.1.

For adjectives formed from nouns we started with our lists of defining formulae and came up with rules for each suffix, which are embodied in the algorithm in Table 4.2. We found confirming examples for all of them in main entries; these are shown in Table 4.3. These rules work much of the time, but not all of the time.

For adjectives formed from verbs, we have two rules which seem to work well. If the suffix is -ABLE or -IBLE and the noun entry is a transitive verb, then we construct the definition: CAPABLE OF BEING <verb>ED. This gives, for example, FIXABLE—capable of being fixed. If the verb is intransitive, then we construct the definition: CAPABLE OF <verb>ING. If the suffix is -IVE or -ATORY, then we construct the definition: SERVING OR TENDING TO as in,

DECORATIVE—'serving or tending to decorate'

We have experimented with a number of noun suffixes. Our rules for -NESS and -ER and -OR are satisfactory. The others are not. -NESS is used to form nouns from

Table 4.1. Algorithm for Creating Definitions for Derived Adverbs in -LY.

```
IF THE MAIN ENTRY IS AN ADJECTIVE X
    THEN CONSTRUCT DEF: IN AN X MANNER
ELSE IF THERE IS AN ADJECTIVE Y EARLIER IN THE LIST
                OF DERIVED WORDS
    THEN CONSTRUCT DEF: IN A Y MANNER
ELSE IF THE MAIN ENTRY IS A NOUN Z
    THEN CONSTRUCT DEF: IN THE MANNER OF A Z
ELSE IF THE MAIN ENTRY IS A VERB W
                AND THE ADVERB ENDS IN -INGLY
    THEN CONSTRUCT DEF: IN A WING MANNER
```

adjectives and past participles. There are a number of these words with main entries in W7, and they use the formula: THE QUALITY OR STATE OF BEING <adjective>. For example,

> DIRTINESS—'the quality or state of being dirty'
> GENTLENESS—'the quality or state of being gentle esp. mildness of manners or disposition'

We decided to adopt this formula ourselves. For nouns formed from verbs by adding -ER and -OR we use the formula: ONE THAT <verb>S. Thus, *feigner* is defined as 'one that feigns.'

The prefix groups contain a sizable number of words. There are 893 words in the UN- group alone. The majority of words in the UN- group are adjectives, but there are a number of adverbs, and a few nouns. At the beginning of this group, the editors have placed an explanation, 'See UN- and 2d element.' If you take this

Table 4.2. Algorithm for Creating Definitions for Adjectives formed from Nouns.

```
IF SUFFIX IS -IC, -ICAL, -AL, -IAL
    THEN CONSTRUCT DEF: OF OR RELATING TO X
ELSE IF SUFFIX IS -AN OR -IAN
    THEN CONSTRUCT DEF: OF OR BELONGING TO X
ELSE IF SUFFIX IS -OUS
    THEN CONSTRUCT DEF: FULL OF OR
                        ABOUNDING IN X
ELSE IF SUFFIX IS -LESS
    THEN CONSTRUCT DEF: DESTITUTE OF X OR
                        HAVING NO X
```

Table 4.3. Confirming Examples from W7 Definitions for Adjectives formed from Nouns.

ATHLETIC	1. OF OR RELATING TO ATHLETES OR ATHLETICS; 2. CHARACTERISTIC OF AN ATHLETE; esp VIGOROUS, ACTIVE; 3. CHARACTERIZED BY HEAVY FRAME, LARGE CHEST, AND POWERFUL MUSCULAR DEVELOPMENT; MESOMORPHIC 4. USED BY ATHLETES.
DEMOGRAPHIC	OF OR RELATING TO DEMOGRAPHY
BARONIAL	1. OF OR RELATING TO A BARON OR THE BARONAGE; 2. STATELY, AMPLE.
CLERICAL	1. OF, RELATING TO, OR CHARACTERISTIC OF THE CLERGY, A CLERGYMAN, OR A CLERIC; 2. OF OR RELATING TO A CLERK OR OFFICE WORKER.
CLAMOROUS	1. FULL OF CLAMOR; NOISY; 2. NOISILY INSISTENT syn - see VOCIFEROUS
VENOMOUS	1. FULL OF VENOM AS A: POISONOUS, ENVENOMED B: VIRULENT, BANEFUL C: SPITEFUL, MALIGNANT; 2. HAVING A VENOM-PRODUCING GLAND AND ABLE TO INFLICT A POISONED WOUND.
WITLESS	DESTITUTE OF WIT OR UNDERSTANDING
BOTTOMLESS	1. HAVING NO BOTTOM (...CHAIR) 2. A. EXTREMELY DEEP B. UNFATHOMABLE C. BOUNDLESS, UNLIMITED.

advice and look at the main entry for UN-, you find that the first definition is 'Not.' This is consistent with the definitions of UN- adjectives which have main entries of their own. For example,

> UNABASHED—'Not abashed'
> UNABATED—'Not abated; at full strength or force'

The adverbs in the UN- group seem to be almost entirely adverbs of manner. Looking at UN- main entries, we found a very frequent formula, illustrated by,

> UNHAPPILY—'in an unhappy manner'

and we use this formula for adverbs in the UN- group. The few nouns in the UN- group are formed from adjectives, mostly with -NESS. The formula which we used for these appears in the W7 definition for

> UNEASINESS—'the quality or state of being uneasy'

The algorithm for the UN- group is given in Table 4.4. These algorithms for creating definitions were implemented by Ross (1982).

The majority of words in the RE- group are verbs, and for these the simplest alternative seems to be the most appropriate—strip off the prefix and stick TO in front of the verb and AGAIN after it. This produces, for example:

REARRANGE—'to arrange again'

Most of the nouns in the prefix group are derived nouns with suffixes that have already been discussed. We used the suffix rules already devised and added AGAIN. Table 4.5 shows some output from the RE- program written by Daniel (1982). This works for about nine words out of ten. The problem in the last line of the Table 4.5 illustrates a typical failure point.

5. THE INFORMATION RETRIEVAL EXPERIMENTS

We hypothesized that lexical-semantic relations can be useful in information retrieval applications. This hypothesis was tested using IRS, an information retrieval

Table 4.4. Algorithm for Creating Definitions for Words in the UN-Prefix Group.

```
GIVEN A WORD IN THE UN- PREFIX GROUP
TAKE OFF THE UN- AND DETERMINE
     THE PART OF SPEECH OF THE 2D ELEMENT
IF THE SECOND ELEMENT IS AN ADJECTIVE OR PP
     CONSTRUCT DEF:  NOT  +  2D ELEMENT
EX:  UNABBREVIATED - adj -  NOT ABBREVIATED
IF THE SECOND ELEMENT IS AN ADVERB
     (ENDS IN -LY AND IS NOT AN ADJECTIVE)
     CONSTRUCT ADJECTIVE x
               FROM WHICH IT IS DERIVED
     CONSTRUCT DERIVED ADV DEF (INSERTING UN-)
               IN AN UN- x MANNER
EX:  UNCANNILY - adv -  IN AN UNCANNY MANNER
IF THE SECOND ELEMENT IS A NOUN
     (ENDS IN A NOUN SUFFIX)
     CONSTRUCT THE ADJECTIVE  x
               FROM WHICH IT IS DERIVED
     CONSTRUCT DERIVED NOUN DEF (INSERTING UN-)
               THE QUALITY OR STATE OF BEING UN- x
EX:  UNTIDINESS - n -  THE QUALITY OR STATE OF
                       BEING UNTIDY
```

Table 4.5. Output from Program which Creates Definitions for Words in the RE-Prefix Group.

READAPT	- TO ADAPT AGAIN
READDRESS	- TO ADDRESS AGAIN
READJUST	- TO ADJUST AGAIN
READJUSTABLE	- CAPABLE OF BEING ADJUSTED AGAIN
READJUSTMENT	- THE ACT OR PROGESS OF ADJUSTING AGAIN
READMISSION	- THE ACT OR PROGESS OF ADMISSING AGAIN

system designed by Vandendorpe. Fox (1981) has also studied this question using the SMART information retrieval system (Salton 1971).

Both studies compare the retrieval performance of a control-group of queries (the baseline) with queries enhanced by lexical-semantic relations. The studies differ in that Fox's retrievals used a frequency weighting of keywords and our study used a weight factor of one.

IRS

IRS was designed as a bibliographic retrieval system and, like all bibliographic retrieval systems, IRS maintains lists of keywords that identify documents. Such systems search for and retrieve documents that are most similar to English descriptions (queries) about the documents. (See Salton 1968, and Salton and McGill 1983.)

Characteristically, these systems use mechanically constructed keyword lists collected from the text of the documents themselves. This keyword-filtering process selects words that occur both in the document and in a controlled dictionary of keywords. Each list is then associated with a document number and is known as a document-vector. The set of all document-vectors is called a document-term matrix and is maintained on a secondary file. To formulate an IRS query, a user writes a paragraph describing the subject matter he or she is looking for. The following is an example of one of the queries used in our experiment:

> How are **matrices stored** in different **systems?** How do different **matrix storage** methods affect the **performance** of **algorithms** for **matrix arithmetic, operations** such as **addition, multiplication,** and **inversion?** How does **paging** interact with these **arithmetic operations?**

A list of the control-dictionary keywords used in a query is made, and this query-vector is compared with the keyword lists that identify the documents. In the example just given, the list of query words printed in boldface forms the query-vector.

In response to the query, documents are listed in descending order of similarity to the query vector. An IRS command controls the content of the response. Document numbers, titles, authors, keywords, and/or the text of the documents themselves can all be included in the list by using this command.

Three IRS design features are unique: the matrices which the system uses to find the best match are efficiently represented with a B-tree data organization (Vandendorpe 1980); matrix elements are identified by pairs of keyword text strings and not by numeric indices; and the system interprets a command-language that simplifies the creation of new experimental configurations. These three features make IRS robust and flexible.

The IRS preprocessor has two additional capabilities that were not used in our experiment: the ability to remove suffixes from the words prior to checking the controlled dictionary; and the ability to weight the significance of keywords by the frequency of their occurrence. The word stem capability was not used in our experiments since we were interested in preserving the suffixes. The frequency count feature was not used because of an undetected programming error that occurred during the parallel development of IRS.

IRS statistically compares document-term matrices by computing the cosine of the angle between the query-vector and each of the document-vectors.

$$\cos(A,B) = \frac{A \cdot B}{|A|\,|B|}$$

The more alike the vectors are, the closer the cosine is to 1, and the smaller the angle. The numerator of the fraction on the right-hand side of this equation is the inner product of the two vectors. This particular measure of similarity was chosen because it is the same measure that Fox used in his study. IRS computes this measure by assuming a vector space of keywords and applying the component formulae. To save computational steps, IRS computes the numerator and the denominator of this equation in parallel, storing both of these values in the same element of the response-vector. This computing technique is efficient because it causes the most frequently accessed portions of the matrix to remain in computer memory rather than on slow, secondary-storage files.

To represent lexical-semantic relations in IRS, matrices that map one set of keywords into another were used. Our experimental procedure was to use the cosine measure to compare the query vector with a relation matrix. When this is done, related keywords are found. By adding these new keyword-vectors to the original query-vector, we hoped to make the original query more explicit. The retrieval results for these enhanced queries are then compared with the baseline retrievals obtained from the original queries.

Two standard measures were used to compare the results—RECALL and PRECISION. RECALL is the percentage of relevant documents retrieved by the system. PRECISION is the percentage of retrieved documents that were actually relevant. When IRS is being evaluated, users are asked to provide lists of documents that are actually relevant to each query. IRS then computes recall and precision pairs on the basis of these lists.

It is a common practice in information retrieval to plot precision values at fixed recall intervals. For a given retrieval, however, there are recall levels for which precision values are not mathematically defined. Fox avoided this problem by using an interpolation method defined by Salton and incorporated in the SMART information retrieval system (Salton 1971). Since our results were to be compared with Fox's, the same interpolation method was used.

The interpolation technique is best seen in the example of Figure 5.1. Shown in this figure are the original data points, marked with the character *, as they would appear before the interpolation. The points marked with the character + distinguish the interpolated points.

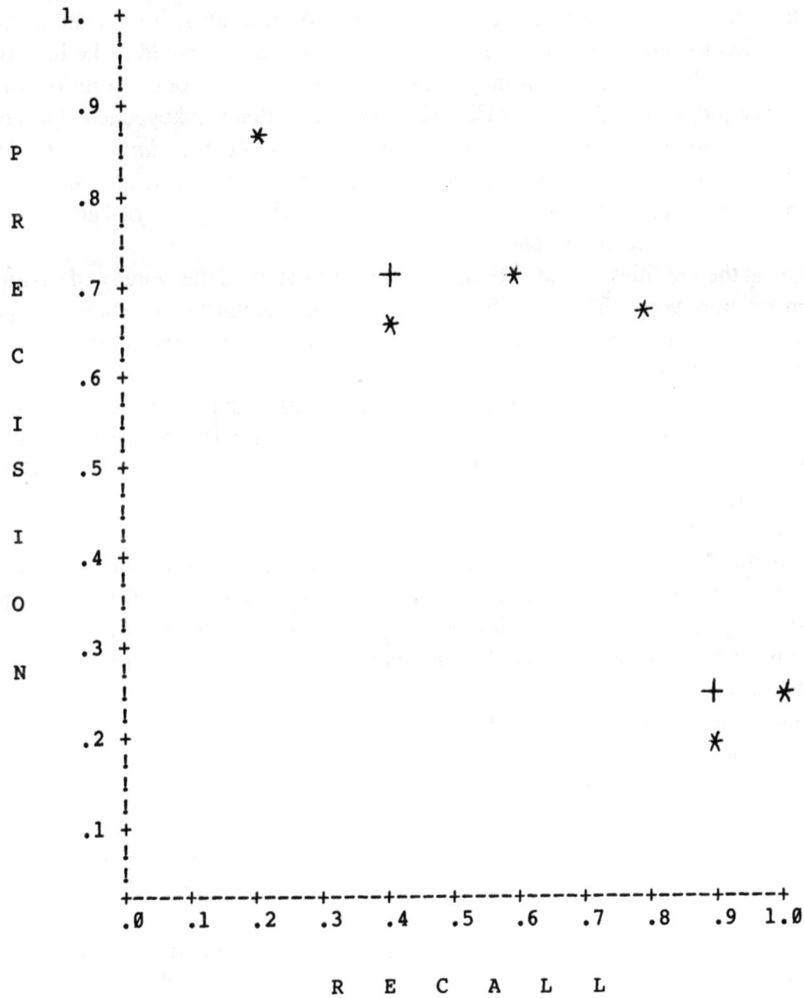

*: Before interpolation.
+: After interpolation.

Figure 5.1. Interpolation method.

The interpolation technique examines the recall and precision pairs that are defined, beginning with the lowest recall value and progressing to a recall value of one. Only the largest precision values that are monotonically decreasing over recall are retained; the other points are discarded. When this process is complete, recall values that have no corresponding precision measure are assigned the precision of the next larger recall.

The Experimental Procedure

The first step in designing the experiment was to choose an appropriate database of documents. Much of the work was to be carried out by the group of graduate students taking Computer Science 580, Information Retrieval, from Vandendorpe. We needed to choose a subject area in which these students could make intelligent queries and documents which they could understand well enough to make correct relevance judgments. An earlier CS 580 class had written and keypunched abstracts for all 222 papers published in the *Communications of the Association for Computing Machinery* between 1961 and 1969. We decided to use these abstracts as data for our experiments and we asked the students to make up 30 queries about important topics in Computer Science.

Using the facilities provided by IRS we made a list of all the words and examined them for stop words. These are function words like conjunctions, articles, prepositions, and auxiliary verbs, which appear in all texts and therefore are useless in discriminating between texts on different topics.

The students took copies of these vocabulary lists and composed a list of all word-relation-word triples which they could find for that relation. Once the students had finished, Klick and Evens went over these lists together, making additions (and a few deletions).

The students next took the list of queries home, carefully reread the abstracts they themselves had typed, and made a list of which papers were relevant to which queries. This list was discussed at length by the whole group, then the authors spent several days going over these relevance judgments. One of the queries was excluded because it was too new for the database and had no relevant documents.

We also chose a subgroup of the 10 'worst' queries. For the other 19 queries the results of the first attempt at retrieval were generally successful without any enhancement—there was not much room left for improvement.

The 10 worst queries seem qualitatively different; these queries are shorter and contain few index terms. The series of experiments were run once with these 10 queries and again with the whole group of 29. The first experiment in each series was a baseline experiment—no enhancement was done. In the second experiment the query was enhanced using the antonymy relation group; that is, the set of index terms in the query was increased by adding all words related to words in the query set by antonymy relations. Then retrieval was performed using this enhanced query set. In the third experiment the query set was enhanced using all relations except antonymy. The fourth experiment used all relations including antonymy. The fifth experiment used the part-whole relation group which includes set and element relations as well. The sixth used collocation relations, the relations which connect words which co-occur in phrases. The seventh used taxonomy and synonymy. The eighth used paradigmatic relations, those which connect different words containing the same concept (such as sun, sunny, and solar).

In all, there were 8 experiments performed using all 29 queries. Recall and precision values were computed by IRS after each response, and these values were interpolated giving precision values at 10% recall intervals. To plot the recall versus precision graph, the mean of the precision values was used. Statistical comparisons used the interpolated data sets.

Results of the Experiments

When we graphed the results of these experiments, we could see that the results of the third experiment were better than all the others. The results of the second experiment, which uses antonymy relations, were consistently worse than all the others. Graphs have been prepared comparing the results of experiments two and three with the baseline experiment. At each recall level we calculated the mean of the interpolated precision values for the current group of queries. It is these mean precision values that are plotted on the graphs. The digits 1, 2, and 3 identify the experiment being plotted.

Two nonparametric statistical tests were used to analyze the results of these experiments, the signed pair test and the Wilcoxon test. These texts were chosen because of the relatively small number of cases (queries) and the absence of any reason to expect a normal distribution. The Wilcoxon test is generally recognized to be the more powerful of the two since it takes into account the size as well as the direction of the difference between the two treatments (Siegel 1956). The null hypothesis for each experiment is that enhancing the query with related words will have no effect. Significance results are given for a one-tailed test. Tables 5.1 through 5.4 show the results of these analyses. The numbers in the tables are the probability that the null hypothesis is correct. Thus, the smaller numbers reflect

Table 5.1. Significance Levels of Results for Baseline vs. All relations but Antonymy.

Number of queries: 10
Summary of statistics: One-sided probability for each test

Recall Level	Sign Test	Wilcoxon Test
0.1	0.109	0.058
0.2	0.016	0.014
0.3	0.004	0.006
0.4	0.090	0.019
0.5	0.254	0.043
0.6	0.254	0.025
0.7	0.500	0.339
0.8	0.090	0.087
0.9	0.090	0.069
1.0	0.002	0.004

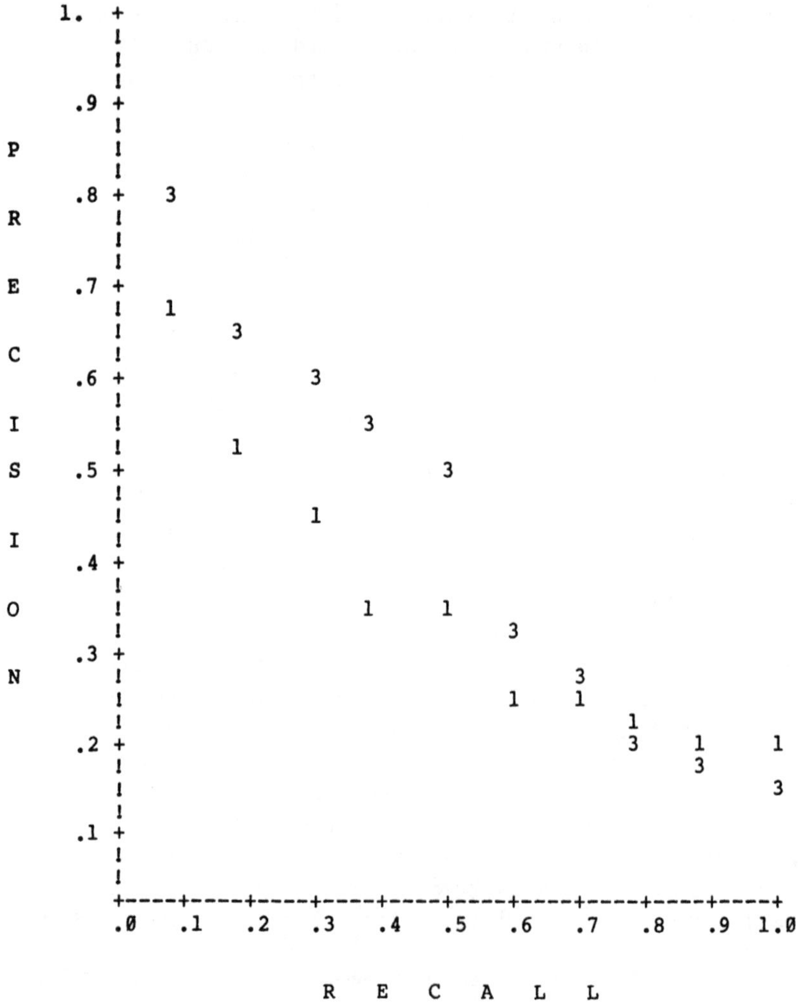

1: Baseline
3: All relations but antonymy

Figure 5.2. Baseline vs. All Relations but Antonymy

better results. A Wilcoxon test value of 0.0485, for example, indicates that enhancement by relations is significantly better than the baseline at 5% level. The necessary computations were made using the BMDP package developed at the University of California at Los Angeles.

Figure 5.2 is a graph of the results obtained when the 10 worst queries are enhanced using all the relations except the antonymy relation. Plotted on the same axes for comparison purposes are the results of the baseline experiment. Table 5.1 gives the significance levels for this comparison. For this series, the use of all relations except antonymy to enhance the set of index terms in the query gives significant improvement in retrieval performance. This improvement is most marked for the first few documents retrieved, but it continues through the 0.7 recall level. Above the 0.7 recall level the graphs cross. The words being added by the relations from this point on do not make the original query more precise. Instead they add words which do not convey the original meaning of the query. Though they enable the retrieval of more relevant documents, they cause the system to retrieve more irrelevant documents as well.

Figure 5.3 shows a graph comparing the results obtained by using antonymy alone with the results from the baseline experiment. This graph may show even

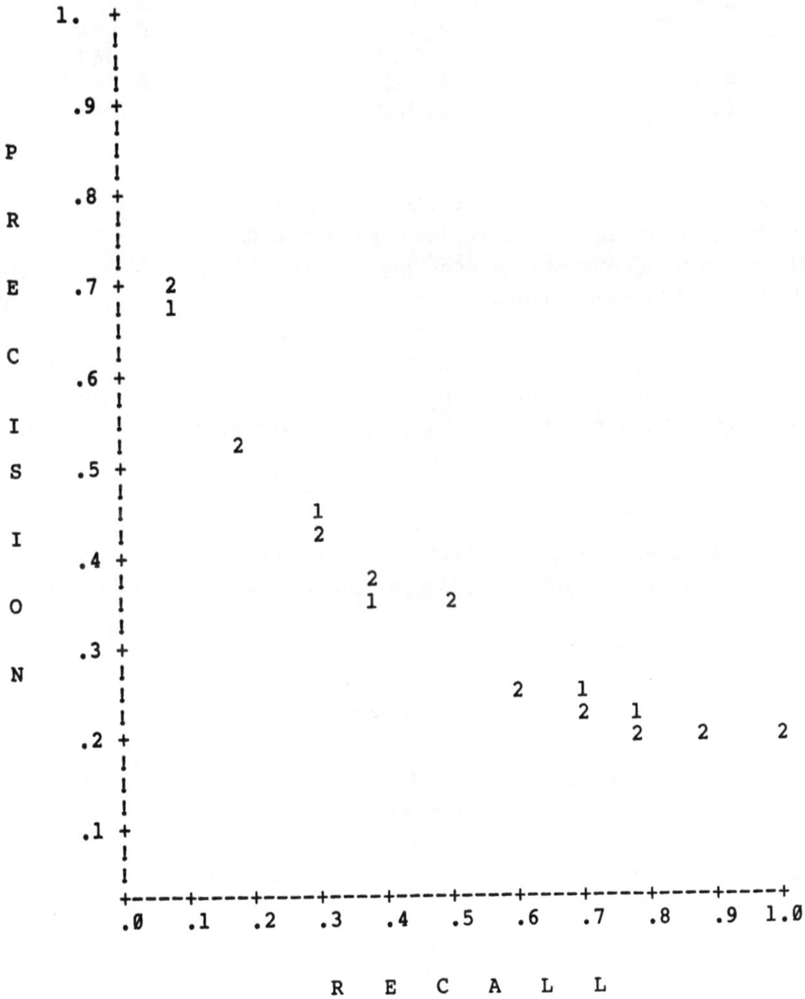

1: Baseline
2: Antonymy

Figure 5.3. Baseline vs. Antonymy Relation for 10 Queries.

Table 5.2. Significance Levels of Results for Baseline vs. Antonymy.

Number of queries: 10
Summary of statistics: One-sided probability for each test

Recall Level	Sign Test	Wilcoxon Test
0.1	0.750	0.327
0.2	0.313	0.357
0.3	0.016	0.014
0.4	0.145	0.221
0.5	0.145	0.221
0.6	0.145	0.337
0.7	0.035	0.081
0.8	0.019	0.043
0.9	0.020	0.043
1.0	0.020	0.043

more clearly than Table 5.2, which contains the significance levels for this experiment, that antonymy does not affect the retrieval results.

The results for all relations but antonymy with these 10 queries agree with Fox's results (1981). The results with antonymy do not. In his experiment he found that the use of antonymy relations made retrieval slightly, but significantly, worse.

If we look instead at the results for 29 queries, we find the results of using all relations but antonymy are rather equivocal, but the results for antonymy bear out Fox's findings. The graph in Figure 5.4 compares the results of using all relations but antonymy with the baseline. The significance levels in Table 5.3 support the impression given by the graph that the improvement is not consistent or significant.

Figure 5.5 shows the graph for antonymy with 29 queries. Here the precision values for the antonymy experiment are consistently below the baseline values, and Table 5.4 shows that this difference is significant except at the lower recall levels.

Discussion of the Results

As we have seen, our best results come with the 10 worst queries. These queries, which contain few index terms, are most susceptible to enhancement from any kind of thesaurus, not just a relational one. When we looked at these results ourselves, we wondered what would happen if we took the bad queries and turned them into good ones. Wang, who was the one most familiar with both the system and the database, took the 10 worst queries and added index terms by hand. When we tried enhancing the rewritten queries with relations, the results were bad. While the index terms added by the system picked out a few documents which were not retrieved without them, they pulled in a great many more useless documents.

Like Fox, we find that our best results come from throwing together all relations which have a positive effect, from using all relations except the antonymy relations. We also found that antonymy does degrade the quality of the retrieval.

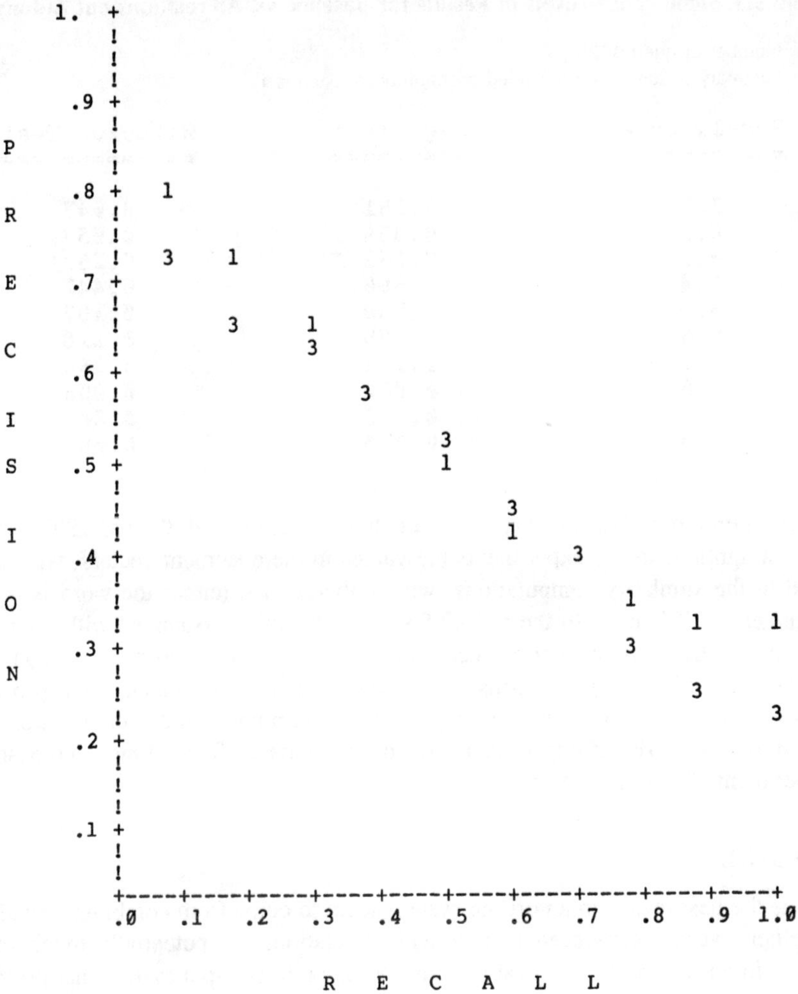

1: Baseline
3: All relations but antonymy

Figure 5.4. Baseline vs. All Relations but Antonymy for 29 Queries.

All of these effects seem likely to happen in any offline system. We are convinced that individual relations or small groups of relations will prove much more effective in an interactive retrieval situation, where the user is actively making decisions about what terms should be added to the query. In this format different relations could be used to pick out new groups of index terms for the user to choose among.

Why are our results less satisfactory than those obtained by Fox? We suspect that

Table 5.3. Significance Levels of Results for Baseline vs. All relations but Antonymy.

Number of queries: 29
Summary of statistics: One-sided probability for each test

Recall Level	Sign Test	Wilcoxon Test
0.1	0.151	0.047
0.2	0.058	0.052
0.3	0.262	0.263
0.4	0.500	0.440
0.5	0.500	0.197
0.6	0.105	0.118
0.7	0.271	0.166
0.8	0.002	0.006
0.9	0.000	0.000
1.0	0.000	0.000

the most important factor is that the system that Fox employed, the SMART system, used weighting. In our experiments the values in the document vectors, which are used in the similarity computations, were either 1 or 0 (either the word is in the document or it is not). In the SMART system the value associated with a term is determined by its frequency of occurrence in the abstract. This same weight was applied as well as to index terms which were added in the enhancement process. IRS was designed to include weighting from the beginning, but this information was lost during the series of experiments. We did not have sufficient funds to repeat the experiments from the beginning.

6. FUTURE WORK

While the best results in an offline system seem to come from combining relations together, we are convinced that individual relations are potentially much more useful in an interactive retrieval system. We hope to set up a system that presents index terms to the user and allows the user to choose those that best convey his or her meaning. Some relations, like the part or member relation, can point to terms which make a query more specific. The taxonomy relation and set relation, on the other hand, can help make a query more general. Collocation relations can guide us to other topics in the same semantic field. IRS was designed with the intent of making it interactive eventually. Wang is examining the problems of designing an interactive interface.

We are continuing to work on the problem of finding relations and extracting relationships from the dictionary. Sager's group has recently sent us a copy of the VAX version of LSP, and we are continuing work on parsing definitions, with special emphasis on adverbs, using some of the tecbniques developed by Ahlswede.

We are starting work on a large relational lexicon for a system to generate reports and answer questions about CAT scanner images. The relational information will be

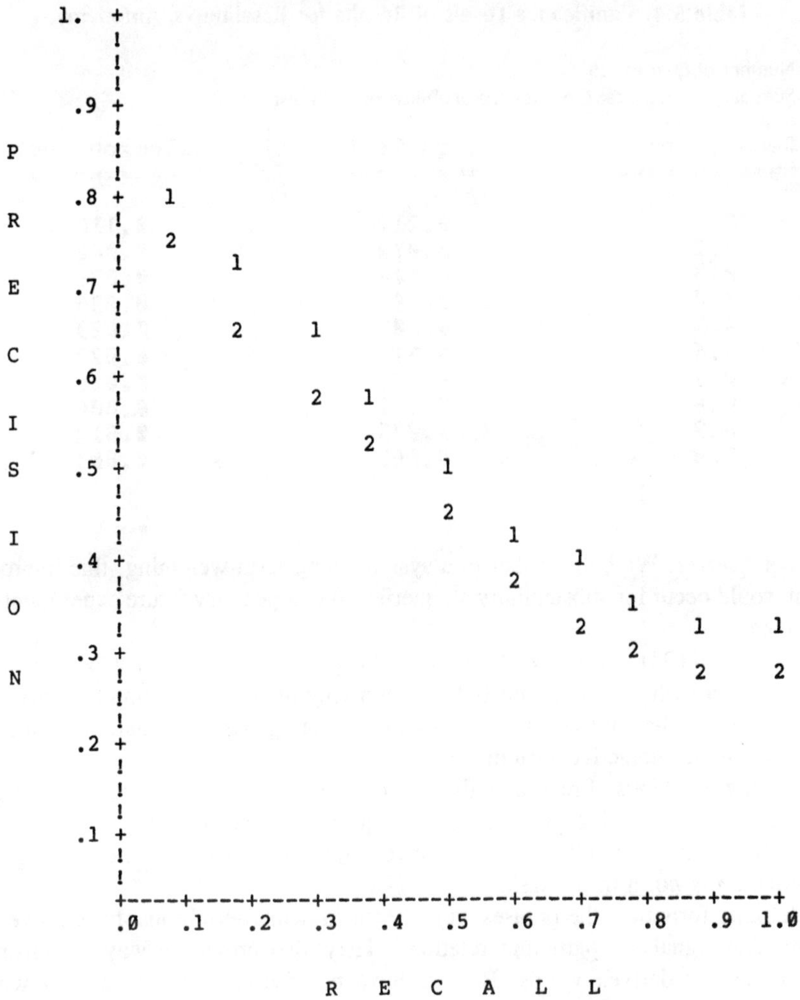

1: Baseline
2: Antonymy relation

Figure 5.5. Baseline vs. Antonymy Relation for 29 Queries.

used by the image understanding module to recognize objects and construct a scene description. It will also be used by the text generation module to find terms to describe these objects.

7. SUMMARY

Our experiments show that the use of a relational thesaurus can improve recall in an information retrieval system, but that improvement was significant only for a group

Table 5.4. Significance Levels of Results for Baseline vs. Antonymy.

Number of queries: 29
Summary of statistics: One-sided probability for each test

Recall Level	Sign Test	Wilcoxon Test
0.1	0.212	0.110
0.2	0.072	0.042
0.3	0.048	0.026
0.4	0.095	0.096
0.5	0.009	0.029
0.6	0.011	0.023
0.7	0.002	0.006
0.8	0.002	0.006
0.9	0.003	0.012
1.0	0.001	0.003

of poor queries. We believe that in a system using term weighting, this improvement would occur for substantially all queries. We hope to try future experiments in this area.

Like Fox (1981), we have found that the greatest improvement occurs in an offline system when all relations but the antonymy relation are acting together. We are convinced that individual relations or smaller groups of relations could be effective in an interactive system.

Before these kinds of relational thesauri can be of practical importance, automatic thesaurus construction procedures are required. A machine-readable dictionary seems to be the most valuable source of relational information, but extracting this information is not a trivial task.

Defining formulae, the phrases which recur in many definitions, have proved to be reliable signals of particular relations. They also provide a way to construct definitions for derived words. But we have not found a way to extract word-relation-word triples from definitions without using some parsing to identify the related words. Sager's Linguistic String Parser has shown itself to be tremendously powerful and adaptable for this task. Much more work is needed however, to actually construct the enormous relational lexicon that practical applications require.

REFERENCES

AHLSWEDE, THOMAS. 1984. A linguistic string grammar of adjective definitions from Webster's Seventh New Collegiate Dictionary. Chapter Seven, this volume.

AMSLER, ROBERT. 1977. Computational lexicology: the search for Noah's arcs. Austin: Computer Science Department, University of Texas.

———. 1980. The structure of the Merriam-Webster Pocket Dictionary. Austin: Computer Science Department, University of Texas, CS TR-164.

______. 1981. A taxonomy for English nouns and verbs. Proceedings of the 1981 Annual Meeting of the Association for Computational Linguistics. Stanford, California, June 29–July 1, 133–138.

______. 1982. Computational lexicology—a research program. Proceedings of the 1982 National Computer Conference, Houston, Texas, June 7–10, 657–663.

APRESYAN, YURI, IGOR MEL'ČUK, and ALEXANDER ŽOLKOVSKY. 1970. Semantics and lexicography: toward a new type of unilingual dictionary. Studies in syntax and semantics, ed. by Ferenc Kiefer, 1–33. Dordrecht-Holland: Reidel.

BMDP. Biomedical Computer Programs, P-Series. 1977. Health Sciences Computing Facility, Department of Biomathematics, School of Medicine, UCLA. Berkeley, CA: University of California Press.

DANIEL, RICKEY. 1982. Prefix group programs. Unpublished. Chicago: Computer Science Department, IIT.

EVENS, MARTHA. 1979. Structuring the lexicon and the thesaurus with lexical-semantic relations. A proposal to the National Science Foundation.

______, BONNIE LITOWITZ, JUDITH MARKOWITZ, RAOUL SMITH, and OSWALD WERNER. 1980. Lexical-semantic relations: a comparative survey. Edmonton, Alberta: Linguistic Research Inc.

______, and RAOUL SMITH. 1978. A lexicon for a computer question-answering system. American Journal of Computational Linguistics, Microfiches 81, 16–24, and 83, 1–98.

FAHLMAN, SCOTT. 1979. NETL: a system for representing and using real-world knowledge. Cambridge: MIT Press.

FOX, EDWARD. 1981. Lexical relations: enhancing effectiveness of information retrieval systems. SIGIR Newsletter, vol. 15, no. 3.

GROVE, ERNEST. 1981. When does a noun deserve a main entry? some alternative hypotheses. Unpublished paper. Chicago: Computer Science Department, IIT.

HENDRIX, GARY. 1975. Expanding the utility of semantic networks through partitioning. Proceedings of the Fourth International Joint Conference on Artificial Intelligence, Tbilisi, August, 115–121.

______. 1979. Encoding knowledge in partitioned networks. Associative networks, ed. by Nicholas Findler. New York: Academic Press.

KINTSCH, WALTER. 1972. Notes on the structure of semantic memory. Organization and memory, ed. by Endel Tulving and Wayne Donaldson, 249–309. New York: Academic Press.

LITOWITZ, BONNIE. 1981. Problems of conceptualization and language: evidence from definitions. Proceedings of the Northwestern University Conference on Adults with Learning Disabilities, Evanston, Illinois, March 18. To be published by Grune and Stratton.

LYONS, JOHN. 1977. Semantics. London: Cambridge University Press.

MERRIAM-WEBSTER POCKET DICTIONARY. Springfield, MA: G & C Merriam Company.

MILLER, GEORGE. 1978. Semantic relations among words. Linguistic theory and psychological reality, ed. by Morris Halle, Joan Bresnan, and George Miller. Cambridge: MIT Press.

NORMAN, DONALD, and DAVID RUMELHART. 1975. Explorations in cognition. San Francisco: W. H. Freeman & Co.

OLNEY, JOHN. 1968. To all interested in the Merriam-Webster transcripts and data derived from them. Document L-13579. Systems Development Corporation, Santa Monica, CA.

PETERSON, JAMES. 1982. Webster's Seventh New Collegiate Dictionary: a computer-readable file format. TR-196, Austin: Department of Computer Sciences, University of Texas at Austin.

RAPHAEL, BERTRAM. 1968. SIR, a computer program for semantic information retrieval. Semantic information processing, ed. by Marvin Minsky, 33–145. Cambridge: MIT Press.

ROSS, JUDITH. 1982. Program for computing definitions of derived words. Unpublished. Chicago: Computer Science Department, IIT.

SAGER, NAOMI. 1981. Natural language information processing: a computer grammar of English and its applications. Reading, MA: Addison-Wesley.

SALTON, GERARD. 1968. Automatic information organization and retrieval. New York: McGraw-Hill.

———. ed. 1971. The SMART retrieval system—experiments in automatic document processing. Englewood Cliffs, NJ: Prentice-Hall.

———, and MICHAEL MCGILL. 1983. Introduction to modern information retrieval. New York: McGraw-Hill.

SCHWIND, CAMILLA. 1975. Generating hierarchical semantic networks from natural language discourse. Proceedings of the Fourth International Joint Conference on Artificial Intelligence, Tbilisi, August, 429–434.

———, and JURGEN JANAS. 1977. Automatic thesaurus construction from natural language definitions. SIGART Newsletter, vol. 61, 49–50.

SIEGEL, S. S. 1956. Nonparametric statistics for the behavioral sciences. New York: McGraw-Hill.

SIMMONS, ROBERT F. 1973. Semantic networks: their computation and use for understanding English sentences. Computer models of thought and language, ed. by Roger Schank and Kenneth Colby, 63–113. San Francisco: W. H. Freeman & Company.

———, and ROBERT AMSLER. 1975. Modeling dictionary data. Directions in artificial intelligence, natural language processing, ed. by Ralph Grishman, 1–26. Courant Institute Report #7. New York: New York University.

SLAVIERO, LINDA. 1981. Phrase counts from the W7 KWIC indices. Unpublished. Chicago: Computer Science Department, IIT.

SMITH, RAOUL. 1978. Computational bilingual lexicography: a la recherche du mot juste. Computer support to translation, ed. by J. Mathiss, 84–112. Washington, DC: National Technical Information Service.

———. 1981. On defining adjectives: Part III. Dictionaries, the Journal of the Dictionary Society of North America, Winter.

———. in press. Conceptual primitives in the English lexicon. Lexicography Today, ed. by W. Frawley. Edmonton, Alberta: Linguistic Research Inc.

VANDENDORPE, JAMES. 1980. A crash tolerant B-tree data structure for data base retrieval systems. Ph.D. Dissertation. Chicago: Computer Science Department, IIT. To be published by UMI Research Press, Ann Arbor, MI.

WEBSTER'S SEVENTH NEW COLLEGIATE DICTIONARY. 1963. Springfield, MA: G & C Merriam Company.

WERNER, OSWALD. 1969. On the universality of lexical/semantic relations. American Anthropological Association Annual Meeting, New Orleans, November.

———. 1974. Intermediate memory, a central explanatory concept for ethnoscience, Communication and Cognition, 7, 3/4, 218–314. Reprinted in Language and Thought: Anthropological Issues, edited by W. C. McCormack and S. A. Wurm, 1977, 131–170. The Hague: Mouton.

ŽOLKOVSKY, ALEXANDER, and IGOR MEL'ČUK. 1970. Semantic synthesis. Systems Theory Research, vol. 19, 170–243.

SEVEN

A Linguistic String Grammar of Adjective Definitions from *Webster's Seventh Collegiate Dictionary*

Thomas E. Ahlswede
Illinois Institute of Technology*

INTRODUCTION

This paper describes an adjective definition grammar (ADG)—see Appendix A—which parses and extracts semantic information from adjective definitions in a machine-readable tape version of *Webster's Seventh Collegiate Dictionary* (W7). The program is written for the Linguistic String Parser (LSP) and is intended as a pilot for a considerably more detailed grammar which will also process noun, verb, and adverb definitions. The parsing process extracts semantic information from the definitions, to be used in constructing a relational lexicon for information retrieval or question answering.

Design of the Lexicon

Every natural language processing system must have some body of prior knowledge—syntactic, semantic, and especially, lexical information. In the past, computer lexicons have been constructed 'by hand' to the exact specifications of the particular systems using them, and have usually been very small.

The difficulty of manually building a large lexicon is one of the factors that have restricted natural language processing systems to small specialized subsets of natural language. Thus, it is obviously desirable to automate the process. Unfortunately, there is nothing like a consensus on the best structure for a computer lexicon. It is probably inevitable that some details of the construction—perhaps even fundamental design features—will remain application-dependent.

Intended Applications. The lexicon to be built with the help of the ADG is primarily intended as a thesaurus which will be used to extend the power of an information retrieval system by enabling the system to search for words related to

* Presently affiliated with R. R. Donnelley & Sons Co., Chicago, Illinois. The author would like to thank Martha Evens for her guidance and enthusiastic support; also Ralph Grishman and Naomi Sager for their help in understanding the Linguistic String Parser, and the National Science Foundation, whose Grant No. IST-79-18467 made the work possible.

given keywords. It should also be easily adaptable for use in question answering and other language-understanding applications, since this is the context in which its basic design was worked out (Evens 1975, Evens and Smith 1978).

A relational network is built around a standard set of possible relations between words. These relations are represented as labeled arcs connecting nodes; the nodes contain words plus any nonrelational information we care to include. The number of distinct relations we need may be fairly large but still far less than a thousand. Finding words related to a given word is easy; we simply access the related words directly through the relational arcs. If a particular relation we are interested in is more complex, we may search through some sequence or sequences of arcs.

Lexical-Semantic Relations

Two lexical-semantic relations that are familiar to everyone are synonymy and autonymy. Synonymy appears in the lexicon as a set of arcs, labeled with a name such as SYN, connecting pairs of synonymous words such as *amusing* and *funny, to help* and *to aid:*

amusing	SYN	funny
to help	SYN	to aid

Lexical-semantic relations can have properties such as reflexivity, symmetry, and transitivity. Synonymy, for instance, is reflexive:

amusing SYN amusing

and symmetric:

amusing	SYN	funny
	iff	
funny	SYN	amusing

Another generally recognized relation is taxonomy, which is used particularly with noun and verb definitions (Amsler 1980):

lion TAX mammal

Taxonomy is transitive:

mammal TAX animal

therefore

lion TAX animal

but not symmetric

*mammal TAX lion

and it is questionable whether it should be regarded as reflexive:

(?)lion TAX lion

Relations in the Analysis of Dictionary Definitions. Our working hypothesis is that a dictionary definition can be analyzed into a set of relations between the defined word on one hand, and various elements of the definition proper on the other hand. We propose to use definitions to generate word-relation-word triples which may then be used as data to build the lexicon.

The Project

The parent project for the ADG is 'Structuring the Lexicon and Thesaurus with Lexical-Semantic Relations', funded through NSF Grant No. IST-79-18467 and directed by Martha Evens. Its purpose is to create a computerized lexicon (which we will call THE LEXICON) in which nodes containing words are linked to each other by labeled arcs corresponding to lexical-semantic relations.

There are three phases to the project:

1. Identification of new relations;
2. Computer analysis of dictionary definitions to reveal specific relations connecting specific words;
3. Use of these specific instances (represented as word-relation-word triples) to generate a thesaurus.

The ADG completes a subset of the project, consisting of Phase 1 and part of Phase 2, carried out on adjectives. A large (though neither exhaustive nor definitive) set of relations is defined for adjectives. The identification of relations is done 'manually'—by human study of the dictionary, with the help of computer-generated indices. (The concept of lexical-semantic relations is still far from the level of exactness where relations could be found automatically, although some patterns can be detected, as we shall see.)

Dictionary definitions of adjectives are then parsed on the LSP to yield:

1. The original adjective—word 1 of the word-relation-word triple.
2. One or more lexical-semantic relations contained in the definition. These are identified by ''defining formulae''—frequently-recurring initial phrases.
3. A parse tree of the remainder of the definition. This remainder will contain one or more 'core' words which are related to the adjective being defined, through the relation(s) already identified.

Completion of Phase 2 (generation of triples) will require further processing of the parse tree of the definition to isolate core words and separate the numerous triples that may occur in a single definition. This step is complicated by the frequent conjoining both of defining formulae and core words.

The final stage of Phase 2 is to identify relations and generate triples for other parts of speech. Some work in this area is presently being done. Vicki Klick has written a simple grammar of adverb definitions. Martha Evens and Linda Slaviero have created a list of noun relations, but there has been no attempt yet (March 1984) to use this list in a grammar of noun definitions. The basic process of creating such a grammar will not be radically different from that described here for adjectives, but the details are sufficiently different that creation of a grammar for noun (or verb) definitions will be a substantial job.

IDENTIFICATION OF DEFINING FORMULAE AND RELATIONS

The Defining Formula

The notion of a DEFINING FORMULA was introduced by Gove (1968) and was used as a tool of analyses by Smith (1981). A defining formula is a word or phrase that frequently occurs in definitions of some part of speech—e.g., *of or relating to . . .* for adjectives, *state of . . .* for nouns, *in a . . . manner* for adverbs.

Relators. We can define the concept of defining formula more exactly by establishing a related phenomenon which occurs throughout the dictionary, the relation-bearing phrase or relator.

An important convention of dictionary definitions is that the definition be syntactically parallel to the defined word—thus, a noun must be defined with a noun phrase, a verb with a verb phrase, etc. An attempt is made to follow this convention with adjectives (Smith 1981), but, while some adjective definitions are clearly adjectival in form (e.g. 'abrupt **adj.** unceremoniously curt'), to the extent that they can be 'plugged in' in place of the defined word, most of them are much less distinctly adjectival. For example, it would be at least awkward to use *of or relating to the atmosphere* in place of *atmospheric* in most text situations.

If, as often happens, an adjective is derived from or best defined in terms of a noun or verb phrase, the definition will consist of that phrase plus another phrase which converts the entire definition to adjectival form, as well as sometimes carrying additional semantic information accompanying the conversion. The additional information may be minimal, as in '*of or relating to* the atmosphere', where the italicized phrase merely denotes the adjectival form of the given noun. Or the semantic information may be considerable. The phrase *capable of* in *clear* **adj.** *capable of sharp discernment* not only relates the adjective to a noun (and ultimately to a verb, since, as it turns out, the noun in a *capable of . . .* definition is always derived from a verb), but denotes, in addition, a notion of potentiality not contained in the original verb or verbal noun.

Converters

The above discussion emphasizes the syntactic role of these phrases; they 'convert' a phrase of one part-of-speech type into another phrase which may be of the same part-of-speech type but is often of a different one. Thus, if phrase A can take another phrase B (which belongs to part of speech X) as a complement, and the combined phrase A-concatenate-B is of part of speech Y, then we can call A an X-Y CONVERTER.

For example: *marked by* is a noun-adjective converter—the adjective calm is defined as *marked by* [*the noun*] *calm. Not* is an adjective-adjective converter—g.g., *easy* **adj.** *not severe.*

It appears that every converter expresses some kind of lexical-semantic relation between the defined word and the complement phrase. We can say, for instance, that the converter not relates the adjective easy to the adjective [phrase] *severe*—in this case, through the relation of antonymy. Converter and relator thus refer to the same thing, defined by its (syntactic) form or its (semantic) function, respectively.

I have not attempted to prove this hypothesis. Since the domain (adjective definitions) of the hypothesis is finite, an exhaustive demonstration might be easier than a proof. Either one, however, must wait for a more rigorous and complete understanding of lexical-semantic relations.

None of this is to say that a given converter always expresses the same relation. The word *affecting,* for instance, serves as a converter in several definitions, including:

> fine **adj.** . . . affecting elegance or refinement
> epidemic **adj.**. affecting many persons at once

which clearly use the word in different senses. Fortunately, the meaning of a converter is usually much more consistent than this example would suggest; and as a broad approximation we can assume that a converter is consistent in its meaning. Note: the definitions referred to throughout this paper follow the format in which they have been adapted from the machine-readable version of W7, for use in the ADG. These do not always match the original W7 definitions, particularly in punctuation.

DEFINING FORMULA can now be defined as a converter/relator which occurs with a frequency greater than some arbitrary minimum—i.e., often enough to justify putting it in a special category.

Identification of Formulae

The first step in the procedure for finding defining formulae is to decide what kinds of phrases are likely to serve as formulae. In a sample of 3,909 adjective definitions from W7, Smith (1981) identified 33 formulae as occurring 10 or more times. Their combined occurrence is 1,763 times, or in about 45% of the definitions. Smith's list and his comments on it have been extremely helpful in the process of finding additional formulae. Smith notes that all of his formulae consist of (1) a present participle, (2) a past participle, or (3) an adjective of some other type. Any of these may be preceded by *not.*

Since the function of a defining formula is to state a relation between its complement and the defined word, we intuitively expect it to come between the defined word and the complement—i.e., at the beginning of definition. For easy recognition, we would like it also to be contiguous, i.e., in one piece. (An example of a non-contiguous formula is the adverb formula *in a . . . manner.*) In practice, we find that adjective-defining formulae are initial unless preceded by adverbs, and are usually (though not always) contiguous.

For the ADG, finding formulae and their associated relations was largely a manual process, although it could be automated to some extent. The first step was to generate a KWIC (Key Word In Context) index of adjective definitions in our sample. (A KWIC index is a sorted list of text subelements, each showing its context. In this case, the KWIC index showed every word of every definition, sorted alphabetically, preceded and followed by the rest of its surrounding definition.) The sample consisted of definitions of all the adjectives from A through P that occurred eight or more times in the Brown University corpus (Kucera and Francis 1967). Each sense of a word was treated as a separate definition. The total size of the KWIC output was 27,469 lines, one for each word.

The Relations

Table 1 contains a list of all relation-bearing phrases encountered 11 or more times in a manual search of the KWIC output. Relations are associated with as many of these as possible.

The following types of words and phrases were assumed to be relation bearers:

1. The present participle of a transitive verb, followed by a noun phrase;
2. An adjective (including a participle) followed by a preposition;
3. An initial adverb.

Only initial phrases were regarded as parseable, with the following exceptions:

1. Phrases conjoined by *or;*
2. Phrases preceded only by initial adverbs;
3. Phrases preceded by the symbols ESP, ALSO, SPECIF.

Description of Important Relations. The *J* at the beginning of a relation name is an arbitrary convention indicating an adjective relation. The formulae associated with each relation are those which occurred 10 or more times in the sample.

The technique for assigning a formula to a relation is entirely subjective. A formula is assigned to an existing relation if it is felt that the formula can be substituted for the most commonly occurring relation in the relation-class without seriously altering the meaning of the definition. Otherwise, a new relation is created for it.

This catalog of relations is very tentative and suggestions for change are eagerly solicited.

JSIMPL (relating to, of, characteristic of, based on, concerned with, dealing with) is similar to AMZ's A(o). It denotes the adjectival form of the object noun or noun phrase.

blue **adj.** of the color blue
criminal **adj.** relating to crime or its punishment
beat **adj.** of or relating to beatniks
missionary **adj.** characteristic of a missionary
formal **adj.** based on conventional forms and rules
cultural **adj.** concerned with the fostering of plant or animal growth
hot **adj.** dealing with radioactive material

Table 1. Formulae occurring 14 or more times in adjective definition sample.

Formula	Complement type	Relation	Total occurrences	Parseable occurrences
relating to	NP	JSIMPL	453	453
having	NP	JCHAR	317	284
not	NP	JANTI	235	186
marked by	NP	JCHAR	130	127
of (initial)	NP	JSIMPL	90	90
lacking	NP	JNHAVE	82	79
characterized by	NP	JCHAR	77	73
being	PP	JBEING	c. 66	c. 66
constituting	NP	JBEING	63	58
being	NP		c. 47	c. 47
free from	NP	JNHAVE	48	42
characteristic of	NP	JSIMPL	42	39
involving	NP	JCHAR	38	37
situated	LP		38	36
having no	NP	JNHAVE	34	34
showing	NP	JMANIF	31	30
capable of	VN	JABLE1	29	28
containing	NP	JCONTN	30	27
belonging to	NP	JPART	27	25
resembling	NP	JLIKE	25	25
based on	NP	JSIMPL	26	24
consisting of	NP	JCOMPO	25	24
very	NP	JMAGN	30	22
capable of being	PsPt	JABLE2	20	20
extending	LP		21	20
conforming to	NP	JAFFIN	18	18
easily	PsPt	JABLE2	24	18
producing	NP	JCAUSE1	19	18
being	AP	JSYN	c. 16	c. 16
causing	NP	JCAUSE1	19	16
full of	NP	JCONTN	17	16
subject to	NP	JINFLU2	17	16
affecting	NP	JINFLU1	16	15
possessing	NP	JCHAR	15	15
concerned with	NP	JSIMPL	16	14
expressing	NP	JMANIF	16	14

NP = noun phrase
AP = misc. adjectival phrase
PP = prepositional phrase
LP = locational phrase (usually prepositional)
VP = verb phrase
VN = verbal noun phrase
PsPt = past participle

JCHAR (having, marked by, characterized by, involving, possessing) denotes the attributive form of the object noun phrase. It appears to be the inverse of a noun-to-adjective relation marked by the formula *the quality or state of being* + adjective.

> passing **adj.** having a brief duration
> distinguished **adj.** marked by eminence, distinction, or excellence
> (Note: one definition of *distinction* is *the quality or state or being distinguished*).

impatient **adj.** prompted or marked by impatience
explicit **adj.** characterized by full clear expression
clinical **adj.** involving direct observation of the patient
consistent **adj.** possessing firmness or coherence

JANTI (not) denotes an antonym. The complement of a JANTI is sometimes a simple adjective, as in

little **adj.** not big

but it can have any internal structure, including converter-type.

naked **adj.** not covered by clothing

Overall, most JANTI complements are adjectival in form.

JNHAVE (lacking, free from, having no, lacking in, ⟨JCHAR⟩ + lack of) is simply a compound of JANTI and JCHAR. It is so common, however, that it is more convenient to treat it as a single relation.

faint **adj.** lacking courage or spirit
honest **adj.** free from deception
null **adj.** having no legal or binding force
passive **adj.** lacking in energy or will
indifferent **adj.** characterized by lack of active quality

JBEING (being + NP, constituting) is difficult to describe. It is also not clear whether *constituting* belongs here or in JSIMPL; 26 of its 58 parseable occurrneces are in conjunction with *of, relating to,* or *or.*

fellow **adj.** being a companion, mate, or associate
final **adj.** constituting the ultimate in degree or development

JMANIF (showing, expressing) is an attributive relation similar to JCHAR but emphasizing that the attribute is manifest rather than latent. This relation, as well as JTEND and possibly JCONTN, might well be lumped together in JCHAR if simplicity is desired; the difference is one of nuance, not fundamental meaning.

distorted **adj.** showing symptoms of emotional illness
grateful **adj.** expressing approval

JABLE1 (capable of + verbal NP, able to + VP) is the same as AMZ's Able(1). It denotes ability to be the agent or instrument of the action expressed in the verb phrase.

moral **adj.** capable of right and wrong action
durable **adj.** able to endure

JABLE2 (capable of being + past participle, easily + past participle) is the same as AMZ's Able(2). It denotes ability to be the recipient of the action of the verb phrase.

movable **adj.** capable of being moved
fragile **adj.** easily broken or damaged

The formula *easily* is interesting: it is the most common of a very few initial-adverb converters that express relations other than various forms of synonymy, antonymy, or taxonomy. All occurrences of *easily* are followed by past participles, and express the relation JABLE2.

JCONTN (containing, full of) is similar to JCHAR.

lemon **adj.** containing lemon
cheerful **adj.** full of good spirits

JLIKE (resembling) denotes a similarity to the object noun.

gigantic **adj.** resembling a giant
fatal **adj.** resembling fate in foretelling destiny

JPART (belonging to) denotes a part-whole relation.

gentle **adj.** belonging to a family of high social station
antique **adj.** belonging to antiquity

JCOMPO (consisting of, composed of) denotes the inverse of JPART.

complicated **adj.** consisting of parts intricately combined
integral **adj.** composed of integral parts

JMAGN (very, extremely, well) gets its name from AMZ's adjective-noun relation Magn, although JMAGN is an adjective-adjective taxonomy or modified synonymy. The JMAGN converters are all adverbs, and their complements are always adjectival (*well* always takes a past particple).

brilliant **adj.** very bright a ' light
fascinating **adj.** extremely interesting or charming
fat **adj.** well stocked

JCAUSE1 (producing, causing, giving) denotes a thing caused by the noun which the adjective modifies.

exciting **adj.** producing excitement
destructive **adj.** causing destruction a ' storm
encouraging **adj.** giving hope or promise

JCAUSE2 (none of 10 or more occurrences, but less common examples would include *produced by* and *formed by*) and JORIGIN (arising from, resulting from) denote the cause of the noun which the adjective modifies. These two might more suitably be lumped together.

arbitrary **adj.** arising from will or caprice
occupational **adj.** relating to or resulting from a particular occupation ' disease

JSYN (being + adjective phrase, unprefaced adjective phrase) is self-explanatory.

else **adj.** being different in identity somebody '
neat **adj.** being orderly and clean

JINFLU (affecting) denotes the object of an influence

international **adj.** affecting or involving two or more nations ' trade

JACTIV (engaged in) denotes an activity.

busy **adj.** engaged in action
industrial **adj.** engaged in industry the ' classes

jneces (requiring) denotes some sort of necessity.

intellectual **adj.** requiring use of the intellect

As indicated in Table 1, relations have been determined only for the more common formulae. A casual perusal of the list suggests that these relations will apply to many of the remaining formulae, but that a great many formulae will represent relations not yet defined.

THE LINGUISTIC STRING PARSER

Sager and Grishman's Linguistic String Parser was chosen to implement the ADG because, as one of the oldest English language parsers in use, it is relatively thoroughly debugged and has been applied to an exceptionally large subset of English grammar. Furthermore, it has been adapted to a variety of systems, including the Univac 1108, which is IIT's mainframe.

Syntactic Types of Adjective Definitions

I have classified adjective definitions into two fundamental types: those where an explicit converter phrase (see preceding section) links the defined adjective to a noun or verb phrase, and those where the definition is more strictly adjectival in form—where the principal words in the definition are themselves adjectives (other than participles of verbs).

Within the category of converter-type definitions, we must draw a line somewhere between those converters which are common enough to be regarded as formulae and those which are not. The line may be drawn anywhere we consider convenient—but it is a very fundamental line. Formulae can be written explicitly into the grammar as literal strings, and, as a result, the relations they embody can be recognized immediately by the parser. On the other hand, there is no way yet to extract a relation from a nonformulaic converter, even where the relation is obvious to the human reader. At present, the grammar parses nonformulaic converters without attempting to yield triples from them.

Although most relation bearers are noun- or verb-to-adjective converters, some are initial adverbs which may begin an adjective-type definition. Several of these are common enough to appear in the ADG as formulae. They usually represent types of synonymy, antonymy, or taxonomy (which three relations are little if at all represented among the noun- and verb-to-adjective converters).

The BNF Component of the Grammar

The bulk of the parsing of a sentence is done using a context-free grammar. This grammar, written by the user in BNF, analyzes the sentence into linguistic strings and further analyzes the strings into their atomic elements, i.e., members of the various word classes. The parse tree thus generated will then be examined and perhaps modified by the restriction part of the grammar (see Figure 1).

The Restriction Component of the Grammar

Restrictions are procedures, written by the user in a special RESTRICTION LANGUAGE, by which the LSP can handle the non-context-free rules of English. The redundant parse tree shown above is an example of one kind of situation that calls for restrictions; another one, simpler to describe, is the following:

Nonformulaic converters take remainders of the form LNR (Left noun-adjunct, Noun, Right noun-adjunct), a type of noun phrase. But some require other strings as remainders: *easily* takes a past-participial phrase, *able* and *tending* take infinitive phrases.

We could accommodate these special cases in a context-free grammar by specifying the type of remainder for each formula. This would be complex and clumsy. Furthermore, the division of an adjective definition into ⟨converter⟩ + ⟨remainder⟩ is intuitively a deep one, comparable to the division ⟨subject⟩ + ⟨predictae⟩ in a declarative sentence. We would prefer to separate the converter and the remainder early in the parsing process.

In a context-free language, once we have separated converter and remainder, we

```
SENTENCE
   |
CENTER ---------------------------------------- '.'
   |
*ADJ - 'ADJ.' - ADJDEF -------------- ADJTAIL
   |                |                     |
evil             CONVTYP               *NULL
             |
          CONVTR
             |
          DSTG — FMLA -------REMDR
             |      |          |
          *NULL  JCAUSE1      LNR
                    |          |
                 causing      LN -- *N -- RN
                               |     |     |
                            *NULL  harm  *NULL
```

Figure 1. Parse tree (slightly abridged) for 'evil *adj.* causing harm.'

must parse them separately, independently of each other. But they are not really independent—the converter *easily*, as mentioned above, must be associated with a remainder consisting of a participial phrase rather than the more usual noun phrase. This is much like the requirements for agreement between subject and verb in English.

The rule for formula-remainder agreement can be stated something like this:

```
REMDR has the form
  TOVO      (TO + Verb + Object—infinitive phrase)
            iff the formula is tending or able;
  VINGO     (Verb + ING + Object—gerund or pres.
            particle plus object)
            iff the formula is capable of;
  VENPASS   (past participle with adjunct phrases)
            iff the formula is easily or
  LNR       otherwise.
```

The Restriction Language statement that expresses this rule is:

```
WAD1 = IN CONVTYP: ALL$TOVO, $VINGO, $VENPASS.
  $TOVO = IF REMDR IS TOVO
          THEN EITHER CORE X1 OF CONVTR IS 'TENDING'
          OR X1 IS 'ABLE'.
  $VINGO = IF REMDR IS VINGO THEN X1 IS 'CAPABLE OF'.
  $VENPASS = IF REMDR IS VENPASS
             THEN EITHER X1 IS 'EASILY'
             OR X1 IS 'CAPABLE OF BEING'.
```

PARSING THE DEFINITIONS

Early Problems

In the early stages of work on the ADG, we considered the possibility of writing our own parser. The LSP, like all large natural language parsers and especially like those which concentrate on syntax with little or no semantic processing, is slow and expensive to run. Since the development of the ADG was going to require a great deal of testing, it seemed possible that we might decide to sacrifice the power of the LSP in favor of the simplicity and speed of a special-purpose parser.

A significant step in this direction was a Snobol program by Judy Ross which identified formulae in definitions and matched them to their corresponding relations. This program thus gave us the first two elements of the word-relation-word triple: the defined word and the relation.

Three serious problems remained. We still had to parse the remainder of the definition in order to extract the third part of the triple; and the grammar necessary to do this with any completeness would be little smaller than that for complete definitions.

Second, we still had to parse definitions which contained no explicit formula. The third problem was that a great many adjective definitions contain conjunctions, especially *or*. (*Or* is by far the commonest word in our definition sample, with 2,387 occurrences.) We had no way of handling conjunctions. The LSP, on the other hand, had a very powerful conjunction-parsing mechanism (Raze 1976).

The Little Grammar. The ADG grew out of a very simple training grammar provided by the LSP group (Grishman, *User's Guide*). This we dubbed the 'little' or sometimes the 'baby' grammar. In one of its versions (see Appendix B), it contained BNF statements to implement a limited use of the conjunction, according to the Raze method.

This conjunction material included a set of special conjunction restrictions without which the BNF statements were useless. We did not suspect the existence of these restrictions until we discovered them in a sample grammar inadvertently buried in the enormous Fortran source file of the LSP. Once we had written in these restrictions, the enlarged 'little grammar' worked beautifully. It was not difficult to rewrite the BNF code and the special restrictions to accommodate the much more elaborate conjunction strings characteristic of adjective definitions.

Semantics of *OR*

Some decisions had to be made about the ubiquitous *or*. In ordinary English, this conjunction is far less common than *and*, and is used in somewhat different ways. The 'full' LSP grammar (Sager 1981) recognizes these differences by designating ⟨ANDSTG⟩ (*and*-string) and ⟨ORSTG⟩ (*or*-string) as distinct nonterminals.

Not only is *or* strikingly common in adjective definitions, but ternary and larger constructions of the form *x, y, or z,* rare in ordinary English, are frequent in the dictionary. The LSP documentation available to us said nothing about how these complex strings are handled, so the method used in the ADG is my own.

And is much less common than *or* in definitions. In the KWIC output, it appears 281 times as against 2,387 times for *or*. In the base sample, it occurs twice, whereas *or* occurs 30 times. Under these circumstances, I found it convenient to ignore the difference between the two words. Furthermore, the distinction between the words in dictionary usage is far less clear than in logic, or even in ordinary English.

In artificial languages influenced by formal logic, such as programming languages, conjunction operators generally have low precedence and an ambiguous statement analygous to that found in:

> formal **adj.** based on *conventional forms and rules* would be resolved
> (1) (conventional forms) and rules rather than
> (2) conventional (forms and rules)

In English, including its dictionary sublanguage, there is no such clear precedence. Sometimes the ambiguity can be resolved semantically: *fierce wolves and rabbits* lends itself to the interpretation (*fierce wolves*) *and rabbits* better than to *fierce* (*wolves and rabbits*).

My feeling is that, in English, coordinate conjunctions have fairly high precedence. The phrase *fierce wolves and rabbits* at least momentarily calls up the image of fierce rabbits, although we are finally led to analyze it the other way. A semantically neutral adjective in place of *fierce* seems to be naturally global: *gray* (*wolves and rabbits*) rather than (*gray wolves*) *and rabbits*.

Writing the Grammar

In the early stages of experimentation, I used the 'little grammar,' with a minimum of added vocabulary and syntax, to parse simple 'artificial' definitions. At this stage, several things remained to be determined.

Fundamental Syntax of Adjective Definitions. As we noted above (p. 110), adjective definitions are basically adjectival in form. It would therefore be possible in principle to analyze adjective definitions according to conventional English grammar, with a few allowances for peculiar terms and usages (see Table 1) and with the basic provision that ⟨adjective⟩ 'adj.' ⟨adj. phrase⟩ be a legal 'sentence' type.

This strategy turns out to be hopelessly uninformative about the semantics of adjective definitions. Furthermore, upon looking at definitions for any length of time, one soon observes syntactic patterns which, although possible in ordinary English, do not normally occur. 'Of or realting to ⟨NP⟩' is so common (196 occurrences) that it could be treated as an atom—but the pattern of fragmented prepositional phrase is ubiquitous in the sample.

> abundant **adj.** existing in or possessing abundance
> aesthetic **adj.** relating to or dealing with aesthetics or the beautiful
> arched **adj.** made with or formed in an arch

Clearly, here is a syntactic structure that subsumes at least three phrase types which we ordinarily consider quite different: preposition, adjective + preposition, and the present pariciple of a transitive verb. The structure seems to be defined by the fact that it takes a noun phrase as a complement, and, concatenated with this noun phrase, forms a more or less adjectival phrase. This is the noun-adjective converter.

The first step toward a successful grammar, therefore, was to introduce the converter as a legitimate syntactic form. The parse tree would now be structured with relational material all together on one side, and target-word information on the other. There still remained the question of how to extract the needed information, particularly that having to do with relations.

Incorporation of Formulae in the Grammar. The solution to the problem was inspired by Ross's program (see p. 19 above). The LSP could read the formulae as literal strings; successful identification of a formula would cause the LSP to create a node in the parse tree—a node named after the appropriate relation. This still did not constitute generation of triples, but it meant that everything needed to generate triples would be explicitly present in the parse tree: the target word or words as terminal nodes in the 'remainder' subtree, and the relation or relations as nonterminals in the 'converter' subtree.

Selecting a Subset

The ADG could not be considered successful until it was capable of parsing real dictionary definitions, preferably typical ones not chosen for simplicity or any other limiting trait. On the other hand, constraints of resources and time dictated that it cover no more than a fairly small subset of the full English grammar. The question was, what constituted a reasonable subset?

I decided to choose a sample set of definitions, as nearly as possible random with respect to syntactic structure and complexity. My early efforts at creating a formula/relation list had resulted in a list of about 40 formulae with a frequency of 10 or greater. The definitions chosen for this sample were selected by looking up each formula in the KWIC index and picking the tenth definition from each formula.

This became the 'base sample.' A second, 'control' sample consisted of the definitions appearing at the top of each of the first 37 pages of the input (instead of the output) of the KWIC index.

I then wrote the ADG to give the best possible performance in parsing the base sample—ideally one successful parse for each definition. Once this grammar was debugged, I tested it on the control sample to get an idea of how powerful it really was.

Multiple Parses

The goal of exactly one parse per definition was in a sense unrealistic, because many definitions are legitimately ambiguous in their syntax (though we hope not in semantics). Two types of such ambiguity are particularly prominent:

1. Scope of conjunctions. We have already discussed this above (pp. 113–114). The two levels of reference of the conjunction are easily distinguished in the LSP: on the basis of intuition I chose to give preference to the lower level, that is, *gray* (*wolves and rabbits*) as opposed to (*gray wolves*) *and rabbits*. It is worth noting that the conjunction restrictions of the 'little grammar' allow only this scope; conjunctions at the higher level cannot be parsed.

2. *Nonformulaic parsing of formulae.* The 'nonformula' node permits nonformulaic parsing of converter-type definitions whose converters are not common enough to be included in the grammar as formulae. Such definitions are not semantically useful yet, but are included for completeness.

The ambiguity arises in the fact that every formula is, by definition, a converter. This means that every formula can be parsed nonformulaically. But if we already have a formula parse, a useless nonformula parse only wastes time and space. I wrote some restrictions which reject a nonformulaic interpretation of definitions whose converters contain words used in formulae.

CONCLUSIONS

Discussion of Results

Since the ADG was built around the base sample of definitions, it is no surprise that its performance on the base sample, as shown in Table 2, is excellent. In fact, the grammar was tuned and polished until further improvement promised not to be worth the effort.

Table 2. Base and control samples.

Definition			Parses
EVIL	ADJ.	CAUSING HARM .	1
PAY	ADJ.	REQUIRING PAYMENT .	1
DEPRESSED	ADJ.	LOW IN SPIRITS .	2
CLEAR	ADJ.	FREE FROM BLEMISHES .	1
DRY	ADJ.	SERVED WITHOUT BUTTER .	2
MOVABLE	ADJ.	CAPABLE OF BEING MOVED .	1
NERVOUS	ADJ.	EASILY EXCITED OR IRRITATED .	3
OBJECTIVE	ADJ.	DERIVED FROM SENSE PERCEPTION .	1
LOST	ADJ.	LACKING ASSURANCE OR SELF- CONFIDENCE .	1
FALSE	ADJ.	TENDING TO MISLEAD ' PROMISE .	1
DANGEROUS	ADJ.	EXPOSING TO OR INVOLVING DANGER .	1
COLONIAL	ADJ.	POSSESSING OR COMPOSED OF COLONIES .	2
COMPLEX	ADJ.	COMPOSED OF TWO OR MORE PARTS .	1
FORMAL	ADJ.	BASED ON CONVENTIONAL FORMS AND RULES .	1
INDUSTRIAL	ADJ.	ENGAGED IN INDUSTRY THE ' CLASSES .	1
CONGREGATIONAL	ADJ.	OF OR RELATING TO A CONGREGATION .	2
GENEROUS	ADJ.	MARKED BY ABUNDANCE OR AMPLE PROPORTIONS .	1
LIGHT	ADJ.	HAVING A CLEAR SOFT QUALITY ' VOICE .	1
COMFORTABLE	ADJ.	GIVING COMFORT ; ESP PROVIDING PHYSICAL COMFORT .	1
DIFFERENTIAL	ADJ.	PRODUCING EFFECTS BY REASON OF SUCH DIFFERENCES .	3
DARK	ADJ.	ARISING FROM OR SHOWING EVIL TRAITS OR DESIRES .	1
LIVELY	ADJ.	FULL OF LIFE , MOVEMENT , OR INCIDENT .	1
JUDICIAL	ADJ.	OF , CHARACTERIZED BY , OR EXPRESSING JUDGMENT .	1
INTELLECTUAL	ADJ.	GIVEN TO STUDY , REFLECTION , AND SPECULATION .	1
OUTSIDE	ADJ.	NOT BELONGING TO ONES REGULAR OCCUPATION OR DUTIES .	1
MOTOR	ADJ.	OF , IN , OR RELATING TO AN AUTOMOBILE .	1
FUNCTIONAL	ADJ.	OF , CONNECTED WITH , OR BEING A FUNCTION .	1
FUNERAL	ADJ.	OF , RELATING TO , OR CONSTITUTING A FUNERAL .	1
INTERNATIONAL	ADJ.	AFFECTING OR INVOLVING TWO OR MORE NATIONS ' TRADE .	1
GENERAL	ADJ.	CONCERNED OR DEALING WITH UNIVERSAL RATHER THAN PARTICULAR ASPECTS .	1

Table 2 (*Continued*)

Definition		Parses
MUNICIPAL	ADJ. OF , RELATING TO , OR CHARACTERISTIC OF A MUNICIPALITY .	2
DIRTY	ADJ. CHARACTERIZED BY A HUSKY , RASPING , OR RAW TONAL QUALITY .	1
COMMON	ADJ. CHARACTERIZED BY A LACK OF PRIVILEGE OR STATUS ' PEOPLE .	1
NEUROTIC	ADJ. OF , RELATING TO , CONSTITUTING , OR AFFECTED WITH NEUROSIS .	1
DISTANT	ADJ. CONCERNED WITH OR DIRECTED TOWARD THINGS AT A DISTANCE ' THOUGHTS .	3
LOW	ADJ. NOT ADVANCED IN COMPLEXITY , DEVELOPMENT , OR ELABORATION ' ORGANISMS .	4
AUTOMATIC	ADJ. ACTING OR DONE SPONTANEOUSLY OR UNCONSCIOUSLY ; ALSO RESEMBLING AN AUTOMATON .	2
JUST	ADJ. HAVING A BASIS IN OR CONFORMING TO FACT OR REASON A ' COMMENT .	1
COMPOUND	ADJ. COMPOSED OF OR RESULTING FROM UNION OF SEPARATE ELEMENTS , INGREDIENTS , OR PARTS .	1
CLUB	ADJ. CONSISTING OF FOODS IN A FIXED COMBINATION OFFERED ON A MENU AT A SET PRICE .	2

The purpose of the control sample (shown in Table 3) is to put into perspective what would otherwise seem to be the peculiarly perfect behavior of the ADG. It also gives an idea how powerful the ADG is—roughly how much of the entire dictionary it could parse without further additions (other than lexical).

Out of 37 definitions in the control sample, 21 were successfully parsed. Most of these, however, yielded more than one parse, for a total of 54 parses.

Work Still to Be Done

The simple adjective definition grammar we have constructed here is only a beginning: it is important not because it has produced immediately useful results but because it has established a strategy for processing dictionary definitions, and has made clear the remaining steps in the job as well as giving some hints as to how they can be tackled.

Transformations. The ADG yields a parse tree for every successful parse of a definition. Some additional steps are necessary before we can generate all of the triples most definitions implicitly contain. The ubiquitous conjunctions, especially *or,* obscure a great many triples. Consider

absent **adj.** not present or attending from which we want the triples

absent	ANTI	present
absent	ANTI	attending

Table 3. The control sample.

Definition		Parses
ABANDONED	ADJ. WHOLLY FREE FROM RESTRAINT AND ESP MORAL RESTRAINT .	0
ABSOLUTE	ADJ. HAVING NO EXTERNAL REFERENCE ' MUSIC .	2
ACID	ADJ. RICH IN SILICA .	2
ACUTE	ADJ. HAVING THE FORM #1208#1 .	1
AFRAID	ADJ. FILLED WITH CONCERN OR REGRET OVER AN UNWANTED CONTINGENCY .	4
ALL	ADJ. NOTHING BUT .	0
AMPLE	ADJ. MORE THAN ENOUGH .	0
ANTIQUE	ADJ. IMITATING OR SUGGESTING THE CRAFTS OR STYLE OF AN EARLIER PERIOD.	3
ARC	ADJ. ' SINE .	0
AUTHENTIC	ADJ. WORTHY OF ACCEPTANCE OR BELIEF .	2
AWKWARD	ADJ. APPEARING ILL-PROPORTIONED , OUTSIZE , OR POORLY FITTED TOGETHER .	0
BASE	ADJ. CONSTITUTING OR SERVING AS A BASE .	2
BEST	ADJ. MOST PRODUCTIVE OF GOOD OR OF ADVANTAGE, UTILITY , OR SATISFACTION .	1
BLACK	ADJ. INVOKING THE SUPERNATURAL AND ESP. THE DEVIL ; SPECIF MARKED BY THE OCCURRENCE OF DISASTER .	0
BLOND	ADJ. OF HUMAN HAIR OF A FLAXEN , GOLDEN , LIGHT AUBURN , OR PALE YELLOWISH BROWN COLOR .	0
BRIEF	ADJ. SHORT IN DURATION OR EXTENT .	2
BULL	ADJ. LARGE OF ITS KIND .	2
CASUAL	ADJ. EMPLOYED FOR IRREGULAR PERIODS .	2
CHEMICAL	ADJ. ACTING OR OPERATED OR PRODUCED BY CHEMICALS .	6
CLASSIC	ADJ. OF RECOGNIZED VALUE SERVING AS A STANDARD OF EXCELLENCE .	2
CLEAR	ADJ. UNHAMPERED BY RESTRICTION OR LIMITATION : AS UNENCUMBERED BY DEBTS OR CHARGES .	6
CLUB	ADJ. OF OR RELATING TO A CLUB .	2
COLORED	ADJ. OF MIXED RACE .	1
COMPARABLE	ADJ. CAPABLE OF OR SUITABLE FOR COMPARISON USU. USED WITH TO .	0
COMPOUND	ADJ. INVOLVING OR USED IN A COMBINATION .	2
CONSCIOUS	ADJ. PERCEIVING , APPREHENDING , OR NOTICING WITH A DEGREE OF CONTROLLED THOUGHT OR OBSERVATION .	6
CONTEMPORARY	ADJ. HAPPENING , EXISTING , LIVING , OR COMING INTO BEING DURING THE SAME PERIOD OF TIME .	0
COOL	ADJ. MODERATELY COLD LACKING IN WARMTH .	2
CREATIVE	ADJ. HAVING THE POWER OR QUALITY OF CREATING .	0
CRYSTAL	ADJ. RELATING TO OR USING A CRYSTAL A ' RADIO RECEIVER .	0
DAILY	ADJ. ISSUED EVERY DAY OR EVERY WEEKDAY .	0
DEAD	ADJ. LACKING ELASTICITY ' TENNIS BALL .	0
DEEP	ADJ. EXTENDING WELL BACK FROM THE FRONT SURFACE A ' CLOSET .	0

Table 3 (*Continued*)

Definition		Parses
DENTAL	ADJ. OF OR RELATING TO THE TEETH OR DENTISTRY .	2
DIFFICULT	ADJ. HARD TO DO , MAKE , OR CARRY OUT A ' CLIMB .	0
DIRTY	ADJ. HIGHLY REGRETTABLE ' SHAME .	1
DIVINE	ADJ. DIRECTED TO DEITY .	2

The LSP Restriction Language permits the writing of "transformation restrictions" which will allow us to expand conjunction strings. Transformation restrictions actually perform reverse transformations on the parsed sentence, creating a deep-structure parse tree (or whatever structure is desired) from the untransformed tree. Thus, a transformation restriction could be used to convert *not present or attending* into *not present and not attending* (see the section above on the semantics of logical operators in English).

Generation of Triples. Besides performing reverse grammatical transformations, transformation restrictions can be used to reduce a definition to a series of word-relation-word triples. Another useful tool in generating triples is the WRITE instruction of the Restricted Language, with which it is possible to output selected nodes of the parse tree to a file from which they can later be read.

Secondary Relations. The triples we have extracted so far generally have a "core" word as their third element. This makes very poor use of some definitions. For example:

abrupt **adj.** marked by sudden changes in subject matter

at present gives only one triple:

abrupt JCHAR changes

But this is not the only, or even the most informative, relation in the definition. We can see that *sudden* tells us most of what we need to know about the meaning of the word *abrupt*—in fact, if we could only get one triple out of this definition, we would probably rather have:

abrupt SYN sudden

Subject matter limits the domain of abrupt in this particular definition. A triple:

subject matter DOMAIN abrupt

might be desirable. (We are not considering the problem of somewhat idiomatic word combinations, like *subject matter*.)

Other Parts of Speech. Prepositions, conjunctions, and other small syntactic words are relatively few in number but also essential for the interpretation of other words. For the purpose of definition parsing, we can regard them as undefined primitives. Other parts of speech which may be parsed in more or less the same manner as adjectives are adverbs, nouns, and verbs.

Adverbs are not very numerous, but may be quite difficult. Verbs and nouns form the bulk of the dictionary, with adjectives a distant third in frequency.

Amsler's work so far (1980, Simmons and Amsler 1975) has concentrated on nouns and verbs; this was one of our reasons for choosing adjectives as a starting point. The most common relation involved in defining nouns and verbs is taxonomy, and much of the process of understanding nouns and verbs consists of fitting them into proper hierarchies. As we have seen, the problems with adjectives are quite different. We find a multiplicity of relations (Table 1) which look vaguely familiar but are subtly different from the corresponding relations between nouns and nouns, or between verbs and verbs. Adjectives are usually defined with reference to nouns, less often with reference to verbs, and rather seldom with reference to other adjectives.

However, I believe the techniques we have developed for processing adjective definitions will serve us well when we attempt to deal with other kinds of definitions. The strategy will be the same: identify formulae and their associated relations; then write a grammar which will recognize the formulae as literal strings and identify the core words pointed to by the relations. The details of the process will be complex, probably at least as much so as in the case of adjectives. It is here that there will be the greatest need to combine our techniques and theory with those of others who have worked on the problem of computer understanding of dictionary data.

REFERENCES

AMSLER, R. A. 1980. The structure of The Merriam-Webster pocket dictionary. Ph.D. Thesis, The University of Texas at Austin, December 1980. Also appeared as CS Technical Report TR-164.

APRESYAN, YU. D., I. A. MEL'CHUK, and A. K. ZHOLKOVSKY. 1970. Semantics and lexicography: Towards a new type of unilingual dictionary. Studies in syntax, ed. by F. Kiefer, 1–33. Dordrecht, Holland: Reidel.

EVENS, M. W. 1975. Semantic representations for question-answering systems, Evanston, IL: Northwestern University. Unpublished Ph.D. Dissertation).

———, B. C. LITOWITZ, J. A. MARKOWITZ, R. N. SMITH, and O. WERNER. 1980. Lexical-semantic relations: A comparative survey. Edmonton, Alberta: Linguistic Research, Inc.

———, and R. N. SMITH. 1978. A lexicon for a computer question-answering system. American Journal of Computational Linguistics 4.1–96.

GOVE, P. B. 1968. On defining adjectives: Part I. American Speech 45.5–32.

GRISHMAN, R. Undated. Linguistic string parser user's guide. New York: New York University, Linguistic String Project.

———. Undated. Restriction language manual. New York: New York University, Linguistic String Project.

HARRIS, Z. S. 1962. String analysis of sentence structure. The Hague: Mouton.

KUCERA, H., and N. FRANCIS. 1967. Computational analysis of present-day American English. Providence, RI: Brown University Press.

RAZE, C. 1976. A computational treatment of coordinate conjunctions. American Journal of Computational Linguistics, Microfiche 52.

SAGER, N. 1981. Natural language information processing. New York: Addison-Wesley.

SIMMONS, R. F., and R. A. AMSLER. 1975. Modeling dictionary data. Directions in artificial intelligence: Natural language processing, ed. by R. Grishman. Courant Computer Science Report #7, New York.

SMITH, R. N. 1981. On defining adjectives, Part III. In *Dictionaries,* the Journal of the Dictionary Society of North America, Winter, 1981.

SMITH, R. N. Conceptual primitives in the English lexicon. In W. Frawley, ed., *Lexicography Today,* Edmonton, Alta: Linguistic Research Inc. In press.

Appendix A. The adjective definition grammar.

```
*OBJSW=T
*BNF
* FORMULA-ORIENTED ADJDEF GRAMMAR
*
<SENTENCE>  ::= <CENTER> .
<CENTER>    ::= <*ADJ> 'ADJ.' <ADJDEF> <ADJTAIL> .
<SA>        ::= <*D> / <*INT> / <PN> / <*NULL> .
<PN>        ::= <*P> <NSTG> .
<NSTG>      ::= <LNR> .
<LNR>       ::= <LN> <*N> <RN> .
<LN>        ::= <TPOS> <QPOS> <APOS> .
<TPOS>      ::= <*T> / <*NULL> .
<QPOS>      ::= <LQ> <*Q> <RQ> / <*NULL> .
<LQ>        ::= <*NULL> .
<RQ>        ::= <*NULL> .
<APOS>      ::= <LAR> <APOS> / <*NULL> .
<LAR>       ::= <LA> <AVAR> <RA> .
<LA>        ::= <*D> / <*NULL> .
<DSTG>      ::= <*D> / <*NULL> .
<AVAR>      ::= <*ADJ> / <*VING> / <*VEN> .
<RA>        ::= <DSTG> / <PN> / <TOVO> .
<RN>        ::= <PN> / <*NULL> .
<TOVO>      ::= TO <LVR> <SA> <OBJECT> <SA> .
<LVR>       ::= <LV> <*V> <RV> .
<LV>        ::= <*D> / <*NULL> .
<RV>        ::= <*D> / <PN> / <*NULL> .
<VINGO>     ::= <*VING> <OBJECT> .
<OBJECT>    ::= <NSTG> / <THATS> / <*NULLOBJ> / <TOVO> / <PN> .
<THATS>     ::= THAT <ASSERTION> .
<ASSERTION> ::= <SA> <SUBJECT> <SA> <VERB> <SA> <OBJECT> <SA> .
<SUBJECT>   ::= <NSTG> .
<VERB>      ::= <LTVR> .
<LTVR>      ::= <LV> <*TV> <RV> .
<VENPASS>   ::= <LV> <*VEN> <RV> .
<CONJSTG>   ::= <OR/AND/RATHER THAN/BUT> <Q-CONJ> /
            ',' <Q-CONJ> ',' (OR/AND) <Q-CONJ> /
            ',' <Q-CONJ> ',' <Q-CONJ> ',' (OR/AND) <Q-CONJ> .
<Q-CONJ>    ::= <NULL> .
<SPCLASS    ::= <*SPWORD> .
* SPECIAL SYMBOLS FOR ADJECTIVE DEFINITIONS
<ADJDEF>    ::= (<JANTI> / <*NULL>) (<CONVTYP> / <ADJTYP>) .
  <JANTI>     ::= NOT .
<CONVTYP>   ::= <DSTG> <CONVTR> <REMDR> .
<CONVTR>    ::= <FMLA> / <NFMLA> .
* RULES DIRECTLY IDENTIFYING RELATIONS THROUGH FORMULAE
<FMLA>      ::= <SIMPL>/<CHAR>/<CONTN>/<MANIF>/<TEND>/<NHAVE>/
                <ABLE1>/<ABLE2>/<CAUSE1>/<ORIGIN>/<COMP>/<NSIMPL>/
              <BEING>-/<PART>/<NECES>/<LIKE>/<ACTIV>/<AFFIN>/
              <INFLU> .
<JSIMPL>    ::= ( OF / RELATING TO / BASED ON / CHARACTERISTIC OF /
                  CONCERNED WITH / DEALING WITH ) .
 <JCHAR>     ::= ( HAVING / MARKED BY / CHARACTERIZED BY / INVOLVING /
                  POSSESSING ) .
 <JCONTN>    ::= CONTAINING / FULL OF .
 <JMANIF>    ::= SHOWING / EXPRESSING .
 <JTEND>     ::= TENDING / GIVEN TO .
 <JNHAVE>    ::= (LACKING / WITHOUT / FREE FROM / BEING WITHOUT) /
                 (<JCHAR> / <JCONTN> / <JMANIF> ) <JNH2> .
   <JNH2>      ::= 'NO' <TPOS> (LACK OF / ABSENCE OF) .
 <JABLE1>    ::= CAPABLE OF / ABLE .
 <JABLE2>    ::= CAPABLE OF BEING / EASILY .
 <JCAUSE1>   ::= CAUSING / PRODUCING / GIVING / PROVIDING .
 <JORIGIN>   ::= DERIVED <RA> FROM / RESULTING <RA> FROM .
 <JCOMPO>    ::= CONSISTING OF / COMPOSED OF .
```

Appendix A (*Continued*)

```
  <JNSIMPL>  ::= AS DISTINGUISHED FROM .
  <JBEING>   ::= BEING / CONSTITUTING .
  <JPART>    ::= BELONGING TO .
  <JNECES>   ::= REQUIRING .
  <JLIKE>    ::= RESEMBLING .
  <JACTIV>   ::= ENGAGED IN .
  <JAFFIN>   ::= CONFORMING WITH / CONFORMING TO .
  <JINFLU>   ::= AFFECTING .
  <JCONTN>   ::= CONTAINING / FULL OF .
* RULES BASED ON IDENTIFICATION AF ADJECTIVE-NOUN CONVERTERS
<NFMLA>     ::= <RN> <*P> / <*VING> .
<REMDR>     ::= <LNR> / <TOVO> / <VINGO> / <VENPASS> .
<ADJTYP>    ::= <JTAXSYN> <LAR> .
<JTAXSYN>   ::= <*NULL> .
* "ADJTAIL" COMPONENTS
<ADJTAIL>   ::= <ADJA> <NEXTDF> <XAMPLE> .
<ADJA>      ::= <*NULL> / 'ESP.' (<DSTG> / <PN>) .
<NEXTDF>    ::= <*NULL> / <INTRO> <ADJDEF> / <JNSIMPL> <REMDR> .
<INTRO>     ::= ';' (ESP / SPECIF / ALSO) .
<XAMPLE>    ::= <*NULL> / <TPOS> '''' <*N> <RN> .
*LISTS
ATTRIBUTE = SINGULAR, PLURAL, NCOUNT, NHUMAN, OBJLIST, NOMINATIVE,
            ACCUSATIVE, NCOUNT2, PVAL.
TYPE STRING = ADJDEF, ADJTAIL, CONVTYP, ADJTYP, ASSERTION, PN, THATS,
              TOVO, VINGO, FMLA, RA, Q-CONJ.
TYPE STGSEG = ASSERTION, VINGO.
TYPE ADJSET = SA, LN, LV, RN, RV, LA, RA, LQ, RQ.
TYPE ADJSET1 = SA, LN, LV, LA, LQ, RN, RV, RA, RQ, CONJSTG.
TYPE LADJSET = LN, LQ, LA, LV.
TYPE RADJSET = RN, RQ, RA, RV.
TYPE LXR = LNR, LTVR, LVR, LAR, QPOS, VENPASS.
TYPE VERBAL = VERB, LVR, VING.
TYPE ATOM = ADJ, D, P, N, Q, VING, SPWORD, TV, VEN, V.
*RESTR
ROUTINE STARTAT (X) = EITHER TEST FOR X OR $DOWN1.
 $DOWN1 = GO DOWN; ITERATET GO RIGHT UNTIL TEST FOR X SUCCEEDS.
ROUTINE ISIT (X) = TEST FOR X.
ROUTINE CORE- = ONE OF $1, $D, $S IS TRUE .
 $1 = TEST FOR ATOM.
 $D = DESCEND TO ATOM NOT PASSING THROUGH ADJSET1.
 $S = DESCEND TO STRING NOT PASSING THROUGH ADJSET1.
ROUTINE CORE = DO CORE-; VERIFY $STACK-TEST.
 $STACK-TEST = ITERATET $STACK-X UNTIL $AND-TO-RIGHT FAILS.
 $AND-TO-RIGHT = GO RIGHT; TEST FOR ANDSTG; STORE IN X100.
 $STACK-X = GO TO X100; DESCEND TO Q-CONJ; GO DOWN; STACK.
ROUTINE L(X) = ITERATE GO LEFT UNTIL TEST FOR X SUCCEEDS.
ROUTINE R(X) = ITERATE GO RIGHT UNTIL TEST FOR X SUCCEEDS.
ROUTINE COEL1(X) = EITHER DO L(X) OR DO R(X).
ROUTINE COELEMENT(X) = EITHER DO COEL1(X) OR $STGSEG.
 $STGSEG = DO COEL1(STGSEG); DO DOWN1(X).
ROUTINE DOWN1(X) = GO DOWN; ITERATET GO RIGHT UNTIL TEST FOR X SUCCEEDS.
ROUTINE ELEMENT(X) = EITHER DO DOWN1(X) OR $STGSEG.
 $STGSEG = DO DOWN1(STGSEG); DO DOWN1(X).
ROUTINE LEFT-ADJUNCT = EITHER $LEFT-TO-LADJ OR $UP-AND-LEFT.
 $LEFT-TO-LADJ = DO L(LADJSET); EITHER TEST FOR LN OR DO CORE.
 $UP-AND-LEFT = GO UP; TEST FOR Q-CONJ; GO UP; DO $LEFT-TO-LADJ.
ROUTINE RIGHT-ADJUNCT = EITHER $RIGHT-TO-RADJ OR $UP-AND-RIGHT.
 $RIGHT-TO-RADJ = DO R(RADJSET); DO CORE.
 $UP-AND-RIGHT = GO UP; TEST FOR Q-CONJ; GO UP; DO $RIGHT-TO-RADJ.
ROUTINE HOST = =EITHER $1 OR $2; DO CORE.
 $1 = EITHER TEST FOR LADJSET OR ASCEND TO LADJSET;
      ITERATE GO RIGHT UNTIL TEST FOR CONJSTG FAILS.
 $2 = EITHER TEST FOR RADJSET OR ASCEND TO RADJSET;
      ITERATE GO LEFT UNTIL TEST FOR CONJSTG FAILS.
```

Appendix A (*Continued*)

```
ROUTINE IMMEDIATE(X) = ASCEND TO X.
ROUTINE PRESENT-ELEMENT = TRUE.
*
WAGREE = IN ASSERTION: BOTH $SINGAGREE AND $PLURAGREE ARE TRUE.
 $SINGAGREE = IF THE CORE X1 OF THE VERB IS SINGULAR THEN $SUBJNOTPLUR.
  $SUBJNOTPLUR = BOTH THE CORE X2 OF THE SUBJECT IS NOT PLURAL
                AND NOT $CONJOINED.
   $CONJOINED = GO TO X2; GO RIGHT; TEST FOR CONJSTG.
 $PLURAGREE = IF X1 IS PLURAL THEN $SUBJNOTSING.
  $SUBJNOTSING = BOTH $CORENOTSING AND X2 IS NOT OF TYPE STRING.
   $CORENOTSING = EITHER CORE X2 OF THE SUBJECT IS NOT SINGULAR
                 OR $CONJOINED.
WCOUNT = IN LNR: IF THE CORE IS N:NCOUNT THAN IN LEFT-ADJUNCT OF
                 CORE TPOS IS NOT EMPTY.
WVERBOBJ = IN OBJECT: IF THE VALUE X1 OF OBJECT EXISTS,
                      THEN CORE OF COELEMENT VERBAL HAS ATTRIBUTE
                      OBJLIST:X1.
DCONJ1 = IN CONJSTG: GO UP; PRESENT-ELEMENT IS NOT EMPTY.
DCONJ4 = IN Q-CONJ: GO UP; GO LEFT; STORE IN X1; STORE IN X2;
                    GENERATE OPTION SPANNING X1 TO X2.
DCONJ5 = IN CONJSTG: BOTH $INXORSTG AND $AFTERX.
 $INXORSTG = GO UP; IF NOT TEST FOR LXR THEN TEST FOR STRING.
 $AFTERX = GO LEFT; NEITHER TEST FOR LADJSET NOR TEST FOR RADJSET.
WCONJ1 = IN Q-CONJ: PRESENT-ELEMENT IS NOT EMPTY.
*
* WCONJ2 -- WHERE BOTH 'LXR' AND 'STRING' PARSES OF A CONJUNCTION
* STRING ARE POSSIBLE, THE LXR IS IN MY OPINION GENERALLY PREFERABLE.
* THIS RESTRICTION ELIMINATES MANY REDUNDANT 'STRING' PARSES.
* (FOR A FULL GRAMMAR IT WOULD BE EXCESSIVELY STRICT.)
*
WCONJ2 = IN CONJSTG: IF $STRING THEN $LADJ.
 $STRING = GO UP; TEST FOR STRING.
 $LADJ = IF BOTH $LXR1 AND $LXR2 THEN
         LEFT-ADJUNCT OF CORE OF X1 IS NOT EMPTY.
  $LXR1 = GO LEFT; DESCEND TO LXR.
  $LXR2 = DO DOWN1 (Q-CONJ); DESCEND TO LXR; STORE IN X1.
WCOUNT2 = IN LNR AFTER N: IF CORE X1 IS N:NCOUNT2 X2
          THEN EITHER IN LEFT-ADJUNCT OF X1 TPOS IS NOT EMPTY
          OR AT IMMEDIATE PN LISTS P AND X2 HAVE A COMMON ATTRIBUTE.
WPNOBJ = IN OBJECT: IF VALUE IS PN X1 THEN BOTH $1 AND $2.
 $1 = CORE OF COELEMENT VERB HAS ATTRIBUTE OBJLIST: PN: EVAL X2.
 $2 = AT X1 LISTS P AND X2 HAVE A COMMON ATTRIBUTE.
*
* ADJECTIVE DEFINITION RESTRICTIONS
*
* WAD1: MOST FORMULAE TAKE REMDR ::= LNR.  THE FOLLOWING DO NOT:
*
WAD1 = IN CONVTYP: ALL OF $TOVO, $VINGO, $VENPASS.
 $TOVO = IF REMDR IS TOVO THEN EITHER CORE X1 OF CONVTR IS 'TENDING'
                               OR X1 IS 'ABLE'.
 $VINGO = IF REMDR IS VINGO THEN X1 IS 'CAPABLE OF'.
 $VENPASS = IF REMDR IS VENPASS THEN EITHER X1 IS 'EASILY'
                                     OR X1 IS 'CAPABLE OF BEING'.
*
* WAD2 EXCLUDES FROM THE 'NFMLA' CATEGORY, CONVERTERS WHICH CONTAIN
* FORMULA WORDS -- WITH A FEW EXCEPTIONS.
*
WAD2 = IN NFMLA: EITHER $NOFM OR $EXCEPTION.
 $NOFM = ONE OF $RN, $P, $VING.
  $RN = EITHER $APOS OR $OTHER.
   $APOS = DESCEND TO LAR; BOTH CORE X1 OF PRESENT-ELEMENT IS NOT FM
                           AND IF LEFT-ADJUNCT X2 OF X1 IS NOT EMPTY
                               THEN X2 IS NOT FM.
   $OTHER = BOTH VALUE X1 OF ELEMENT RN IS NOT APOS
```

Appendix A (*Continued*)

```
          AND CORE OF X1 IS NOT FM.
  $P = ELEMENT P IS NOT FM.
  $VING = ELEMENT VING IS NOT FM.
 $EXCEPTION = ONE OF $PLAINPREP, $CONJSTG, $SUBREMDR.
  $PLAINPREP = BOTH ELEMENT RN IS EMPTY AND ELEMENT P IS NOT 'OF'.
  $CONJSTG = EITHER $STRING OR $LXR.
   $STRING = DESCEND TO STRING; PRESENT ELEMENT HAS ELEMENT CONJSTG.
   $LXR = DESCEND TO LXR; PRESENT-ELEMENT HAS ELEMENT CONJSTG.
  $SUBREMDR = BOTH VALUE X1 OF RN IS VINGO
            AND ELEMENT OBJECT OF X1 IS NOT EMPTY.
*WAD3 ELIMINATES REDUNDANT ADJTYP PARSES.
WAD3 = IN ADJTYP: BOTH CORE X1 OF LAR DOES NOT HAVE ATTRIBUTE FM
                  AND IF LEFT-ADJUNCT X2 OF X1 IS NOT EMPTY
                      THEN CORE OF X2 DOES NOT HAVE ATTRIBUTE FM.
WAD4 = IN CONVTYP: IF ELEMENT DSTG EXISTS THEN
                   VALUE OF DSTG DOES NOT HAVE ATTRIBUTE FM.
WAD5 = IN REMDR: IF ELEMENT LNR EXISTS THEN CORE OF LNR IS NOT FM.
* ELIMINATE REDUNDANT PARSES OF <VING> <P> WITH EMPTY OBJECT
WAD6 = IN NFMLA: IF ELEMENT P EXISTS THEN BOTH $VINGO AND $VENPASS.
 $VINGO = IF VALUE X1 OF RN IS VINGO
         THEN ELEMENT OBJECT OF X1 IS NOT EMPTY.
 $VENPASS = IF VALUE X1 OF RN IS VENPASS
           THEN ELEMENT RV OF X1 IS NOT EMPTY.
*WD
```

(Base sample and control sample each had a lexicon similar to that of the little grammar but consisting of about 200 words. These have been left out for brevity.)

Appendix B. The little grammar.

```
*OBJSW=T
*BNF
* THIS GRAMMAR ALLOWS CONJOINING OF X AND X IN LXR ONLY.
* IF X IS CONJOINED THE CORE ROUTINE WILL STACK THE CONJUNCT OF X .
* IF THE RESTRICTION WHICH CALLED CORE IS SUCCESSFUL, IT WILL BE
* RE-EXECUTED BY THE RESTRICTION INTERPRETER SUBSTITUTING THE VALUE
* STACKED BY CORE IN PLACE OF THE CORE ROUTINE.
*
<SENTENCE>  ::= <CENTER> .
<CENTER>    ::= <ASSERTION> .
<ASSERTION> ::= <SA> <SUBJECT> <SA> <VERB> <SA> <OBJECT> <SA> .
<SA>        ::= <*D> / <*INT> / <PN> / <*NULL> .
<PN>        ::= <*P> <NSTG> .
<SUBJECT>   ::= <NSTG> .
<NSTG>      ::= <LNR> / <LPROR> / <NREP> .
<LNR>       ::= <LN> <*N> <RN> .
<LN>        ::= <TPOS> <QPOS> <APOS> .
<TPOS>      ::= <*T> / <*NULL> .
<QPOS>      ::= <*NULL> .
<APOS>      ::= <*ADJ> / <*NULL> .
<RN>        ::= <PN> / <*NULL> .
<LPROR>     ::= <LPRO> <*PRO> <RN> .
<LPRO>      ::= ONLY / EVEN / <*NULL> .
<NREP>      ::= WHAT <SUBJECT> <SA> <VERB> <SA> .
<VERB>      ::= <LTVR> .
<LTVR>      ::= <LV> <*TV> <RV> .
<LV>        ::= <*D> / <*NULL> .
<RV>        ::= <*D> / <PN> / <*NULL> .
<OBJECT>    ::= <NSTG> / <THATS> / <*NULLOBJ> / <TOVO> / <PN> .
<LVR>       ::= <LV> <*V> <RV> .
<THATS>     ::= THAT <ASSERTION> .
<TOVO>      ::= TO <LVR> <SA> <OBJECT> <SA> .
```

Appendix B (*Continued*)

```
<ANDSTG>    ::= <AND> <Q-CONJ> .
<Q-CONJ>    ::= <NULL> .
<SPCLASS    ::= <*SPWORD> .
*LISTS
ATTRIBUTE = SINGULAR, PLURAL, NCOUNT, NHUMAN, OBJLIST, NOMINATIVE,
            ACCUSATIVE, NCOUNT2, PVAL.
TYPE STRING = ASSERTION, PN, NREP, THATS, TOVO, Q-CONJ.
TYPE STGSEG = ASSERTION.
TYPE ADJSET = SA, LN, LPRO, LV, RN, RV.
TYPE ADJSET1 = SA, LN, LPRO, LV, RN, RV, ANDSTG.
TYPE LADJSET = LN, LPRO, LV.
TYPE RADJSET = RN, RV.
TYPE LXR = LNR, LPROR, LTVR, LVR.
*RESTR
ROUTINE STARTAT (X) = EITHER TEST FOR X OR $DOWN1.
 $DOWN1 = GO DOWN
 ITERATET GO RIGHT UNTIL TEST FOR X SUCCEEDS.
ROUTINE ISIT (X) = TEST FOR X.
ROUTINE CORE- = ONE OF $1, $D, $S IS TRUE .
 $1 = TEST FOR ATOM.
 $D = DESCEND TO ATOM NOT PASSING THROUGH ADJSET1.
 $S = DESCEND TO STRING NOT PASSING THROUGH ADJSET1.
ROUTINE CORE = DO CORE-; VERIFY $STACK-TEST.
 $STACK-TEST = ITERATET $STACK-X UNTIL $AND-TO-RIGHT FAILS.
 $AND-TO-RIGHT = GO RIGHT; TEST FOR ANDSTG; STORE IN X100.
 $STACK-X = GO TO X100; DESCEND TO Q-CONJ; GO DOWN; STACK.
ROUTINE L(X) = ITERATE GO LEFT UNTIL TEST FOR X SUCCEEDS.
ROUTINE R(X) = ITERATE GO RIGHT UNTIL TEST FOR X SUCCEEDS.
ROUTINE COEL1(X) = EITHER DO L(X) OR DO R(X).
ROUTINE COELEMENT(X) = EITHER DO COEL1(X) OR $STGSEG.
 $STGSEG = DO COEL1(STGSEG); DO DOWN1(X).
ROUTINE DOWN1(X) = GO DOWN; ITERATET GO RIGHT UNTIL TEST FOR X SUCCEEDS.
ROUTINE ELEMENT(X) = EITHER DO DOWN1(X) OR $STGSEG.
 $STGSEG = DO DOWN1(STGSEG); DO DOWN1(X).
ROUTINE LEFT-ADJUNCT = EITHER $LEFT-TO-LADJ OR $UP-AND-LEFT.
 $LEFT-TO-LADJ = DO L(LADJSET); EITHER TEST FOR LN OR DO CORE.
 $UP-AND-LEFT = GO UP; TEST FOR Q-CONJ; GO UP; DO $LEFT-TO-LADJ.
ROUTINE RIGHT-ADJUNCT = EITHER $RIGHT-TO-RADJ OR $UP-AND-RIGHT.
 $RIGHT-TO-RADJ = DO R(RADJSET); DO CORE.
 $UP-AND-RIGHT = GO UP; TEST FOR Q-CONJ; GO UP; DO $RIGHT-TO-RADJ.
ROUTINE HOST = =EITHER $1 OR $2; DO CORE.
 $1 = EITHER TEST FOR LADJSET OR ASCEND TO LADJSET;
      ITERATE GO RIGHT UNTIL TEST FOR ANDSTG FAILS.
 $2 = EITHER TEST FOR RADJSET OR ASCEND TO RADJSET;
      ITERATE GO LEFT UNTIL TEST FOR ANDSTG FAILS.
ROUTINE IMMEDIATE(X) = ASCEND TO X.
ROUTINE PRESENT-ELEMENT = TRUE.
*
WAGREE = IN ASSERTION: BOTH $SINGAGREE AND $PLURAGREE ARE TRUE.
 $SINGAGREE = IF THE CORE X1 OF THE VERB IS SINGULAR THEN $SUBJNOTPLUR.
  $SUBJNOTPLUR = BOTH THE CORE X2 OF THE SUBJECT IS NOT PLURAL
                 AND NOT $CONJOINED.
   $CONJOINED = GO TO X2; GO RIGHT; TEST FOR ANDSTG.
 $PLURAGREE = IF X1 IS PLURAL THEN $SUBJNOTSING.
  $SUBJNOTSING = EITHER CORE X2 OF THE SUBJECT IS NOT SINGULAR
                 OR $CONJOINED.
WWH = IN NREP: CORE OF VERB HAS ATTRIBUTE OBJLIST:NSTG.
WCOUNT = IN LNR: IF THE CORE IS N:NCOUNT THAN IN LEFT-ADJUNCT OF
                 CORE TPOS IS NOT EMPTY.
WVERBOBJ = IN OBJECT: IF THE VALUE X1 OF OBJECT EXISTS,
                      THEN EITHER CORE OF COELEMENT VERB HAS ATTRIBUTE
                              OBJLIST:X1,
                      OR CORE OF COELEMENT LVR HAS ATTRIBUTE
                              OBJLIST:X1.
```

Appendix B (*Continued*)

```
DCONJ1 = IN ANDSTG: GO UP; PRESENT-ELEMENT IS NOT EMPTY.
DCONJ4 = IN Q-CONJ: GO UP; GO LEFT; STORE IN X1; STORE IN X2;
                    GENERATE OPTION SPANNING X1 TO X2.
DCONJ5 = IN ANDSTG: BOTH $INLXR AND $AFTERX.
 $INLXR = GO UP; TEST FOR LXR.
 $AFTERX = GO LEFT; NEITHER TEST FOR LADJSET NOR TEST FOR RADJSET.
WCONJ1 = IN Q-CONJ: PRESENT-ELEMENT IS NOT EMPTY.
WCOUNT2 = IN LNR AFTER N: IF CORE X1 IS N:NCOUNT2 X2
          THEN EITHER IN LEFT-ADJUNCT OF X1 TPOS IS NOT EMPTY
          OR AT IMMEDIATE PN LISTS P AND X2 HAVE A COMMON ATTRIBUTE.
WPNOBJ = IN OBJECT: IF VALUE IS PN X1 THEN BOTH $1 AND $2.
 $1 = CORE OF COELEMENT VERB HAS ATTRIBUTE OBJLIST: PN: EVAL X2.
 $2 = AT X1 LISTS P AND X2 HAVE A COMMON ATTRIBUTE.
*WD
 'A'              T.
 '.'              .
 MY               T.
 WHAT.
 AND  SPWORD:(ANDSTG).
 CAT   N:(SINGULAR,NCOUNT).
 CATS   N:(PLURAL).
EGG  N:(SINGULAR,NCOUNT).
EGGS  N:(PLURAL).
MEANS  N:(PLURAL), TV:(SINGULAR, OBJLIST:(THATS, NSTG, TOVO)),
     V:(OBJLIST:(THATS, NSTG, TOVO)).
MEAN  N:(SINGULAR, NCOUNT), TV:(PLURAL, OBJLIST:(THATS, NSTG, TOVO)),
     V:(OBJLIST:(THATS, NSTG, TOVO)), ADJ.
EATS  TV:(SINGULAR, OBJLIST:(NSTG, NULLOBJ)).
EAT  TV:(PLURAL, OBJLIST:(NSTG, NULLOBJ)), V:(OBJLIST:(NSTG, NULLOBJ)).
FISH  N, TV:(PLURAL, OBJLIST:(NSTG,NULLOBJ)),V:(OBJLIST:(NULLOBJ)).
SLEEPS  TV:(SINGULAR,OBJLIST:(NULLOBJ)), N:(SINGULAR), V:(OBJLIST:
       (NULLOBJ)).
HAPPY  ADJ.
GENERALLY  D.
WITH  P.
HE  PRO:(SINGULAR,NOMINATIVE,NHUMAN).
HIM  PRO:(SINGULAR,NOMINATIVE,NHUMAN).
SHE  PRO:(SINGULAR,NOMINATIVE,NHUMAN).
HER  PRO:(SINGULAR,NOMINATIVE,NHUMAN).
THEY  PRO:(PLURAL, NOMINATIVE).
THEM  PRO:(PLURAL, ACCUSATIVE).
THAT .
EVEN .
         TO  P: ('TO').
         GIVE  TV: .12,PLURAL.
         GAVE  TV: .12
         BED  N: (NCOUNT2: ('IN'), SINGULAR).
         IN  P: ('IN').
        'AND/OR'/
ONLY .
*CLOSE()
```

EIGHT

Episodic Organization and Language Acquisition

John W. Oller, Jr.
University of New Mexico

The purpose of this chapter is to offer some reflections on the nature of episodic organization from the vantage point of applied linguistics, especially the study of second language acquisition. In the course of the discussion, some of the recent work in artificial intelligence will be drawn upon, but the focus will be on episodic organization as it relates to second language instruction.

Before launching into the topic, it may be useful to anticipate three objections to the investigation of episodic organization. Some will claim that any such investigation is doomed to fail because of the sheer complexity of the subject matter. This first objection may be due in part to an appreciation of the difficulty of the undertaking, but its force may be reduced somewhat by approaching the problem programmatically, as has been done in the whole field of artificial intelligence. I have in mind, for instance, such efforts as Rumelhart's well-known attempt to formulate a story grammar (1975), or the burgeoning theory of episodic memory by Schank (1975, 1980), or of text processes by de Beaugrande (1980).

A second objection that will be raised concerns whether or not episodic organization has any universality. Some are inclined to argue that, in fact, what has frequently been termed 'episodic structure' would be better labeled 'Western thought' or something of the sort. This objection, I think, misconstrues the nature of episodic organization. Although the organization of episodes of experience may be influenced by culture, it may be argued that there is nonetheless a universal physiological basis for it and that the principal constraints upon it are as much a matter of physical event structures as of psychological tendencies.

A third objection is that the current interest in episodic organization is merely a passing fad, that we must eventually return to "sentence" linguistics. While it seems to me that the present interest in episodic organization may indeed be trendy, and though trends come and go like the tides, I believe that the need to understand and characterize episodic organization is going to be with us into the foreseeable future.

Of course, it would also be wrong to infer that, because the interest in episodic organization is currently faddish, it is therefore new. Actually, concern for the temporal organization of experience has been with us for a long time, and even the more intriguing question of how sequences of events are linked to structures in discourse is not a new concern. For instance, John Dewey stressed in the preface to his *Essays on Experimental Logic* that it was the *temporal development* of experience which he sought to characterize and to explain. He often referred to this temporal aspect as having a 'genetic' character. In fact, he used the term 'genetic' with reference to *particular* episodes of experience much the way that Jean Piaget (1947, 1980, 1981) used it when speaking of the whole scope of child development and learning.

Although Dewey's *Essays* were not assembled into book form until about 1916, he was very much a contemporary of Otto Jespersen, who may be noted as among the first linguists to express serious concern for the importance of episodic organization in language teaching materials. In fact, it was the conspicuous *absence* of such structure in the French textbooks of his day that Jespersen commented on clear back in 1904. Not without humor, he observed:

> The reader often gets the impression that Frenchmen must be strictly systematical beings who one day speak merely in futures, another day in *passé définis* and who say the most disconnected things only for the sake of being able to use all the persons in the tense which for the time being happens to be the subject for conversation while they carefully postpone the use of the subjunctive until next year (1904:17).

Jesperson insisted that:

> we ought to learn a language through sensible communications; there must be (and this as far as possible from the very first day) a certain connection in the thoughts communicated in the new language . . . One cannot say anything sensible with mere lists of words. Indeed not even disconnected sentences ought to be used. . . (1904:11).

More recently, this theme was carried into practice in a Spanish program published by Encyclopaedia Britannica Films. The author's preface states:

> We believe that language on the useful, everyday level is situational and sequential and that the moment a student can react automatically . . . to a given situation identified with his own experience, he 'knows' the foreign language used in *that* situation. The proper procedure then is to immerse the student in the world in which this language is used, a world inhabited by people about whom he knows and cares. This sharing of everyday experiences with people of a foreign tongue creates the climate of sympathy necessary and establishes the *sine qua non* for the teaching of the language, the desire of the students to learn to communicate with the people of that language . . . (Oller 1963:ix).

Presently, the interest in episodic organization continues to be pursued on several fronts. Among them is the very interesting work in artificial intelligence already alluded to, as well as research in applied linguistics. For instance, there is the intriguing work of Di Pietro and his collaborators on what he calls 'strategic interaction' (1981, 1982).

With the foregoing background in mind, we will now proceed to consider four working hypotheses about second language acquisition. These hypotheses will then provide the basis for the rest of our discursive investigation of episodic organization. Finally, I will conclude with some observations about texts to be used for language instruction.

THE INPUT HYPOTHESIS

In 1980, Steve Krashen stated explicitly an idea that many language teachers and even some theorists had been considering for a long time. He called it "the input hypothesis." Roughly put, this hypothesis says that THE ACQUISITION OF A SECOND LANGUAGE DEPENDS ON ACCESS TO AND UTILIZATION OF COMPREHENSIBLE INPUT. Krashen's hypothesis makes it clear that more than mere 'access' is required. Or, as the author of the above-cited Spanish program put it:

> All teachers of foreign language know that simple "exposure" is not enough . . . We all know that until a language becomes an integral part of the student's experience, until he can react to and activate automatically language which has been MADE A PART OF HIS EXPERIENCE, he cannot communicate effectively in the language (his emphasis; Oller 1963:ix).

Of course, this 'hypothesis' is not really testable in the traditional sense of experimental science. It is rather a working theory—a sensible basis for practice—and, no doubt, many would also agree that it has some theoretical value as well.

In an interesting way, the input hyopthesis helps us to formulate the theoretical problem of second language acquisition. By implication, the input hypothesis differentiates mere 'input' from 'intake', where the latter is taken to be input that gets comprehended. This helps us to formulate the following question: How does input become intake? The question can be represented diagrammatically, as shown in Figure 1. The problem is to explain how the leap is made from the manifest elements of the target language (INPUT) to comprehension (INTAKE).

This leads to the formulation of three other hypotheses which have roughly the

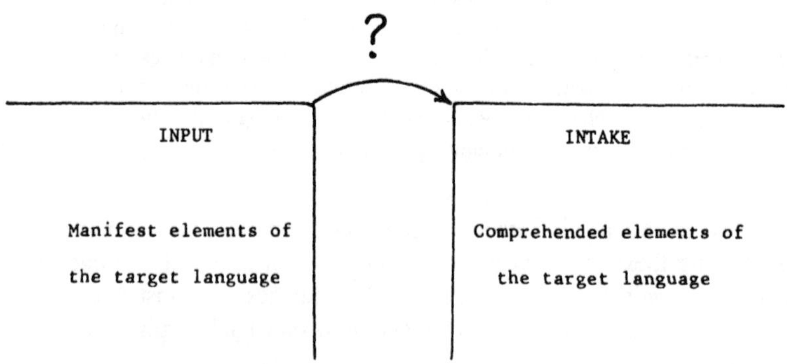

Figure 1. A schematic representation of the language acquisition process as expressed in the input hypothesis.

same character as the input hypothesis—i.e., they too are working hunches. Before going into any of them in detail, it may be useful here to preview all three.

The first of them, THE TEXTUALITY HYPOTHESIS, is the assertion that the events of experience have a textural character—that they are temporally organized and arranged in a sequence. The second, THE EXPECTANCY HYPOTHESIS, calls attention to the cognitive momentum that seems to attend the dynamic processes of producing or comprehending discourse; and, finally, THE EPISODE HYPOTHESIS suggests that text (in the sense of any stretch of discourse) will be easier to produce, to understand, to recall, and in general to profit from if it is episodically organized. (It will be possible to be more explicit about the nature of episodic organization as we discuss each of these hyoptheses in greater detail below.)

These three hypotheses, together with the input hypothesis, can be understood in relation to the process of pragmatic mapping—that is, the systematic linking up of discourse structures with the events of ordinary experience. If we expand Figure 1, as shown in Figure 2, the rough outlines of the process of pragmatic mapping emerge. Pragmatic mapping may be understood as the process by which the event sequences of experience are set in meaningful correspondence with discourse structures.

Input in a second language is merely one of the many manifest types of event structures which constitute ordinary experience. Therefore, the left side of Figure 1 is expanded upon in Figure 2 so as to encompass the broad range of 'facts of experience'—abbreviated with a lower case *e*. On the right side of Figure 2, are represented the utterances (or written forms) of discourse, or texts—abbreviated *u*. As with the input hypothesis, the problem is to determine how the inferential leap is made from the facts of experience to the comprehension of discourse. In order to call attention to the inferential, pragmatic linkage of the facts of experience with the strings of verbal elements in discourse, the bridge in Figure 2 is labeled with the Greek letter *pi* (this, it may be hoped, also adds a certain scientific flavor to the whole discussion).

At the miscocosmic level, the problem is to explain the comprehension of any

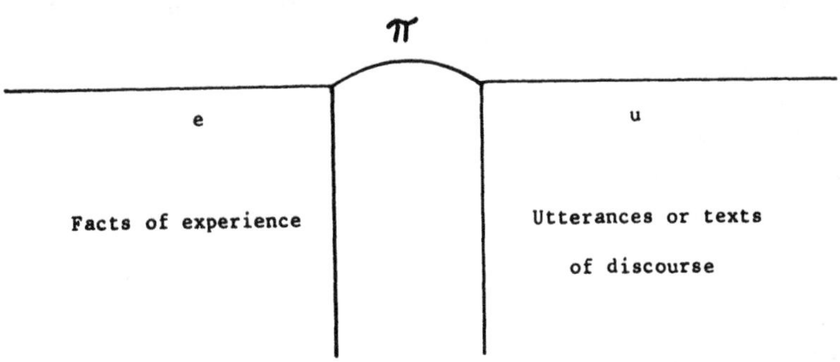

Figure 2. A schematic representation of the process of PRAGMATIC MAPPING—the linking of elements of experience with the texts of language.

text or portion thereof—to explain the conversion of input to intake, or of experience to text, and vice versa. At the macrocosmic level, the problem is to explain the acquisition of language and, still more generally, the advance of knowledge and the maturation of the ability to make sense of experience.

In a rough and ready manner, the whole formula for pragmatic mapping may be pictured somewhat allegorically as a journey taken by the proverbial homunculus, call him Pilgrim Elf, who presumably operates the controls of the great information processing center inside the head of the ideal-speaker hearer (reputed to reside in Cambridge, Massachusetts), or perhaps some less exalted brain of a plebian language acquirer (probably living somewhere west of the Mississippi).

Imagine that the intrepid Pilgrim begins his search for meaning with his feet planted firmly on the solid soil of experiential facts. However, as he plods along beyond where 'the roads run out and stop.' as Kipling might have said, Pilgrim comes to a vast chasm. There he reads various signs which have been left by previous explorers to help guide his across the uncharted frontiers of human discourse at the far side of the canyon. The signs warn of great peril. One of them, whose faint inscription seems to bear the signatures of Pierce, James, and Dewey, says that travelers who attempt to cross Intelligence Gap without using the Pragmatic Bridge must invariably come to harm. In fact, according to the sign weathered with age, some travelers have already crashed to their death on the rocks of experience, while others have been swept away by the River of Reason that flows deep (no one knows how deep) through Intelligence Canyon.

This same sign has an arrow carved in it which points Pilgrim in the direction of the Pragmatic Bridge. The latter is suspended above the river. Pilgrim notices that its wooden understructure, roughly in the shape of numerous branching trees, is anchored in solid concrete pilings that he supposes must reach to the very Bedrock of Innate Ideas which is believed, by many, to undergird the whole landscape. Venturing out onto Pragmatic Bridge, Pilgrim pauses momentarily to look down at the River of Reason which rages on its course far below. For a dizzy moment, he wonders if it might not have been at this very spot where a certain research team from MIT tried to float across the river on a raft of logs cut from syntactic trees. According to the newspapers, Pilgrim recalls, due to the manner in which the logs were cut they had petrified and, of course, the raft had sunk and the researchers were all drowned.

For a while, rapt in awe, Pilgrim just stands there, leaning against the rail, contemplating the fact that his right hemisphere is oriented analogically (as it were) toward the holistic facts of experience on the near side of the canyon, whereas his left is oriented (more or less digitally) toward the highly temporalized texts of discourse at the far side. It occurs to him that the bridge on which he stands is not unlike the corpus callosum of the human brain through which so much information is communicated between the two hemispheres.

But the analogy is an imperfect one, and he soon forgets it and crosses over to the discourse side of the canyon. Later, as we might have expected, he finds it necessary to make many trips back and forth across the bridge. Even later still, he applies for an MIT research grant in order to purchase a Helicopter of Abstraction, with the aid of which he eventually discovers that the Pragmatic Bridge only appeared to be stationary, that in fact it is dynamically interacting with the two sides of Intelligence Canyon. Further, he concludes that the River of Reason, to his amazement, was only apparently moving. Actually, he surmises, it was the entire landscape that was moving. He later comes to believe (whether rightly or wrongly who can say?) that it is the River of Reason which is actually secure and unmovable.

At this point, we leave Pilgrim as, in any case, he too begins to contemplate the quandaries of the several hypotheses which form the basis for the rest of this paper.

THE TEXTUALITY HYPOTHESIS

Whereas the diagram of Figure 2 might suggest that the facts of experience are static and solid, the textuality hypothesis suggests that the elements of experience themselves are dynamically interrelated and must of necessity be represented in a temporalized logic (sequentialized) in order for us to make sense of them. Further, this hypothesis claims that the highly temporalized event-structures of experience are propostionally complex. Simply put, the textuality hypothesis says that THE EVENT-STRUCTURES OF EXPERIENCE ARE TEXTUAL IN NATURE. This idea seems to underlie the following remarks by Karl Lashley, from his well-known paper on 'The Problem of Serial Order in Behavior':

> . . . the organization of language seems to me to be characteristic of almost all other cerebral activity. There is a series of hierarchies of organization; the order of vocal movements in pronouncing the word, the order of words in the sentence, the order of sentences in the paragraph, the rational order of paragraphs in a discourse. NOT ONLY SPEECH, BUT ALL SKILLED ACTS SEEM TO INVOLVE THE SAME PROBLEMS OF SERIAL ORDERING, EVEN DOWN TO THE TEMPORAL COORDINATIONS OF MUSCULAR CONTRACTIONS IN SUCH A MOVEMENT AS REACHING AND GRASPING (emphasis mine; 1951:187).

Of course, what Lashley is talking about has nothing to do with 'Western civilization'. He is talking about BRAIN FUNCTIONS—especially the analytic temporalizing functions that seem to be the specialty of the left hemisphere. These functions, probably, are relatively unaffected by differences in the details of culturally determined experience.[1] In other words, the textuality hypothesis argues that event-structures are propositional in nature quite independently of any cultural overlay that may, over the course of development, result in adjustments in their interpretation.

Lashley, however, was focusing his attention explicitly on motoric behavior. The textuality hypothesis is broader in scope. There is an important sense in which all event-structures are temporalized—even when viewed from the vantage point of an independent observer rather than a participant actor. For instance, consider the

[1] However, there is some evidence that the DISTRIBUTION of brain functions may be determined in part by certain cultural variables in experience (see Sibatani 1980).

following example, which was originally offered in a slightly different form by someone who was seeking to refute the textuality hypothesis. Suppose that we are observing a worker at an American Embassy somewhere in the Middle East. We note that the crowd outside the Embassy is growing increasingly unruly. Suddenly a brick comes crashing through a window above the worker. He sees it coming and ducks his head just in time. The brick crashes harmlessly to the floor near where he is sitting.

To illustrate the textuality hypothesis, it will help if we take a closer look at the event sequence. The important thing to see is that the event sequence itself has a kind of grammatical (propositional) as well as presuppositional and implicational structure.

Why did the brick come crashing through the window? For one thing, it had sufficient momentum to break the glass. But before that could happen, it had to acquire the momentum somehow. We infer that it was thrown by someone. Now, notice the sequence of events that is crucial to an appropriate interpretation of the episode. Some unknown person, an agent, throws the brick. That is, the agent acts upon an instrument (the brick), which results in a whole new state of affairs which can be characterized in a proposition or, indeed, in a whole series of them. The brick hurtles toward the window. After a brief lapse of time, the window becomes a direct object, whose structure is radically altered by the impact of the brick. The momentum of the brick can be construed as a predication associated with it by the act of the thrower. In order to understand and react to the situation appropriately, it is first necessary to appreciate the fact that the trajectory of the brick would pass through the space now occupied by the head of the worker, if said worker did not negate that propositional possibility by ducking his head. Otherwise, we infer correctly that undesirable consequences would result. To understand this is to take account of a good deal of knowledge about bricks and heads. Setting aside the motoric response of the person who ducks, even for an independent observer to understand this action requires an appropriate interpretation of the textual elements of the event sequence—all of which goes to confirm the textuality of ordinary experience.

THE EXPECTANCY HYPOTHESIS

Another hypothesis which relates in fact to both sides of the schematic given in Figure 2 is the expectancy hypothesis. It says that THE ACTIVATION OF CORRECT EXPECTANCIES WILL ENHANCE THE PROCESSING OF TEXTUAL STRUCTURES. This hypothesis logically applies both to event structures in experience and to the sequences of verbal elements that constitute discourse.

The importance of the effects of expectancies is perhaps best illustrated through errors, or through texts that deviate from the expected form and thus cause us to do a mental double-take at one or many points while processing them. For example, consider the sentence *The pen was lost by the pier*. The structure is such that we expect an agent (e.g., *by the newswoman*) instead of a location *by the pier*. What we seem to do, in such a case, is like putting on our mental brakes, cramming the gear lever into reverse, and driving by again hoping not to miss the turn. (Expectancies of this sort can conveniently be represented in the sort of grammatical system characterized by Woods 1970, 1978, as an augmented transition network. For a variety of similar examples, see de Beaugrande 1980:47–48.)

Expectancies of the most complicated sorts enter into even mundane motoric routines. For instance, one of my favorite examples came from a certain professor I knew in graduate school. It seems he had just purchased a new cigarette lighter and was driving down the highway at the speed limit. It was a warm summer day and he had the window down. Absently he lit up, shook out the flame, and tossed the lighter out the window. He had developed an expectancy for using matches to light up and continued on automatic pilot to behave as if he had just lit his cigarette with a match instead of a brand new lighter. His error is one of anticipatory mind-set. A sort of cognitive momentum that is set up by a false expectation. Although this example illustrates a problem in the event-structure side of Figure 2, it is not unlike common lexical confusions that occur on the verbal side of intelligence.

For an example of the latter sort, consider the tragically prophetic error of Sadat some years ago. He was asked what he would do if the peace talks with Israel did not bear fruit. He answered that he would turn in his 'assassination.' He corrected himself immediately and said 'resignation,' but the fearful motivation for his slip of the tongue had already revealed an anticipatory mind-set—which as it turned out was not unwarranted. Of such errors was Freudian psychology made.

Interestingly, slips of the mind and tongue may also be accompanied by slips of the whole body at times. For instance, I remember an incident where a certain lawyer was preparing to take leave of a tired group of conferees. The long discussions of the day were concluded and people were beginning to look forward to a more pleasant evening. It was the sort of occasion where people are brightening up and congratulating one another on their congeniality. At just such a moment, the lawyer said he would meet the rest of us in the lobby shortly. Then, he turned briskly and ran into the door jamb. Speaking to the wall, he said, 'Oh, excuse me,' and at the same moment gave it a couple of pats, as if to say, 'I hope you're not injured.' Then, casting a glance over his shoulder in our direction, he hurried into the corridor and out of sight.

The lawyer's speech act shows that he had formed certain expectancies based on the crowded surroundings and his previous successes at getting through doorways. He apparently was more prepared to run into a person than a door jamb. His error reveals the sequential articulation required between understanding, intention, and action.

One final example will serve to illustrate that this coordination involves a delicate synchronization of more than one level of meaning and intention. Not long ago, I was checking out at a grocery store. It was late in the day, and the store was crowded and noisy. The clerk said something to me as I was picking up the bag of groceries to leave. I didn't understand and asked for a repetition. She repeated herself. I still missed it, and asked for another shot. She obliged, a bit louder. I still couldn't quite make out what she had said. On the fourth try, her words were loud enough and mean enough to have stopped the front line of the Pittsburgh Steelers. She shouted, 'I said 'T-H-A-N-K Y-O-U!!!' You might have thought that E. F. Hutton had begun to speak. Every head in the store turned.

On what Watzlawick, Beavin, and Jackson (1967) term the CONTENT LEVEL, she was apparently intending to say that she was glad I stopped by and that she hoped I would come again. However, due to the difficulty of putting this message (perhaps an insincere one) through the channel, on what Watzlawick et al. term the RELATIONSHIP LEVEL she ended up saying something like, 'You idiot, if I never see you again, it'll be too soon.'

What this example shows is that plans to communicate must be coordinated in terms of content and relationship information, and also that, as John Dewey observed long ago, the things that people say may often surprise themselves as much as anyone else.

Now we turn to a consideration of the hypothesis that provides a basis for linking the input, textuality, and expectancy hypotheses together.

THE EPISODE HYPOTHESIS

The episode hypothesis says that TEXT (I.E., DISCOURSE IN ANY FORM) WILL BE EASIER TO PRODUCE, UNDERSTAND, AND RECALL TO THE EXTENT THAT IT IS MOTIVATED AND STRUCTURED EPISODICALLY. A corollary to this hypothesis is that the acquisition of a second language will be facilitated to the extent that the texts used in the instructional process are episodically organized. There are two aspects to 'episodic organization'—motivation (or affect) and logical structure. Generally, it may be said that selling authors respect both of these (Braine 1974, Peck 1979, and Swain 1980).

I'll have more to say about both the motivation and structure of episodically organized texts in a moment, but first I want to emphasize how I see the episode hypothesis and its corollary as relating to second language teaching. It seems to me that THESE IDEAS LEAD TO THE SUPPOSITION THAT PERHAPS SECOND LANGUAGE TEACHING WOULD BE MORE SUCCESSFUL IF IT INCORPORATED PRINCIPLES OF GOOD STORY WRITING ALONG WITH THE BENEFITS OF SOUND LINGUISTIC ANALYSIS. This supposition underlies all of the preceding discussion. We will return to it shortly, to consider some of the ways in which it may help to bolster practical approaches to language teaching, but now it is time to illustrate more explicitly what episodic organization is.

As with the expectancy hypothesis, episodic organization may be clarified by examining cases where it is violated. There are two principal ways in which episodic organization can be made light of. The first common violation is to generate unmotivated (or poorly motivated) text. The result, as Peck observes, is 'boring, boring, boring,' and most writers who do it, unless they happen to write for ESL or FL publishers, generally remain unpublished. Speakers who do it are rarely invited back for a second engagement. The person who persist in it, sad to say, is regarded as a bore.

A second common violation is to generate illogical (or jerky) text. The latter may prove interesting in the short term (provided it is motivated), but usually it loses ita audience much as a devilish bronc unseats many a would-be rider. The result of the two types of violation together is almost always fatal to the text. The first violation usually quenches the spirit of any potential interpreter, and the second skins the shins and twists the nose of the unfortunate Pilgrim until he gives up and goes home.

Let's take the problem of textual logic first. My favorite example of an apparent narrative which jerks and twists and turns with tortured logic comes from the 19th century humorist, Samuel Foote. It is a useful piece of text because, though it violates the principle of episodic STRUCTURE, it has a surprising episodic MOTIVATION, which we will come to in a moment. But first a look at the test:

> So she went into the garden to cut a cabbage leaf to make an apple pie: and at the same time a great she-bear coming up the street pops its head in the shop. "What! No soap!" So he died, and she very imprudently married the barber: and there were present the Picninnies, the Joblillies, and the Garcelies, and the great Panjandrum himself, with the little round button at the top, and they all fell to playing the game of catch-as-as-catch can, till the gunpowder ran out the heels of their boots (S. Foote, ca. 1854, as cited by Cooke 1902:221ff.).

My father used to quote this passage as part of a general sales pitch on the importance of "meaningful sequence" (alias "episodic structure") in materials to be used for teaching a foreign language. His point was that the logic of the text is not terribly unlike that found in many exercises written for the consumption of foreign language students. Except for its vague resemblance to narrative and its syntactic heterogeneity, Foote's prose could well pass for many an ESL or FL pattern drill from a now, we may be grateful, fading era.

The trouble with Foote's prose is not so much its violation of what might be construed as a purely Western style of episodic organization of discourse; rather, it is a problem of how to make an apple pie, and of the habits and haunts of she-bears. It is a matter of shaving soap, mortality, and barber shops, of weddings and the kind of folk who celebrate them, of gunpowder and boot heels.

However, if we look back at the time and place where Foote's text was created, we discover that in fact his prose was not 'unmotivated' in the sense in which we used this term above. That is, Foote himself had a pragmatic purpose in mind. His text made a point. It was a practical experiment proving one aspect of the episode hypothesis. To see this, we must look back at the context of his creation.

It seems that Foote had been attending a series of lectures where a certain Professor Macklin was holding forth on the art of oratory. On the evening in question, Macklin boasted that using the techniques of memorization which he had ardently recommended throughout, and which he himself had mastered, he could repeat from rote any passage of prose up to a hundred words in length after having read it aloud only once. Foote casually wrote the text about the she-bear and the barber shop on the back of a scrap of paper, handed it to Macklin, and challenged him to read it once and repeat it from memory.

To the great delight of Mr. Foote, Macklin read the text, but, alas, after only one pass through it, was unable to repeat it from memory. With a single stroke of humorous fantasy, Foote reduced Macklin's boast about his memory to a scrambled mess of apple pie and cabbage leaves. The trouble was that Macklin COULD memorize up to a hundred words in a single pass, provided the words fell into the sort of meaningful sequence characteristic of the logic of ordinary prose.

In retrospect, we look back and say that Foote's prose was pragmatically MOTIVATED by Macklin's boast, but the text itself violated many of the constraints that govern ordinary narrative. His prose lacked the internal episodic structure of ordinary discourse.

Of course, there are lots of examples of texts that are poorly motivated, and/or poorly structured as well. In fact, lack of motivation especially may be singled out as one of the most common faults in texts that are written for the consumption of second language learners. For instance, consider the following conversation that supposedly took place on an air plane while Mr. and Mrs. Miller were en route to Hong Kong. They had run into Miss Yamada again, a stewardess they had met on an earlier flight. Miss Yamada had begun to show them pictures of family and friends, and then the following dialog is supposed to have ensued:

> Miss Yamada: This is my best friend. Her name is Fumiko.
> Mrs. Miller: She's very pretty. Is she older or younger than you?
> Miss Yamada: She's one year younger.
> Mrs. Miller: Aren't you thinner than she is?
> Miss Yamada: Yes, I am. Fumiko loves to eat.
> Mr. Miller: So do I. I hope it will be time for lunch soon
> (National Council of Teachers of English 1973:73).

This text is odd because it lacks motivation. For instance, we might ask why the dialog takes place. Does it have anything to do with getting to Hong Kong? Actually, in a tangential way it does, but it does not seem to contribute toward that end in any SIGNIFICANT way. (It is not the sort of thing that one would be apt to write home about.) More particularly, we might ask why Mrs. Miller is curious about the relative ages of the stewardess and her friend. Or why Miss Yamada happens to take out the picture album in the first place. However, once the pictures are out, why is Mrs. Miller so curious about the relative sizes of Fumiko and Miss Yamada? Is the picture so bad, or the stewardess's uniform so ill-fitting, that the question is not superfluous—not to mention impertinent?

It isn't so much that the text lacks structure. On the contrary, Mrs. Miller seems to have an abiding concern for 'structure'—especially comparatives. (She is probably an ESL teacher of the old school). There is even a kind of temporal development in the conversation, as, for instance, the mention of eating causes Mr. Miller to remark upon the fact that it is lunch time. What is missing is a motivation for Miss Yamada to take out the pictures in the first place, or for Mrs. Miller to ask about relative ages and weights, or alternatively to quiz Miss Yamada on her ability to use English comparatives. Also, there is the general question as to why this conversation is reported in the course of a trip to Hong Kong.

What exactly is missing from the Miller text, and from many similar ones in ESL and FL texts? Or, putting the question differently, how come the episode does not seem to make any essential contribution to the Miller's experience, or even to their trip to Hong Kong? Wouldn't it make more sense to delete the dialog and just report, 'The Millers went to Hong Kong by plane'? Apparently, the hidden agenda is to give the ESL students practice in the use of comparatives. This is probably the true motivation not only for the dialog, but for the chance meeting on the plane, and perhaps even the trip to Hong Kong in the first place. However, any such motive is simply insufficient if we take the pragmatic basis of trips to Hong Kong and the like seriously. Yes, giving practice in the use of comparative structures is a KIND of pragmatic motive (to an ESL textbook writer), but it is too esoteric as a motive to contribute to an interesting story. The interpreter (listener-reader-hearer-learner) remains unmotivated. The outcome is dull, dull, dull.

What is missing?

A little more than seven decades ago, John Dewey (1910) noted that reflective thinking is always occasioned by trouble. A difficulty arises in experience and provides the incentive for reflection. Without any trouble, there just isn't anything much worth bothering your head about. Not only is there nothing to write home about, there isn't even anything to converse about. Dialog that contains no implicit conflicts, that wrestles with no troubles or difficulties, is a lot like reflective thinking without any motive. It is, in short, unmotivated.

Interestingly, Dewey's analysis of thinking presupposes that human behavior is goal-directed. There can be no trouble except in relation to thwarted purposes or desires. The very definition of the term 'trouble' implies a cognitive superstructure with goals and plans to achieve them. (For an interesting analysis attempting to characterize such structures more explicitly, see Schank and Abelson 1977, although we may note in passing that Rumelhart's story schema does not say anything significant about the beginnings and ends of stories precisely because he does not concern himself to explain where conflict enters and exits.)

Perhaps the single most common goal-orientation of human beings (something that can be taken for granted in ALMOST all contexts of ordinary life) is the struggle to preserve life against the threat of death. This is a very practical version of the classic conflict of most novels which portray the battle between good and evil in one form or another. It is just such a classical structure that also motivates all of man's religious activities, which are oriented toward achieving enlightenment and immortality. Even scientific endeavors, in a very general sense, can be construed as attempts to differentiate false propositions from true ones—correct theories from nonsense. Presumably the fact that false ideas and superstitions in the end promote disease, poverty, and injustice is the primary motivation for the pursuit of scientific thinking and research.

Or, putting the whole perspective of episodic organization in a nutshell, we may refer to Robert Newton Peck's observation that "a plot is two dogs and one bone." Conflict in the pursuit of desired ends provides the motive for conversation, for writing home, and for telling stories as well as listening to them. A meaningful episode, one worth generating text about, is one that involves an experiencer pursuing a desirable goal in the face of opposition—the more severe the opposition, the more desired is the goal, and the more motivated will be the telling, comprehending, recalling, and retelling of the story. Or, casting the whole matter in Piagetian terms (see, especially, Piaget 1981), it may be argued that conflict is the principle source of the affective fuel that powers the cognitive engine. Dwight Swain (1980) and other teachers of writers have also often commented on the importance of feeling as a reaction to conflict and as a motivation for story telling.

The episode hypothesis thus asserts that to the degree a text is episodically organized (motivated and structured episodically), it will be easier to produce, understand, recall, and otherwise to benefit from for any practical purpose. To illustrate this, consider the fact that there are answers to many questions concerning episodically organized texts which elicit only a blank stare when asked about less organized texts. For instance:

- Why did the she-bear amble up the street?
- Who died in the barber shop?
- What killed him, the lack of soap or the bear?
- How did the gunpowder end up inside the boots of those at the wedding?
- What is the game of catch-as-catch-can?

For these questions there are no determinate answers, because the text in question lacks the requisite level of episodic structure (i.e., meaningful sequence).

The same is true, though less dramatically so, of the Miller text:

- Why did Miss Yamada take out her picture album?
- Why does Mrs. Miller ask about the relative ages of Fumiko and Miss Yamada?
- How does the conversation with Miss Yamada relate to the Miller's trip to Hong Kong?

Compare the absence of any determinate answers for the foregoing questions with the following:

- Why did the Embassy worker duck his head.
- What would have happened if he hadn't ducked?
- What caused the brick to come crashing through the window?

Or consider the determinacy of the answers concerning the Foote text if we focus on the broader episodic context which motivated Foote's creation:

- Why did Foote write such an extraordinary text?
- Why couldn't Professor Macklin repeat it?
- What does Foote's demonstration prove about memory?
- Who had the better understanding of memory, Macklin or Foote?

And, obviously, many other questions could be adduced.

However, my point is by now established: TO THE EXTENT THAT A GIVEN TEXT IS EPISODICALLY MOTIVATED AND STRUCTURED, IT WILL GIVE A RICHER PRAGMATIC

YIELD OF INFORMATION. Quite simply, it contains a larger quantity of accessible information than a less structured text.

SOME IMPLICATIONS

So where does all of this lead us? What can we conclude from the input, textuality, expectancy, and episode hypotheses? It seems to me that several significant implications can be drawn for second language instruction, and for education in a more general sense as well. These can perhaps best be summed up as caveats which, as I have indicated above, have their roots in successful story writing techniques. I am thinking here primarily in terms of second language instruction, but no doubt some of the implications which I will try to make explicit seem to have applications to other instructional objectives in other areas of school curricula.

First, I think that unmotivated texts should be avoided. We should walk wide around them, just as we would circumvent polecats with their tails in the air. Since, as we saw above, motivation seems to hinge on meaningful conflict, a text that lacks conflict relevant to the pursuit of a desired goal should not be used. This will HELP to relieve a lot of classroom boredom.

Second, the story line should be carried primarily by stageable action. This piece of advice is really not my own, but comes from the most successful fictionalist of all time, Erle Stanley Gardner, and has been echoed many times by other successful writers. By 1979, Gardner had sold 310 million copies of his novels—mainly the mystery novels featuring Perry Mason and company. According to a 1981 publisher's release (Ballantine Books in New York), Gardner still outsells Agatha Christie, Harold Robbins, Barbara Cartland, and Louis L'Amour combined. Therefore, it seems that the advice he wrote in a letter to an aspiring writer is worthy of our attention:

> Don't say that the villain is a mean man with a wicked wallop. Show him sliding down from his horse in a rage because the animal jerks away from him. Show him swing a terrific fist and crash the horse on the nose. That gives the reader the idea of the wickedness of his wallop. Then when the villain advances toward the hero with doubled fist the reader gets some suspense because he's seen what happened to the horse. But if you tell the reader the villain is bad and has a mean wallop it's history, and the less history you get into a yarn the better (as cited by Fugate and Fugate 1980:79).

Or, in the words of Robert Newton Peck, 'Don't tell'em: show 'em.'

If this advice were heeded in the preparation of materials to be used in teaching languages, texts would be easier to dramatize, easier to understand, and much effort presently wasted trying to make sense out of nonsense could be better used.

Third, if the action of the story is to be stageable, it must respect the logic of experience. (And to a surprising degree this is even true of fantasy!) That is to say, the sort of pattern drill nonsense that goes through every imaginable permutation of a given surface form without respect to meaning should never be used. In other words, we should not ask language students to practice saying drills like the following:

John is a pilot.
John is not a pilot.
Is John a pilot?
If John were a pilot, he could fly an airplane.
John is not a pilot so John cannot fly.
John is a pilot so John can fly.
If John were not a pilot, he could not fly.
Be a pilot, John, so you can fly.
Fly to the John, pilot.
Ask the pilot where the John is, John.
The John is not a pilot.
The pilot is not a John.

For the non-native speaker, there is little possibility of comprehending drills which permute structures without regard for meaning, and even less motivation to do so. In fact, meaningfulness is contrary to the intent of meaningless drills in the first place. However, meaningless drills are not logically necessary. Pattern drills, where they are used, may be anchored in pragmatically motivated text. For instance, in one Spanish program the author wrote:

> Even the structure drills . . . are either based upon the known facts of the story or are cued by means of cartoons so as to render comprehension automatic . . . (Oller 1963:x).

Fourth, from the earliest stages of second language acquisition it makes sense to present the experience side of the pragmatic mapping first, and then to go on to analyze in greater detail the discourse side. In other words, the teacher should first make sure the students know what happens in the story, who is there, where it all takes place, what difference the events make to the characters, and what goals are being sought and thwarted. Then the student will be in a position to begin to work out an understanding of the subtleties of the target language used in that text, in much the same manner, presumably, that the first language acquirer develops the usual sort of native-speaker 'intuitions.'

Fifth, if the text is long it may be broken down into manageably smaller chunks. Understanding a long text is like eating an elephant in this respect: both must be consumed one bite at a time. This principle allays many a complaint that texts in general are 'too complicated for learners at stage X' (read *X* as any point between ground zero and native speaker competence).

Sixth, it will be possible with episodically organized material to work through each episode in multiple cycles, where the depth of understanding and the range of comprehension increases on each pass. On the first pass through a text or segment, only the bare outlines may be understood. On the second and subsequent passes, progress is made from the principal facts of who, what, and where, to the meatier details of when, why, and how, and eventually to presuppositions, associations, and implications at whatever depth suits the purpose of the instructor.

In the final analysis, the process of pragmatically linking input in the target language with the facts of experience depends, as Krashen (1980) has argued, on comprehension. This process can be facilitated by capitalizing on the textuality of ordinary experience, respecting its logic, harnessing the cognitive momentum that this logic creates, and in general by employing good story telling techniques in preparing, packaging, and presenting language teaching materials.

REFERENCES

BOBROW, D. and A. COLLINS (eds.) 1975. Representation and understanding. New York: Academic.

BRAINE, J. 1974. Writing a novel. New York: McGraw Hill.

COOKE, W. 1902. The table talk and bon mots of Samuel Foote. London: Myers and Rogers.

DE BEAUGRANDE, R. 1981. Text, discourse, and process. Norwood, NJ: Ablex.

DEWEY, J. 1910. How we think. Boston: D. C. Heath.

______. 1916. Essays in experimental logic. New York: Dover.

DI PIETRO, R. J. 1981. Discourse and real-life roles in the ESL classroom. TESOL Quarterly 15. 27–33.

______. 1982. The open-ended scenario: a new approach to conversation. TESOL Quarterly 16. 15–20.

FUGATE, F. L. and R. B. FUGATE. 1980. Secrets of the world's best-selling writing: The story telling techniques of Erle Stanley Gardner. New York: Morrow.

JESPERSEN, O. 1904. How to teach a foreign language. London: Allen and Unwin.

KRASHEN, S. D. 1980. The input hypothesis. Current Issues in Bilingual Education, ed. by J. E. Alatis. Washington, DC: Georgetown University. Also in J. Oller, (ed.). 1983. Issues in language testing research. Rowley, MA: Newbury House.

LASHLEY, K. 1951. The problem of serial order in behavior. Cerebral mechanisms in behavior, ed. by L. A. Jeffress. New York: Wiley. Reprinted in S. Saporta, ed. 1961. Psycholinguistics: A book of readings. New York: Holt, 180–197.

NATIONAL COUNCIL OF TEACHERS OF ENGLISH. 1973. English for today, Book Two: The world we live in. 2nd ed. New York: McGraw Hill.

OLLER, J. W. 1963. Teacher's manual: El espanol por el mundo, primer nivel. Chicago: Encyclopedia Films.

PECK, R. N. 1980. Secrets of successful fiction. Cincinnati, OH: Writer's Digest.

PIAGET, J. 1947. The psychology of intelligence. Totowa, NJ: Littlefield Adams.

______. 1980. Genetic epistemology, tr. by E. Duckworth. New York: Norton.

______. 1981. Affectivity and intelligence, tr. and Ed. by T. A. Brown, C. E. Kaegi, & Mark R. Rosenzweig. Palo Alto, CA: Annual Reviews.

RUMELHART, D. 1975. Notes on a schema for stories. Representation and understanding, ed. by D. Bobrow & A. Collins, 211–236. New York: Academic.

SCHANK, R. 1975. The structure of episodes in memory. Representation and understanding, ed. by D. Bobrow & A. Collins, 237–272. New York: Academic.

______. 1980. Language and memory. Cognitive Science 4.243–284.

SCHANK, R., and R. ABELSON. 1977. Scripts, plans, goals, and understanding. Hillsdale, NJ: Lawrence Erlbaum.

SIBATANI, ATUHIRO. 1980. The Japanese brain. Science, December.24–27.

SWAIN, D. L. 1980. Techniques of the selling writer. Norman, OK: University of Oklahoma.

WATZLAWICK, P., J. BEAVIN, and K. JACKSON. 1967. Pragmatics of human communication. New York: Norton.

WOODS, W. A. 1970. Transition network grammars for natural language analysis. Communications of the Association for Computing Machinery 13.591–606.

———. 1978. Generalization of ATN grammars. Research in Natural Language Understanding, ed. by W. Woods and R. Brachman. Cambridge, MA: Bolt, Beranek, and Newman (Quarterly Progress Tr 4, 3963).

NINE

Patterns of Textual Cohesion in Genre-Specific Discourse

William J. Frawley
University of Delaware

Raoul N. Smith
GTE Laboratories, Inc.

INTRODUCTION

Researchers in texlinguistics from the various branches of linguistics and allied disciplines have been basically struggling with the following question: what makes a text a text? Despite the plethora of models in answer to this question, those working in textlinguistics either explicitly state or presuppose that a text is a text by virtue of the means by which its constituents COHERE: a text is such because of its peculiar connectivity.

Petöfi's (1975) and van Dijk's (1977a, 1977b) work on texts, for example, reveals a distinct attempt to capture the internal structure of texts in terms of the connectives of formal logic, and the external grounding of texts in terms of the logic of pragmatic coherence. Similarly, Grimes' (1975) well-known rhetorical model of texts relies heavily on connectives. His typology of rhetorical predicates, which functions as an anchor to both Grimes' and other rhetorically oriented researchers' models (such as Meyer 1977), is essentially a typology of rhetorical connectives in texts: a typing of the methods by which texts sequence and index rhetorical structures. Likewise, Kintsch's (1977) propositional model is predicated upon the hierarchical connection of semantic information in texts; a text, for Kintsch, is such because it is hierarchy of propositions. Schank and Abelson's (1977) representative AI text model works on the assumption that a text is a sequence of atomizable propositions: Schank's (1972) famous Causal Syntax is an elaborate description of the causal connections across statements, and without the Causal Syntax, or something like it, AI systems would be unable to generate or parse natural language texts AS TEXTS (instead of as simply sentences). Finally, Halliday and Hasan's (1976) study of connectivity in English text clearly shows that the fundamental property of a text is its internal cohesion, which, according to Halliday and Hasan, provides a text with TEXTURE.

Given this point of research agreement, and the fact that most text research has been directed toward the devices which texts in general employ in order to achieve connectivity, it is reasonable to inquire whether or not certain types or GENRES of texts hold together in different or the same ways. That is, we pose the problem of whether texts which fall into certain genres can be categorized as doing so because they possess patterns of connection at once peculiar to other texts in those same genres, and different from patterns in other genres. This is a problem motivated not only by the assumption that genres are, intuitively, homogeneous, but also by the fact that very little research has been done on cross-genre patterns of connectivity. In truth, most of what has been done on connectivity has been done exclusively on NARRATIVE, yet there are other equally interesting genres to investigate for connectivity.

We pose the problem of cross-genre patterns of connectivity for three purposes. First, we want to discover what makes a genre a genre. Second, we want to discuss these patterns of connectivity in terms of the nature and logic of the discourses involved. Third, we want to speculate about the implications of genre-specific patterns of textual connection.

In order to study this problem, we have chosen to examine the most used device of COHESION (Halliday and Hasan 1976) in English text: REFERENCE. We have chosen it because its cohesive function has been well documented. Our purpose in looking at reference is to consider the distribution and cohesive function of pronouns, since they have a broad range of cohesive effect: they accomplish endophoric, exophric, and other connections, and differential distribution of referential indexing may contribute to our knowledge of the nature of the discourses involved.

To study these problems, we have investigated 16,000 word samples of fiction, journalism, religion, and science from the Brown English Corpus. Using APL, we have completed frequency distribution studies both lexically and syntactically on the corpora, and we are reporting on what we have discovered thus far about the differential distribution in the genres of the connective device called reference.

COHESIVE REFERENCE

Referential cohesion has been amply documented in the literature on text grammar as a critical device in the unity of texts, and is thus a potentially revealing cohesive phenomenon. We will limit our discussion to an examination of only personal pronouns and their cohesive function in the four genres.

The first type of reference we will consider is the use of third person singular nominative pronouns. This type of pronoun is germane to the cohesion of a text since the third person pronoun 'is inherently cohesive, in that a third person form typically refers anaphorically to a preceding item in the text' (Halliday and Hasan, 1976:48). Thus, the appearance of this type of pronoun is an indication of the endophoric (intratextual) cohesion in a particular text: a measure of how the text holds together in itself.

The total use (hereafter called ABSOLUTE CHOICE) of this type of pronoun in the four genres appears in Table 1. The total number of tokens out of 16,000, and the rank of this total within the entire count of the syntactic phenomena in the corpora, are given.

Some interesting differences across the four genres emerge from this tabulation. Fiction has the highest use of the third person pronouns, which means that there is a

Table 1. Distribution of exophoric pronouns.

Genre	Amount	Rank
Journalism	80	29
Fiction	289	18
Religion	263	14
Science	32	41

great deal of endophoric pronominal cohesion in this genre. On one level, this is a very peculiar finding, since it is a known fact that fiction is a highly VERBAL genre. Smith's (1982) study of this matter reveals that fiction employs about 50% more verbs than the other genres under consideration here. Thus, one would expect, simply from frequency, that fictional texts would cohere verbally, but the data suggest that this is not the case (Ellegard's 1978 study also bears this out).

However, the high frequency of these pronouns in fiction can be understood if one considers the structure of fictional texts in general. Gutwinski (1976) remarks that one peculiar feature of narrative texts is that they contain a clearly marked line of individuals involved in the sequence of events in the narrative. Endophoric pronouns, such as the third person, serve the function of marking this seriation of participants in fictional texts. Gutwinski says, about the fiction of Henry James, 'this (participant) line consists wholly of third person pronouns and personal possessives' (1976:148). It appears, then, that the high frequency of these pronouns in fiction is a consequence of their function in fictional discourse of allowing the line of participants to cohere in narrative.

While fiction employs this cohesive device to a great extent, science does not. The paucity of such pronouns in science is both peculiar and understandable. As to the peculiarity, Smith (1982) has found that scientific texts are almost wholly NOMINAL, with about 50% more nouns in scientific texts than in texts from the other genres in question. One would assume that the highly nominal nature of these texts would contribute to, or at least allow, a great deal of pronominal reference. But this is decidedly not the case, a fact which has been noted in passing by Ellegard (1978) and Gopnik (1972).

Why is it that scientific texts do not cohere through pronominal endophora? Two explanations come to mind. The first is that, unlike fiction, scientific texts have no need for a participant line, since scientific texts do not proceed in a narrative fashion. Thus, this sort of endophoric cohesion is ruled out by the nature of the discourse. The second reason is perhaps more interesting. It appears that, although science does not employ endophoric pronominal cohesion, it does employ endophoric cohesion through lexical repetition. A look at Gopnik's study reveals that there are many lexical items in scientific texts which are CONTENT WORDS. Cohesion appears to be effected by the recurrence of content words, which supersedes the use of pronominal cohesion. And this is perfectly in line with the nominal nature of scientific texts: science is characterized by a plethora of nominals which recur identically, or through other lexically related words, to allow scientific texts to cohere.

But if science and fiction are so different, journalism and religion are rather similar in the utilization of this cohesive device. Like fiction, journalism and religion employ a great deal of pornominal endophora. This is understandable for journalism, which is something of a narrative genre: journalism can be logically expected to have a participant line since, like fiction, journalism is a description of facts, events, and participants in those events; Ludvíková (1979) has in fact made similar observations about the distributions of such pronouns in Czech journalism.

But religion is a different case altogether. Why should religion have pronominal endophora to a great extent? It may be that religious discourse is very much related to narrative. Moreau (1961) has argued that theological discourse has its origin in mythic and literary discourse. It may be this historical connection to narrativity which allows religious texts to cohere in a manner quite unlike science, but like other genres which create participant line and systematic endophoric pronominal cohesion.

If the patterns of endophoric pronominal cohesion have revealed differences in cohesion across the four genres, then patterns of pronominal reference which are exophoric (extratextual reference) might also be illuminating. To look at exophoric pronominal reference, we must catalogue the patterns of usage of first and second person pronouns, which, as Halliday and Hasan say, 'Do not normally refer to the text at all; their referents are defined by the speech roles of speaker and hearer, and hence they are normally interpreted exophorically, by reference to the situation' (Halliday and Hasan 1976:48).

The absolute choice of such pronouns in the four genres appears in Table 2 (again with the total number of tokens out of 16,000 given, as well as this rank in the complete tabulation).

Several very interesting differences across the genres are evident in the use of such pronouns. First, it is obvious that science has the lowest frequency of these types of pronouns, which suggests that science has the least exophoric reference. The lack of such is explainable, first, from the general lack of pronouns in scientific texts to begin with, and second, from the nature of scientific texts. It may be accurate to say that scientific texts are neither audience- nor speaker-directed, and therefore can do without exophoric pointing. For one thing, scientific texts seem to be asituational. Under ideal conditions, scientific information is supposedly timeless and objective, which means that the texts which contain such information ought to be accessible to any reader in the field for the purpose of replication of the results. It does not matter, of course, whether or not scientific information actually IS objective; as a matter of fact many philosophers of science have argued that it is not (e.g., Feyerabend 1972). All that matters is that the information be perceived as such, which is the norm in the scientific readership. Scientific texts are thus not required to capture an audience (or at least not in traditional exophoric ways), so there is no need to have the texts cohere exophorically for speaker and hearer.

Another reason why scientific texts seem to be rather self-contained is that they

Table 2. Distribution of endophoric pronouns.

Genre	Amount	Rank
Journalism	230	18
Fiction	653	10
Religion	250	15
Science	75	26

do not need exophoric reference for their logic. Blanton (1982) has pointed out the rigor of the self-contained scientific text, and Gopnik (1972) has shown that, while science is normally thought to be referential discourse (and hence ought to point outside of itself for cohesion), most scientific texts are self-referential or intertextual (refer to other texts). It appears, then, that the nature and function of scientific discourse militate against exophoric reference.

None of this is true, of course, for fiction, which is highly exophoric. There is a strong tendency for fictional discourse to be situationally located, with speaker and hearer clearly marked throughout the discourse. But this stands to reason, since fiction, unlike science, has no set audience, is often dialogical, and must therefore rely on marked cohesion to define and sustain its situationality.

Interestingly enough, religion employs about as much exophoric reference as does fiction, which again points up the parallels between these two genres. Undoubtedly, the prominence of exophora (as well as endophora) in religious texts is another consequence of the narrative/literary origins of theological discourse.

Finally, it is curious to note that journalism has very little exophora. For such a strictly referential discourse as this, journalism ought to have a great number of extratextual connections. But the same assumptions prove untenable for science, an ostensibly referential discourse. Journalism is, in fact, much like science in its discourse functions. Journalism is asituational: the texts are assumed to be readable by anyone. Even though journalism is dialogic to a great extent (with reported speech, which would allow for exophoric pronouns), there is evidently little need in this genre to mark speaker and hearer. The texts stand on their own, and cohere more endophorically than exophorically (as the statistics in Ludvíková's 1979 study also imply for publicist prose written in Czech).

These two facts of pronominal endophora and exophora, in combination, allow us to establish some convenient parameters for the categorization of genres by their cohesive devices. First, it is evident that, from a comparison of endophora/exophora choice, there is much more endophora than exophora in all of the genres. Statistical tests of the four genres for endophora versus exophora show that the difference is significant ($\chi^2 = 78.39$; $p < .001$). What this means, of course, is that intratextual pointing is more important for all texts than extratextual pointing, of, in other words, that texts are such because of their internal connectivity, as was argued in the beginning of this paper.

However, while it is true that endophora is more crucial than exophora for textuality in general, a closer look at the data reveals that the differences between endophoric and exophoric pronominalization are most critical for some genres than others. If endophora and exophora are represented as axes, one can plot the genres in question according to the ratios of pronominal endophora and exophora, which gives the RELATIVE CHOICE of endophora over exophora in the genres. (See Figure 1. The ratios are represented in parentheses.)

It appears that, given the choice of endophora and exophora in the production of text, fiction, journalism, and science are more likely to have the endophoric pronominalization device than religion is. In other words, fiction, journalism, and science cluster around the choice of endophoric cohesion as a dominant cohesive device. Statistical comparison of the raw data for the genres bears this out: journalism/fiction, $\chi^2 = 2.5$, $.1 < p < .25$ (functionally not significant); journalism/science, $\chi^2 = .58$, n.s.; fiction/science, $\chi^2 = .049$, n.s. However, a comparison of these genres to religion shows consistent statistical difference: journalism/religion, $\chi^2 = 51.03$, $p < .001$; fiction/religion, $\chi^2 = 59.05$, $p < .001$; religion/science, $\chi^2 = 16.35$, $p < .001$.

While it is clear that the above data show a distinct clustering of the genres in their overall choice of cohesive referential devices, these data in no way invalidate the claims made previously regarding, say, the intimate connection between fiction and religion. Religion stands out here as a unique genre insofar as its relative choice of endophora over exophora is concerned; in absolute choice, however, of these referential devices, fiction still shows a marked similarity to religion. In fact, if religion is indeed a historical derivative of fiction and narrative, the divergence of religion from fiction and narrative may be found in this distinction of relative choice of cohesive devices; but this is only speculation, and a detailed study of the development of the genre, in the sort of epistemological archaeology suggested by Foucault (1972), needs to be done to settle this matter.

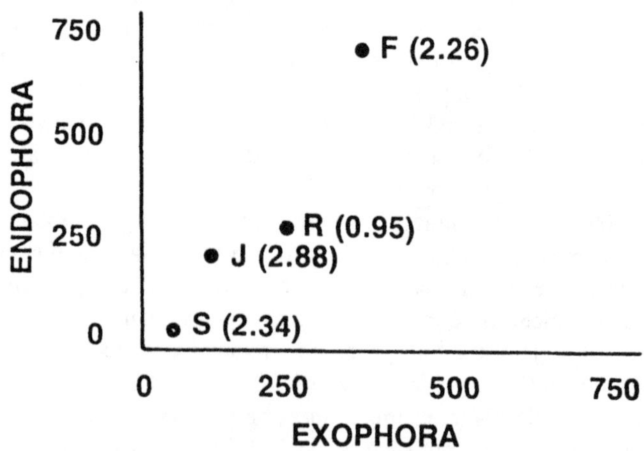

Figure 1. Ratios of endophoric to exophoric reference.

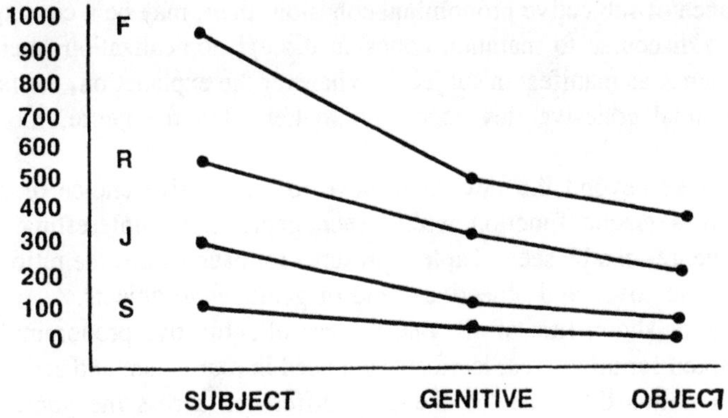

Figure 2. Distribution of pronouns by syntactic function.

For a final perspective on the referential cohesion characteristic of these four genres, let us turn to an examination of the referential devices by syntactic function. Figure 2 presents the absolute choice of all subject, genitive, and object pronouns in the genres (the genitives are represented by only the possessive determiners, since they have only one cohesive function; see Halliday and Hasan 1976).

Interestingly enough, the trend in pronominal usage according to syntactic function of the pronoun is the SAME for all of the genres. Subject pronouns dominate, genitives are the second most frequent, and objects are the least frequent. This is rather peculiar, but noteworthy. It means that, despite the radical differences outlined above in pronominal patterning and cohesive functions for the four genres, all of the types of discourse are the same at some level of analysis. This suggests that written discourse, no matter what the genre, is subject to fairly rigorous conditions on pronominal choice, irrespective of the pattern of referential cohesion which characterizes the genre.

It is no surprise, however, that subject pronouns dominate in all four of the genres. Recent studies of syntactic phenomena related to personal pronouns cohesively, relative pronouns, reveal that subjective constructions are the most frequent in written discourse. Keenan (1975) demonstrated this in his study of relativization in fictional, journalistic, and philosophical texts; Frawley (1982) also found similar patterning in his study of the prose of sophisticated and unsophisticated writers. There is something about the logic of subjective constructions which transcends the logic of choice within genres. It may be that subjective constructions are the most natural, universal, and most easily processed—as Keenan and Frawley argue—and thus the predominance of pronominal cohesive ties in subjective constructions could be a function of a condition on discourse to maintain (pronominal) cohesion according to the most natural structures available.

Another reason for the predominance of subject pronouns may be that the syntactic category of SUBJECT is closely related to, and quite often indistinguishable from (in some languages), the category of TOPIC (see Givon 1979 for this point). The predominance of subjective pronominal cohesion, then, may be a consequence of a tendency in discourse to maintain cohesion through topicalization, thematization, and prominence as manifest in subjects. Whatever the explanation, the fact remains that pronominal cohesive ties occur, no matter what the genre, most often as subjects.

If one looks beyond the raw data above to the relative choice of pronominal cohesion by syntactic function within each genre, some interesting differences across the genres can be seen. Table 3 presents for each genre, the ratios of subject pronouns to genitives and objectives, and of genitives to objects.

These ratios show, first of all, that the use of subjective pronominal cohesion, though marked for all genres, is most often used in journalism and science. In fact, it looks as if this difference is the only difference across the genres as far as syntactic function of the pronominal cohesive tie. Note that all of the other genres have fairly close ratios for the other syntactic functions. Thus, it appears that subjective pronominal cohesion may be the true indicator of differential cohesion patterns in genres, as far as reference goes.

Another interesting fact in the ratio table can be related to the clustering of genres noted in the discussion of endophoric and exophoric cohesion. As with the absolute choice of endophoric and exophoric reference, fiction and religion appear to be very much the same in their choice of pronominal cohesion according to syntactic function: they have the smoothest distribution of these items. This means that fiction and religion cohere similarly, as far as reference goes, in that they each have a broad range of syntactic choices for the pronominal cohesive devices. This may again be a function of the literary origins of religious discourse, as pointed out above; nonetheless, the similarity across the two genres is striking, and this finding, in conjunction with the similarity in absolute choice of endophoric and exophoric reference, suggests homogeneity across these two genres.

SUMMARY

In this paper, we have argued that the fundamental problem in achieving textuality is the text's connectivity. We have briefly examined various views of textual connectivity and have proposed an analysis of one type of textual connectivity, cohesion by reference, in four genres of English text.

Our study has revealed the following. In terms of absolute choice of referential

Table 3. Ratios of pronomial choice by syntactic function.

Genre	S/O	S/G	G/O
Journalism	5.74	2.11	2.72
Science	6.29	2.81	2.24
Fiction	2.45	2.34	1.05
Religion	2.36	2.71	1.43

cohesion, fiction employs a great deal of enodphora and exophora, as does religion; journalism employs a great deal of endophora and little exophora, while science employs little endophora and little exophora. In terms of relative choice of referential cohesion, fiction, science, and journalism are similar in their ratios of endophora to exophora; religion differs from these three genres in relative choice. In absolute choice of pronouns according to syntactic function, all genres have a predominance of subjective pronominal cohesion (which no doubt relates to thematization in texts), followed by genitive and objective pronominal choice. In relative choice of pronouns according to syntactic function, the choice of subjective pronouns is more crucial for journalism and science; fiction and religion have smoother and similar distributions, which points up the arguments made for the close conceptual connection between the two, especially insofar as religious discourse may have literary or narrative origins.

REFERENCES

BLANTON, MACKIE J-V. 1982. The pragmatic structure of rhetorical maturity in the sciences. Linguistics and literacy, ed. by William Frawley, 125–44. New York: Plenum Press.

ELLEGARD, ALVAR. 1978. The syntactic structure of English texts. Goteborg: University of Goteborg.

FEYERABEND, PAUL. 1972. Against method: Outline of an anarchistic theory of knowledge. London: New Left.

FOUCAULT, MICHEL. 1972. The archaeology of knowledge. New York: Harper & Row.

FRAWLEY, WILLIAM. 1982. Universal grammar and composition: Relativization, complementation, and quantification. Linguistics and literacy, ed. by William Frawley, 65–90. New York: Plenum Press.

GIVON, TAMLY. 1979. Understanding grammar. New York: Academic Press.

GOPNIK, MYRNA. 1972. Linguistic structures in scientific texts. The Hague, Mouton.

GRIMES, JOSEPH. 1975. The thread of discourse. The Hague: Mouton.

GUTWINSKI, W. 1976. Cohesion in literary texts. The Hague: Mouton.

HALLIDAY, M. A. K., and R. HASAN. 1976. Cohesion in English. London: Longman.

KEENAN, EDWARD L. 1975. Variation in universal grammar. Analyzing variation in grammar, ed. by R. Fasold and R. Shuy, 136–48. Washington, DC: Georgetown University.

KINTSCH, WATLER. 1977. On comprehending stories. Cognitive processes in comprehension, ed. by M. A. Just & P. A. Carpenter. Hillsdale, NJ: Erlbaum.

LUDVÍKOVÁ, MARIE. 1979. Pronouns in newspaper texts. The Prague School Bulletin of Mathematical Linguistics 32.33–56.

MEYER, BONNIE J. F. 1975. The organization of prose and its effect on memory. Amsterdam: North-Holland.

MOREAU, JULES. 1961. Language and religious language. Philadelphia: Westminster.

PETÖFI, JANOS. 1975. Beyond the sentence: Between linguistics and logic. Style and text, ed. by H. Ringbom et al. Stockholm: Skriptor.

SMITH, RAOUL N. 1982. A statistical syntactic study of four English genres.

SCHANK, ROGER. 1972. Conceptual dependency: A theory of natural language processing. Cognitive Psychology 3.552–631.

SCHANK, ROGER, and ROBERT ABELSON. 1977. Scripts, plans, goals, and understanding. Hillsdale, NJ: Erlbaum.

VAN DIJK, TEUN. 1977a. Connectives in text grammar and text logic. Grammars and descriptions, ed. by T. van Dijk & J. Petöfi, 11–63. New York: De Gruyter.

______. 1977b. Text and context: Explorations in the semantics and pragmatics of discourse. London: Longman.

TEN

Computers and Their Frame of Mind— The Linguistic Component

Klaus K. Obermeier
The Ohio State University

We are no longer anything more than slaves, working toward our own destruction, in the service—and for the greater glory—of the Almighty God of the Mechanical.
(Alain Robbe-Grillet, *Djinn*, 1982, Grove Press, p. 69)

My goal in this paper is to show the epistemological and ethical impact of automated linguistic data processing on the understanding of natural language. The advent of viable and already implemented natural language understanding programs (e.g., KRL, SAM, KLONE, GUS) has brought forth not only new theories of understanding, but also a renewed interest in the relation between man and machine. In particular, some scientists (Scriven 1953, Dreyfus 1979, Searle 1980) would like the limit the potential of programs that emulate human intelligent behavior by fiat to a solely sophisitcated simulation procedure. Computer programs, in their opinion, serve the purpose of testing theories and cannot manifest intelligent behavior, mainly because they lack consciousness and intentionality (Searle 1980). Researchers in the area of artificial intelligence, however, claim that some programs already emulate intelligent behavior in limited domains (Schank 1975:4, Winograd 1972:2). Their avowed goal can best be characterized by a well-known quote from Winograd (1972:2): 'We want to understand what intelligence is and how it can be put into computers. Language is one of the most complex and unique of human activities, and understanding its structure may lead to a better theory of how our minds work.' In this context language is considered to be a tool, a means to an end. The description of language understanding programs goes beyond the structural aspect of language, and will lead to psychological and philosophical insights into the human mind.

In this ongoing controversy between proponents of 'weak' AI (i.e., people who consider the program as a useful tool only) and 'strong' AI (i.e., people who believe that a program is a mind), I will espouse and justify the latter position. The central question to be asked is, 'What does it mean and what does it take for a computer program to "understand" natural language?' This paper shows that understanding is primarily linguistic and not biological in nature, i.e., communication via a symbol system is possible for carbon-based as well as for silicon-based entities. I do not intend to give an 'existence proof' for a model of human intelligence. I would like to emphasize, however, that major advances in the modelling of intelligent behavior by a computer program will have a strong impact on the perception and evaluation of human attributes, and should therefore not be seen as monolithic scientific feats.

EPISTEMOLOGY

Natural language programs that go beyond linguistic trickery (e.g., ELIZA) reflect, even if not explicitly stated, epistemological tenets held by their creators. If successful, the programs constitute theories of linguistic information processing with respect to encoding and decoding of meaning, modifying and maintaining information, and drawing inferences from the current discourse situation. If a program meets all the requirements of communicative competence, some philosophers remain skeptical, mostly on a priori grounds, about the sufficient condition of understanding: 'The formal symbol manipulations by themselves don't have any intentionality; they are quite meaningless; they aren't even SYMBOL manipulations, since the symbols don't symbolize anything' (Searle 1980).

I have argued elsewhere (Obermeier 1982b) that intentionality is a possible, not a necessary, by-product of a discourse, whereby the projection of a meaning onto an utterance is not the intention itself, but an interpretation of the utterance. It is the function of an utterance in a specific context that is a conditio sine qua for 'understanding.'

Understanding

The philosopher Wittgenstein characterizes the process of understanding as follows: 'To understand a sentence means to understand the language. To understand the language means to be master of a certain technique' (1971:127). Wittgenstein separates the act of understanding 'as performance' from understanding as feeling (Wilks 1976:231). Opponents of the 'strong' AI approach (Searle 1980, Dreyfus 1979) clearly confuse what we do versus what we feel when we do it.

Understanding is the function of an utterance in an actual situation. As a process, it is based on the meaning qua use of the words, together with the context which is partly determined by the specific use of the words. We are cognizant of the fact that while we use words with a certain meaning qua use in mind, their meaning potential is subject to dynamic changes. We use a word to refer to a concept, with the tacit assumption that, although the linguistic artifact remains constant, its meaning is in flux. We make good use of this change by employing various figures of speech derived from the sphere of visual perception (Waltz 1981). The dynamics of the understanding process that should also comprise plausibility criteria is adequately represented in frames or scripts (Schank 1973), with their default values that are modified depending on the situation.

Understanding is primarily a linguistic process that is contingent on plausibility, representability, and computability of a sentence. 'Meaning and the constellation of mental attitudes that exhibit it, are manufactured products. The raw material is information,' which is 'an objective commodity, something whose generation, transmission, and reception do not require or in any way presuppose interpretive processes' (Dretske 1981:vii). We understand an utterance because we are familiar with the conventional meaning that contains the information.

In phenomenological terms, the essence of an entity is preceded by its existence. Information is not information about language but information on the basis of language. Language on the one hand enables us to classify and categorize entities, and, on the other hand, develops into an autonomous system of rules and processes. The function of language in the information process is that of a substrate, and at the same time of a superstrate, of meaning (Obermeier 1982a).

Entities are delineated via language while at the same time being evaluated by the very fact that they are categorized and labelled. We will have terms for the salient features of an object, yet what criteria do we apply while choosing them? Understanding an utterance depends on inferences and expectations that we conjure up in a given situation. This process of making the necessary connections, although complex, can be emulated by a program provided we realize the importance of separating the constitutive force from the evaluative force of language.

A further dichotomy should be pointed out here. We use language not only to state but also to justify mental or physical states. If programs understand human language, one might submit, they are truly not in a position to emulate feelings or other states characteristic of carbon-based life? How does a human being understand a sentence like *I am in ecstasy?* After hearing someone say it, I could detect a logical-conceptual link between the linguisic and nonlinguistic behavior of the speaker. If I asked him to justify his statement, he could simply respond *Because I am ecstatic,* rather than providing further evidence. The crux of the matter is that reporting a state of being does not imply a previous computation on the part of the speaker (Putnam 1960:81). By the same token, a computer program reporting *I am in subroutine Y* is not required to provide further evidence for the statement. It is obvious that stating something without prior act of judgment is not different for a program or a human.

Consider, however, the difference in saying *I am in state X* versus *Z is in state X*. The former utterance, as a statement about oneself, need not be justified; the latter has to be justified. The person who claims that *Z is in state X* might have never been in state *X*, yet, on a verbal level, he or she can understand what it means to be in state *X*. By the same token, a computer program can output *Z is in state X*, and the meaning representation of this utterance is justification enough to attribute to the program a sufficient degree of understanding.

Understanding an utterance does not entail a previous use of the same utterance by the listener; we will respond to a person in distress by saying *I know what you are going through* even if we have never been in a similar state before. Thus, requiring from a computer program to have been in a certain state previous to its description is equally pretentious, since the program only reports that *Z* is in state *X*.

The concept of understanding is frequently invoked to show the uniqueness of man vis a vis a machine. As we have seen so far, even some rudimentary investigation of its components does not substantiate any of the sweeping claims about a computer program never being able to 'understand' natural language.

The Mind-Body Problem

The distinction between understanding as a linguistic versus a biological phenomenon has some theoretical impact on the mind-body problem. Understanding as a biological phenomenon allows us to identify mental with physical states in humans. Since computers and humans differ in their biochemistry, understanding is qualitatively different. There is, however, an isomorphism of man and machine that not only renders the 'two-state' argument unimportant but also enhances the humanoid disposition of the computer. The states of the computer can be likened in abstracto to those of human beings, in that logical and structural states correspond to mental and physical states, respectively. If we adopted the biological foundation of understanding, the argument above would only show that there exists a possible dichotomy between mental and mechanical phenomena in humans and in computers. The crux of the mind-body problem so far is that it does not explain anything; it is a 'purely verbal' problem (Putnam 1960:96).

The explanatory value of considering the understanding process by means of a computer program becomes evident once we have realized that understanding is a linguistic process. Under the assumption that programs achieve communicative competence, we could demonstrate that cognitive abilities related to language can be dealt with outside the body-mind dichotomy that seems to be still rampant amongst epistemologists. Language in this context reports about states, be they mental or physical; it never requires a mental state for its proper use. Language does not mediate mental states, but translates them into its semantic component. The study of automated linguistic data processing has not solved the mind-body problem, but rather has shown that it is ill-conceived and epistemologically vacuous.

Thinking

Language is more than a manifestation of the reproductive understanding process; it is evidence for 'creative' cognitive processes commonly referred to as 'thoughts.' A computer program that uses natural language successfully should be able to generate 'thoughts,' while drawing inferences and responding to expectations. The understanding process requires a selection among alternatives of meaning. By the same token, thinking requires an organization of cognitive constructs. The difference between understanding and thinking is not a qualitative one, but rather a quantitative one. While understanding something, I will limit my selections of alternatives to the immediate context and its implications, whereas thinking requires the recourse to all of my cognitive recourses. These remarks should in no way be taken as an endorsement of limiting intelligent behavior to elaborate search strategies. They are meant to discern understanding from thinking, while pointing to the striking similarities between the two processes.

A common misunderstanding about computer programs is manifest in the unwarranted claim that these programs are only as capable as their creators. In a trivial sense, this is certainly true as far as the logistics go. The actual task, however, can very well be performed by a program excelling the 'creative' capabilities of its creator. A case in point would be chess programs: even program designers who are not good chess players are able to write excellent chess programs that will checkmate their own creators.

Language is an ostensive manifestation of thinking. Thinking is not mediated by language; rather it is translated into language. The understanding process relies on the linguistic transfer of 'thoughts.' The proper decoding and encoding of the meaning of a linguistic utterance requires a system of rules for the translation process, together with an assessment of its cognitive structures.

Natural language programs make apparent the need for a strict separation of cognitive and linguistic structures. If this proves to be successfully implemented, we could arrive at a viable alternative to other information processing theories.

COGNITION

Cognition is commonly defined as 'the activity of knowing: the acquisition, organization, and use of knowledge' (Neisser 1976:1). Natural language programs constitute the interface between cognitive and linguistic structures. The activity of knowing entails for the program as well as for the human being fusing the two structures in order to be able to communicate. The program performs two activities at the same time: knowing the language, and knowing based on language.

The analogy between human knowledge and knowledge stored in and by a program depends on two tacit assumptions: humanoid intelligent behavior is optimal, and should therefore be emulated; humanoid intelligence is different from artificial intelligence. It is my contention in what follows that both are ill-conceived stipulations that lead to autoverification of psychological, linguistic, and philosophical theories, while at the same time providing critics of AI with the opportunity to point to deficiencies of programs in the emulation process.

Reality

The fact that a parsing strategy or the maintenance of a knowledge base comes close to humanoid behavior is considered to be a major advantage for a program. If programs were only used for the implementation of established theories, the fact that they process information successfully would be a merit of the cognitive theory. In this sense, programs are tools for testing purposes. Autoverification is present when scientists try to place explanatory significance on the simulation process: a theory should not be favored on the basis of its programmability. Along these lines, scientists seem to work under two assumptions that lead to a fallacy par excellence: that human information processing is optimal, and that programs fare better by imitating and emulating human intelligence. It is important to note that this contention leads to a fallacy of 'faulty hypostatization.' The use of human behavior as a criterion for success or failure of emulation procedures should always be regarded in relation to the qualitative differences between man and machine. A program might be in a position to excel in intelligence due to an apparent lack of human qualitites and dispositions (e.g., feelings, fatigue). If a program is too successful, scientists who like to maintain the human uniqueness factor are quick to point out those differences between man and machine that they took the liberty to suspend when starting the testing procedure.

By the same token, current programs in AI are not yet in a position to abstract from one level of structure to the next. A case in point is the chess program that cannot focus on partial board configurations, thus giving way to a combinatorial explosion of possible moves. The program, however, is much more consistent when it comes to the set of moves that ends a game successfully. In this context, cognitive processes like forgetting and remembering become significant for the evaluation of human versus machine performance. Using programs for any scientific research is only satisfactory if the study of intelligence is not limited to human intelligence as the ultima ratio, but transcends it. Intelligence should not be distinguished on the basis of what organism uses it. In this sense, programs are reflections of reality in that they manifest genuine intelligent behavior idiosyncratic of their structure.

Artificial Intelligence

Intelligence is commonly treated as a tangible commodity that humans have and machines only have in an artificial way. If the notion of artificiality were used to point to a qualitative difference, it would serve a useful purpose. It is, however, mostly used to establish a strict separation between human and machine intelligence in an evaluative sense: intelligence is intrinsic to humans but extrinsic to machines; therefore, programs will never have genuine intelligence.

This prevalent conjecture about intelligence can be refuted. If we consider the function of a system in a certain environment, we will see that the system adapts itself or is adapted with respect to the tasks and goals set by the environment (Simon 1969). In this situation, the system constitutes an interface between an inner and outer environment. The inner environment adapts itself to the outer one by means of the 'artificial' system that mediates between them. In Simon's view, both man and man-made artifacts are artificial systems in regard to their behavior.

Intelligence is not system-specific, in that it encompasses the property any system must have to function as an interface. This operational definition puts artificial intelligence on a par with human intelligence, at the same time setting the stage for an investigation of intelligence sui generis. Intelligence is the ability to apply existing knowledge to new situations by means of a process called abstraction. Thus, the implementation of intelligence by an organism requires a cognitive act that has a common denominator, yet manifests itself in different forms. Natural language understanding requires a type of abstraction from certain contexts that is based on visual perception. The following sentences taken from Waltz (1981) illustrate the case in point:

1. The dog bit the mailman.
2. The dog bit the mailman in the neck.
3. The dachshund bit the mailman in the neck.

Sentences 1 and 2 are instantiated without problems by the human understander. Sentence 3, however, requires some further processing. It is harder to understand for reasons of plausibility. We imagine (visually?) the tall mailman and the small dog during the scene described by 3. We abstract from the scene certain primitives; e.g. the difference in height, the act of biting, together with the necessary conditions for their plausibility. All our knowledge goes into the decoding of the utterance. The understanding process goes through a number of stages, ranging from the linguistic level to the visual level. The plausibility of sentences like *A bachelor is an unmarried man* can be assessed on the linguistic level. Logical plausibility needs to be invoked for *It is raining or it is not raining*. Empirical plausibility is called for in a sentence like *Carter was the 49th president of the US*.

Intelligence is required to process or understand sentences that contain the same word but with a different meaning. Consider the following sentences:

4. The cube fell into my lap.
5. The cube destroyed Oscar's confidence.
6. The cube turns if two people push it.
7. The cube is enough for one cup of soup.

In all four sentences, we seem to detect a prototype of the concept 'cube.' Between 4 and 5, we notice the meaning conflict that involves the tangible object 'cube,' and in 4 also a tangible object 'lap' versus an abstract concept 'confidence' in 5.

In 6, a further complication arises: the size together with the state of events require abstraction and some conjectures on the part of the understander. In 7, it is still another factor that plays a role in the decoding process: the consistency of the cube is relevant for the proposition. The cognitive factors used in these understanding processes are based on the capability of abstraction that promotes percepts to the next higher level of perception. The organization of programs in terms of tree structures that culminate in more and more abstract constructs seems to capture the process in essence. If isomorphisms between the human and the program can be established, artificial intelligence will no longer be an inferior surrogate for human intelligence. At the same time, it should become clear that isomorphism does not encompass an 'existence proof' for human cognitive processes.

Perception

Perception takes place where reality and cognition meet (Neisser 1976:9). In order to perceive certain things, an organism has to be in a position to know what and how to perceive. The organism has to have some advance knowledge of what to look for. The process of perception, according to Neisser (1976:14), is guided by preexisting structures or schemata that help us to notice entities in real life. The notion of schematas is the underlying principle for all forms of cognition (e.g., speaking, thinking, listening). It is akin to Minsky's frames and Schank's scripts. We take part in a conversation, enter a house, order a meal, play chess, all with preconceived ideas and expectations. We notice the unusual and take for granted the usual (as 'default' values). The implementation of these structures presupposes a precise delineation of perceptual wholes. Perceptual structures consist of relations between concepts. Concepts are prototypes that are subject to change; therefore perceptual structures change. Linguistic structures and elements do not change as rapidly as cognitive structures they express, thus creating the illusion that CHAIR still stands for the same entity as it did two years ago. The perceptual cycle that encompasses Piaget's processes of accommodation and assimilation causes some intricate problems for its implementation. It requires a program that contains dynamic and constantly modifying procedures. Once successfully deployed, these procedures could deal with the phenomena of forgetting and remembering.

Perception as a link between reality and cognition is thus more intricate as simple pattern matching. Structural and functional idiosyncrasies abound; the mode of perception has a significant impact on the percept. For a program, the most common form of input consists of linguistic and visual information. Although the analogy between human and machine perception breaks down at the neuron and micro-chip level, on the functional and structural level we find a considerable degree of correlation. From this brief discussion of perception, we have learned that, as a process, it does not crucially depend on the biological origin of the organism, but rather on invokable principles that are feasible for a computational implementation.

LANGUAGE

The title of this paper proclaims two basic contentions that have had a strong impact on the previous sections. My first contention is that, inasmuch as we can use a vague term as 'mind,' it can be applied to computer programs with respect to their intelligent behavior. My second contention is that the concept of mind is characterized to a large extent by a linguistic component. 'Mind' in this context stands for an entity that emanates intelligent behavior in terms of an adaptation process between an inner and outer environment. The impact of language on the mind is not to be taken in a Whorfian sense, but rather in an information processing sense that also includes other resources of information (e.g., vision).

The processing of language by a computer program is comparable to the human linguistic processing: in both systems, we find a translation process (Fodor 1975:116) that takes as input physical strings of linguistic items and 'compiles' from them the meaning of the information. In the computer, compilers translate higher level languages into machine code, whereas, in the human understander, acoustic or graphic information gets transformed by the nervous system into a semantic equivalent. This is a two-stage process that needs to be refined into structural levels. The structure of the linguistic component is modular, not only to promote computability, but also to incorporate the knowledge gained by linguists in regard to the different levels of structure. Special attention will be paid to the control problem: what module is responsible at what stage for the parsing process?

Language processing has to deal with two tasks at once: the translation of information into meaning, and the proper functioning of the linguistic system itself.

The Control Problem

Language is described by a grammar which consists of a quadruple $G=(T,V,P,S)$, whereby T constitutes the set of terminal symbols (lexical items), V the set of nonterminal symbols (category names), P the set of production rules, and S the category for sentences. The parser is an algorithm that accepts only sentences that belong to the language. Although there are different types of parsers, their task is to analyze the sentence in terms of its constituents and their dependencies. Parsing a sentence involves a multi-level analysis that consists of passing control from the phonological to the morphological, syntactic, and semantic component. Equivocal analyses arise if the ambiguity goes beyond the word level. Most ambiguities can be resolved by the context, be it linguistic or non-linguistic. We can distinguish there major models that deal with the control problem that arises in linguistic automated processing, and for that matter also in humans.

- THE HIERARCHICAL MODEL uses a sequence of levels that is accessed in a top-down or bottom-up fashion. If there is more than one analysis possible, we have to allow for back-up or look-ahead procedures that can lead to the floundering of the system, or to the wrong interpretation in the worst case.
- THE HETERARCHICAL MODEL (Woods and Makhoul 1973) uses the components all at once; any one component can pass information to the control unit that decides, on the basis of these suggestion rules, which analysis to choose. The different modules also communicate amongst each other.
- THE PANDEMONIUM MODEL (Reddy 1973) uses the components independently from one another. The linguistic experts pass suggestions to the control unit that can change, add to, or support the already-existing hypothesis.

The control unit has to finalize the analysis on the basis of incoming information and on its own knowledge base. It is at this point of the analysis that linguistic and cognitive structures constitute an interface. The control unit receives linguistic information in the form of already analyzed meanings and matches it with 'schemata' and linguistic knowledge (e.g., associative priming, ellipsis, implicatures, conversational maxims). A further complication, related to faulty input in terms of errors, requires a certain robustness of the parser itself (Hayes and Mouradian 1981).

The interaction between the various components not only has to be supervised but also guided to facilitate successful decoding. The result of the parser has to be stored in the knowledge base with regard to new linguistic and nonlinguistic information. The system has to 'learn' from every new bit of information. The dynamics of this process require multi-level processing, whereby information is passed to various memory areas of the system at the same time. Again, the structural idiosyncrasies of the computer program separate the human understander from the machine. Even if we find a 'flawless' system, the strongest claim to be made is one about isomorphism between the two systems. At various points in the information process, human physiological and psychological limitations will necessarily produce results that are different from the computational outcome.

Creativity and Productivity

Using language successfully requires us to make infinite use of finite means. The number of linguistic elements is finite; their proper concatenation is subject to nonlinguistic constraints that are derived from what we know about the world and its structure. It is not sufficient to store encyclopedic knowledge in a computer in order to be able to understand utterances or even produce appropriate linguistic output. The two-way process of information exchange adds another dimension to the requirements for a natural language understanding program. The system should be in a position to instigate the process on the basis of its needs. At some point, we would want it to realize the difference between knowing the meaning of an expression and knowing that the expression has a certain meaning.

The understanding program is an interface between linguistic and cognitive structures. Scientific insight does not lie primarily in a solution to this translation process, but in the reasons for making one choice over another. In the previous sections, our choices for one alternative were guided by metatheoretical principles. The idea underlying this investigation is that we try to structure the world we live in. Language is a primary medium for this structuring process. Knowledge is mediated by language. Linguistic and cognitive structures are not real (in the sense of philosophical realism) but constructs of human endeavor to survive in a particular environment. Notions of creativity and productivity are labels for the dynamic adaptation of information processing to ever-changing structures. Intelligence enables systems to abstract from a previous structure to a novel situation; thus it makes possible the 'learning' process. Language is one of the major tools used in a system of symbols that communicates between the inner and outer environment.

CONCLUSION

Antony Jay once remarked that 'the uncreative mind can spot wrong answers, but it takes a creative mind to spot wrong questions.' This is true for some scientists who study artificial intelligence in general, and natural language processing in particular. The solution to the question 'what is intelligence?' does not lie in an 'existence proof' of human intelligence, nor is it the painstaking search for underlying human principles. The implication of the question biases the scientists in favor of the uniqueness of human intelligence, rather than the search for intelligence per se. By the same token, automated linguistic processing is not adequately dealt with in terms of the human use of language. In both instances, intelligence and language have to be viewed from a structural standpoint that enables the scientist to look at these phenomena in regard to isomorphic systems that have to be evaluated by their respective merits, and not by how well they fare as theoretical substrates for one another.

On the basis of this crucial distinction, epistemological and ethical pitfalls can be avoided when it comes to automated information processing. In epistemology computer programs serve two functions: (a) As testing procedures which do not, however, provide additional support for a theory, since they only help the scientists with the mechanics and logistics of a theory. In this context, autoverification is rampant that is comparable to Hugo Dingler's operationalism, in that a program that does not add anything to the theory is used as supportive evidence for the theory, and (b) as autonomous systems, they provide us with a different form of intelligent behavior that might turn out to be isomorphic to the human system and, taken on its own merits, shed light on the essence of intelligence.

Ethical implications of successful intelligent programs concern the wrong assumption that, once we can put intelligence into a computer, man will be viewed as another mechanical construct, and, transcending this problem, the ultimate fear that machines will supersede mankind. Machines that respond to humans in a natural language seem to pose a particular threat to the uniqueness of man. Only a clear understanding of the function of language in our world can dispense with these erroneous fears.

Language is a symbol system that facilitates the transfer of information via meaning. It serves as a vehicle to help us realize structural dependencies, see connections between phenomena, and function in an ever-increasingly complex environment. Computer programs will use language in the same capacity as humans: to organize data, to facilitate its storage, and to access it appropriately and efficiently. Therefore, natural language understanding programs serve useful purposes, while at the same time making us understand the function of language in the communication process. The 'Almighty God of the Mechanical' will only be a threat if mankind ceases to use language as a manifestation of intelligence.

REFERENCES

DRETSKE, FRED. 1981. The flow of information. Cambridge, MA: MIT Press.

DREYFUS, HERBERT. 1979. What computers can't do. Revised ed. The limits of artificial intelligence. New York: Harper and Row.

FODOR, JERRY. 1979. The language of thought. Cambridge, MA: Harvard University Press.

HAYES, PHILIP, and GEORGE MOURADIAN. 1981. Flexible parsing. American Journal of Computational Linguistics 7.4.232–242.

NEISSER, ULRIC. 1976. Cognition and reality. Principles and implications of cognitive psychology. San Francisco: W. H. Freeman.

OBERMEIER, KLAUS. 1982a. Die Bedeutung des Zweifels als Grundlage des Wissens in der Existenzphilosophie. Language and ontology. Proceedings of the 6th International Wittgenstein Symposium, ed. by Elisabeth Leinfellner and Adolf Hübner-Werner. Vienna: Hölder-Pichler.

———. 1982b (in press). Wittgenstein on language and artificial intelligence. The Chinese room thought experiment revisisted. Synthese. Dordrecht: Reidel.

PUTNAM, HILARY. 1960. Minds and machines. Minds and machines, ed. by A. R. Anderson, 72–97. Englewood Cliffs, NJ: Prentice Hall.

REDDY, D. R., L. D. ERMAN, R. D. FENNELL, and R. B. NEELEY. 1973. The Hearsay speech system: An example of the recognition process. Advance Papers, Third International Joint Conference on Artificial Intelligence, 185–193.

SHANK, ROGER. 1973. Identification of conceptualization underlying natural language: Computer models of thought and language, ed. by R. Schank & K. Colby. San Francisco: Freeman.

———. 1975. Conceptual information processing. Amsterdam: North Holland.

SCRIVEN, MICHAEL. 1953. The mechanical concept of mind. Minds and machines, ed. by A. R. Anderson, 31–42. Englewood Cliffs, NJ: Prentice Hall.

SEARLE, JOHN. 1980. Minds brains and programs. The behavioral and brain sciences 3. Cambridge, England: Cambridge University Press.

SIMON, HERBERT. 1969. The sciences of the artificial. Cambridge, MA: MIT Press.

WALTZ, D. L. 1981. Toward a detailed model of processing for language describing the physical world. Proceedings of the 7th IJCAI-=International Joint Conference on Artificial Intelligence. 1, 1–6.

WILKS, YORICK. 1976. Philosophy of language: Computational semantics. An introduction to artificial intelligence and natural language comprehension, ed. by E. Charniak & Y. Wilks. Amsterdam: North Holland.

WINOGRAD, TERRY. 1972. Understanding natural language. New York: Academic Press.

PART II

COMPUTER-ASSISTED INSTRUCTION

ELEVEN

Designing Effective Computer-Assisted Courseware

Stephanie Paulauskas
Susanne Holunga
Department of National Defence Language School, Canada

Microcomputer technology has created a revolution in the classroom, permanently altering the traditional educational framework. No longer is the debate in educational circles over whether the new technology should be applied to education, for its integration into the school curriculum is now seen as inevitable and even necessary. The new and growing concern is with the development and evaluation of quality courseware.

While we hear of great strides being made in computer hardware, little is being said about developments in computer courseware, except that it cannot keep pace with the advancements made in the former. Questions concerning the nature and the effectiveness of the courseware developed have rarely been considered, even up to now. The general consensus is that the microcomputer is an effective instructional tool. No such general consensus exists with regards to the instructional effectiveness of courseware. But perhaps it is with good reason, since much of the existing commercial courseware is developed by computer programmers and teachers who not only lack expertise in instructional design, but also remain far removed from courseware purchasers and the target audience for whom the materials are intended.

Such lack of cooperation and coordination amongst producers, purchasers, and target audiences, coupled with a lack of expertise in instructional design, has led to the development of a plethora of inappropriate and poor quality courseware. Further, this inefficient use of, or misapplication of, microcomputer technology will persist unless remedial action is taken to reverse the trend. This paper, thus, addresses itself to the specific problems of courseware design and offers an approach to designing Computer-Assisted Instruction (CAI) courseware that is both instructionally effective and aesthetically appealing.

Clearly, though, upgrading the quality of CAI courseware will require more than smiply establishing links amongst producers, purchasers, and target audiences, or hiring teachers or curriculum specialists to write programs. For, although these measures may prove effective in ameliorating the courseware dilemma somewhat, they can never be considered as more than mere stopgap solutions. A more broadly-based, fundamental solution to the dilemma is required if uniformly high quality standards in courseware design, both in terms of format and instructional content, are to emerge. In other words, a holistic and systematic response is needed. Such a response is embodied in the principles and practices of instructional design of the systems approach. The design process (see Figure 1), whether conducted on the macro level (the instructional system level) or the micro level (the course level), is complex, but it answers only three questions as Robert Mager (1975) has succinctly summarized them:

> Where am I going? (objectives)
> How will I get there? (strategy)
> How will I know when I've arrived? (evaluation)

It cannot be expected, however, that a thorough knowledge of the instructional design process alone is the perfect panacea that will see an end to the production of poor quality courseware. For that end can only come about if instructional design expertise is wedded to computer expertise (Gleason 1981). Without an understanding of the computer's potential and capacity, even the most carefully and effectively designed courseware can prove to be an instructional disaster because of its unadaptability to the microcomputer. In order to be truly instructional and effective, courseware must be designed specifically with the microcomputer in mind. That is not to say that courseware developers must be both expert instructional designers and computer programming experts, although such a combination would be ideal. Practically, it is doubtful that there will ever be sufficient numbers of individuals with training in both these highly specialized fields. As a result, the most viable solution, which has already been implemented, is the establishment of professional organizations or consortia, like CONDUIT, MICROSIFT, and MECC, made up of experts in instructional design, computer programming, various subject matters, and evaluation, to act as clearinghouses for the barrage of software and courseware flooding the market. With the establishment of more organizations modelled after the three consortia, there is little doubt that much of the low quality courseware that is able to find its way into the market place will eventually be eliminated. But such an eventuality depends on the coordinated and concerted actions of many people.

The instructional design process, though not a panacea in itself, is nonetheless crucial to the development of quality courseware, since it provdes the guidelines necessary to establish uniform standards of high quality. And by applying the instructional design process to the design of CAI materials, indeed to all instructional courseware, it becomes at once obvious how efficacious it is in ensuring the production of high quality materials, both in terms of instructional content and format, as the remainder of this paper will show.

The instructional design perspective, essentially the design process, is a problem-solving one. That is, an instructional outcome, whatever it may be, is looked upon as a solution to an instructional problem, a problem being defined as a discrepancy between the actual outcome and the anticipated outcome defined by the aims of the instructional system (Romiszowski 1981, Briggs 1977).

Should a discrepancy occur, it is fully analyzed at the first stage of the process

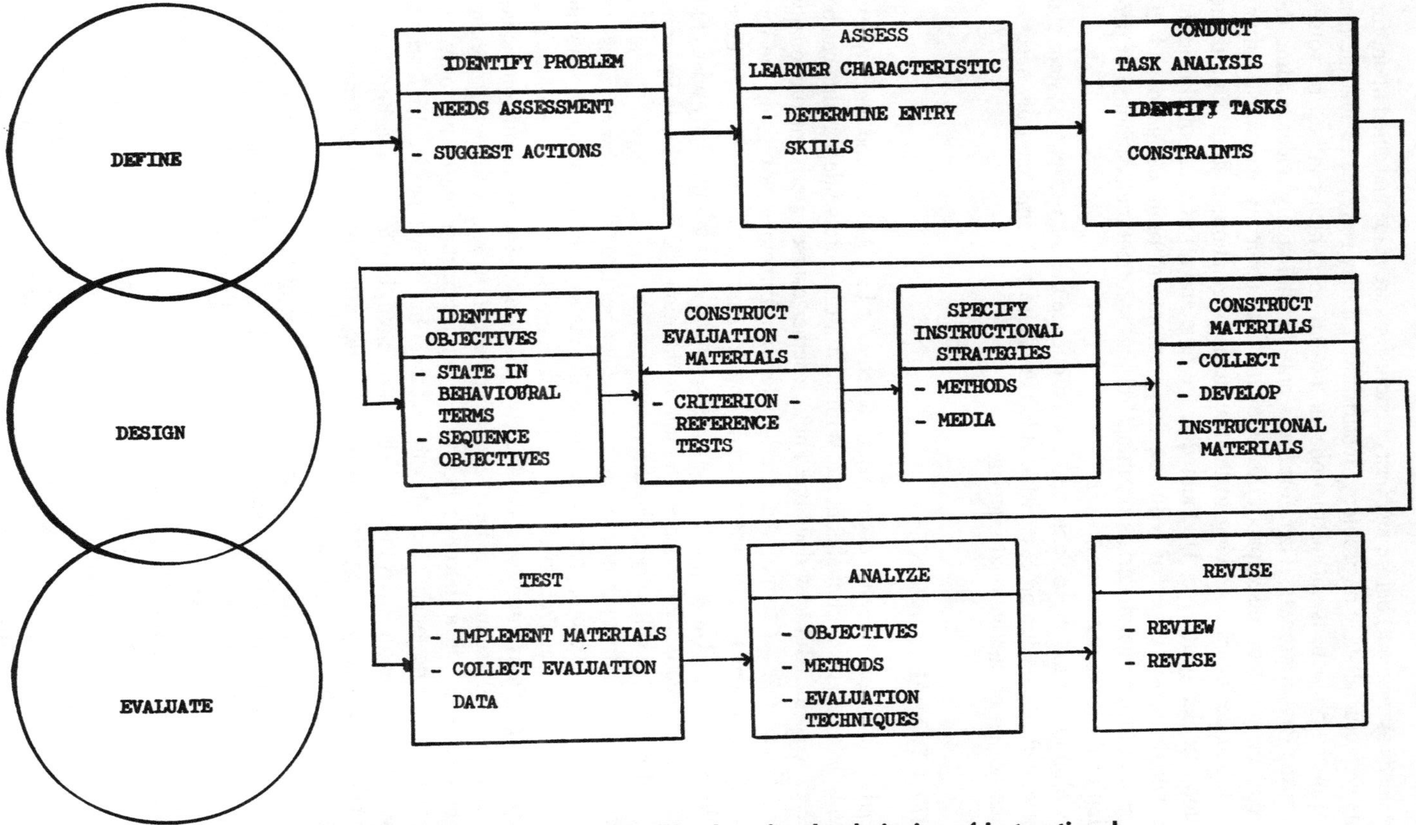

Figure 1. Format and content flowchart for the designing of instructional courseware.

(i.e., needs assessment) before any hasty conclusions are made and acted upon, for, at this very crucial stage of problem identification, it may be revealed that the true nature of the problem is not instructional at all, but one which can best be solved outside the design process. Therefore, it is only by thoroughly understanding the nature of the problem (discrepancy), by viewing it systemically and holistically as instructional designers do owing to their systems orientation, that an appropriate solution can clearly emerge. Undoubtedly, the time and effort spent on this initial stage will have the effect of reducing the development of ill-designed and ill-conceived instructional materials resulting from an incorrect understanding or perception of the problems to be solved.

By eliminating those problems best solved outside the instructional system and hence outside the design process, what is left are those problems that truly necessitate the design of instructional materials.

INSTRUCTIONAL CONTENT

Unequivocably, good quality courseware, whether it be CAI or some other types, depends on sound instructional content. Without it, little worthwhile learning can be expected to result. But how does one know whether courseware is instructionally sound? What makes it sound? Are there underlying principles governing the formulation and presentation of instructional content? And if there are, how are those principles revealed? These questions are systematically and scientifically answered by the instructional design process, and not by intuition and subjective judgments, as is, unfortunately, still very often the case.

With the shift in focus in education from the teacher and the teaching process to the learner and the learning process, it is woefully inadequate to make judgments on the soundness or effectiveness of instructional content based on such nebulous and amorphous criteria as intuition and subjective judgments. Sound instructional content, and especially sound CAI instructional content, if its aim is to increase learning, mut be based on a thorough knowledge and understanding of not only the subject matter to be taught, but also the learner, his or her needs, the learning process, and communications theory. What is required, in effect, is a technology of instruction, technology being defined as a holistic, scientific, and systematic approach to the solution of problems.

The instructional design process is in every sense of the word a technological process; in fact, it is the only technological process available to solve instructional problems which more and more require technological solutions.

Learner Characteristics

The first essential prerequisite in the design of effective courseware content is that it must be based on learner characteristics such as level of intelligence, entry skills, maturity, motivation, reading ability, socioeconomic status, age, and attention span. The more details the profile of learner characteristics a design is able to obtain, the better equipped he or she is to design instruction most suited to the group's needs and level of competence, thereby ensuring optimal learning.

Based on the profile obtained, the designer is then able to make decisions on the appropriate level of language he or she must use, the length of the program or lesson, the type of lesson (e.g., drill and practice, tutorial, or simulation), the most appropriate kinds of activities, the number and nature of prompts, the extent of learner control, and the extent of interactiveness between the learner and the computer.

Task Analysis

Effective content design is also dependent upon a thorough analysis of the tasks involved in acquiring the intended learning outcomes established by the needs assessment. These all-inclusive learning outcomes, according to Gagné (1977), can be categorized into the following five domains: verbal information, intellectual skills, cognitive strategies, motor skills, and attitudes (see Table 1). Moreover, these outcomes, and the nine external events of instruction with their corresponding internal processes of instruction (see Table 2), are not artibrarily arrived at; they are derived from research and theories of learning (Gagné, 1981). Understanding instructional tasks within the framework presented by Gagné enables the instructional designer to structure his or her learning environment in order to ensure that both meaningful and intended learning outcomes result. Whether the designer accepts Gagné's taxonomy or chooses some other, for example that of Bloom, to aid in conducting his or her task analysis, this process is nonetheless essential in delineating, in concrete and understandable terms, the knowledge and skills that must necessarily be developed to achieve the intended outcomes.

At this stage as well, the designer not only identifies the relevant tasks to perform, but sequences them hierarchically so that tasks requiring the acquisition of simpler skills are presented before the more complex ones. It must be remembered, though, that often a designer does not have sufficient knowledge of the subject matter to be able to adequately analyze and sequence the tasks and the skills involved. Consequently, at this point in the process, the designer must work with subject matter experts, who can reveal the inherent structure of the subject to be

Table 1. Gagné's (1977) five domains of the learning outcomes.

Learning Outcome	Examples
1. Verbal information	Stating the components of a simple sentence
2. Intellectual skill	Showing how to do the following:
Discrimination	Distinguishing a sentence fragement from a simple sentence
Concrete concept	Identifying the components of a simple sentence
Defined concept	Classifying a group of words as a simple sentence
Rule	Writing a simple sentence
Higher-order rule	Generating rules for punctuating a sentence, given various kinds of simple sentences
3. Cognitive strategy	Planning and developing a topic for an expository paragraph
4. Attitude	Choosing writing as a preferred mode of expression
5. Motor skill	Printing exercises

Table 2. Gagné's (1977) internal learning process with corresponding external instructional events.

Internal Learning Process	External Instructional Event
1. Alertness	1. Gaining attention
2. Expectancy	2. Informing learner of lesson objective
3. Retrieval to working memory	3. Stimulating recall of prior learning
4. Selective perception	4. Presenting stimuli with distinctive features
5. Semantic encoding	5. Guiding learning
6. Retrieval and responding	6. Eliciting performance
7. Reinforcement	7. Providing informative feedback
8. Cueing retrieval	8. Assessing performance
9. Generalizing	9. Enhancing retention and learning transfer

taught and ensure that the instructional content of the CAI lesson or program is presented in a coherent and meaningful way.

Objectives

As a direct result of the task analysis, the designer is in a position to establish the objectives of the CAI lesson or program, state them precisely in behavioral terms, and sequence them hierarchically from simple to more complex. Understandably, it is essential to state objectives in terms of observable behaviors; it would be impossible, otherwise, to determine whether the objectives should be precisely stated to mean exactly the same thing to everyone.

To ensure uniformity and avoid ambiguity, a standardized procedure for constructing objectives must be followed. Such a procedure has been established by many authors (Gagné and Briggs 1974, Mager 1975, Popham 1969), and although authors differ somewhat in their prescriptions for designing objectives, each author's prescription contains certain criterial elements that must be present in all objectives. These criterial elements include an action verb that expresses the intended observable behaviour (e.g., states, writes, names) within one of the three domains of learning outcomes (cognitive, affective, or psychomotor), the standard performance required (most often mastery, as defined by the nature of the learning tasks) and the conditions under which the performance is to be carried out. A typical example of an objective is the following:

> Given a topic, the student will be able to write a clear and coherent paragraph using a topic sentence, developmental sentences, and a concluding sentence within one half hour.

Assessment Instruments

Based on the objectives, assessment instruments in the form of criterion-referenced tests, or tests designed to measure an explicit set of objectives can be devised. Criterion-references tests are constructed at this point in the model because they correspond on a one-to-one basis with the objective; that is, the performance required in the objective must match the performance required in the test item (Dick and Carey 1978). Moreover, with the test items already constructed, they can serve as a guide to instructional designers in developing an appropriate instructional strategy. The development and inclusion of tests applicable to objectives, and the definition of mastery level for each objective, is a vital step in the development of materials, for they provide the means for evaluating the CAI lessons or program itself as well as the performance of the individual learners (Gagné and Briggs 1974). On the basis of the test results, revisions can be made to improve upon the final product.

To accurately assess student progress or mastery, an instructional designer would be wise to administer multiple tests at various points in the lessons or program. For example, an entry-skills test is useful to administer before instruction to determine whether the learner possesses the necessary prerequisite skills to receive the instruction. Pre- and post-tests are two very common and excellent assessment instruments for measuring the objectives taught in the lesson or program. Finally, test items can be constructed and inserted throughout the lesson or program to assess performance and provide the learner with immediate remedial instruction, should he or she wish to branch into it.

Instructional Strategy

Having completed the five previous steps, the CAI instructional designer is able to use the information to select and sequence the steps that will lead to successful achievement of the skills and knowledge prescribed in the instructional objectives. In addition, as there is no one correct sequencing of steps to fit all learning situations, an appropriate strategy must be developed based on the nature of the subject matter; that is, its inherent logical structure, known teaching strategies, notably discovery learning (Bruner 1960), expository learning (Ausubel 1960), backward chaining (Gilbert 1971), learning hierarchies (Gagné 1970), the algorithm and heuristic approaches, and spiral sequencing (Bruner 1960), the capacity of the medium with its unique features, and the creative insights and innovations of the designer.

The learner strategy for sequencing learning in a CAI lesson or program need not conform to any one particular formula, as long as it is logically organized and meaningful (Ausubel 1978). However, it seems that Gagné's hierarchical model of learning, which describes the process of learning in terms of an information processing, has proved to be the most useful and adaptable, particularly in developing individualized instructional materials for various media. The nine external events of instruction are related specifically to those processes which most cognitive theorists favoring the information processing view of learning assume are essential for efficient acquisition and retention of knowledge and skills. Specific guidelines for designing CAI materials, based on the learning outcomes most frequently occurring in CAI, have been comprehensively outlined by R. Gagné, W. Wager, and A. Rojas (1981).

Instructional Materials

Using the instructional strategy developed in the previous step as a guideline, the designer can then produce appropriate materials. However, if CAI materials are available at a reasonable cost or if existing materials can be modified, it may be more cost-effective in the long run to purchase new materials or modify existing ones rather than develop them. For it has been estimated that at least 100 hours' worth of development time is needed to produce a 1-hour CAI lesson (Wager 1981). A decision on whether to purchase, modify, or develop CAI materials must take into consideration such factors as the type of learning outcomes, available resources both physical and human, the availability of relevant existing materials, and the instructional environment.

Formative Evaluation

Once the CAI materials have been presented, it is essential to evaluate them in order to determine their instructional effectiveness. Based on the data generated from such formative evaluation tools as surveys, questionnaires, tests, observation records, and checklists (see Table 3), revisions can be made to ensure that the final product is free of defects. The formative evaluation process is characteristically informal (Gagné and Briggs 1974); thus, it varies quite widely. However, despite variations in collecting procedures, certain fundamental kinds of data are sought in all formative evaluations. They include information about the way in which the materials are exploited, the extent to which the students and teachers follow the specified procedures, the difficulties encountered in conducting the lesson, the degree of student interest and motivation, and the extent to which the students were successful in achieving the objectives of the lesson.

Once the data have been collected and interpreted, they determine whether the CAI lesson or program can be kept as is, revised, reformulated, or discarded (Gagné and Briggs 1974).

INSTRUCTIONAL FORMAT

Besides sound instructional content, effective CAI courseware depends, to a great extent, on the way in which the content is presented; that is, it depends on format. For no matter how effective the instructional content of a CAI lesson is, its effect on learning and retention will be inhibited if it is inappropriately presented. Research on learning has consistently and clearly shown that learning and retention of new information is significantly affected by its organizational structure (Ausubel 1960, Bruner, 1960, Bartlett 1932, Anderson 1977). Specifically, the literature has shown almost conclusively that instructional content must be organized in a way that builds upon the learners' existing knowledge base. In that way, the learnability of the content is increased because it is made meaningful to the learner.

The research is less conclusive about formatting, however, as no optimal organizational patterns or principles have emerged. Despite this deficiency, it is generally recognized that optimal organizational presentation depends on the nature of the

Table 3. Checklist for the evaluation of CAT materials.

CONTENT	YES	NO	N/A
1. OBJECTIVES ARE STATED CLEARLY.			
2. ENTRY SKILLS ARE STATED CLEARLY.			
3. INSTRUCTIONS ARE STATED CLEARLY.			
4. TYPE OF LESSON - DRILL AND PRACTISE - IS STATED.			
TUTORIAL			
SIMULATION			
5. LESSON MATCHES THE OBJECTIVES.			
6. THERE ARE A VARIETY OF ACTIVITIES AND A CHOICE OF CONTENT.			
7. LESSONS ARE INTERACTIVE.			
8. TESTS HAVE SPECIFIC PURPOSES.			
9. TESTS ARE MATCHED TO OBJECTIVES.			
10. CONTENT IS APPROPRIATE FOR INTENDED AUDIENCE.			
11. CONTENT HAS LEARNER CONTROL.			
12. FACTS AND CONCEPTS ARE SEQUENCED.			
13. CONTENT IS ACCURATE, CORRECT, AND COMPLETE.			
14. FEEDBACK IS COMPLETE.			
15. CONTENT IS APPROPRIATE LENGTH.			
16. REINFORCEMENT IS MEANINGFUL.			
17. PROMPTS ARE APPROPRIATELY USED.			
18. PROMPTS ARE POLITE AND PERSONAL.			
19. CONTENT IS COMMUNICATIVE.			
20. CONTENT FITS INTO EXISTING CURRICULUM.			

instructional materials, the target audience, and the type of medium (Salomon 1979).

With respect to designing CAI materials, it is essential to adapt the instructional materials to the unique features and capabilities of the computer. A complete lack of regard for the medium's potential will inevitably lead to the creation of materials that are ill-suited for the computer, thereby reducing the effectiveness of both the materials and the medium. Clearly, maximum efficiency and effectiveness depend on a sophisticated knowledge of both instructional design principles and computer presentation strategies.

CAI courseware writers can facilitate learning by making appropriate and judicious use of a variety of cueing devices offered by most computers (see Table 4). These devices can serve many purposes. For example, in designing course ware for children, extensive use of graphics, animation, and color in place of text can greatly enhance learning because of its ability to arouse and sustain interest and motivation, two requisite conditions of learning (Gagné 1977). Moreover, these as well as other nonverbal cueing devices, such as graphs, charts, diagrams, etc. can not only serve as powerful attention devices, directing the child and adult learners' attention to the essential concepts to be learned, but also facilitate the retention of concepts presented, since iconic or pictorial memory is less resistant to forgetting than verbal memory (Duchastel 1978, Fleming 1979). Finally, the inclusion of a menu can function as an advance organizer, preparing the learners' cognitive structure to process the forthcoming instructional material more effectively.

Other essential formatting considerations that directly affect the learnability and retention of instructional materials are listed in Table 4. Most are common-sense recommendations (e.g., 3, 4, and 6), but the others relate specifically to the unique features of the computer. The computer is especially well-designed to offer learners individual instruction through its branching and feedback capabilities, so, to ensure maximum individualization, extensive use of these two capabilities should be made.

CONCLUSION

Designing CAI lessons can no longer be done by intuition or based on ambiguous purposes and casual subjective judgments. Since a computer-based system is a highly sophisticated technological tool, it logically follows that a highly-sophisticated technological approach to designing CAI lessons must be applied. The systems-based instructional design process provides just such an approach. It is a process of systematic planning that establishes a way to examine instructional problems and a procedure for solving them as well as for evaluating the results. It is a flexible process that involves skilled personnel: designers, teachers, subject-matter experts, curriculum experts, students, programmers, and technicians. Armed with the scientific approach outlined in this paper, it seems an almost inevitable result that highly qualified personnel will produce quality materials in terms of both instructional content and format.

Table 4. Computer cueing devices for courseware design.

FORMAT	YES	NO	N/A
1. A VARIETY OF CUEING DEVICES ARE INCORPORATED:			
a. COLOUR AND COLOUR CODING			
b. GRAPHICS AND ANIMATION			
c. FLASHING			
d. INVERSE			
e. PAUSES			
f. MENUS			
g. SPACING			
h. SOUND			
i. SCROLLING			
j. NON-VERBAL DEVICES (TABLES, GRAPHS, DIAGRAMS, ETC.)			
2. LESSONS ARE SELF-PACED WITH AMPLE BRANCHING			
3. INSTRUCTIONS ARE CONSISTENT			
4. REQUESTED INPUT IS CONSISTENT			
5. PROMPTS ARE USED			
6. LESSONS ARE EASY TO USE			

REFERENCES

ANDERSON, RICHARD C., RAND J. SPIRO, and WILLIAM E. MONTAGUE (eds.) 1977. Schooling and the acquisition of knowledge. Hillsdale, NJ: Erlbaum.

AUSUBEL, DAVID PAUL. 1978). Educational psychology: A cognitive view (2nd ed.) New York: Holt, Rinehart and Winston.

AUSUBEL, DAVID PAUL. 1960. The use of advance organizers in the learning and retention of meaningful verbal material. Journal of Educational Psychology 51.267–272.

BARTLETT, F. C. 1932. Remembering. London: Cambridge University Press.

BLOOM, B. S. (ed.). 1956. Taxonomy of educational objectives. New York: David McKay Company, Inc.
BRIGGS, LESLIE J. and WALTER W. WAGER. 1979. Handbook of procedures for design of instruction. Pittsburgh: American Institute for Research.
———. 1977. Instructional design. Englewood Cliffs, NJ: Educational Technology Publications, Inc.
BRUNER, J. S. 1960. The process of education. Cambridge, MA: Harvard University Press.
DICK, W., and L. CAREY. 1978. The Systematic Design of Instruction. Glenview, IL: Scott, Foresman and Company.
DUCHASTEL, P. 1978. Illustrating instructional texts. Educational Technology 11.36–39.
FLEMING, M. 1979. On pictures in educational research. Instructional Science 8.235–252.
GAGNÉ, ROBERT MILLS. 1977. The conditions of learning (3rd ed.). New York: Holt, Rinehart and Winston.
———. 1970. The conditions of learning (2nd ed.) New York: Holt, Rinehart and Winston.
———, and LESLIE J. BRIGGS. 1974. Principles of instructional design. New York: Holt, Rinehart and Winston.
———, WALTER W. WAGER, and ALICIA ROJAS. 1981. Planning and authoring computer-assisted instruction lessons. Educational Technology 21.17–26.
GILBERT, T. F. 1970. Mathetics: The technology of education. Instructional design: Readings, ed. by M. D. Merrill Englewood Cliffs, NJ: Prentice-Hall.
GLEASON, G. 1981. Microcomputers in education: The state of the art. Educational Technology 21.7–18.
KEMP, J. 1977. Instructional design. Belmont, CA: Fearon-Pitman Publishers, Inc.
KIDD, M., and G. HOLMES. 1982. Courseware design. Computers and Education 6.299–303.
MAGER, R. 1975. Preparing instructional objectives. Palo Alto, CA: Featon Publishers.
MARKLE, S. 1969. Good frames and bad: A grammar of frame writing. New York: John Wilby and Sons, Inc.
POPHAM, W. (ed.). 1969. Instructional objectives. Chicago: Rand McNally.
ROMISZOWSKI, A. J. 1981. Designing instructional system: Decision-making in course planning and curriculum design. London: Kogan Page.
SALOMON, G. 1979. Interaction of media, cognition and learning. San Francisco: Jossey-Bass.
WAGER, W. 1982. The software evaluation dilemma. AEDS Monitor April. 5–6, 10–12.

TWELVE

The MENTOR System: An Answer to Problems of Computer-Aided Language Teaching

Roland Sussex
University of Melbourne
Victoria, Australia

University language departments in Australia are currently going through the same financial malaise which has been affecting language departments in North America and Europe—albeit slightly later, and probably not to such a radical extent. As funds decline, nontenured positions are not filled, and new positions are not advertised. And yet in Australia the overall picture of language teaching is not wholly one of decline; while there has been a steady though undramatic drop in the numbers of students taking 'established' languages like French, the 'community languages'—that is, the languages used by the major immigrant ethnic groups in Australia—have continued to grow. This increase has been particularly marked in the last five years, when community languages have become available for Higher School Certificate, and in a small but growing number of universities. With declining funding, however, it is impossible for a department to maintain its teaching in traditional terms, let alone increase it. This was the familiar problem which led us, in the Department of Russian at the University of Melbourne, to become involved in Computer-Assisted Instruction (CAI).

There is not much of a tradition of CAI in Australia. Some departments in our 19 universities have acquired software packaged from overseas—usually from the U.S.A. or England—for special purposes like teaching statistics to psychologists, or harmony and counterpoint to students of music. There are only two projects concerned with language-teaching CAI—one at the University of Queensland, which has a bias towards microcomputers, and our MENTOR Project at the University of Melbourne, which is associated with recently founded projects in French at Monash and La Trobe Universities. These projects have a common need for tutorial and drill hours for elementary and intermediate language teaching, and we need this facility as soon as possible.

For some reason, Russian has fared rather better than most other languages in the CAI arena—despite the difficulties of handling the Cyrillic alphabet on hardware which was usually designed to manage English. There are a number of people in the U.S.A. who are concerned with developing Russian CAI: Barry Scheer at

Dartmouth; Walter Tuman at Hollins College; Joseph van Campen at the Stanford Project; Constance Curtin at the University High School, University of Illinois; Gil Rappaport at the University of Texas at Austin; Ed Purcell at U.S.C.; Ernest Scatton at SUNY—Albany; and Dick Leed at Cornell. And of course there is some Russian instructional material on PLATO. But all these teaching materials suffer from the usual difficulties of portability between hardware installations, and suitability for different classes of students in different places and under different conditions. Our initial intention was to use ready-made courseware. But none of the material which we viewed quite met our requirements. And altering programs to fit in with our teaching patterns was altogether too expensive and complicated. A particularly clear example of this difficulty occurred with some otherwise most attractive programs developed by Corbett and Ahmad at the University of Surrey in England. They have four programs for teaching Russian morphology and morpho-syntax. These programs are written in FORTRAN 77 as once-off lessons. Altering these programs is impossible for anyone but an experienced programmer with a knowledge of both Russian and FORTRAN programming.

We therefore began to look at authoring systems. There are now quite a few of these about, including the system developing at the University of Leeds in England, PILOT, and several others. We were particularly interested in PLATO, since its size and sophistication makes it very much a benchmark in this business. But full mastery of the PLATO authoring package takes about 240 hours at the terminal. None of the teachers in our department, or in our university, had such quantities of time to spend—particularly in a faculty which shows great resistance to mechanical aids in the humanities! And there was an additional problem of cost: PLATO is far too expensive for our purposes. The University of Delaware has made a firm commitment to PLATO, and with coordinated policy comes strength and support—of both hardware and software. But our university system is just entering this arena. It was unwilling to invest such enormous sums of money in either PLATO hardware or software, and the teaching staff were very dubious about the amount of time required to master the authoring system. Having done some preliminary estimates of costs and goals, we decided to develop a compact system ourselves.

The initial requirements of the MENTOR System were these:

1. portability
2. accessibility to teachers
3. generality: the ability to handle not only foreign language teaching, but also other subjects
4. versatility: the ability to handle foreign language character sets, and preferably graphics and colour as well
5. general user-friendliness
6. in principle, convertible to use on microcomputers, which dominate secondary school use in Australia
7. a MENTOR language of about 20 terms for structuring and presenting the lessons, written in something close to plain English, for teachers to create their lessons

8. a fully menu-driven author package, for teachers with no experience of computer use
9. extensive reporting facilities, so that the system could not only report on student progress and error patterns, but also act as a base for research into CAI itself
10. modular design, allowing easy extension and development

This kind of list is familiar to most people who have developed or used CAI systems. What is more unusual about MENTOR is that it is a general-purpose system which began from a humanities base; we got it working in 6 months, and into teaching use in 8 months; and the total development cost is so far under $5,000, consisting entirely of programming charges. Almost all the work has been done by myself and Stephen Young, of the university's Software Contracts Group. The system is virtually being donated to other university users in Australia, and the University of Melbourne is willing to offer the system on a similar basis to selected universities in North America and Europe.

MENTOR is up and running. It is less powerful than PLATO and DEC's DIMENSION, but is probably more powerful than the majority of the other authoring systems currently available. It consists of the elements outlined below:

1. The MENTOR Language, a set of 20 commands in plain English, accompanied by parameters for certain lesson structures
2. The AUTHOR Program, a menu-driven interactive lesson-creation program which writes the lesson text files for the inexperienced teacher
3. The STUDENT Program, which runs the lessons
4. The AUTHORIZED STUDENTS FILE, which screens students for admission to MENTOR sessions
5. The REPORTING FILES, which collect information about the performance of the students and the lessons, and write the results into reporting files for the use of the teacher and researcher
6. The character-set library
7. The graphics library

If the teacher does not use the AUTHOR Program to create lessons, he or she can use standard DEC editors (EDT, etc.) or commands like CREATE. Files are displayed with EDT, TY, or through a special SCROLL program which allows scanning either backwards or forwards.

This configuration allows us to perform a variety of teaching functions:

1. initiate a lesson
2. load character sets
3. display a screen of text
4. initiate one or two types of interactive question-answer routines with the student
5. display a recurring message with each question
6. ask a question

7. check for a specified right answer (absolute match)
8. check for a specified right included answer
9. check for a specified wrong answer (absolute match)
10. check for a specified wrong included answer
11. display messages with any right or wrong answer
12. display a default message following an unspecified wrong answer
13. keep score
14. display a score
15. assess the student's progress in the most recent question-answer session
16. assess the student's progress over the whole lesson
17. insert a nonprinting comment
18. record errors made by the student
19. allow a student to retake a question
20. record retakes
21. record a variety of information about the progress of the student, the errors made during the lesson, and the effectiveness of the questions
22. initiate a branching message dialogue with the student; this message structure can be nested to any depth
23. include a text file from outside the lesson
24. include a graphic file from outside the lesson
25. terminate a lesson

The driver program—the STUDENT Program—is written in FORTRAN 77, with the exception of one segment which, for reasons of recursive routines, is written in PASCAL. The total package contains about 6,000 lines of source code, and allows lesson files of up to 2,000 lines (160,000 bytes). The system has been designed on a VAX 11/780 computer running under VMS. This chioce was partly dictated to us by the mainframes available at the University of Melbourne; it also agreed with our intention to keep to a computer of at least middle size for the development phase. so as to avoid being cramped by the limitations of micros. And the choice of the VAX ensures a reasonable degree of portability. Although MENTOR will support any VT52 or ANSI terminal, we have concentrated on the GIGI, which allows an efficient means of handling graphics, character sets, and colour. We have used the DEC character set editor to generate character sets for a number of European languages, including Russian; and the DEC graphics editor to produce a number of basic graphic files. The user can implement all these facilities from within the AUTHOR Program under menu-driven control. Or he or she can write lessons with the MENTOR Language, inserting the appropriate GIGI and ReGIS commands in the text of the lesson as he or she goes.

The text of a typical MENTOR lesson, seen from the point of view of the student, appears like this:

```
Bon jour!
Today we are going to test French verbs.
Here are five questions on French verb endings.
                    [Press any key to continue]
```

```
    TEST ON FRENCH VERBS
    Type the correct form of the verb:
    Je (aller, past perfect) à la maison
:
[student types]
suis allé
Correct
Current score: 1 out of 1
```

The lesson text file for this sequence looks like this:

```
.LESSON.
FRENCH VERBS
.LOADCHARSET,FRENCH.
.SCREEN.
   ^NBonjour!
   ^OToday we are going to test French verbs.
   Here are five questions on French verb endings
.QDIALOGUE,5,5,C,YES.
TEST ON FRENCH VERBS
.RECPROMPT.
Type the correct form of the verb:
.QUESTION,1,R,YES,YES.
^NJe (aller, past perfect) à la maison
.RIGHT,suis allé,R.
^OCorrect.
.RIGHT,suis allée,R.
^OCorrect.
```

This lesson contains two 'YES' parameters in the QUESTION command, signalling the recording of retakes and errors. There are four error files on the system. They record information as follows:

- The .LOG file:
- the student's name
- the percent scored
- the date
- The .INS (initial score) FILE:
- the student's name
- whether he or she has been successful (T) or not (F) in the lesson
- the percent score he or she achieved at his or her first attempt
- the number of times he or she has taken the lesson
- The .ERR error FILE:
- the title of the exercise
- the number of each question
- the wrong answers made by the student
- the date
- The .RET retake LOG FILE:
- the title of the exercise

- the number of each question
- the number of initial takes
- the number of correct answers
- the number of wrong answers
- the number of retakes
- the number of correct answers or retakes
- the number of wrong answers on retakes
- the number of other answers on retakes

The MENTOR.AUT file is the authorized students' file. The teacher sets up this file with the names of the students permitted to use the system. If a student enters a nonauthorized name, or a name spelled incorrectly, the system will not allow him or her to take the lesson.

The MENTOR system is currently in teaching use, in a tutorial/drill support role, at the University of Melbourne. We have begun with students of Russian 3, who have sufficient maturity in the language not to be terrified by a new technology. Next year we shall be using the system for elementary and intermediate tutorial and drill sessions in Russian 1–3, for both beginners and nonbeginners. Courseware is being written for French at Monash and La Trobe Universities; and other departments at the University of Melbourne, including the section for English as a Second Language, expect to take up the system early in 1983. The student reaction has been very positive, even though we have been conducting the lessons so far on a trial basis. There is rather more resistance from the teachers. But the secondary teachers are becoming more attracted to the idea of authoring their own lessons. Mathematicians are about to start using the system with the addition of a .CALCULATOR. command, for classes in statistics and complex numbers; and we expect that other departments will shortly follow suit.

The next stages in the development of the MENTOR System have been planned to ensure expansion in two main directions: a broadening of the teaching base of the system, and an increase in the capacity of the MENTOR language.

The broadening of the system's teaching base depends on a number of factors. First, the distribution of the system is being encouraged by the University of Melbourne's policy of virtually donating the system to other educational institutions. This means that copies of MENTOR are already being distributed through a representative part of the tertiary education system in Australia, in return for a sharing of courseware and experimental results. The University is also encouraging such mutual sharing arrangements in North America and Europe, with a view to promoting and coordinating the development of courseware in a wide range of subject areas and teaching contexts. We are organizing a users' group to act as a focus point for this activity. And the University of Melbourne is considering the establishment of a software maintenance contract arrangement, whereby users can have their lessons and software monitored by specialist staff. The university's Software Contracts Group will also undertake contract work for special-purpose extensions to MENTOR for individual users.

The longer-term aims of MENTOR include the investigation of the relation between new educational technology—specifically CAI—and language-teaching policy and implementation, course and curriculum policy, and staffing matters. More immediate aims include the investigation of the properties of the system itself, particularly its interactive aspect: we wish to determine which of the types of interaction with the student are educationally more effective, and what are the ways in which the system is falling short of its expressed goals in terms of educational flexibility and effectiveness. We wish to enhance the reporting functions of MENTOR, not to make it a more omniscient big brother, but rather to increase its ability to function as a source of valuable information to the teacher, and as a research tool and a test base for CAI in general.

Our experience with MENTOR has confirmed some of our worst fears about resistance within the humanities disciplines. In a university which teaches nineteen languages at undergraduate level, only three departments have shown positive interest in using the system, even though we have taken pains to emphasize its supportive role. There is, within the humanities disciplines as a whole—and this applies not only to Australia—a genuine and deeply-rooted suspicion of things electronic. What we all need is something like the British Government's program on computer literacy, which is making some progress in educating the public about the shape of a society structured around the new technology. More than this, however, the educational systems—in Europe and North America, as much as in Australia—need general education in the nature and implications of micro-processor technology, from its technical to its sociological and educational aspects. Our attempts at interesting teachers in the humanities—and subsequently outside the humanities—in Australia have led to a geographically broadly-based interest in MENTOR and its possibilities. Nonetheless, the depth of interest within individual disciplines is sporadic and ill-defined. A real attempt to make the best use of CAI systems will require a more systematic expression of interest, and a more systematic implementation, than we have seen so far.

With these problems in mind, we plan to continue to expand the user-friendly aspect of MENTOR by developing ELE-MENTOR, an ultra-simple version of the MENTOR language. This version of the MENTOR Language will be downwards-compatible, in the sense that by making use of the default values of MENTOR commands, the teacher can construct a lesson with the minimum difficulty in using arguments and other exotica. For instance, the MENTOR command

```
.QUESTION.
```

will function as the equivalent of

```
.QUESTION,1,R,NO,NO.
```

—or, in other words: ask a question, give one point for the correct answer, replace ('R') the question in the stack once it has been used, do not ('NO') record errors, and do not ('NO') record retakes. In our experience, the accessibility of the system's operations to uncertain and fearful teachers is a factor of vital importance.

Our basic position in constructing the MENTOR language was to keep it as simple as possible, so that it will function as a positive interface between the teacher and the system, and not as a barrier to use and implementation. Teachers who have acquired some expertise in using the MENTOR language, first by using AUTHOR, and then through ELE-MENTOR, will be able to progress to handling the full capabilities of the MENTOR language.

Our other main software thrust will be in the direction of making the system more flexible, both in its present terms, and in the variety of educational structures which it can handle. We began by creating a hierarchically-structured language, with five levels of commands. This structure imposed limitations on the types of teaching interaction which the system would support, and also directed the structuring of the software itself. We now perceive that the system itself needs to be more flexible, and in fact less structured. What the system has to do, in other words, is to get away from the interactive dialogue model as we originally conceived it, and to become a more flexible medium. At the present time, the system is fundamentally linear, in the sense outlined by Gagné, Wagner, and Rojas (1981). That is to say, although a question can elicit a number of different controlled and uncontrolled responses, its next step takes it back to a single departure point (see Figure 1). We have already varied this too-highly structured format in two main ways: first, by allowing INCLUDE and GRAPHIC commands; and second, in the message structure. Nonetheless, the text or graphic material introduced into the lesson through these two commands must still obey the syntax of the commands under whose aegis they are introduced. The system's only approach to a genuine branching logic is in the message command, and the structure of nested messages does allow some branching decision-making in the dialogue between the student and the system. However, the provision of more powerful branching technqiues is obviously necessary, not only for enhancing the types of educational strategies which can be modelled with the existing system, but also to make the system capable of handling some types of teaching and learning which are at present conceptually outside its capacity. Note that the addition of branching capabilities will not of itself convert MENTOR from CAI to CDI ('computer-directed instruction') or CMI ('computer-managed instruction'). Our original intention was to provide a teaching support system, and this remains a primary goal for the innovations proposed here, just as it has directed our work so far. Nonetheless, we are looking at the question of adding on CDI structures to MENTOR's underlying CAI architecture. The modular structure of the overall system, and the lines of development which we have followed, should make this development a matter of technical extension rather than radical rebuilding.

In concrete terms, the next step into more complex lesson structures will involve the provision of a finite-state automaton simulation on the system. At the present time, the system is able to emulate experiments in a restricted way, by using the GRAPHIC command to include graphic files from outside the lesson. But the progress through the experiment is still essentially linear, as we remarked above; what is required is an ability to emulate an experiment through a very large number of successive alternative states. This capacity is provided by a finite-state automa-

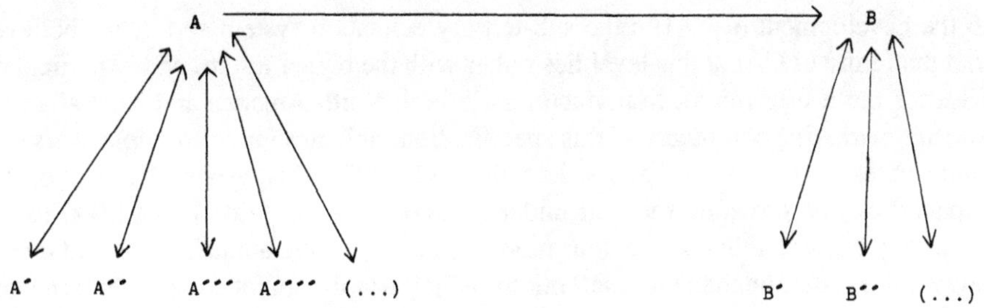

Figure 1. Structural question/answer format.

ton, which allows the system to follow an experiment from one state to another through a finite but possibly quite large number of possible states. If a potentially explosive mixture is distilled at the right temperature, successive states of distillation can be shown; if the heat chosen by the student is too high, an explosion will result. The GRAPHIC command can easily summon a general-purpose explosion piece of graphics from outside the current lesson to make the point with the maximum visual impact.

In a broader educational context, we plan to pursue the adaptation of MENTOR for secondary-school use, and for uses in industry and other areas. These include the application of MENTOR to multi-lingual Prestel-type information services for migrants in Australia, as well as adult migrant education, English as a Second Language, English for Special Purposes, and other related areas. And we shall be exploring hardware applications outside the present configuration of VAX + GIGI. The GIGI is very serviceable, precisely because of its semi-intelligent nature. Although we make no use of the GIGI-resident BASIC, we do make extensive use of the ReGIS graphics command language. The more information that has to be passed explicitly in uncompressed form from the host program—in the form of long and complex vectors for graphics manipulations, or vectors for drawing characters in nonstandard character sets—the longer the lessons will take, and the longer will be the gaps and delays in the presentation of the lesson material. For this reason, a semi-intelligent terminal like the GIGI makes it possible to handle graphics more efficiently, and to store character-sets locally rather than send them from the host as individual vectors on each occasion. In our view, this level of intelligence on the part of the terminal is of significant importance in organizing efficient and effective CAI. MENTOR already supports VT52 and ANSI terminals; we shall be exploring the possibilities of adapting other terminals for MENTOR use, particularly for lessons requiring no graphics or special character sets.

We also expect to have non-VMS versions of MENTOR available fairly soon. A UNIX version is planned, to be followed by RMS, using standard FORTRAN and PASCAL routines, rather than the VMS-specific routines which are employed to a limited extent in the present version. We shall also be looking at smaller mainframes, though probably not of the ordinary micro size represented by Apples and TRS-80's. Whatever the merits of such computers, and in spite of their contribution to the development of CAI in the sub-tertiary education system so far, we believe that the future of CAI at this level lies rather with the bigger micro, and in particular with the multi-user micro. Manufacturers in both North America and Australia are already marketing computers of this specification, able to support multiple users (in some cases in excess of 16) for less than $10,000. This means that computer capacity can be provided for well under $1,000 per user. Add (say) $2,000 for a semi-intelligent terminal and colour monitor, and you have a much faster and more powerful installation than the small micro, which simply cannot compete in terms of versatility. Consequently, we shall be concentrating on a version of MENTOR for a micro of this general specification, with a view to the school which can afford perhaps $12,000 for CAI, and would prefer a multi-user larger micro to stand-alone micros of the smaller variety. It goes without saying that larger numbers of users make the larger micro even more cost-effective in comparison with the smaller micros.

At the present time, MENTOR is limited to keyboard input and screen output. There is nothing stopping users from having PARALLEL installations for audio and video: it is easy to include an instruction on the screen to direct the student to an adjacent cassette recorder, slide projector, or video-tape installation. We eventually plan, however, to interface MENTOR with both audio and video capabilities. Language teachers are already clamoring for comprehension teaching facilities which will combine the display of video tape with structured questions about the material viewed. We are also working on a preliminary model for integrating MENTOR with the CAPASOL Project, a computer-based facility for phonetic analysis, which is also based in the Department of Russian at the University of Melbourne.

No CAI system will succeed without a wide range of courseware. And that courseware must be as portable as possible. Note that MENTOR LESSONS are not hardware-specific: they will run on any installation which is running the MENTOR STUDENT program, since MENTOR lesson files are text files. This is the kind of solution which we think will provide not only for the spread of the system itself, but also—and far more importantly—for the personalization and individualization of education, as well as the democratization of educational resources in an era when manpower is being priced out of the market—just at a time when computers are pricing themselves into contention. MENTOR is deliberately not a teacher replacement, but a teacher support, and an aid to understanding CAI itself. We believe that this system could fill a gap in the current range of CAI software, and that it could form a valuable teaching aid for the new generation of teachers and students who are aware of the potential of CAI, and are willing to put some effort and imagination into making it work.

REFERENCES

GAGNÉ, ROBERT, M., WALTER WAGNER, and ALICIA ROJAS. 1981. Planning and authoring computer-assisted instruction lessons. Educational Technology, Spetember, 17–26.

HOWE, J. A. M., and P. M. ROSS (eds). 1981. Microcomputers in secondary education. London: Kogan Page.

O'NEIL, HAROLD F. (Jr.). 1981. Computer-based instruction: A state of the art assessment. New York: Academic Press.

RUSHBY, N. (ed.). 1981. Readings in computer-based learning. London: Kogan Page.

THIRTEEN

Cohesion in EFL Programs: An Automated Approach to Text Analysis*

Ahmed A. Thabet
Georgetown University

1. BACKGROUND

The current state of linguistic theory has provided us with a heap of broken images in the attempt to give a scientific and objective answer to a very basic and still mysterious question: what is language? Such a scientific answer has been epitomized by various and still controversial models of centrality in linguistic description, namely: the syntactic-centered model of Generative Grammar; the semantic-centered models of Case Grammar and Generative Semantics; and the pragramatic-centered models of Speech Acts, Conversational Implicatures, Discourse Analysis, and Presuppositions.

Proponents of such models are in a turmoil of disagreement with each other, within their own disciplines and among each other's disciplines, the result of which is a hazy picture of linguistic theory which has presented no defined, clear and objective answer to that very basic question: what is language?

However, recent linguistic research marks a shift of emphasis from syntax-centered models to semantic-centered ones. Such a shift of emphasis has been characterized as a shift from linguistic competence—a knowledge of sentences, to communicative competence—a knowledge of how sentences are used in the performance of communicative acts of different kinds (Hymes 1970, Campbell and Wales 1970).

What is most clear is that, even after the emphasis in linguistic research shifted to the communicative aspects of language, both textbook writers and teachers in almost all foreign environments remained language textbook writers and teachers . . . language meaning the grammar and a limited vocabulary of the language concerned. EFL textbook writers have based selecting, grading, sequencing, and presentation of materials on structural criteria of implicitly suggested procedures, and teachers have concentrated on the teaching of sentences as self-contained units. In other words, both have paid little attention to the way sentences are used in combination to form pieces of cohesive texts or stretches of coherent discourse.

* This paper is based on portions taken from the Ph.D. dissertation submitted by the author to the Graduate School of Georgetown University. R. Ross Macdonald is the mentor of this dissertation.

Previous research on the study of English discourse, EFL composition, and EFL courses and syllabuses has left us with the following major problems:

1. A lack of objective criteria for the development or evaluation of instructional materials in foreign language education or research in the teaching of EFL or ESL.
2. A lack of research on the assumed knowledge of students of EFL.
3. A lack of research into automatic analysis of EFL multipurpose texts by computer.
4. A deeply-rooted, sentence-oriented pedagogy which has led teachers and textbook writers to assume that the sentence must be the basic pedagogical unit for foreign language teaching. The result of this has been that most of the tools designed to teach writing are based on the traditional school grammar. Both the rhetoric of a tightly organized paragraph, and the logical presentation of ideas, have remained as foreign to the foreign student as the language of English itself.

The Purpose

The main thrust of this paper focuses on the constraints imposed on Egyptian learners of English by the nature of the EFL programs and pedagogy in Egypt, and on the impact of these constrains on the students' proficiency in EFL.

This paper seeks to answer the following unsolved key questions: (a) are the existing EFL elementary and pre-intermediate programs pedagogically cohesive? (b) how do they help EFL students acquire and adopt the grammar of cohesion, or grammar of composition? and (c) how can we make use of computational linguistics in providing a satisfactory data-base which will yield a conclusive statistical analysis useful in selecting, grading, sequencing, and presenting EFL materials?

To this end, the paper seeks to integrate three autonomous fields of inquiry in linguistics: (a) Textlinguistics on the plane of cohesion, (b) Applied Linguistics on the plane of EFL material preparation and pedagogy, and (c) Computational Linguistics, particularly TXTPRO, a text-processing package for use in computational linguistic work. Collaborative efforts of the scholars of these fields are almost lacking in the literature. The study sets a pattern for such a collaboration and points to its impacts on EFL material preparation and pedagogy.

The Corpus

The voluminous corpus that this research project analyzed with the aid of the computer was excerpted from two major sources: (a) EFL textbooks, and (b) students' compositions.

EFL Textbooks. The textbooks encompass the three EFL instructional program series which are currently taught in the Egyptian public education system: (a) Abdallah et al. (1967/1979), *Living English,* coded as series A (1,2,3); (b) Allen and Mclean (1973/1977), *Progressive Living English,* coded as series B (1,2,3);

and (c) Alexander (1967/1978), *Practice and Progress,* coded as series C (C1 encompasses units 1–36, C2 encompasses units 37–72, and C3 encompasses units 73–96). Series A and Series B are elementary courses and taught in preparatory schools (Junior High), and series C is a pre-intermediate course and taught in secondary schools (Senior High).

All the multipurpose texts that these three EFL series contained were keypunched, verified, and stored for computational analysis.

Students' Compositions. Composition samples were collected on a field trip to Egypt. Two random samples of 230 excerpts each have been selected from two groups for data entry and processing:

Group 1: Students from third-year preparatory school and the first-year secondary school, and

Group 2: Students from third-year secondary school and the first-year of university.

Again, all samples were keypunched, verified, and stored for computational analysis.

Table 1.1 gives the reader a global idea of how voluminous a corpus was prepared for processing and analysis.

In a research project of this size, the preparation of text in a form which can be read by the computer is a major task. Keypunching of all EFL multipurpose texts and composition samples was undertaken by the Georgetown Language Processing Center (LPC) punch operators. Special programming was done by Leonard Shaefer, the Executive Director of LPC and developer of TEXTPRO, the computer package used in the analysis of data. Academic guidance was provided by R. Ross Macdonald, the mentor of my dissertation and the Director of the LPC.

Computational Linguistics

The study was carried out with the aid of TXTPRO. This is a text-processing package for use in computational linguistics. The TXTPRO program is written in PL/1. It has been compiled (translated into machine language) and stored in a library of such pre-compiled programs within the Georgetown University Computer System. It provides the following processing options:

1. Listing of input text with line numbers.
2. Word-frequency listing in alphabetic order of text item.
3. Word-frequency listing in descending order by frequency of occurrence.
4. Word-frequency listing in reverse alphabetic order (the words are alphabetized on the basis of their final letters).
5. Most frequent two-word collocations by descending order of frequency of occurrence.
6. Most frequent two-word collocations by alphabetic order of the words in the collocation.

Table 1.1. Data summary

Textbook	Total Lines of Input Data	Total Number of All Words	Total Number of Distinct Forms
	(a) Textbooks		
A1	329	2862	433
A2	576	5961	1005
A3	760	8007	998
B1	251	2545	432
B2	670	7093	1052
B3	1066	10870	1486
C1	385	4224	1053
C2	505	5416	1406
C3	400	4350	1262
	4942	51328	9127
	(b) Compositions		
Level 1	1597	12880	1434
Level 2	2012	19293	2170
	3609	32173	3604

7. Most frequent three-word collocations in this text by descending order of frequency of occurrence.
8. Most frequent three-word collocations in this text in alphabetic order by first word of the triad.
9. Alphabetical concordance of text items with line numbers (KWIC-ALPHA).
10. Reverse alphabetical concordance of text items with line numbers (KWIC-REVERSE).
11. Key-word-out-of-context KWOC (each word of the text is listed once, accompanied by the numbers of the lines in which it occurs in the text).
12. Distribution of text items by text segments.

Such a list of processing options enables us to produce a conclusive statistical description which enables us, in turn, to provide objective and verifiable answers to the questions posed for this research to resolve.

2. PEDAGOGICAL COHESION: ANALYSIS OF DATA AND FINDINGS

In any given EFL environment, and particularly where two levels of the target language (TL) coexist, certain basic assumptions should be made to justify such levels separation and to create, in consequence, a pedagogically cohesive TL environment.

Alexander has stated that 'the material in *First Things First*, the beginners' course which precedes this one [referred to here as series C], has been designed to "overlap" this course. Students who have completed it will have no difficulty whatever in continuing where they left off. Students who have learnt English from other elementary courses and now wish to continue their studies with this course should have a fair working knowledge of the structures listed below. The list may be formidable, but close inspection will reveal that there is nothing in it that would not be found in the average elementary course.' (Alexander 1967: xiii).

He also makes a distinction between two aspects of assumed knowledge: active and passive. A student has active compound of a pattern if he can use it in speech or writing. He has passive command of a pattern if he can understand it when he hears or reads it, but is as yet incapable of using it. In the list below, this distinction is drawn by the following designations: ability to recognize and to form (active knowledge), and ability to recognize (passive knowledge).

1. Elementary uses of the verbs *be* and *have* in the present and past.
2. The Present Continuous: ability to recognize and to form.
3. The Simple Present: ability to recognize and to form with *-s, -es,* or *-ies* in the third person.
4. The Simple Past: ability to recognize and to form with common regular.
5. The Past Continuous: ability to recognize.
6. The Present Perfect (simple): ability to recognize.
7. The Past Perfect: ability to recognize.
8. The Future: ability to recognize and to form with *going to, shall,* and *will.*
9. Auxiliary Verbs: elementary uses of *can, may,* and *must.* The ability to recognize the forms *could, might,* and *would.*
10. The ability to form questions and negatives with auxiliary verbs including *do/does* and *did.* The use of interrogative pronouns and adverbs.
11. The ability to answer questions beginning with auxiliary verbs and question words.
12. Adverbs: ability to form with *-ly* and *-ily.* The ability to recognize exceptions like *well, hard,* and *fast.*
13. Articles: definite and indefinite: elementary uses of *a/an* and *the.* The use of *some, any, no, much, many,* and *a lot of* with countable and uncountable nouns.

14. Nouns: the ability to form the plural with *-s, -es,* and *-ves;* common irregular plurals: *men, women, children, teeth,* etc.
15. Pronouns: personal, possessive, reflexive, apostrophe *s*.
16. Adjectives: elementary uses. Regular comparison, irregular comparison: *good, bad, much/many,* and *little*.
17. Prepositions: the use of common prepositions of place, time, and direction.
18. Relative Pronouns: the ability to recognize and to use *who, which,* and *that*.

Miscellaneous Features:

19. *This/that; these/those.*
20. Elided forms: *It's, I'm, isn't, didn't,* etc.
21. *There is / it is; there are / they are.*
22. The Imperative.
23. The day of the week, dates, seasons, numbers, and points of time (today, yesterday, tomorrow, etc.).
24. Telling the time.

Since the elementary EFL courses currently used in Egyptian public prep schools do not include Alexander's *First Things First,* the beginner's course, we found it very relevant to test them against such a list of assumed knowledge items, seeking an objective answer to the first questions posed for this research: Do the currently used elementary EFL programs provide the main components of the knowledge assumed to be acquired by those EFL students upon completion of such programs? And, if so, how far does the currently used pre-intermediate EFL program succeed in building up the students' EFL knowledge from where they left off? In other words, are the existing elementary and pre-intermediate EFL programs pedagogically cohesive?

From such a list of assumed knowledge items, the analysis was focused on those which relate to verb tenses, articles, prepositions, interrogative pronouns and adverbs, pronouns, and relative pronouns, and which form stumbling blocks for Egyptians EFL students.

Findings

The analysis of data provides the following striking findings on both active and passive assumed knowledge items:

Active Assumed Knowledge. Infrequent use or total lack of:

1. questions with auxiliary verbs (see Table 2.1).
2. interrogative pronouns and adverbs (Table 2.2).
3. possessive and reflexive pronouns (Table 2.3).
4. simple prepositions of place, time, and direction (Table 2.4).
5. relative pronouns (Table 2.5).

Passive Assumed Knowledge. Moderate to frequent use of the present continuous and present perfect tenses, and the auxiliary verbs *could* and *would,* can be

Table 2.1. Questions with auxiliary verbs

Item	A1	A2	A3	B1	B2	B3
am	1	0	0	0	0	0
was	0	0	0	0	0	1
were	1	1	0	0	0	1
have	0	5	0	8	8	0
has	0	1	0	1	1	0
had	0	0	0	0	0	0
does	4	0	1	1	1	0
will	0	0	2	0	0	0
would	2	5	0	1	1	1
could	0	0	0	0	0	1
may	0	3	1	0	0	0

noticed. For a complete distribution of these passive assumed knowledge items, check Table 2.6.

The preceding findings indicate that some of the active assumed knowledge items are either rarely used or totally lacking, and that some of the passive assumed knowledge items are more frequently used than other active ones. Such a state of affairs creates a predagogically noncohesive TL environment in which the elementary EFL programs do not provide the basic assumed items; and, consequently, the pre-intermediate program is built upon nonexisting foundations. A good course of instruction is pedagogically cohesive.

Table 2.2. Interrogative pronouns and adverbs

Item	A1	A2	A3	B1	B2	B3
when	2	1	0	0	3	27
whose	8	0	0	1	0	1
whom	0	0	0	0	0	0
which	0	1	0	0	4	3

Table 2.3. Possessive and reflexive pronouns

Item	A1	A2	A3	B1	B2	B3
mine	3	0	1	0	2	2
yours	4	0	0	0	4	1
ours	1	0	1	0	1	0
his	1	0	0	0	0	0
hers	1	0	0	0	0	0
its	0	0	0	0	0	0
theirs	1	0	0	0	0	0
myself	0	0	0	0	0	0
yourself	1	0	3	0	0	1
ourselves	0	1	2	0	0	0
himself	0	0	0	0	0	3
herself	0	0	0	0	0	0
itself	0	0	1	0	0	0
themselves	0	3	5	0	0	0
yourselves	0	0	0	0	1	0

3. GRAMMATICAL COHESION: ANALYSIS OF DATA AND FINDINGS

'The study of grammatical cohesion,' it has been suggested, 'has direct relevance to the teaching of text, since it aims to discover the characteristics of a text as distinct from a collection of sentences' (Hasan 1968:24).

Moreover, Widdowson indicates that 'The importance of work on grammatical cohesion is that it is a description of the devices which are used to link sentences together to form text and provides the language teacher with an inventory of points he must incorporate into exercises to develop a knowledge of this aspect of language use' (1979:55). Materials of that sort will affect the transformation from grammatical competence to communicative competence.

Allen and Widdowson point out that 'English language overseas is taking a new character as a result of the need for many advanced students to use the language as a tool in the study of scientific and technical subjects. In this situation, the oral inductive methods of the conventional syllabus are no longer adequate . . . An English course of this level should be concerned both with discourse and with text.

Table 2.4. Simple prepositions of place, time, and direction

Item	A1	A2	A3	B1	B2	B3
above	0	0	2	0	2	1
along	0	0	2	7	8	0
around	0	6	12	0	0	2
below	0	0	3	0	2	0
beside	0	0	1	0	0	4
off	0	2	1	3	5	2
since	0	1	2	0	7	6
till	0	0	1	0	2	0
through	0	0	11	0	2	0
under	0	0	1	2	4	1
untill	0	0	1	0	1	3
without	0	0	0	0	2	0

The first of these involves the ability to recognize how sentences are used in the performance of acts of communication and the second, the abilities to manipulate the formal devices which are used to combine sentences in creating continuous passages of prose' (Allen and Widdowson 1974:1).

Widdowson and Corder point out that papers presented at the Neuchatel Colloquia on Applied linguistics (1972–1975) have led to reconsideration of linguistic structure and communicative effect beyond the sentence level. These papers center around the themes of discourse analysis, communicative competence, and communicative language teaching. The term DISCOURSE ANALYSIS should be restricted to

Table 2.5. Relative pronouns

Item	A1	A2	A3	B1	B2	B3
who	0	2	13	0	0	6
whom	0	0	0	0	0	0
which	0	1	15	0	0	1
that	0	3	8	0	0	0

Table 2.6. Passive assumed knowledge items

Item	A1	A2	A3	B1	B2	B3
was + v - ing	0	0	4	0	3	19
were + v - ing	0	1	4	0	3	14
have + p.p.	0	31	16	2	47	43
has + p.p.	0	6	12	1	16	19
had + p.p.	0	0	3	0	0	43
could	0	2	7	0	5	18
might	0	0	1	0	0	0
would	4	30	11	0	4	25

inquiries related to the (Labovian) functional realization of linguistic elements in communicative interaction; the study of formal manifestations should be referred to as TEXT ANALYSIS. There are textual cohesion features which also require extension of the scope of grammar to structures beyond that of the sentence: propositional linkage and implicational linkage. Analyzing these features leads to the conclusion that the ability to produce and perceive discourse is a part of communicative competence that cannot easily be described via linguistic rules (Widdowson and Corder 1976).

Candlin points out that studies in textual cohesion form one of 'the areas of inquiry which are commonly accepted among applied linguistis as contributing to the study of discourse, and which are drawn on in the development of communicative syllabuses for language learning' (Candlin 1976:238).

Halliday and Hasan (1976:4–6) indicate that 'the concept of cohesion is a semantic one; it refers to relations of meaning that exist within the text, and that define it as a text. . . Cohesion is expressed partly through the grammar and partly through the vocabulary.' Halliday & Hasan refer therefore, to grammatical cohesion and lexical cohesion. Reference, substitution, and ellipsis are grammatical. Reiteration is lexical. Conjunction is on the border line of the two: mainly grammatical, but with lexical component in it.

They also point out that the analysis of cohesion leads in all kinds of directions: 'it is likely to mean one thing in the context of automatic analysis of text by computer, another thing in the context of the teaching of composition, and something different again in the context of stylistic studies' (p. 332).

This study links together the automated analysis of EFL multipurpose texts and students' EFL compositions by taking the systematic study of grammatical cohesion as a point of departure.

Grammatical Cohesion in EFL Programs

Halliday and Hasan indicate that 'a text has a texture and that is what distinguishes it from something that is not a text' (1976:2). Text texture is realized by certain linguistic features referred to as COHESIVE TIES.

In this section we would like to give an account of EFL multipurpose texts patterns of texture, and, more specifically, the frequency distribution of cohesive tie in the multipurpose texts contained in the three EFL series taught in Egypt.

A dictionary of 231 cohesive ties was selected. The schematic subclassification of those ties were adopted from Halliday and Hasan's *Cohesion in English* (1976).

The concordances produced by TXTPRO made it possible to check for the functional distribution of those selected ties in the context of the multipurpose texts contained in the three EFL series under analysis. Sedelow and Sedelow (1967:182) point out that 'a concordance may show not only where a word occurs in the text, but also the context in which the word occurs. With only an index of word occurrences, the scholar must look up every entry in order to select those of interest to him. By providing the immediate context as well, the concordance may greatly improve the researcher's efficiency.'

The TXTPRO processing option KWIC-ALPHA produced a concordance, or KWIC-INDEX line (KWIC = Key Word In Context), for each item in the input text unit. Each line of KWIC contains four parts, which appear in the printout from left to right: first, the segment of the text which precedes the key word; second, the item being indexed, that is, the key word; third, the segment of text which follows the key word; and fourth, the number of the line of text in which the key word occurs. The items listed by KWIC-ALPHA are given in alphabetical order.

Findings

1. It was found that many classes and subclasses of cohesive ties are either rarely used or totally lacking as text-forming devices in the multipurpose texts contained in the three EFL series. Their frequency distribution is as follows:

a. *Across All Three Series: Cohesive Ties which do not occur at all:*
- *Reference:*
- *Comparative:*
  Identity: equal, identical, identically
  Similarity: likewise, similar, similarly
  Difference: differently, otherwise
  Numeratives: additional, fewer, further
- *Ellipsis:*
  Specific Deicties: his, hers, its, theirs
  Nonspecific Deicties: both, each, either
  Ordinals: last
  Indefinite Quantifiers: few, a few, fewer, little, lots, most, much dozen, end, pack, quarter, set.
  Auxiliaries: have, had

Model Operators: shall, should, may, might, ought to
Infinitive—To: used to, need to

- *Conjunctions:*

Temporal: before that, currently, firstly, recently, thirdly, from now on, hereafter, henceforth, henceforward, in conclusion, in short, nowadays, previously, thereafter, yet.

Additive: alternatively, besides, by the way, elsewhere, for instance, further, furthermore, identically, in addition, in other words, likewise, moreover, similarly.

Adversative: adversely, as a matter of fact, at any rate, at least, conversely, counteractingly, despite, I mean, nonetheless, nevertheless, notwithstanding, on the contrary, otherwise.

Causal: accordingly, as a result, aside from, consequently, for this purpose, hence, in consequence, in this regard, to this end, with reference to.

b. *Across All Three Series: Cohesive Ties occurring once only:*

- *Reference:*

Possessive Determiners: *his, hers, theirs* (A1)
Comparative Numeratives: less (C2)

- *Ellipsis:*

Nonspecific Deictics:	*neither* (C1)
Ordinals:	*first* (B1)
	second (B3)
	next (B3)
Indefinite Quantifiers:	*many* (B1)
	half (B3)
Auxiliaries:	*was* (A3)
	be (B3)
	were (C1)
Model Operators:	*could* (B3)
Indefinitive—To:	*going to* (C2)

- *Conjunctions:*

Temporal:	*at the same time* (B2)
	second (A3)
	by this time (C2)
	ever since then (C3)
	in the meantime (C3)
	whenever (C3)
Additive:	*that is* (C2)
Adversative:	*in any case* (B3)
Causal:	*in this respect* (A3)
	thus (A3)
	for this reason (C1)
	in that case (C2)
	therefore (C3)

c. *Across All Three Series: Cohesive Ties which are frequently used:*
- *Reference (see Table 3.1):*
  Personal Pronouns: he, she, it, they, him, her, it, them
  Personal Determiners: his, her, its, their
  Demonstratives: this, that, here, there, the
  Compartaive: same, so, different, else, other, more
- *Substitution and Ellipsis (see Table 3.2):*

Substitution:
Nominal: one
Verbal: do, doing
Clausal: so
Ellipsis:
Specific Deictics: mine, yours
Non-Specific Deictics: all
Post Deictics: others

- *Conjunctions (see Table 3.3):*
  Temporal: after, before, first, immediately, later, since, soon, then
  Additive: also, and, too
  Adversative: but, however, rather, still, although
  Causal: because, for, so

2. The preceding frequency distribution of cohesive ties indicates that the multipurpose texts contained in the three EFL programs were used to train the EFL students to gain only sentential proficiency. That is, the multipurpose texts were not presented as graded samples of cohesive texts and EFL students were not, in turn, trained to gain more than sentential proficiency. Consequently, the students entering higher education in Egypt with an experience of 6 or more years of instruction in English have considerable difficulty in coping with language in its normal communicative use. They still have major difficulty with reading comprehension, précis and paragraph writing, and composition.

Grammatical Cohesion in Students' EFL Compositions

In the preceding sections, we have focused on the constraints imposed by the nature of EFL instructional programs and pedagogy in Egypt, and particularly on the manner in which they presented English grammar and the grammar of cohesion.

Here, we will focus on the impact of such prescribed EFL pedagogy on the Egyptian students' EFL proficiency, and specifically on the extent to which they use the grammar of cohesion in their written composition.

The students' EFL compositions were analyzed from three crucial and complementary perspectives: (a) native language interference and target language peculiarities, (b) grammar of cohesion or grammar of composition, and (c) learner's views and expectations.

Such a threefold analysis enabled us to provide reasoning for the existing problems presented by previous researches, and to answer some of the major questions such as these raised by Candlin and Breen (1979:91) on directionality in EFL

Table 3.1. Reference

Cohesive Ties	A1	A2	A3	B1	B2	B3	C1	C2	C3
1. Personal									
Pronouns:									
he	61	61	37	44	45	156	87	110	38
she	30	33	5	17	24	60	50	44	12
it	63	63	77	24	80	188	44	56	46
they	26	65	109	23	59	94	29	19	44
him	5	9	14	2	13	30	14	34	11
her	7	2	0	6	27	46	13	1	3
it	2	44	31	12	45	46	24	28	16
them	2	31	34	7	28	33	9	6	9
Determiners:									
his	20	30	47	20	39	38	26	30	12
her	4	13	7	6	27	46	13	16	3
its	0	4	6	0	1	8	1	0	3
their	13	21	43	0	19	7	9	4	11
2. Demonstratives:									
this	0	0	10	0	0	15	8	6	8
that	2	23	12	1	18	24	4	3	3
here	6	5	18	5	15	35	3	5	7
there	5	20	15	2	18	8	4	3	7
the	44	329	503	164	317	564	223	382	325
3. Comparative:									
same	0	1	0	0	0	3	4	0	6
so	0	0	5	0	1	1	2	2	1
different	0	0	2	0	2	0	1	1	1
else	0	2	1	0	0	2	1	0	1
other	0	6	10	0	5	14	1	2	6
more	0	6	7	0	1	6	3	5	2

Table 3.2. Substitution and ellipsis

Cohesive Ties	A1	A2	A3	B1	B2	B3	C1	C2	C3
1. Substitution:									
Nominal:									
one	0	5	3	0	11	3	2	0	1
Verbal:									
do	8	2	0	0	1	0	0	0	3
doing	10	0	0	6	1	0	2	2	1
Clausal:									
so	0	1	3	0	0	3	0	2	0
2. Ellipsis:									
Specific Deictics:									
mine	3	0	1	0	2	2	0	0	0
yours	4	0	0	0	4	1	0	1	0
Non-Specific Deictics:									
all	0	0	5	0	0	2	0	4	0
Post-Deictics:									
others	0	2	5	0	3	1	2	0	0

material and pedagogy: (a) Is account taken of the learner's initial repertoire (aspects of the mother tongue, and aspects of the target language the learner may imperfectly know)? To what extent? In what ways? (b) Is account taken of the learner's initial competence (initial communicative knowledge and abilities)? To what extent? In what ways? (c) Do materials make allowance for the learner's expectations of what the target language requires? (d) Do the materials allow for the learner's own definition of learning needs? (e) Are the learner's own specific interests and motivation accommodated?

The analysis of data processed on two levels of writing proficiency: Level 1 represented those who had received 3 years of instruction in English, and Level 2

Table 3.3. Conjunctions

Cohesive Ties	A1	A2	A3	B1	B2	B3	C1	C2	C3
1. Temporal :									
after	4	6	4	0	0	17	6	14	8
before	0	1	1	0	0	3	0	0	3
first	0	1	1	1	2	1	1	3	0
immediately	0	0	0	0	0	2	2	5	2
later	0	0	0	0	0	1	3	7	2
since	0	0	2	0	1	6	2	5	0
soon	0	0	3	0	1	1	0	5	1
then	0	8	8	1	20	48	10	5	2
2. Additive:									
also	1	26	33	0	5	2	0	4	2
and	6	8	23	4	43	50	24	30	27
too	18	10	8	9	21	13	3	0	0
3. Adversative:									
but	0	3	26	3	16	90	36	30	20
however	0	0	0	0	0	3	6	9	4
rather	0	1	0	0	5	2	0	1	1
still	0	2	8	0	6	16	4	7	2
although	0	1	1	0	0	3	0	2	0
4. Causal:									
because	0	0	2	0	0	3	4	2	2
for	0	0	1	0	0	0	1	5	2
so	0	10	2	0	14	29	9	6	1

represented those who had received 6 years of instruction in English. The purpose of such a level separation is threefold. It allows us: (a) to reflect upon the students' initial linguistic repertoire, native and target; (b) to measure the impact of both elementary and preintermediate programs separately; and (c) to judge the nature of the cohesion-forming pedagogy of the textbooks.

Findings

The analysis of the processed data has provided the following conclusive and database supported findings:

1. Elementary EFL students have given clear proofs that they are ready to start writing and are capable of gaining a higher level of proficiency if they are trained at an early stage of foreign language learning in this aspect of language use.
2. At an early stage of foreign language learning, students' motivation and expectations are high; as they proceed to higher levels, they gradually lose motivation. Such a loss of momentum was clear in their writings. It is not exaggerating to say that students' EFL writing proficiency at the elementary level is the same as that of the pre-intermediate level, and that they share the same shared stumbling blocks of mother tongue interference, target language peculiarities, and deeply-rooted sentence-level pedagogy.
3. The students' limited linguistic input provided by the EFL programs has minimized their active linguistic output and badly affected their written communication skills.
4. Students experience major difficulties with the various aspects of grammatical cohesion—namely, reference, ellipsis, substitutions, and conjunctions.
5. Classes of comparative reference and elliptical uses of specific deictics (determiners) were almost lacking; there was also an infrequent use, or total lack, of adversative, causal and temporal conjunctions.
6. The study supported previous research findings which indicated that:
   a. the cultural thought patterns that are revealed by an Arab involve his infrequent use of subordinations and the overuse of coordinate constructions (Kaplan 1966), and
   b. The rhetoric of tightly organized paragraph and logical presentation of ideas is as foreign to Arabic-speaking students as the language of English itself (Yorkey 1977).

Based on such research findings, the study calls for certain pedagogical considerations to be given due attention and priority in EFL predagogy in Egypt.

1. Maximizing students' receptive linguistic knowledge, to help them produce a legible output.
2. Extending the scope of EFL pedagogy to include the discourse level as its legitimate level of attainment. That is, due attention must be given to the teaching of how both text cohesion and discourse coherence are brought about.
3. Selecting, grading, and presenting the multipurpose texts in EFL programs so that they serve as good graded samples of written discourse. Such a methodology will help the EFL students acquire, in a systematic manner, competence in reading comprehension and written communication skills.

COMPUTERS AND COMPUTATIONAL LINGUISTICS IN EFL TEXT ANALYSIS

The use of the computer and a program such as TXTPRO allowed for a much more thorough and comprehensive study than would otherwise have been possible. Automated EFL multipurpose text analysis provided us with a satisfactory data-base, which enabled us in turn to:

1. Provide a conclusive statistical analysis useful for selecting, grading, sequencing, and presentation of EFL materials;
2. Speculate on the various linguistic aspects needed for vocabulary expansion, morphological, syntactical and semantic dimensions of contained data, and presentation of high vs. low-frequency lexical and syntactical items and collocations,
3. Analyze the existing status of EFL programs, evaluate and diagnose their pros and cons, and provide some objective procedures and techniques for curing any linguistic ills;
4. Think of computers and computational linguistics as diagnostic and remedial tools within the frame of a generative model that takes the existing limited linguistic repertoire as its input and produces maximum utilization as its output. (Such a procedure could also enhance the students' linguistic repertoire and increase their command of the target language);
5. Lay great emphasis on selecting our texts for language teaching, and provide an objective pedagogical procedure for the presentation of these texts in terms of their lexical, syntactical, and semantic loads;
6. Provide the most objective procedures for developing and updating of the glossaries provided by the EFL textbooks—glossaries could serve as a highly-needed pedagogical facility for teachers, testers, and students if they were carefully prepared;
7. Judge the semantic load that the processed data contained; i.e., a case grammar study of the propositional content contained in EFL instructional programs is feasible; and
8. Provide some objective procedures for judging the effectiveness of EFL textbooks in a given foreign language environment.

CONCLUDING REMARKS

Hartmann (1975:99–100) points out that 'in selecting teaching materials we rely to a large extent on the help of (a) the user specialist whose field we want to capture and (b) the statistician and computer expert who can advise on the problems of data processing. The former issue is related to our understanding of the various functional styles current within and across different fields of study, the latter to the availability of a satisfactory data-base. Both issues are far from being resolved. Collections of textual materials from different registers are rare (cf. Crystal and Davy 1969, Ager 1970, Mcdonald and Sager 1974), linguistic and statistical description inconclusive (Erk 1972, Makin 1973). In analyzing textual materials, linguists frequently acknowledge the value of text corpus for analysis and description, but they can be rightly criticized for not giving enough guidelines on how this should be done.'

Di Pietro (1970:61) indicates that 'no course of instruction is perfect. No teacher is perfect. But if we do not have some generative framework of language in mind, we will be reduced to a fragmentation of our teaching into units of unrelated bits and pieces. A good course of instructions is cohesive.'

Strevens (1977:270–271) points out that the higher the general standard of the teachers, the less important the course books and other teaching materials. But when the standard of teachers is low, as it inevitably is for a time in conditions of rapid expansion of education, then the standard of teaching materials assumes a great importance. Insufficiently trained teachers working with poor materials face a considerable handicap. When this occurs, it is a defect of the system, for whose remedy a three-way collaboration is necessary between publishers, administrators, and teachers.

Sharing Hartmann's views on the collection and analysis of textual materials and development of a satisfactory data-base which is viable in the selection of teaching materials, DiPietro's statement that 'a good course of instruction is cohesive', and Strevens' teachers/materials equation, this study has tried to provide some objective answers to questions relating to pedagogical cohesion, grammatical cohesion, and the use of computational linguistics in providing a satisfactory data-base which yields a conclusive statistical analysis viable in selecting, grading, sequencing, and presentation of EFL materials.

The findings make major contributions to mechanical methods of text analysis and EFL material preparation and pedagogy. This study sets a pattern for other, similar studies in other countries where English is taught.

REFERENCES

ABDALLAH, ALBERT G., HELMI M. ABOUL-FETOUH, and SAAD M. GAMAL. 1979. Living English. Book 1. Cairo: Moharram Press.

———. 1978. Living English. Book 2. Cairo: Moharram Press.

———. 1978. Living English. Book 3. Cairo: General Organization of Government Printing Offices.

ALEXANDER, L. G. 1978. Practice and progress. Part 1. London: Longman.

———. 1978. Practice and progress. Part 2. London: Longman.

ALLEN, J. P. B., and H. G. WIDDOWSON. 1974. English in physical science. Teacher's edn. 1. London: Oxford University Press.

ALLEN, W. STANNARD, and ALAN C. MCLEAN. 1977. Progressive living English. Pupils' book 1. London: Longman.

———. 1978. Progressive living English. Pupils' book 2. London: Longman.

———. 1978. Progressive living English for the Arab world. Pupils' book 3. London: Longman.

CAMPBELL, ROBIN, and ROGER WALES. 1970. The study of language acquisition. New Horizons in linguistics, ed. by John Lyons. Penguin.

CANDLIN, C. N. 1976. The communicative language teaching and the debt to pragmatics. Semantics: theory and application, ed. by Clea Rameh, 237–256. Washington, D.C.: Georgetown University Press.

———, and MICHAEL P. BREEN. 1979. Evaluating, adapting and innovating language teaching materials. On TESOL '79: the learner in focus, ed. by C. A. Yorio, K. Perkins, & J. Schachter, 86–108. Washington, DC: TESOL.

DI PIETRO, R. 1970. Student competence and performance in ESL. TESOL Quarterly 4.49–62.

HALLIDAY, MICHAEL A. K., and RUQAIYA HASAN. 1976. Cohesion in English. London: Longman.

HARTMANN, R. R. K. 1975. Understanding texts. System 3. 98–105.

HASAN, R. 1968. Cohesion in written and spoken English. Programme in linguistics and English teaching. Paper 7. London: Longman.

HYMES, D. 1970. On communicative competence. Directions in sociolinguistics, ed. by J. J. Gumperz & Dell Hymes. New York: Holt Rinehart and Winston.

KAPLAN, ROBERT B. 196B. 1966. Cultural thought patterns and inter-cultural education. Language Learning 16.1–20.

SEDELOW, S. Y., and W. A. SEDELOW, Jr. 1967. Stylistic analysis. Automated language processing, ed. by Harold Borko, 181–213. Santa Monica, CA: System Development Corp.

SHAEFER, L. 1979. TXTPRO: A text processing package for use in computational linguistics work. Washington, DC: Georgetown University Computer Facility.

STREVENS, PETER. 1977. Causes of failure and conditions for success in the learning and teaching of foreign languages. On TESOL '77: teaching and learning of English as a second language: trends in research and practice, ed. by D. Brown, C. A. Yorio, & R. H. Crymes, 266–277. Washington, DC: TESOL.

WIDDOSON, H. G. 1973. Directions in the teaching of disourse. Theoretical linguistic models in applied linguistics, ed. by S. P. Corder & E. Roulet. Paris:AIMAV/Didier. Reprinted in The communicative approach to language teaching, ed. by C. J. Brumfit and K. Johnson, 49–60. Oxford, England: Oxford University Press.

———, and S. P. CORDER. 1976. Discourse analysis, interpretative procedures and communicative language teaching. Bulletin CILA 23.56–64.

YORKEY, R. 1977. Practical EFL techniques for teaching Arabic-speaking students. The human factor in ESL, ed. by J. E. Alatis and R. Crymes, 57–85. Washington, DC: TESOL.

FOURTEEN

Les Quatre Cents Mots: A French Vocabulary Computer Lesson*

Theodore E. D. Braun
George W. Mulford
University of Delaware

A triple-format computer program, an integral part of the new first-semester course at the University of Delaware, had pilot student use in the Spring of 1982. The lesson was designed to help students acquire a vocabulary in excess of 400 words, which were divided into 24 lists introduced at the rate of about two per week.[1] Primary acquisition of the language—and of the vocabulary—takes place in the classoom, where the method of instruction is Total Physical Response.[2] An original-script language-laboratory program and the computer lesson review the word lists, the lab stressing aural comprehension and sound discrimination, and the computer the written form of the language.

Indeed, much of the students' exposure to written French during the first semester, and virtually all their active writing for the first 10 weeks or so, take place at the PLATO[3] terminal, freeing the classroom for oral work. PLATO tracks student errors, and it makes sure that missed words will be drilled extensively. When a student makes an error, PLATO tells him or her what it is. PLATO is proficient enough in French to recognize as misspellings such common errors as transpositions, omissions of letters or accents, doubling of letters, wrong accents, additions of letters or accents, and some faulty substitutions of one letter for another. It can tell students that they have made gender errors or used an inappropriate word. It can provide English translations and can help students recall and write out a word by giving them, on demand, letter by letter, the correct spelling. In a word, it acts like

* The authors gratefully acknowledge the support of the Center for Advanced Study, the Office of Computer-Based Instruction, and the Department of Languages and Literature of the University of Delaware.

[1] These lists were derived from the first 400 words (with additional items taken, where appropriate, from the second 400 words) in Savard and Richards 1970. In all, between 550 and 600 items appear in the data base.

[2] For an explanation of the methodology of TPR, see Asher 1979, 1981a. A fuller treatment is included in Asher 1981b.

[3] PLATO is a registered trademark of the Control Data Corporation.

a tutor, giving each student individual attention and help with written French in response to each individual's demonstrated needs.

Les Quatre Cents Mots has a large database fed by a word editor and a picture editor. Some 500–600 words have been entered and about 200 pictures created for the project. The words are accompanied by articles, English translations, right-answer commentaries for certain items and wrong-answer commentaries for others, synonyms, irregular forms of adjectives, and similar information. PLATO makes use of this wealth of material to judge, analyze and comment upon student responses.

The 'help' key, standard on PLATO keyboards, provides the correct answer on demand, one letter at a time, allowing students to complete as much of the word as they can. The act of pressing the 'help' key marks the word for review by the individual student, and enters the item in the student data bank, in which information generated by student use of the lesson is stored. (By contrast, a call for the translation is transmitted to the student data bank, but does not mark the word for review.) The student data can be retrieved in a variety of forms via a data reader lesson, which provides rich material for analysis.

On entry, PLATO presents the student with two lists: a review list consisting of up to 20 items drawn from the two previous lists the student has worked on and including where possible all of his or her errors on those lists, and up to 40 words from the current list. At this point, the students can choose to take an optional pre-test. Then they choose to study the word list in one of three formats: a picture format, a visual arrangement format, and an audio format. An optional post-test is also available for each list.

From the student's (but not the programmer's) point of view, the picture format is simple in design: basically, it consists of a cue and a response. The cue is made up of a picture and a question, followed by an incomplete sentence; to respond, the student must complete the sentence. Figure 1 illustrates the cue and response. The

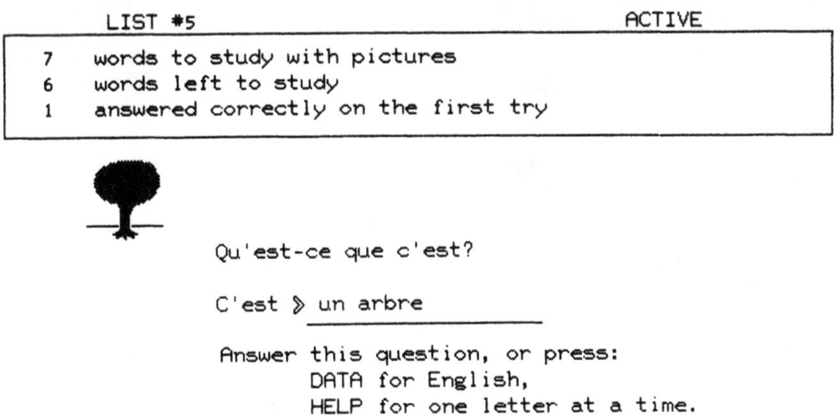

Figure 1. Picture format: standard cue.

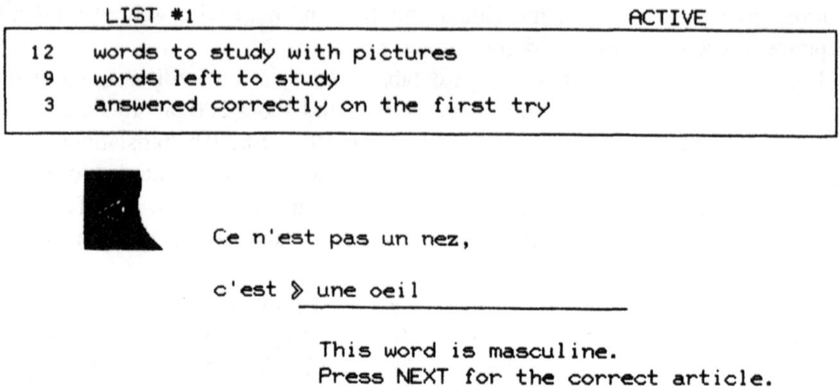

Figure 2. Picture format: alternate standard cue.

cue is the standard one, and the response has been typed but not judged. An alternative standard cue, used for parts of the body, consists of a picture accompanied by an incomplete sentence, as can be seen in Figure 2. In this case, the student has typed in the right word, but has used an incorrect article. The machine gives instructions for obtaining the correct form. Variants based on this alternative standard cue are used for many adjectives and nouns (e.g., *Ce n'est pas un garçon, c'est* ______. *Le crayon n'est pas court, il est* ______). These variants often present two pictures, one of which has been crossed out, to emphasize the contrasts. A third standard cue represents Rodin's Thinker thinking a cartoon character's thoughts, in a balloon, as in Figure 3. Only the infinitive is required (including, with reflexive

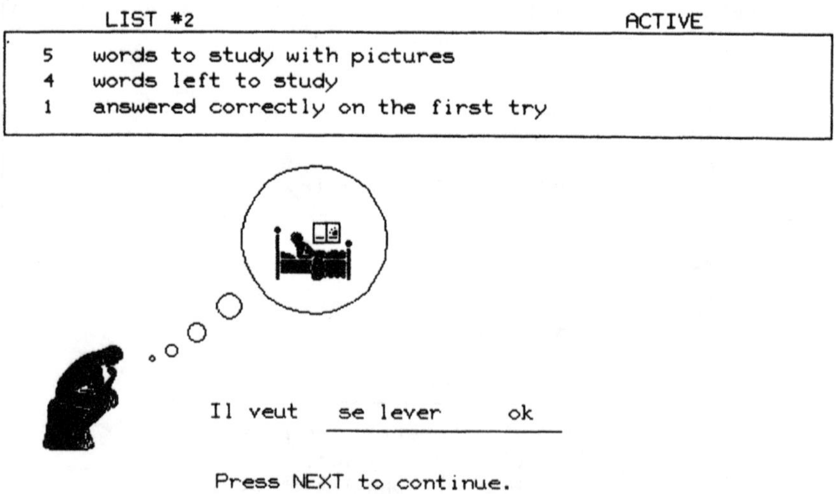

Figure 3. Picture format: third standard cue.

verbs, the pronoun *se*). Finally, some cues, usually based on these three standard cues, had to be scripted for individual words.

In general, we tried to require only the dictionary form of the words: adjectives are therefore usually masculine and singular, verbs are presented in the infinitive, and nouns are almost always singular. Nevertheless, a feminine or plural form of an adjective, or the plural form of a noun, was a more logical choice at times, and was thus called for in such cases (for instance, the word for 'eye' is *oeil,* that for 'eyes' is *yeux;* both forms appear as separate entries).

This brings us to the question of gender, which we touched on with reference to Figure 2. Since one of the premises of this lesson is that the essential thing is the word itself and not its various inflected forms, it was clear that we could not logically count a gender error as a mistake. Thus a student who typed *une* for *un,* as in the example, would not have to review the word *oeil* but would nevertheless be obliged to correct the error so as to see the word with the correct form of the article before proceeding to the next word. A note indicates the nature of the error.

The visual arrangement format is adapted from a PLATO lesson designed by University of Delaware psychology professor John P. McLaughlin. This is the only format programmed to drill ALL the vocabulary: not every word can be conveniently illustrated, and, because of limitations of space and time, only 15 words per list have been incorporated into the audio format. Note, however, that the record of all words missed or correctly answered is shared by all three formats.

The machine scans the available words from the two lists, combines them, and presents up to 16 of them at a time to the student, who arranges them in a logical or random order, as he or she chooses, by using the touch-sensitive screen of PLATO (Figure 4). The student can learn the meaning of a word by touching the space marked TRANSLATION. Once all the words have been mastered in this learning/memorization step, PLATO presents the student with the English for each word in the place where the French word had been. A correct answer automatically causes the French to replace the English on the screen; a wrong answer elicits an appropriate commentary (wrong accent, misspelled, not on list, etc.). In Figure 5, the student has typed the correct answer for *little, small* but has not yet pressed the "next" button. This translation/testing step requires a correct response on at least 80% of the words in order for the student to pass on to the following list. A final drill asks the student to replace empty spaces by the French words. Forgotten words are indicated to the student but not put on a review list.

The third format utilizes random-access tape recorders in conjunction with PLATO terminals. In many respects, this is the most exciting and most promising of the three formats.

Fifteen words from each of the 24 lists—a total of 360 of 1440 sentences. Where possible, three of these sentences are put in predetermined contexts; the fourth sentence repeats one of the contexts. These contexts are: for nouns—subject, direct object, object of preposition; for present-tense verbs—any person in the singular, first or second person plural, third person plural; for adjectives—at least one masculine, one feminine and one plural. This lesson, currently being programmed, will

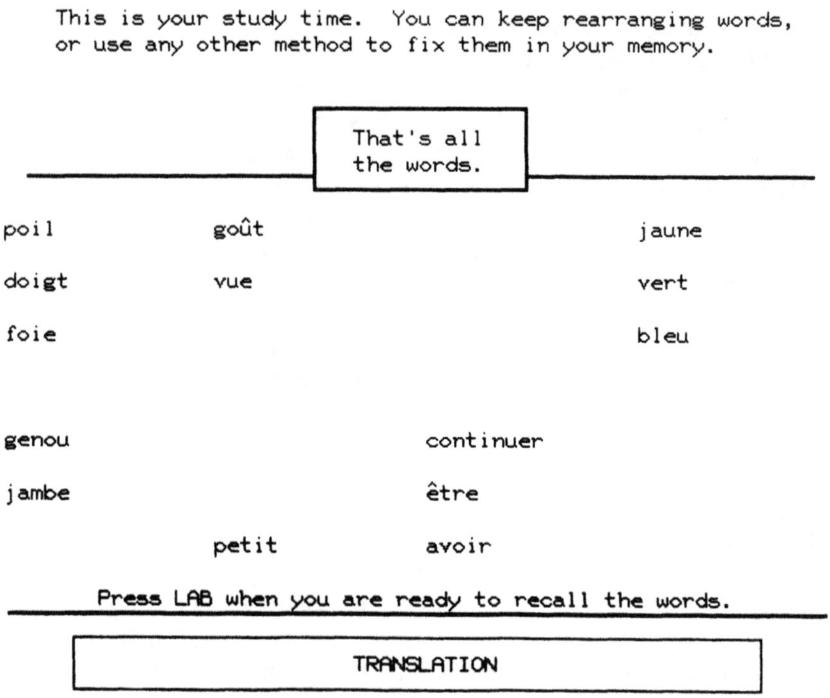

Figure 4. Visual arrangement format: learning/memorization step.

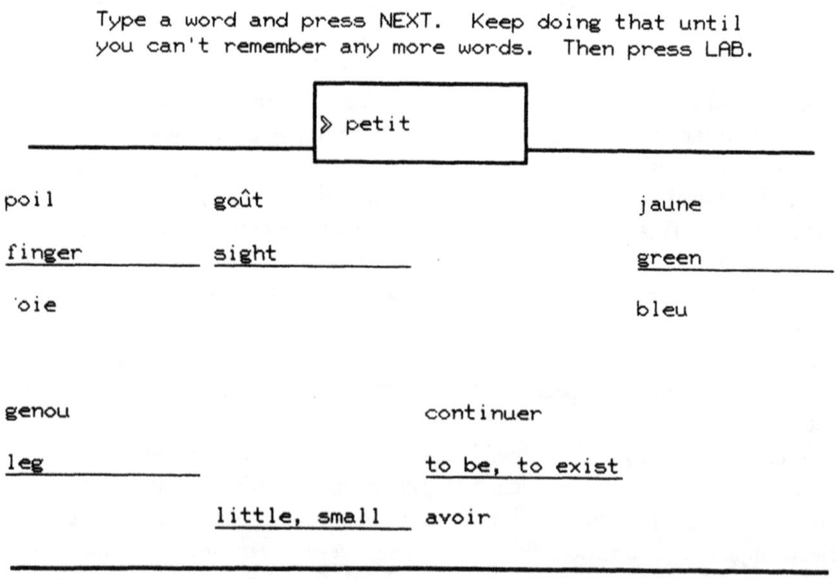

Figure 5. Visual arrangement format: translation/testing step.

be student-ready by January 1983. The sentences have been recorded by two young native speakers, speaking and acting rather than reading.

The audio format combines the sounds of French with written texts and computer-driven randomization. The student hears a sentence and simultaneously sees on the screen the same sentence with the targeted word left blank. The sentence can be heard as often as the student wants, until he or she is ready to type in the correct answer. PLATO presents one sentence per word for a first round, and then proceeds to a second round. The fifteen sentences of the second round are augmented by one additional sentence for each word incorrectly typed. A third round provides further drill on words missed during the second round. Thus, students will see and hear only two of the four recorded sentences if they answer correctly. But if they make a mistake, the third and possibly the fourth sentences are presented to them for additional drill.

Future development involves both the picture format and the audio format. The database has been designed so that a passive mode may be created, that is, multiple-choice questions for both formats. Instead of typing in the correct answer, the student will indicate whether the word flashing on the screen is correct or not. Since only one word appears in the answer box at any one time, the student is forced to judge each response proposed on its own merits rather than seeking the right answer from among three or four offered simultaneously, as is the case in print media. In this case, the computer has a unique capacity that is not available in a book.

In addition, for the audio format, the machine will be able to offer the student a choice between typing a single word or an entire utterance, even an entire sentence. This option would provide students with a significant amount of additional drill in writing, and would take further advantage of PLATO's capabilities. Alternatively, PLATO could also ask students to translate the French sentence they hear into English, and could judge the accuracy of the translation within the parameters of the information it has been given (e.g., it could be taught to tolerate alternative responses, such as *she walks* as well as *she is walking*).

If, from the student's point of view, the program has the advantages of variety in format and flexibility in mode, it also offers a rich resource to the researcher: thanks to the data reader lesson referred to above, vast amounts of student data are accessible in raw form or organized in different categories.

The data collected up to now are only preliminary, since scarcely 120 students have as yet been exposed to the two operative formats, and for only a half-semester and a summer session at that. Yet even with this limitation kept in mind, the data have already proven themselves to be useful and have had an impact on the lessons.

For example, we interpreted a call for an English translation in the picture format as an indication that the picture or the cue might be unclear or ambiguous. Examination of the cues and pictures did indeed indicate the need for some changes and revisions, and appropriate action has been taken. These corrections could not have been made so quickly, conveniently, and economically in the print media.

Similarly, when we examined the wrong answers made by randomly-chosen students, we discovered that some other pictures were ambiguous, and we have corrected them too. Some students answered without asking for help or a translation (e.g., one student wrote *je ne sai* when he could not remember the word for airplane); this has led us to have each class go through a practice session with PLATO so that each student will be reasonably familiar with the lesson before starting on List 1.

Other kinds of mistakes—spelling mistakes in particular—have led to other remedies. Many of these were simply typographical errors—transpositions, hitting the wrong key, hitting a letter one time too often, etc. And there were surprisingly few errors in accents—missing, misplaced, or wrong accents were rare in our sample, and, like other student mistakes, the findings in the group analyzed were corroborated by random checks of the students not analyzed. Curiously, errors in accents became relatively more frequent in the classroom, that is, when students were not at the computer terminal.

Omitted letters frequently included infinitive endings (*mont* or *monte, chant* or *chante, pousse, boir*), or a final *-e* (*port* for *porte, jamb* for *jambe*). Some of these errors indicate a failure to recognize inflected forms, while others betray faulty pronunciation (pronouncing final *-e* like final *-er,* or pronouncing the final consonant of a word). Yet other cases indicate some first-language interference (*doight* for *doigt*) or simple mispronunciation (*courteau* for *couteau*). Finally, a few cases of an incorrect inflected form occurred (*yeux* for *oeil, veille* for *vieux;* in the latter example, the incorrectly inflected form is also misspelled).

As a result of this analysis, more care is being given to combat these errors at the source: the computer has proven to be a valuable tool for helping improve the quality of instruction in the classroom.

Student reaction to the exercise of placing words on the screen and then remembering them was vociferously negative in the first semester of use. Two successive revisions of the program have made it more meaningful to the students. In the light of the program's novelty and initial poor reception, data from the 1982 summer session were examined to determine: (a) whether students were making an effort to place the words, (b) what criteria for placement were being used, and (c) whether it made any difference how words were placed. The results lack formal validity because of the small size of the test group, the informal method of sampling, and the loose circumstances of administration (students were free to use paper and pencil, for instance). 'Thumbing through' the completed screen arrangements does show, however, that a majority of the students used some system to place the words, and that care taken in placement did not decrease over the semester: there is no indication that students gave up on the method. Table 1 shows the total number of word placements as a percentage of word presentations. The figures exceed 100% to the degree that students changed the position of a word after its first placement—a good rough indicator of the deliberateness of their placement.

The arrangements made show one very strong tendency: students placed verbs apart from other words. The arrangement made by student 'a' (Figure 6) is typical of a 'least effort' placement: the words are simply plunked down in the order presented, but verbs are deliberately isolated.

Table 1. Number of word placements as a percentage of number of presentations

List	Percent	List	Percent	List	Percent
1	109%	9	125%	17	121%
2	132%	10	117%	18	111%
3	156%	11	121%	19	103%
4	135%	12	132%	20	126%
5	123%	13	126%	21	114%
6	134%	14	119%	22	108%
7	121%	15	110%	23	158%
8	119%	16	142%	24	104%

Student 'b' was one of the more systematic users of the program. Earlier in the semester, this student was one of the few to alphabetize words. The arrangement shown in Figure 7 is clearly designed to form associational groupings, including even the verbs.

An analysis of 40 screens like these suggests that words placed with care are more often remembered, whereas words lost in the interior of large groups are more often forgotten. The rough data shown in Table 2 indicate the feasibility of a more rigorous study of students' associational strategies and their results.

```
                         Student a

List 2Ø
Words in group: 11    Time in lesson: 14 minutes
Times word was moved (including original placement): 11

* = forgot word    ◆ = asked for translation of word
         Numbers shown are order presented.

1     charbon     3     rappeler

2     sujet       8     obliger

4     intérêt     9     tuer

5     armée

6     possible

7     repos

1Ø    nom

11    guerre
```

Figure 6. Visual arrangement format: arrangement made by student 'a'.

```
                         Student b

   List 20
   Words in group: 13    Time in lesson: 36 minutes
   Times word was moved (including original placement): 34

   * = forgot word    ♦ = asked for translation of word
 ___________ Numbers shown are order presented. ___________


                        5      armée
                                                    4 *   vie
      8 *   sûr        10      garde
                                                   11 *   tuer
      2     certain
                                                   13     repos
     12 *   condition
                              9     article
      3     gaz
                              1     nombre
      6     obliger
                              7     truc
```

Figure 7. Visual arrangement format: arrangement made by student 'b'.

ASHER, JAMES J. 1979. Motivating children and adults to acquire a second language. SPEAQ Journal 3.87–99.

———. 1981a. The total physical response (TPR): Theory and practice. Native language and foreign language acquisition, ed. by H. Winitz. The Annals of the New York Academy of Science 379.324–331.

———. 1981b. Learning another language through actions: The complete teacher's guidebook. 3rd ed. Los Gatos, CA: Sky Oaks Productions.

SAVARD, JEAN-GUY, and JACK RICHARDS. 1970. Les indices d'utilité du vocabulaire fondamental français. Québec: Les Presses de l'Université Laval.

Table 2. Apparent effect of word placement on rate of successful recall

Situation	Words So Placed as % of Total Words	Words Forgotten as % of Words So Placed
Isolated	8%	14%
Top or bottom of group	41%	23%
Inside group	50%	32%
In little group (five words or less)	52%	23%
In big group	48%	31%
In clear sense group	54%	23%
Not in sense group	46%	30%

FIFTEEN

On the Role of the Computer in Foreign Language Instruction

James P. Lantolf
University of Delaware

The intent of the present paper is to discuss the ways in which computers have been and are being used as aids in foreign language programs in light of the research literature on second and foreign language acquisition. At issue is not whether computers can or cannot impact on foreign language learning in a significant way, but whether their use, as reflected in current programs and those under development, provides adequate input to enable learners to acquire language in a way that will allow them to use it spontaneously. The focus of what follows is not on the quality of program design, since there would appear to be no reason to disagree with Schwartz (1982:114), who believes that most programs are sound in this regard; rather, attention will center on the content of the programs in view of the language learning process as it has been discussed in the literature on second language acquisition.

It is imperative that careful consideration be given to the impact which computers may or may not have on language learning before we proceed with the development and implementation of computer-assisted language instruction (CALI) programs in an extensive way. It will be recalled that the language teaching profession's first encounter with machine aids was anything but a resounding success. During the 1960s and early 1970s, language laboratories were seen as a panacea for teaching languages. Unfortunately, the results of studies such as the Pennsylvania Project and the excellent study of Sandra Savignon (1972), which demonstrated that use of language labs had no discernible effect on language achievement, did not appear until long after teaching programs had invested large sums of money and a great deal of time and effort in hardware and software. Despite the findings of these studies, however, there continues to be a reluctance on the part of the profession to eliminate lab programs and materials associated with them. Inertia is a powerful force indeed.

Some scholars (see Underwood 1981, and Schneider and Bennion 1980) have maintained that the failure of the language lab to bring students to the anticipated level of proficiency is in large measure due to the constraint that a tape format allows only linear action and does not permit any nontrivial interaction involving the language learner: 'the lab was seen as a tireless assistant that could drill the mechanical aspects of language, freeing the teacher for more creative activities'

(Underwood 1981:98). The difficulty is that, because of its linear design, the lab is incapable of processing learner responses. The lab produces the same kind of output, and progresses at more or less the same rate of speed, regardless of how students respond. There is no built-in monitor of student performance.[1] What is more, tape programs bear little resemblance to real communication. The students, in essence, communicate or rather verbalize with themselves (Underwood 1981:105).

To remedy the shortcomings of the language lab, researchers began to look to the computer in order to provide what was believed to be the necessary practice that could not be supplied by tape programs. As early as the mid 1960s, researchers interested in CALI believed that languages were among the subjects to which the computer was best suited (Nelson et al. 1976:28). Among the reasons for this conviction were the following: the number of class hours could be reduced without reducing learning; the rigid and narrowly-defined responses demanded of language students in exercises and drills were ideally suited to computer programming, and the teacher could, as a consequence, be freed to do more interesting activities during class time; student error could be corrected immediately, a feature notably missing from lab programs (Nelson et al. 1976:28). To this list, Underwood (1981:107) adds that the computer is able to provide students with individual attention on an extended basis, an aspect often lacking in many language programs due to the large numbers of students frequently enrolled in foreign language classes.

Despite the positive aspects of CALI, Underwood expresses concern that the lack of an audio component detracts significantly from its efficacy. Recently, however, several programs have been given the capacity to utilize audio output. The program under development at Brigham Young University, for example, combines videodiscs and audio tapes to interact with users (see Schneider and Bennion 1980). Underwood also remarks that some of the early programs, such as Dartmouth's CARLOS, were unduly complicated and were often not transferable from one institution to another because of the lack of interface between computer systems. Judging from recent developments, however, it would seem that this difficulty has also been surmounted. Another important consideration that should be mentioned is that many teachers often have a natural skepticism about using devices such as computers, and are frequently wary of the possibility that they may someday lose their jobs to machines (Underwood 1981:107). The NEH-sponsored institute on CALI held on the campus of the University of Delaware this past summer no doubt went a long way toward disabusing teachers of any fears they may have had in this regard.

[1] Underwood believes that the language lab does have one obvious strength, which is its ability to enhance listening comprehension. The kind of listening activities that are included in many lab programs, however, do not meet the requirements for comprehension as discussed in the second language research literature. Consequently, these programs would appear to provide little more than exposure to another language, and as Krashen (1982) argues, exposure is not likely to become intake, which is necessary for language acquisition.

In order to assess the prospects of CALI, it is necessary to consider in some detail two of the most important notions to come out of second language research in recent years: monitor theory and the input hypothesis. Any language teaching program, including CALI, would do well to give careful consideration to the research related to these two concepts.[2]

Among the insights to come out of the work of Stephen Krashen is the distinction between conscious and subconscious language learning. Krashen refers to the former phenomenon as LANGUAGE LEARNING, and uses the term ACQUISITION to characterize the latter process. According to Krashen (1982:12), acquisition in adults is similar and perhaps identical to the way in which children acquire their native language. It is natural, informal, implicit learning in which one is aware not of the process of learning a language but of the attempt to communicate with other human beings. Learning, on the other hand, represents conscious knowledge of the rules of language, be they first or second language rules, and the ability to talk about the rules. While learning and acquisition play a role in the development of language competence, acquisition alone serves as utterance initiator and is solely responsible for spontaneous natural language performance (i.e., fluency), whether spoken or written. The learned aspect of language has a relatively limited role to play in linguistic performance—a role that is restricted to monitoring or editing what has been generated by the acquired competence. Monitoring can take place before or after an individual actually speaks or writes. If it occurs after the fact, the process is referred to as REPAIR.

Krashen claims that language learners use the monitor only if three conditions are met: (a) when there is sufficient time to call up the rule in question and apply it; (b) even if there is time to monitor, as can happen in written discourse, the user must be focusing on the form rather than the meaning of an utterance; (c) the learner must know the rule which is to be applied. The final condition is particularly significant when we realize that linguists to date have been able to describe only fragments of natural language in any satisfactory way (Krashen 1982:16). Moreover, it would appear that there are restrictions on the types of rules which qualify for monitor use.[3] Krashen maintains that only rules which are morphologically, syntactically, or semantically simple can be utilized by the monitor. For example, a rule which specifies that in Spanish *de* plus *el* contract to *del* is sufficiently simple for the monitor to handle, while a rule dealing with *wh*-question formation in English is

---

[2] As a greater understanding of the language learning process has developed over recent years, we have come to realize that, in addition to the linguistic aspects related to language learning, it is essential to consider psychological and sociological factors as well. A discussion of these factors, however, is beyond the intent of the present paper. This is not to say that they are any less important than the linguistic factors.

[3] The term RULE here does not refer to explicitly formulated pedagogical principles as exemplified by descriptive statements included in textbooks and other teaching materials; rather, rule in this case is intended as the linguistic principles that learners internalize on the basis of their own inferences about how a particular structure might be generated in a target language.

syntactically too complex to qualify for monitor use and can only serve the learner if it is acquired.[4] The only value that Krashen sees in learning rules consciously is for use in polishing written or spoken performance when the three conditions for monitor use are met, and, even then, conscious knowledge of language makes only a small contribution, if any at all, to communication (Krashen 1982:112).

We now turn out attention to the input hypothesis. In essence, the input hypothesis states the conditions which are both necessary and sufficient for second language acquisition to occur; that is, input must be of sufficient quantity, it must be comprehensible, and there must be negative input provided for the learner. The first two conditions will be taken up here, while the third is more profitably left for the discussion of error correction to be taken up below. Suffice it to say at this point that negative input entails more than correction of learner error.

The question of quantity of input has yet to be resolved satisfactorily. While we know that learners must receive a great deal of input, at present it is not known precisely how much input is sufficient, nor is there certainty about how to optimally structure input for all learners. It may be the case, for instance, that brief but regular doses of input over an extended period is best suited for some learners, while for others, it may be more beneficial to provide larger doses over shorter periods (Schacter 1982).

The COMPREHENSIBILITY CONDITION states that people acquire language when they comprehend messages that are couched in structures slightly beyond their level of competence at any given moment. For linguistic data to qualify as comprehensible input, they must be embedded in a context that is pragmatically or communicatively so rich that learners may even forget that the message is coded in a foreign language (Krashen 1982:66). By comprehension, it is not intended that every word of every utterance must be understood, as is often advocated by some methodological schools; rather, comprehension means that the acquirer is able to understand, in a general way, the meaning of a linguistic exchange. Implied in the comprehensibility condition is that learners must interact linguistically and in a meaningful way with their environment. Without interaction, linguistic data does not qualify as input, becoming nothing more than meaning-less exposure (see Krashen 1982). Surely no one would expect a child to acquire a native language on the basis of exposure to linguistic data provided by a radio or television set, even if the apparatus were playing 24 hours per day for a lifetime.[5] The means of insuring

---

[4] Some scholars, such as Stevick (1982), argue that learning and acquisition may not be separated phenomena but the extremes of the same heuristic process. As will be discussed below, however, the evidence seems to support Krashen's position, although the issue has yet to be resolved conclusively.

[5] Sachs et al. (1981) report on a case study of two children raised by deaf-mute parents whose primary linguistic input was provided by television programs. At the time the children were discovered, they had not developed a linguistic system that was anywhere near what would normally be expected in children at their age level. Sachs and her colleagues conclude that, for language acquisition to take place, simple exposure to linguistic data is not sufficient input, and extensive interaction with one's environment is indispensable.

that the necessary interaction will take place is to engage the learner in language use as it was intended to be used: to communicate real meaning. As Newmark so appropriately pointed out more than a decade ago, 'the odd thing is that despite our ignorance as experts, as human beings we have always known how to teach other human beings language: use it ourselves and let them immitate us as best they can at the time' (1970:224).

There may be some who would argue that the apparent structural randomness implied by the input hypothesis will make language learning too difficult for any adult to achieve; yet this is precisely what is required if learners are to acquire fluency in a second language. What is advocated by the input hypothesis is nothing more than what every normal human being knows intuitively: 'unless a learner has learned instances of language in use, he has not learned them as language, and if he has learned enough such instances, he will not need to have analyses and generalizations about the whole made for him' (Newmark and Reibel 1970:236).

A survey of CALI programs reveals that the majority of the early programs reflected tenets of either of two schools of language teaching: audio-lingual philosophy of instruction, or cognitive-code theory of teaching. In a paper typical of audio-lingual methodology, Adams et al. (1968:3) state that 'active practice is an essential ingredient of language learning, and quick or frequent remediation is very valuable to forestall the learning of poor language patterns.' Consequently, for Adams, CALI exercises must stress pattern practice over grammatical analysis, correct student error immediately, and correspond to skills actually acquired of the student. As an advocate of cognitive-code teaching, Rosenbaum (1969:457) argues that, for CALI to be effective, it must compel the student to 'take creative action in the target language,' which for Rosenbaum is the generation of an utterance based upon the comprehension of another utterance. To attain the desired goal, Rosenbaum contends that students must know how sentences of the target language are constructed. Therefore, CALI programs, according to Rosenbaum, must provide the learner with sufficient practice in such activities as substitution and transformation drills and translation. More recently, Nelson et al. (1976), also cognitive-code advocates, claim that the purpose of CALI is to teach active skills in which students learn to form sentences in the target language. To achieve this end, they argue that the computer's role should be to inform students where their mistakes are, and then proceed to analyze them so that students become aware of the principles underlying the correct structures. Once this has been done, the students must be constantly on their guard so as not to make mistakes in the future. Nelson and his colleagues believe that the computer can provide the incentive necessary for students to avoid errors by stopping them every time an incorrect structure is produced.

On the basis of the preceding discussion, it would appear that effective CALI programs should incorporate in some form or other the following features: drills of type, error correction, and structural analysis. Indeed, many of the programs currently in use (e.g., CARLOS, PLATO, MONIQUE, SPAN, CONDUIT, ZAP) have incorporated into their format, in some form or other, drills (morphological, syntactic, lexical, or phonological), error correction, and rule analysis.[6] The difficulty with this approach is that it destroys the integrity of language by segmenting it into bits and pieces which are isolated from pragmatic contexts, thus making the learning of language an impossible task (Oller 1979:216). People do not learn languages in order to generate well-formed sentences, and, as the input hypothesis maintains, they do not learn languages by learning principles of linguistic structure. People learn languages by using them to communicate information, express feelings, and, as Di Pietro (1981) convincingly argues, to negotiate strategies and fulfill social and psychological roles.

Some may argue, as Underwood has, that if a learner sticks with the pieces long enough to gain a thorough understanding of language structure, facility in the

---

[6] Some CALI programs such as CONDUIT and SPAN make no pretense about their relevance to language use, and simply engage students in exercises on low-level morphological manipulation in which learners are expected to do nothing more than convert an item like *sentarse* (*nosotros*) 'to sit down (we)' into *nos sentamos* 'we sit down' (Underwood 1981:110). ZAP, developed by Decker (1976) and used at the University of California at Riverside, incorporates a novel twist into its program format. Instead of asking students to perform grammatical operations on strings, ZAP asks users to key in their own sentences and then punch a number to trigger the computer to perform the desired grammatical operation. A student, for example, can key in a declarative sentence and then instruct the computer to transform it into an interrogative or negative configuration. According to Decker (1976:26), ZAP is based on the pedagogical assumption that learning language is learning first to make sentences and subsequently learning how to perform grammatical operations on them. From what has been said above, however, language learning involves much more than the ability to perform structural manipulations.

Although originally developed for Latin instruction at the University of Illinois, PLATO has been extended to use in foreign language programs as well. Despite the fact that the core of PLATO consists of drills, Curtain et al. (1976:280) point out that PLATO goes beyond traditional exercises like substitution and transformation practice, and incorporates activities intended to draw student attention to problems of grammatical structure, agreement, word order, and even pronunciation and intonation phenomena. The program is capable of asking students about such grammatical detail as which Russian case ending is to be used when translatings specific English sentences into the target language. Be that as it may, the format of PLATO is still discrete-point and form-focused, and, as will be elaborated below, this format is unlikely to have a significant effect on a learner's spontaneous use of a target language. In addition, the technique that PLATO uses for dealing with suprasegmental phenomena in language has been shown to be linguistically unsound (see Lieberman 1965).

CARLOS, developed at Dartmouth, features the computer's ability to distinguish between real errors and typos and other non-errors. CARLOS is also able to indicate to students how close their response is to the correct answer, and has the capacity to maintain a diary of student errors. It can also tell users how long it takes them to respond to items, in order for them to increase the pace of their work (see Allen 1972, and Turner 1970). Once again, it must be pointed out that, no matter how novel and innovative these techniques may seem, they are discrete-point and stress grammatical accuracy rather than real language performance.

MONIQUE is a program for drill work in French devised by Robert Terry (1977) at the University of Richmond. Similar to the other programs, MONIQUE engages students in drills, translations, and rewrites. According to Terry, MONIQUE was developed in order to help students in required language courses overcome lack of motivation. As Terry (1977:191) puts it, his program is an attempt to answer the question 'What else can I do to learn the grammar?,' the assumption being that learning grammar is an essential condition for learning grammar. Learning grammar, however, is learning about language, or as Krashen has said on several occasions, learning grammar is nothing more than language appreciation.

language will eventually develop. Krashen contends, however, that learning does not become acquisition. While the evidence is not overwhelming, several cases have been reported on in the literature in which unsuccessful attempts have been made at converting conscious learning of isolated bits and pieces of language into the ability to use those pieces in spontaneous discourse. Krashen (1982:103) reports on a study conducted by Sascha Felix in which an EFL class in Germany was given intensive and extensive instruction on learning the correct use of elliptical sentences in English of the type *Is it a dog? Yes, it is.* The instructor explained the rule to the students and drilled the construction on a daily basis over a 3-month period. Yet Felix discovered that, in spontaneous conversation, correct elliptical forms were supplied only randomly by the students, who instead of the correct *Yes, it is* tended to produce *Yes, it isn't.*

Schumann, in his important 1978 study on the pidginization process in second language acquisition, undertook to teach on a tutorial basis, often claimed as an advantage of CALI, the rule for negation in English to an adult learner whose native language was Spanish. Schumann's intent in focusing on a single structure was to determine if direct conscious intervention would have an effect on the acquired system of the learner; i.e., whether learning would turn into acquisition. The subject received instruction over a period of several months on the proper use of negation in English. At each session, he was given an explanation of how negation operates and was then provided with numerous sets of positive sentences, which he was to negate. Schumann then compared the elicited negatives with negative utterances produced by the subject in natural spontaneous speech. Prior to the tutorial sessions, the subject had produced negatives accurately only 10% of the time in elicited tasks; following instruction, his performance improved significantly to 64% accuracy. In his spontaneous speech, however, the situation was found to be quite different. Before intervention, the subject had produced well-formed negatives in 22% of the cases; after instruction, his use of accurately-formed negatives showed no improvement, with his rate of accuracy actually decreasing slightly to 20%. Schumann concludes that 'instruction had radically improved his performance in an artificial, or highly monitored task, but had virtually no effect on his normal communication with native speakers of English' (1978:109).

One of the time-honored techniques of discrete-point teaching is that of pattern drills. The purpose of pattern drills is to consolidate what has been learned about the target language and to provide a means for overlearning of the structures in order to make correct speech habits automatic, so that they can be accessed successfully in future target language speech interactions (Lamendella 1979a:433). In other words, drills represent an attempt to convert the learning of structures into the ability to use the structures spontaneously. Computers would appear to be particularly well-suited for drill activities, since 'drill and practice can work well on the computer (even after the novelty fades) because the exercises can give the student a sense of mastery' (Schwartz 1982:144). A sense of mastery, however, is not the same thing as true mastery, i.e., acquired competence. As any experienced teacher can attest, there is rarely if ever transference from drills to natural language use. This is because drills do not provide input that can be utilized in any significant way for language acquisition (Lamendella 1979b:435).

Lamendella (1979b) furnishes evidence from research on transcortical aphasia to demonstrate the irrelevance of drills to communicative language use. It has been found that patients with lesions in certain areas of the language centers of the brain are able to communicate effectively but are unable to carry out simple pattern drill activities like repetition, imitation, and substitution drills; nor are they able to perform smiple editing tasks on ungrammatical strings. On the other hand, if a lesion occurs in a different area of the speech center, subjects are unable to communicate but have no difficulty with pattern drill tasks. Lamendella contends that the evidence from such studies suggests the existence of separate neurofunctional systems: one which governs interpersonal communication, and another which controls intrapersonal cognitive information. According to Selinker and Lamendella (1981:208), activation of specific neurofunctional systems is determined by the type of input received by the brain. If the input is form-focused, as in the case of pattern drills and grammatical analysis, the cognitive system and not the communicative hierarchy is activated and the responsibility for learning is delegated to the former neurofunctional system. If the input is informal and embedded in a pragmatic context, the communicative system assumes the responsibility for learning. The problem, however, is that information stored in one system cannot be transferred to the other system. Thus, knowledge attained through the operation of the cognitive neurofunctional system is unavailable to the communication hierarchy.

Moreover, there is evidence that, when learners engage in pattern drills, they tend to disassociate such activities from higher level language processing, much in the same way a typist disassociates the meaning of a text from its form (Lamendella 1979b:14). In a series of interviews conducted with beginning-level French students, Hosenfeld (1976) discovered that learners indeed appeared to separate form from meaningful language use when doing pattern drills. One student included in Hosenfeld's study, for example, made the following remarks with regard to how she went about carrying out structural drills: 'Well . . . because . . . I'm a pretty verbal person . . . mixing up the sentence and moving the pieces around . . . it's just frustrating to have to continually do this . . . and after a while you don't even know what all this stuff means. I know what the directions are and I know what I'm supposed to do, but I don't know why I'm supposed to be doing it . . .' (Hosenfeld 1976:122).

In real-world discourse, successive utterances rarely share the same grammatical structure as is the case in successive items in contrived structural exercises; yet they almost never lack the textural cohesion so clearly missing in pattern drills (Newmark and Reibel 1970:238). For Newmark and Reibel, structural drills force students to formulate sentences the use of which is nearly impossible to grasp unless the students can create situations for every item presented in the drill. Drills, then, destroy the cohesive properties of language which are essential for learners to grasp if they are to acquire the ability to use the language in a wider context, and what is more, these, along with other discrete-point techniques, induce learners into constructing 'freak grammars' that are of little use to them in real language performance (Oller 1979:202, 216).

As mentioned earlier, error correction has also been an integral feature of CALI programs. In most cases, learners are not permitted to proceed from one step to the next until they are able to produce accurately what has been called for in a given drill, or until the computer has provided them with what the programmer considers to be a sufficiently adequate analysis of a given grammatical problem. Without such treatment, it is believed that learners somehow run the risk of assimilating inorrect structures into their target language competence. As Kasper (1982:106) correctly points out, in foreign language teaching the formal aspect of language is stressed, often to the detriment of interpersonal communication, which is usually carried out in the learners' native language. Consistent focus on formal accuracy, however, frequently leads learners into adopting a strategy in which they seek to avoid use of certain structures, or in some cases, to avoid use of the target language entirely, for fear of making a mistake. More importantly, perhaps, if Krashen's monitor model is accurate, and the evidence presented by the research of Schumann and Felix would appear to be supportive of his position, the elimination of errors on discrete-point, highly monitored tasks is likely to have a minimal impact at best on spontaneous language use.

It is interesting to note, as Roger Brown and his colleagues observed, that, in first language acquisition, while parents indeed provide negative feedback for their children, the focus of this feedback is only rarely on linguistic form (occasionally parents endeavor to correct mispronunciations and certain verb irregularities); rather, adult feedback to children emphasizes the truth value of the child's utterances (Krashen 1982:13). Schacter (1982) argues that, in adult second language acquisition in a natural setting, negative feedback, or as she labels it, negative input, provided by native speakers of a target language likewise focuses primarily on content rather than on form. In native/non-native interactions, according to Schacter, negative input is furnished by natives in the form of confirmation checks (expressions used to insure that the intended message has been understood), clarification requests (in which learners are required to supply additional information or to recode the original message), or failure to understand (in which immediate evidence is given to the learner that transmission failure has occurred). The serious kind of negative input in natural situations only sporadically focuses on utterance form—for example, if an agreement has been reached beforehand that a native should attempt to correct grammatical errors in the learner's performance—but even in these cases concern with form rarely lasts for an extended period of time, especially if the topic of conversation is of interest (see Lantolf and Kanji 1983). If a non-native produces an utterance such as **There are two glass on the shelf,* the native is much more likely to respond with something like *Shall I get them* rather than with *No, two glasses*. Since the context has built-in redundancy, the native probably will not even notice such low-level morphological errors. To be sure, teachers and computers notice such mistakes and do not readily let them pass unattended. Content-focuses rather than form-focused negative input may be a necessary condition for acquisition, because it creates the required disequilibrium in the language acquisition mechanism, which in turn causes learners to modify their output (Schacter 1982). Without this kind of negative input, fossilization is likely to occur.

It would seem that CALI programs which utilize drills, error correction, and grammatical analysis have no more hope of making a significant imprint on learners' natural language abilities than did these techniques when they were used by teachers in classroom settings. Does this mean that computers have no potential value in foreign and second language instruction? If programs can be developed that incorporate in some way the conditions necessary for acquisition to take place, the answer may well be yes. Potentially successful CALI programs would be those which focus on content in a manner that is intensely interesting to the learner.

Underwood (1981) is in the process of developing and refining a program for Spanish called FAMILIA. FAMILIA is based on a program devised by Joseph Weizanbaum at MIT known as ELIZA, which is capable of maintaining a plausible human conversation by giving the appearance that a message has been understood even when it has not. If a learner keys in a sentence that the computer cannot process, it simply reacts as a therapist might and hedges with a response like *Why do you say that? Go on,* or it changes the topic. In experimenting with this program, Weizenbaum found that people were often willing to divulge their most intimate secrets to the computer. In terms of language acquisition, the interaction provided by a program like ELIZA may in some way be of sufficient interest for the learner to enhance his or her natural language ability in a target language. Schwartz (1982) argues strongly for open-ended programs like ELIZA which do not need the capacity to process all possible student input. She says that 'to suppose we can anticipate all possible supportable answers is to deny to our students what we cherish for ourselves, human creativity and the need to reinterpret the words in terms of our own experience' (Schwartz 1982:147). One drawback of programs like ELIZA, however, is that users must still type in their responses, a procedure which at times may cause learners to be overly concerned with form. Research underway at the University of Delaware on the use of computers in constructing scenarios in the strategic interaction method indicates, nevertheless, that language learners are able to key in responses without paying undue attention to their formal quality.

Despite its basis in an open-ended program like ELIZA, Underwood's FAMILIA continues to make extensive use of remediation. Thus, if a student keys in **Bueno, mi madre está de Boston* 'Okay, my mother is from Boston,' the computer responds with *Se usa ser con de; por ejemplo soy de Boston* '*Ser* is used with *de;* for example I am from Boston'; or if the computer asks (only the English is provided here) *Is there anyone else in your family who is a teacher?* and the student answers with *No,* the computer promptly retorts with *No, what?,* a clear request for the student to answer in a complete sentence. The problem here is not with the computer but with the assumptions of the programmer. In traditional foreign language teaching, whenever there is a conflict in which the instructor must choose between pedagogical goals and the reality of communication in the natural setting, priority is given to pedagogical concerns, the rationale being that speaking in complete sentences increases practice with morphological rules, despite the fact that people do not use language in such a way (Kasper 1982:106). For acquisition purposes, it would seem that Underwood's program would be more valuable if it did not insist on disrupting the flow of discourse through remedial intervention.

A program under development at Brigham Young University also has as its aim communicative interaction between learners and the computer. Schneider and Bennion (1980) report that their program is intended to increase the amount of spoken language the learner hears. To this end, they employ a videodisc tied to a computer-controlled cassette tape recorder, thus freeing the learner from having to key in a given response. A prototype lesson begins with a camera spanning the *plaza* of a Mexican village. It then focuses on a man leaning against a wall at one end of the *plaza*. The man walks toward the foreground and asks *¿Es Ud. un turista norteamericano(a)?* 'Are you an American tourist?' The action is then frozen and a set of possible responses is displayed on the screen in English. The student makes a selection from among the alternatives, translates it into Spanish, records it on tape for the instructor to critique, and then hears a surrogate student utter the choice on the screen. Although use of a surrogate is akin to reliance on a knower or counselor in communicative methodologies like community-language learning and strategic interaction, the limiting of possible responses to a predetermined set destroys the spontaneity of natural language performance. In all fairness, however, the Brigham Young CALI program is still in the early stages of development, and it would be premature to pass judgment until the program is fully operational and adequately tested. This brings us to the final topic of discussion in the present paper: the testing of CALI programs.

One of the reasons it took so long for us to discover the drawbacks of language lab, as mentioned earlier, was a neglect of adequate testing of materials in order to determine their efficacy. It was generally assumed, although often erroneously, that labs were effective adjuncts to classroom instruction. As one reads the literature on CALI, one is struck by the frequency with which researchers have made strong claims about the positive impact of their programs without actually having undertaken to verify their conclusions through valid testing procedures. Schneider and Bennion (1980:16) go so far as to make the following statement regarding their interactive program: 'the urge to explore the town will motivate several hours of listening to and speaking the language.' The curious fact about their contention is that, at the time their paper was published in 1980, the program was still in the prototype stage. Such claims, nevertheless, are indeed attractive to those in the market for innovative instructional techniques.

The only evaluation of Terry's (1977) MONIQUE program was based solely on student opinion, which was elicited through a simple questionnaire containing items like *Do you find CA drill work beneficial?*. While the discovery of student attitudes toward teaching techniques is important, it represents only part of the picture. Students often maintain that particular instructional techniques are helpful in learning a language (on this point, Terry's students were no exception), but the ways in which this learning usually manifests itself is through classroom activities and testing procedures that focus almost exclusively on linguistic form rather than on natural language use. It is not surprising, therefore, that under these conditions students perceive the usefulness of engaging in discrete-point practice on computers.

In a trial run of the PLATO program at the University of Illinois reported on by Curtain et al. (1976:290), the impact of the program was assessed on the basis of final grades in language courses. As we know, however, final grades are not necessarily a reflection of language proficiency, since many additional factors usually enter into the computation of final grades.

There have been some attempts to set up controlled experiments to evaluate the effectiveness of CALI programs. One of the earliest experiments of which I am aware was conducted in the German department at SUNY Stonybrook and was reported on separately by Morrison and Adams (1968) and Rosenbaum (1969). In the Stonybrook study, two groups of students received classroom instruction in German according to the principles of discrete-point methodology. The experimental group was given supplemental intervention by means of two 50-minute computer labs per week, whereas the control group was provided with two 25-minute traditional language labs per week. The groups were matched for aptitude and general academic achievement. The CALI lessons consisted of transformation and substitution drills, translation, dictation, and comprehension activities. Following treatment, both groups were given the MLA Cooperative Examination. A comparison of performance on the exam showed that the E group performed as well as the C group on speaking and listening, while surpassing their control counterparts significantly in writing, and doing slightly better in reading. Despite the fact that there were several flaws in the design of the experiement, as readily admitted to by Morris and Adams (e.g., the C group did not remain constant throughout the course of the experiment), one might be somewhat encouraged at least by the superior performance of the E group on reading and writing.[7] Of no less importance than the design flaws in the experiment is the testing instrument used to evaluate the two groups. The MLA Cooperative test is a discrete-point examination, which is normed on the basis of non-native performance on the test (Oller 1979:202). Consequently, it is a test, the validity of which is determined on the basis of the previously-mentioned FREAK GRAMMARS that are induced by discrete-point teaching. Such a test is in part, at least, insensitive to the kinds of knowledge a native grammar specifies, as has been verified by some of Oller's research in which it was found that many items on tests like the MLA Cooperative exam are often more difficult for natives than for non-natives.[8] This is because 'the ability of non-native

[7] The E group, of course, spent their time out of class working on activities that were focused on reading and writing. As will be seen below, however, the test used to assess these activities must suspect in terms of what actually was tested. Also, the fact that there was no significant difference between the two groups on listening and speaking is not at all surprising, given what has been said about the effectiveness of language labs.

[8] In a study of the TOEFL exam conducted at the University of New Mexico, Oller discovered that, on the writing portion of the test, natives performed less well than non-natives on 21% of the items. It

speakers to answer certain discrete items correctly may be unrelated to the kinds of ability that native speakers display when they use language in normal contexts of communication' (Oller 1979:200). Discrete-point tests, therefore, are not necessarily a valid means of assessing the effectiveness of second-language instructional techniques, the aim of which is the development of natural language ability in learners.

As a further illustration of the danger of invalid testing of instructional programs, I would like to cite a recent study conducted by Schaeffer (1981). Schaeffer set up a more tightly controlled experiment than was the case in the Stonybrook study. He used two experimental groups, both of which engaged in computer practice, while the control group received no intervention beyond the classroom setting. The content of the CALI program for one E group consisted of structural drills in which the students were asked to convert sentences from present to present perfect in German. The other E group was given practice with so-called semantic drills, which forced the students to select the appropriate verb for each of a series of sentences from a list of verbs provided by the computer. Both E groups were given feedback on accuracy and were also furnished with the appropriate grammatical rules where necessary. Following treatment, all three groups were tested through the implementation of structural and semantic multiple choice tests. As might be expected, both E groups surpassed the C group on the tests, and the E group which was given semantic practice outscored the E group that was given structural practice on both tests, although the difference between the E groups was significant only in the case of the semantic test—also not a surprising result.

On the basis of the results, Schaeffer draws an astonishing conclusion: 'meaningful learning or meaningful practice is not dependent upon interaction between people. As shown by the performance of the semantic group in the experiment, a deeper level of processing (meaningful content processing) resulting in better understanding can also take place by interacting with a medium such as a computer. Thus, these findings suggest that interpersonal interactions do not necessarily seem to be a sine qua non for meaningful language practice' (Schaeffer 1981:136). While Schaeffer's experiment did indeed incorporate semantically meaningful sentences, from the perspective of real language use the sentences were meaning-less. The activities of both E groups were in no way reflective of what native speakers do with language. A multiple choice test is no less discrete-point than are tests like the MLA Cooperative exam. Moreover, as Hosenfeld (1976) clearly demonstrates, in doing drills, meaningful or otherwise, students do not necessarily follow the strategies that materials writers and teachers think they do. Hosenfeld found this to be the case especially with exercises like those utilized by Schaffer in his study. When asked how they go about doing drills like *Demain je (croire/venir) a l'école pour étudier* 'Tomorrow I (believe/come) to school to study', the students interviewed by

should be noted that the written portion of the TOEFL requires knowledge of discrete aspects of grammar and style which non-natives are usually taught in language classes, but which natives do not normally learn about their language (see Oller 1979:202).

Hosenfeld responded that they did not read the entire sentence for its meaning, as is often assumed by those who formulate such drills, but that they know *école* is a place and so the correct choice must be *venir* (Hosenfeld 1976:121). When the students were then asked what they looked at first in doing meaningful drills, one student answered, 'the words after the dash, you don't need that part (the beginning) of the sentence at all' (Hosenfeld 1976:121). This statement appears to confirm Lamendella's contention that drills do not require students to attend to the complete semantic content of a sentence, since they can be carried out with a minimal knowledge of word classes and low-level coocurrence restrictions, which has little relevance for natural language use (Lamendella 1979a:435).

In light of Hosenfeld's findings as well as the questionable testing procedures used by Schaffer, it is difficult to perceive any relevance in his study with regard to the effect of CALI on foreign language acquisition. While experimentation is needed, not only must the design of CALI experiments be carefully planned, but the means of assessing results must be valid in terms of what they indicate about the impact of computers on learners' natural language abilities.

REFERENCES

ADAMS, EDWARD N., H. W. MORRISON, and J. M. REDDY. 1968. Conversation with a computer as a technique of language instruction. Modern Language Journal 52.3–16.

ALLEN, J. R. 1972. Individualizing foreign language instruction with computers at Dartmouth. Foreign Language Annals 5.348–349.

CURTAIN, CONSTANCE, CLAYTON L. DAWSON, NOLEN PROVENZANO, and PHILIP COOPER. 1976. The PLATO system: using the computer to teach Russian. Slavic and East European Journal 20.280–292.

DECKER, HENRY W. 1976. Computer-aided instruction in French syntax. Modern Language Journal 60.263–267.

DI PIETRO, ROBERT J. 1981. Discourse and real-life roles in the ESL classroom. TESOL Quarterly 15.27–33.

HOSENFELD, CAROL. 1976. Learning about learning: Discovering our students' strategies. Foreign Language Annals 9.117–129.

KASPER, G. 1982. Teaching-induced aspects of interlanguage discourse. Studies in Second Language Acquisition 4.99–113.

KRASHEN, STEPHEN D. 1982. Principles and practice in second language acquisition. Oxford: Pergamon Press.

LAMENDELLA, JOHN T. 1979a. Lamendella replies. TESOL Quarterly 13.433–437.

———. 1979b. The neurofunctional basis of pattern practice. TESOL Quarterly 13.5–19.

LANTOLF, JAMES P., and RAJAI KANJI. 1983. Non-linguistic parameters of interlanguage performance: Expanding the research paradigm. Ninth LACUS Forum, ed. by Adam Makkai. Columbia, SC: Hornbeam.

LIEBERMAN, PHILIP. 1965. On the acoustic basis of the perception of intonation by linguists. Word 21.40–54.

MORRISON, H. W., and E. N. ADAMS. 1968. Pilot study of CAI laboratory in German. Modern Language Journal 52.279–287.

NELSON, G. E., JEAN R. WARD, S. H. DESCH, and ROY KAPLOW. 1976. Two new strategies for computer-assisted language instruction. Foreign Language Annals 9.28–37.

NEWMARK, LEONARD. 1970. How not to interfere with language learning. Readings in applied transformational grammar, ed. by Mark Lester, 219–227. New York: Holt, Rinehart and Winston.

———, and DAVID REIBEL. 1970. Necessity and sufficiency in language learning. Readings in applied transformational grammar, ed. by Mark Lester, 228–252. New York: Holt, Rinehart and Winston.

OLLER, JOHN W., Jr. 1979. Language tests at school. London: Longman.

ROSENBAUM, PETER S. 1969. The computer as a learning environment for foreign language instruction. Foreign Language Annals 4.457–463.

SACHS, JACQUELYN, B. BARD, and M. C. JOHNSON. 1981. Language learning with restricted input: Case studies of two hearing children of deaf parents. Applied Psycholinguistics 2.33–51.

SAVIGNON, SANDRA. 1972. Communicative competence: An experiment in foreign language teaching. Philadelphia: Center for Curriculum Development.

SCHACTER, JACQUELYN. 1982. Inside the nutritional needs of language learners: Sufficient input and negative input. Paper read at TESOL Convention, Hawaii.

SCHAEFFER, REINER H. 1981. Meaningful practice on the computer: Is it possible? Foreign Language Annals 14.133–137.

SCHNEIDER, EDWARD W., and JUNNIUS L. BENNION. 1980. Half a conversation on videodisc: A language instruction program. Pipeline (Fall). 15–17.

SCHWARTZ, HELEN J. 1982. Monsters and mentors: Computer applications for humanistic education. College English 44.141–152.

SELINKER, LARRY, and JOHN T. LAMENDELLA. 1981. Updating the interlanguage hypothesis. Studies in Second Language Acquisition 3.201–220.

STEVICK, EARL. 1982. Teaching and learning languages. Cambridge: Cambridge University Press.

TERRY, ROBERT. 1977. Students work with MONIQUE and learn French. Foreign Language Annals 10.191–197.

TURNER, ROBERT C. 1970. CARLOS: computer-assisted instruction in Spanish. Hispania 53.249–252.

UNDERWOOD, JOHN HARVEY. 1981. Chomsky, De Sauze and the computer: A humanistic approach to language teaching (with special reference to Spanish). Ph.D. dissertation, UCLA.

SIXTEEN

Computers, Linguistics, and Basic Writing

Elaine Chaika
Providence College

1. INTRODUCTION

To many traditionally-trained instructors of composition, both linguistics and computers are anathema, and for opposite reasons. They have tried linguistics, and they haven't tried computers. Not only can the English teacher point to the carcasses of dead linguistic theorizing, but also to Chomsky himself. This revolutionizer of modern linguistics has repeatedly claimed that his formulations may have no practical value, a conclusion with which I heartily concur. Convoluted argumentation about this or that little wrinkle in linguistic theory serves no useful purpose for English teaching that I can see. And, in fact, many modern linguists, taking scienta linguarum out of the closet and into the world, have long eschewed esoteric theorizing. This does not mean a total rejection of Chomskyan theory or of anyone else's. Rather, those insights which explain—or teach—real life phenomena are being used in studies as diverse as social stratification, psychotherapy, and rhetoric.

2. THE PROBLEM OF TEACHING RHETORIC

What has long been considered tried and true in teaching writing has, in the past decade or so, been tried and found not to be so true. Neither handbooks, essay reading, red-penciling compositions, nor even the most cherished of our personal attentions, the student/teacher conference, has survived the crucible of teaching the TV generation. However, all is not lost. If some of the old ways fail, still others seem to work, as do a new trick or two. Specifically, collaborative learning and paraphrase exercises including sentence combining (SC in this paper) have been shown to be especially effective, even for those lacking elementary expository skills (Chaika 1974, 1978, Brufee 1980a, Daiker, Kerek, and Morenberg 1979, 1980). Fortunately, that other new development, the microcomputer, is especially well adapted to these techniques for teaching writing, making them even more effective.

2.1 The New Methodologies and Why They Work

It is not surprising that students learn to write better by collaborating with peers than by listening to teacher talk. We know from acquisition studies that humans learn language skills by partaking in social routines, and collaborating involves social routines. Language learning also demands a great deal of self-practice. This is why sentence-paraphrasing exercises are so effective. They are analogous to the constant chatter of young children as they experiment with speech forms. It has long been known that humans do not learn language solely by imitating. In fact, it is very difficult for people to imitate forms unless they have first figured out the rules that produce those forms. This is why children make so many funny mistakes as they are learning to speak. Perhaps, also, for this reason, having students read great essays in the hopes that these will teach writing does not seem to work, especially today when students are not exposed to years of literature as they would have been in former ages. Then, too, thanks to multiple choice questions and fill-in-the-blanks, they have not learned to formulate their thoughts in writing. Furthermore, since foreign language studies are no longer required in many schools, students often have not had the benefit of learning to heed fine points of structure as those of us weaned on traditional language studies did. In short, our freshman classes are loaded with people who have not had much opportunity to phrase their thoughts in writing, to study the structure of language, or to read enough to start learning the language of literacy.

Such students are, in writing, akin to the 3-year-old still mastering the rules of spoken discourse. They may know the basic rules for simple sentences, but have not yet mastered all the finer points of syntax, much less which type is appropriate for a given discourse situation. Nor has the 3-year-old yet learned just how much he or she must utter in order for listeners to follow an anecdote, just as our composition students do not know what to include in an essay.

Sentence paraphrasing exercises and collaborative learning simulate the conditions under which humans learn language in the first place. It is not suprising, then, that they are successful.

2.2 Validation of Sentence Combining Methodology

Ironically, it is Chomsky's own view of language that forms the basis of SC. Kerek, Daiker, and Morenberg (1980:85) show that students taught to write by SC showed highly significant improvement by every measure over those conventionally taught: holistic grading, forced choice (which of two themes was better), and increase in T-units. A variant of SC, paraphrasing exercises based upon case relationships between verbs and their nouns, is similarly successful (Chaika 1972, 1974), and for the same reasons. Case grammar is but another expression of transformational grammars. Both conceive of a deep structure meaning which may be paraphrased according to rule. Both SC and case grammars concur with the Chomskyan formulation that native speakers are competent to judge paraphrase and grammaticality, but cast doubt on the notion that transformations do not change meaning. To the contrary, what people recognize as paraphrases often does change meaning slightly, if only for emphasis. Fillmore (1968:48–49, Footnote 49) shows that one must allow for transformations which do have semantic import. Indeed, it has always seemed to me that if paraphrases within a language did not change meaning, then languages would be most inefficient, given the number of paraphrases which speakers and writers can think up for any given sentence. Moreover, it is most clear that beginning writers do have to be taught to look for the nuances in paraphrases. Undoubtedly, one reason that SC and case grammars have been so successful is that they focus learners on the semantic and stylistic consequences of paraphrase.

3. THE MACHINE

Before elaborating on this, however, let us consider that other anathema to those trained in the ways of Wadsworth and Wilde—the computer. Here, we will be talking about microcomputers fitted out with a word processing program, as this is what most teachers find available. The programs, like anything typed on the computer, are written onto diskettes which look like 45 RPM records. Machines that are just word processors may be available, as well as time on a large mainframe. It makes no difference. All work substantially the same way, hence will be referred to in this paper as *word processors*.

3.1 The Machine and the Humanities

Most of the people now teaching composition were never trained to teach it. Their forte is literature. They not only celebrate the great artists, but their analyses of great works are themselves prized for originality, even idiosyncracy. To such people, indeed to all of us in our naivete, computers, with or without word processing programs, dredge up images of robotized students and, worse, robotized professors. The very term WORD PROCESSOR sounds like a verbal Cuisinart, the antithesis of creativity and intelligence, much less Art. 'Oh,' many concede, 'computers are all right for teaching mechanics, but what else can they teach?' Or, one hears, 'Learning to write is such a glacial process; computers can't really speed it up.' True, computers are very handy for teaching the mechanics: agreement, punctuation, the difference between *infer* and *imply*. Certainly, instructors are delighted not to have to bore more classes with discussions on capitalization, but this is not all that computers can do. Exercises in mechanics don't even begin to tap the computer's potential (Schwartz 1982, Wresch 1982).

3.2 Hardware (to be skipped by those conversant with the beast)

What, perhaps, computer novices are unprepared to find is that the new machinery, used correctly, actually unleashes creativity, both in writers and in teachers. Word processors do not directly type on paper, as do typewriters. Rather, all typing is done onto a screen (known as a CRT 'cathode ray tube') which typically displays about 25 lines of text as a time. Any part of the larger text can be brought up on the screen as the writer needs it, however, giving the writer as much convenience as manuscripts typed on paper do.

This does not sound like the stuff of revolutions, in teaching or otherwise, but it is; for the word processor allows one to type over errors, or rapidly expunge anything from a word to a page. Furthermore, one can move words, phrases, and paragraphs around with but a flick of the finger or two. One is free to move from any part of the composition to any other, again by pressing a key or two. One may insert a word, a character, or even a whole page wherever and whenever the spirit moves. One can even tell the computer to replace one word with another, or with a phrase, or a phrase with a word, commands that take, literally, seconds—if that. Of course, if one doesn't like what one has wrought, one can ask the computer to reverse the process. The computer not only makes the changes, but automatically makes adjustments in lines, as well as margins, and page numbering after such operations.

3.3 Collaborative Learning

Fortunately, few schools have enough computers in any one room so that each student can have his/her own. I say fortunately because then two to three students have to work together in each class. The teacher need not lecture. He or she need only direct students at the keyboard in making certain changes, allowing students to discuss with each other the consequences. Since only one person can type in a response at one time, the students at each computer discuss each move with each other. This, of course, forces collaboration. Furthermore, whereas a student might feel inhibited about voicing his or her thoughts about language to a professor or the class as a whole, there is no such inhibition in speaking to one or two others. A great deal about language and rhetoric goes on all of the time in every class, discussion that stimulates students above and beyond the class exercises. Everyone in the class, even the quietest and shyest, discusses language, style, and grammaticality for the entire class and in each and every class. That can not happen with a blackboard, overhead projector, worksheets, or handbook. Students are focused on language and talking, even arguing, about it while the instructor floats from machine to machine, listening, answering, or questioning.

4. RAMIFICATIONS

From the outset, students are surprised to discover that they can comment on the effect of transformations as well as make decisions about grammaticality and style. In turn, this focuses the student on language in a way that traditional handbook techniques do not. Students quickly realize that language does have grammar, grammar that they are capable of discovering, and that the professor's criticisms are not arbitrary or mean. Thus an excellent atmosphere for learning is created (Chaika 1972, 1974, 1978).

4.1 The Significance of Speed

It is not that one cannot correct errors or insert or move around material by conventional means. One can. It is that, with the word processor, all is done so rapidly. This alone, as just about everybody who composes on one testifies, allows one's writing to keep up with one's mental processes, helping to make even an experienced writer's productions smoother. In the computer classroom, any lesson involving paraphrase not only proceeds almost as rapidly as students and teacher can think up variations, but the students get visual reinforcement of mental processes. As they move words around and insert new ones, they see the changes almost instantly. The display on the CRT seems almost as fluid as language processes in one's head.

4.2 Involvement

As impressive as all this is, still, perhaps the most important thing to remember is not the speed with which changes are made, but that every student in every class is undergoing every mental operation for him or herself. No more falling asleep while the teacher or the class talkers do all the composing. Those fortunate enough to be in a school such as mine, in which the computer labs are open long hours, can even set up lessons that those who cut classes must do on their own time. Thus, every student does all of the work in the semester. Computer-aided instruction, (hereafter CAI) allows, even demands, that students participate totally in the writing process, and that they become totally involved with it.

The exercises are set up to lead students to formulate rules of written discourse on their own (another important process in attaining language skills). Because they are working in teams, the students constantly talk about and analyze language throughout the entire composition class. Perhaps most importantly, each student has to compose in the process of learning how to write. Because of the extent of student involvement, CAI is intense.

5. THE ROLE OF CURRENT LINGUISTICS

One need not be wedded to any single theory of syntax or teaching methodology to take advantage of the creative potential of CAI. Except for programmed instruction in mechanics, lessons should be centered around revising sentences, paragraphs, and even whole themes. For example, paraphrasing exercises are obvious candidates for computerized teaching. Since these need not involve any technological jargon, even when they are based upon transformational or case grammars, teachers with no training in the theories behind them can still use them effectively. My own preference is to use the students' own sentences for such exercises, using canned examples only to introduce each lesson. For instance, if faulty coordination is the day's text, then I type sets of sentences on computer diskette, some of which can and some of which cannot be coordinated. After the students have revised and discussed these, then samples of faulty coordination or failures to coordinate taken from their own themes are presented.

5.1 For Instance, the Passive

Recent work in discourse and text analysis also can be translated into composition lessons, providing both superb error analysis and insights into rhetorical practise. For instance, recently the passive has become a veritable whipping boy. However, students do not even know what the passive is, much less what to do to avoid it. Yet, if the construction is in the language, one supposes it must have developed for a reason which must be discovered. Then, after one determines the proper ways to use the passive, one is faced with the problem of knowing when to delete the agent. All these lessons are easily taught on the computer, as issues related to the requirements of discourse.

Students can be taught to recognize the passive by transforming active sentences into passives, and vice versa. I find this more effective than discussing goals of action or receivers of action. They quickly learn the concept of subject position and the paraphrase that puts something in object position into subject position. Once they have mastered this for verbs of all tenses and aspects, students can be asked what can be deleted in the passive, but not the active. The students delete with the flick of a finger. Thus, they learn that one function of the passive is to omit mention of agent or cause. A discussion is encouraged about when this is desirable and when not. This can be demonstrated by having them type in phrases or sentences to create a context. For the sentence *The Japanese regularly slaughter dolphins,* students see that *Dolphins are slaughtered regularly by the Japanese* emphasizes that it is the Japanese who are responsible, and that this is both normal and desirable if the context is something like . . . *not the Russians* or *Although you wouldn't believe it,* . . . If one were Japanese and at a Greenpeace meeting, then one might want to delete the agent. As it happens, this is usually the first lesson in my composition classes, as it immediately focuses students on language structure, the possibilities and consequences of paraphrase, and its relationship to the text as a whole. Moreover, it is highly doable, and students are not threatened by it.

5.2 Subordination

The concepts of subordinating are especially easily taught on a computer. Besides what by now are virtually traditional SC exercises, creating one sentence out of two or more, one can present an entire composition consisting of simple sentences. Students then are asked to combine them, using whatever linguistic devices are necessary for well-formedness, e.g., deletion, adding morphemes like *-ing* or words like *for . . . to*. In this exercise, attention has to be paid to the requirements of the text as well as to the feasibility of combining. Students can be asked to justify the decisions they have made, trying to formulate rules whenever appropriate. For instance, subordinating one sentence to another may make cause and effect explicit rather than implicit, or a nominalization may effectively cut off any discussion of truth value. Alternatively, by keeping the sentence intact rather than converting it to a gerund or other nominalized sentence, one may be inviting discussion of whether or not it is true. The students themselves articulate exactly what semantic and stylistic consequences have accrued as a result of their joining two or more sentences into one. I move from computer to computer, having the team at each tell me what they have done and why. Far from being robotized, students are gently forced into participation in the learning process.

5.4 Ordering the Text

It is not only at the sentence level that CAI excels. The very fluidity of word processors means that larger concerns, such as ordering of paragraphs, are a joy to teach on computers. Students can move paragraphs around at will, as well as sentences within paragraphs. They can revise either as the spirit moves, and see the consequences in a fraction of the time that blackboards take. True, overhead projectors and prepared mimeos can be used to show different versions of the same essay, but these are not manipulated by the student, thereby giving him or her the crucial practice of formulating for him or herself.

5.4 What to Include

One persistent problem in essay construction is that of how much to include. One has to explain, on the one hand, why the student has information gaps between sentences, and, on the other, why they have included more than the reader needs to know. One way to handle this is to put on diskettes paragraphs from student themes which have instances of both faults. Students can be asked to highlight or bracket all the new information.[1] After this is done, they literally see the flow of information, and whether or not it follows the optimal order [orienter]-[old information]-[new information], with old information including what is known by all members of a given culture (Chaika 1982:178, Williams 1981:107, 109, 111–112, 121). If there is a departure from this order, students can be asked to justify it. Perhaps a special focusing transformation has been invoked, such as clefting, e.g., *It was the brown suit that he wore* from *He wore a brown suit.* If not, then students know where to make changes. In any event, gaps are readily seen, as well as overdetailed, known material.

5.5 Dialogues and Computer Correction

Schwartz (1982) describes some innovative programs that engage the writing student in dialogues. These can be purchased ready made, or clever programmers can find inspiration to formulate their own. The better ones actually ask students probing questions. For instance, one, based upon Aristotelian topics (Schwartz 1982:147) asks the students to clarify the purpose of his or her paper, first by completing the sentence *The purpose of this paper is to . . .* If the student responds, for instance, with *fear of death,* he or she is then asked a series of questions like *What objects do you associate with fear of death?* (or any other topic chosen by student). Thus is the student led to a full development of a topic.

Wresch (1982) discusses a program that reads a composition and shows students that their sentences are too convoluted (p. 489) or contain other stylistically poor choices.

---

[1] Whether one uses highlighting or brackets depends upon the capabilities of the word processing program and computer being used. Not all have highlighting.

6. THE COMPOSING PROCESS

6.0 Getting Started

Even in the all-important problem of getting started (Brufee 1980b), word processors are of inestimable help. Brufee claims, and I think rightly, that one must know the order or form of the entire before one can start to write. This does not mean that one can not change the order or form as one composes, or even after. Clearly, we all do that. Indeed, we often change sentences in midstream, both in writing and in speech. Such false starts give transcripts of spontaneous speech a disjointed air (e.g., Schenkein 1978, Chaika 1981). However, in order to get started, one seems to need some map of where it is all to go.

We might avail ourselves of D'Angelo's (1975, 1980) insights in getting our students started. He advises setting up paradigms for different kinds of themes. For instance,

> Introduction (states the thesis)
>
> Example
> (1 . . . n)
>
> Conclusion
> (restates the thesis, summarizes, . . .)
> (D'Angelo 1980:42).

Students, after choosing a topic, select the paradigm they think appropriate. The students then type in phrases or words under the headings, later fleshing them out. These may be in any order in which ideas come to mind. Of course, one may simply jot down random thoughts on the topic as they come to mind, then elaborate on them and reorder them into a theme. D'Angelo's paradigms are more structured, making them more valuable to some beginning students. Either way, the word processor allows the writer to build up from the notes by bleeping out or typing over the original paradigm headings and/or jottings, so that he or she progresses from outline to notes to finished product. However, this transition is unlikely to be linear.

6.1 The Way People Compose

Recent extensive studies into the composing processes of both skilled and unskilled writers have shown that they write, plan, review, revise, and anticipate, moving back and forth among these different operations (Hairston 1982:85). Writers do not neatly first outline, then write, then revise the entire, as conventional methodologies imply. CAI encourages the student in the natural cycling through various operations. It enables them to go swiftly through several possibilities, and test them all out, at every level of writing—from word choice to text organization.

Wresch (1982:489) tells also of a dialogue program that can be used for prewriting. Here, when a student tells the computer *I don't know what you want me to say* (about Dreiser's dramatic technique), the computer responds with *Concentrate now on seeing Dreiser's dramatic technique. What features stand out the most? Describe. Your turn, Karen.* And so the computer gets the girl started. Wresch says the student remained for 40 minutes of questioning, and left with 18 pages of transcript.

7. IN SUM

7.0 The Need for CAI

The current crisis in literacy facing the nation's colleges may well be resolved, indeed may only be solvable, by the advent of relatively inexpensive microcomputers fitted out with word processing programs. Basic Writing courses today are expected to do what 12 years of schooling and a good deal of recreational reading once did: acquaint people with the written language. CAI allows an intensity of instruction not possible in older methods. This intensity is fostered in two ways: by visually presenting changes in text almost as fast as the brain can produce and comprehend them, and by involving every student in the class in every bit of creating and analyzing.

7.1 How to Set Up CAI

If your school has not yet made computers available for writing instruction, the best and simplest way to implement it is to cast longing eyes at your microcomputer labs. If there are any computer programming courses taught there, your school probably has at least one such lab. If not, then they must have a mainframe with terminals that students and faculties can use. So long as there is a word processing program, either facility can be used. Visit your local computer department, and ask if they will allow you to use the computer room for one of your classes on an experimental basis. That's how I got my first chance at CAI. The computer people were so delighted with the prospect of extending computer literacy to the English department that they let me have it for one class, even though their own students had to be denied use of the machines for 3 hours a week. If you both begin and end the semester with appropriate testing to determine objectively the efficacy of the computer instruction, you then should have ammunition to campaign for more computer time—or computers for the Basic Writing courses.

8. TWO LESSONS

8.0 Cases in Point

The knotty problem of "awkward" sentences and what they actually are plagues us, and, even more, our students. Suzette Elgin (1982) and Joseph Williams (1981) each provide a different solution to the problem of showing students what is awkward. Never being ashamed to borrow, I adapted both of their wise treatments to CAI. The lessons were typed onto diskette, and then transferred by a simple copying routine to the students' diskettes. These lessons are not being presented as the last word, or even as anything approaching the best. They are simply illustrations of what may be done either when an idea hits you, or when someone else's does.

8.1 What is *Awkward?*

The following appears on the computer screen. Students read it at their own speed and do any operations asked:

How frustrating to see your sentences marked AWKWARD. What is awkward? Why is one sentence awkward, but another not? Many violate no rules of the language, but are still not felicitous. It is most aggravating to be told that you simply must develop an ear or get a feel for sentences. If you haven't done so, then clearly you haven't figured out how to. Telling clumsy writers to stop being awkward is a little like telling a short person to become tall. How does one do it?

Fortunately, some concrete answers have been forthcoming, answers that allow writers to check their own sentences for awkwardness.

For sentences to be clear and graceful, they must not be difficult for the human mind to process. Now this seems almost absurdly obvious—but there is a wrinkle. Long ago, a psychologist, George Miller, showed that the number of chunks of information that a human being can manage to deal with efficiently is about seven. He called this the MAGIC NUMBER SEVEN PLUS OR MINUS TWO. As Suzette Elgin (1982:14) comments,

> It's no accident that telephone numbers have seven digits, broken into handy groups of three digits plus four digits. It's no accident that when little kids learn the alphabet they chunk it like this: ABCDEFG, HIJK, LMNOP; QRS and TUV. It's no accident that our Social Security numbers are nine digits long, and that the digits are broken up for us into groups of three and two and five. Everywhere in the real world business and government and other centers of power (not to mention wise little children!) make use of the natural limitations on memory for information processing in the human mind. (Elgin 1982:14).

When Professor Elgin analyzed thousands of sentences marked *awkward,* she found that, a large percentage of the time, such sentences contained sequences that violated the constraints of the 'magic number seven plus or minus two' Let's test that contention out. Examine 1.–5.

1. That Max insisted on puffing on a cigar even though it obviously was making the woman sitting next to him cough annoyed me.
2. It annoyed me that Max insisted on puffing on a cigar even though it obviously was making the woman sitting next to him cough.
3. For Max to insist on puffing his cigar even though it obviously was making the woman sitting next to him cough always annoyed me.
4. Max's insistence on puffing his cigar even though it obviously was making the woman sitting next to him cough always annoyed me.
5. Whether Max insisted on puffing his cigar just to be annoying or because he disliked this woman sitting next to him wasn't known.

Mark every sentence that seems awkward with an asterisk (*). Put a slash before every sentence that is difficult to understand on the first reading. Did you mark the same sentences? Mark the beginning and end of every block that seems to be making the sentence awkward or difficult to understand.

Most people find number 2 the least awkward and the easiest to understand. Mark the complete subject in each sentence. Except for number 2, does this coincide with the block you marked as being awkward or difficult? Count the number of words in these complete subjects. Does your count verify or refute Elgin's theory of the magical number seven plus or minus two. Subjects with more than nine words burden the memory, so that it is difficult to remember which word, as simple subject, goes with the predicate verb, such as *annoyed me* or *wasn't known*.

Now, mark off both the matrix and embedded sentences in 2.[2] Next, count how many words, if any, are between the simple subject and predicate of each of these sentences. How does 2 differ from the rest of the sentences:

a. in the way that sentences are embedded into the matrix?
b. in the size of constructions intervening between subjects and predicates, including those in embedded sentences?

On the basis of your counts, have you modified your agreement (or disagreement) with Elgin about the magical number seven plus two? Explain your answer.

(Here I give three or four awkward sentences from their own papers for them to rewrite.)

8.2 Another View of Awkwardness

Joseph Williams explains awkward sentences a bit differently. He focuses on relative clauses. We have already seen that these typically come between subjects and predicates, but still they, too, may be implicated in awkwardness:

6. A discovery that will change the course of world history and the very foundations of our understanding of who we are and our place in the scheme of things is imminent.
7. A marketing approach that will allow us to take advantage of shifting demographic patterns and changing tastes has been developed (both examples from Williams 1981:96).

We have already seen many times that heavy constructions can be zapped to the end of a sentence. Here, too, this is a cure. Mark the relative clauses in 6 and 7. Now move them after the predicate verbs in each sentence, respectively. Which version of each is easier to understand, and which seems less awkward?

Does your first formula for avoiding awkward sentences work for these? In the light of 6 and 7, does Elgin's explanation still seem to hold?

Consider previous lessons on passive voice, starting sentences with *it* and

---

2 My students learn this early on as a result of SC exercises.

there—and the zapping of heavy constructions to the ends of sentences. How do these relate to the concept of awkwardness discussed here? Do they fit into your formula?

(Here I take some awkward sentences from the students' own themes for them to correct on the computer.)

8.3 Another Kind of Awkwardness

Now consider the following sentences.

8. New car model tire durability enforcement is a Federal Trade Commission responsibility.
9. Corporation organization under state law supervision has resulted in federal government inability as to effective implementation of pollution reduction measures.
10. Early childhood thought disorder misdiagnosis often occurs as a result of unfamiliarity with recent research literature describing such conditions.
11. The city's sale tax position toward an increase contradicts the State Finance Office's recent announcement.

Does your formula for awkwardness prevent sentences like 8–11? Does the "magic number seven plus two" seem to be implicated in these?

Bracket those constructions which seem awkward.

Bracket those constructions which are hard to understand.

Did you bracket the same constructions for both?

Even though they do not violate the magic number constraint, why do these seem overloaded? What grammatical construction are the bracketed portions of the sentences? Can you think of deep structure sentences that underlie these noun phrases? Consider the subject of 8, for instance:

8a. *New car model tire durability enforcement*

Change *enforcement* back to a verb. Now make 8a into a sentence.

(They come up with: *Someone must enforce the durability of tires for new car models . . . or the like.)*

Reading further on in the sentence, we see that someone is the Federal Trade Commission. The original author of 8 apparently also wished to emphasize that this is their responsibility (Williams 1981:22).

Rewrite the rest of this sentence, and 9–11, so that they are no longer awkward. (Again, here they have to rewrite sentences from themes.)

REFERENCES

BRUFEE, K. 1980a. A short course in writing, 2nd ed. Cambridge, MA: Winthrop Publishers.

______. 1980b. Getting started. Language and Style 13. 52–60.

CHAIKA, E. 1972. Models of grammar and the pedagogical problem. Unpublished Brown University dissertation.

———. 1974. Who can be taught? College English 35. 575–583.
———. 1978. Grammars and teaching. College English 39. 770–783.
———. 1981. How shall a discourse be understood? Discourse Processes 4.71–88.
———. 1982. A unified explanation for the diverse structural deviations reported for adult schizophrenics with disrupted speech. Journal of Communication Disorders 15. 167–189.
DAIKER, D. A., A. KEREK, and M. MORENBERG. 1979. The writer's options: College sentence combining. New York: Harper and Row.
———. 1980. The effects of intensive sentence combining on the writing ability of college freshmen. Language and Style 13. 81–90.
D'ANGELO, F. 1975. A conceptual theory of rhetoric. Cambridge, MA: Winthrop Publishers.
———. 1980. Paradigms as structural counterparts of Topoi. Language and Style 13. 41–51.
ELGIN, S. 1982. The great grammar myth. Occasional Paper No. 5. Berkeley, CA: National Writing Project.
FILLMORE, C. 1968. The case for case. Universals of linguistic theory, ed. by E. Bach and R. Harms, 1–88. New York: Holt, Rinehart, and Winston.
HAIRSTON, M. 1982. The winds of change: Thomas Kuhn and the revolution in the teaching of writing. College Composition and Communication 23. 76–88.
SCHENKEIN, J., ed. 1978. Studies in the organization of conversational interaction. New York: Academic Press.
SCHWARTZ, H. 1982. Monsters and mentors: Computer applications for humanistic education. College English 44. 141–152.
WILLIAMS, J. 1981. Style: Ten lessons in clarity and grace. Glenview, IL: Scott, Foresman, and Company.
WRESCH, W. 1982. Computers in the English class: Finally beyond grammar and spelling drills. College English 44. 483–490.

SEVENTEEN

Microcomputers in the Composing Process

Helen J. Schwartz
Oakland University

Computers offer new ways to implement composition theory throughout the composing process. Existing programs (most available for microcomputers) can be used. However, the expertise of classroom instructors is and must remain essential for the sensible use of such programs.

Although different writers will use different processes for different kinds of writing, most writers, at some stage in the process of composition, will engage in the following practices (written, some spoken aloud or to themselves):

1. Invention: finding something to say, whether by a search of memory, by observation, or through research.
2. Organization: forming a meaning by deciding on a purpose and planning what to include and how to present it to affect an audience.
3. Writing down the meaning as it is discovered.
4. Revision: reformation for revised meaning and suitability for purpose and audience, for clarity, and for cohesion.
5. Polishing: editing for readability, style, and correctness.

These practices are not separate, mutually exclusive, or strictly sequential. If we pay attention to our own process of writing, we can see these activities cropping up in different ways in different stages. In the midst of re-vision we may see a need for additional information and do additional research. Or, in the midst of writing, we may pause to edit a turn of phrase or change the order of paragraphs.

Many times, however, the emphasis in writing classes is on steps one, two, and three. Even if there were time for re-viewing, there seems to be too little time (or money) for retyping, and editing is either too mysterious or time consuming. Here computers can be especially useful (in addition to their use for the first three steps), because they make revision convenient, quick, and interesting. And it is re-viewing and editing that are often most crucial for completing the act of communication successfully for the writer.

For once we have discovered what we mean, and perhaps have even written it down, the act of communication is not over. Someone, usually, will read our writing and try to decipher the meaning there. People always try to find meaning. If the meaning doesn't seem very important, they may not try very hard, but they will try. That's the way the world makes sense to them and the way they come to feel they can make their way in the world.

INVENTION

Invention means finding something to say. This may involve a systematic search of the writer's memory, analysis (especially according to disciplinary conventions), and research. Computers can help with all three aspects of invention.

Computer programs written by Hugh Burns can help students with a systematic search of memory. Burns has written three programs: BURKE is based on Kenneth Burke's 'pentad' asking questions about act, agency, agent, scene, and purpose; TAGI is based on the tagmemic matrix, which explores a topic by thinking of it as a particle (a thing in itself), a wave (something that changes through time), and a field (as part of a larger group); finally, TOPOI is based on Aristotelian topics for persuasion, such as definition, cause and effect, discussion of consequences, or associations.

Using Burns's program, BURKE takes the management decision out of the writer's hands. That is, instead of deciding which question to work with, the program supplies the questions. The writer is given the option of choosing a particular kind of question (on act, agency, agent, scene, or purpose), and he or she can get further explanations of questions, but generally he or she simply responds to the programmed questions.

I tried using the computer program on a topic I knew nothing about, 'petuntze production'. (Petuntze is a kind of ground stone used in the manufacture of porcelain.) After being asked for a one- to three-word description of my topic, I was advised to check for recent research on the topic and then quizzed about my purpose for the paper. (Notice that the program takes my input 'petuntze production' and uses it as a string variable in some of the subsequent questions to individualize the procedure to my interests.) Since I really hadn't decided on a focus, I kept my answer rather general. (In the examples, my input is in lower case letters after the program's prompting question marks.)

> BRIEFLY DESCRIBE THE PURPOSE OF YOUR PAPER BY COMPLETING THIS STATEMENT:
> THE PURPOSE OF MY PAPER IS TO . . .
> ? discuss something about petuntze production

The directions and program comments advised me that I could change my purpose later. And the program prompted me to do so at several points, though the choice to narrow or reword the topic was up to me. The pentad procedure on the computer produced the following dialogue:

> WHO ESPECIALLY CARES ABOUT PETUNTZE PRODUCTION?
> EXPLAIN THEIR REASONS.
> ? porcelain manufacturers care bec. it is a crucial ingredient.

? the people who live near the mining site care bec. there may be ecological impact.
WHAT'S SO SIGNIFICANT ABOUT PETUNTZE PRODUCTION? IN OTHER WORDS, 'SO WHAT?'.
? porcelain is a luxury item. it makes especially fine china—thin, translucent. Also, for fine art work. possible to do more detail with porcelain than other clays.
DO YOU WISH TO CHANGE OR NARROW YOUR SUBJECT?
? the effect of petuntze production on the fine and decorative arts
THAT'S A MOUTHFUL, HELEN. MAKE IT SHORTER—LIKE A TITLE.
? pp and the arts
DESCRIBE OR LIST WHAT OTHERS MAY NOT KNOW ABOUT PP AND THE ARTS.
? how petuntze is mined
? how political & historical events have affected production
? comparison of porcelain to other clays to show superiority of porcelain
WHERE DOES PP AND THE ARTS OCCUR? DESCRIBE.
? my friend Barbara uses it [porcelain.]
? she is a semi-professional potter, but it's largely used in china making
? Lynn in Wyoming also seemed to be using it for her 'cattle skull' sculptures. check.
WHO ESPECIALLY THINKS ABOUT PP AND THE ARTS? WHY? EXPLAIN.
? potters. I need to find out whether petuntze is mined other than in china
THAT'S THE IDEA, HELEN. GIVE ME SOME MORE INFO NOW.
? change! [The command, followed by an exclamation point, directs the program to allow me to change my topic. Here I took the initiative.]
PLEASE TYPE IN YOUR NEW SUBJECT:
? potters & petuntze
(REASONS ARE IMPORTANT TOO—THE MORE, THE BETTER.)
WHAT CAUSES POTTERS & PETUNTZE? EXPLAIN.
? potters are concerned about the cost and availability of raw materials because cost affects the prices they can charge and availability may affect their artistic development, hampering them or causing them to experiment with new media.
HOW IS THE PURPOSE OF POTTERS & PETUNTZE PART OF A LARGER PURPOSE?
DESCRIBE THIS LARGER PURPOSE.
? explain! [This command asks for more information.]
WHAT'S THE BIG PICTURE? HOW DOES POTTERS & PETUNTZE FIT INTO THE OVERALL SCHEME? WHAT ARE YOU THINKING NOW?
? it's really a little part. Exploration and commerce can affect the style of arts bec. of materials or cultural exchange of ideas. For example, Picasso's cubism seems influenced by African art, and china makers of the 19th century were influenced heavily by chinese art and discovery of Tutankahmen's tomb started an Egyptian revival in 20th century.
GOOD, HELEN. ADD TO YOUR RESPONSE NOW.

? also, Manet's strong outlines derived from influence of Eastern, oriental art.
SUPER, HELEN! ANYTHING ELSE?
? continue!
WHAT AUTHORITIES KNOW ABOUT POTTERS & PETUNTZE? ARE THEY RELIABLE?
? I could write to Lynn and Barbara and ask about petuntze in particular and the effect of raw material prices and availability in general.
GOOD, HELEN. ADD TO YOUR RESPONSE NOW.
? Check mining or encyclopedia publications or the card catalog and check history of China. Ask Shelly for suggestions, too, or ref. libe.
SUPER, HELEN! ANYTHING ELSE?
? maybe check Chinese embassy to see if they have any handout info.
WHAT PURPOSE DOES POTTERS & PETUNTZE HAVE?
? change! [This allows me to change my topic.]
PLEASE TYPE IN YOUR NEW SUBJECT:
? craftspeople and the world
HOW ARE PEOPLE CONSCIOUSLY OR UNCONSCIOUSLY INVOLVED WITH CRAFTSPEOPLE AND THE WORLD?
? agent! [This command directs the program to produce a question concerning the agent in petuntze production.]
WHAT AUDIENCE WOULD MOST APPRECIATE KNOWING MORE ABOUT CRAFTSPEOPLE AND THE WORLD?
? junior craftspeople (teen or pre-teen?); craft mag.; general public like Smithsonian
WHATEVER YOU THINK BEST, HELEN. YOU DECIDE.
? scene! [This requests a question on scene.]
WHAT IS THE SETTING FOR CRAFTSPEOPLE AND THE WORLD? DESCRIBE.
? the workshop of Lynn or Barbara and a mine for making petuntze
? act!
HOW IS CRAFTSPEOPLE AND THE WORLD LIKE A RAINBOW?
? explain!
ANALOGIES ARE OFTEN FRUITFUL WAYS TO THINK ABOUT A TOPIC. A RAINBOW CAN BE A SYMBOL OF HOPE, A SHORT-LIVED PHENOMENON, OR SOMETHING WHICH DEMONSTRATES A RANGE OF COLORS. IS CRAFTSPEOPLE AND THE WORLD LIKE A RAINBOW? YOUR TURN, HELEN.
? a rainbow links 2 parts of the world by where it begins & ends and it's also beautiful.
? so too, something as mundane as petuntze production links the history, politics and economy of China and the work, economy and spirit of Lynn in Laramie, Wyoming as Lynn strives to find beauty and form and understanding of the American experience.
TERRIFIC, HELEN. ANYTHING ELSE?
? stop!

Would you have come up with a different focus? Could you see where I was going with the paper topic? I found that I 'knew' more about petuntze than I thought. But when you review the example, I really didn't. What I did was remember peripheral information (based on my experience and knowledge) that revealed an approach to the topic, a way to focus my further research.

Furthermore, I've been assuming that the purpose in writing was rather general, and that the focus was up to me and the audience was a general one (intelligent strangers). If the topic had been more proscribed and limited (for example, discuss the companies involved in petuntze production and evaluate their profitability over the last 5 years), then my responses would have been different and perhaps it would have been better if I conducted research before using the heuristic. But, as it was, I used the pentad to search my memory and come up with ideas to explore further for a paper.

Finally, notice that, with a free topic, the pentad helped me get an angle and limit the topic (especially the rainbow question!) but that I still have to do research. Nevertheless, the pentad helped me narrow the field for research (Lynn, mining, and Chinese history) and got me started on a plan of research (write Lynn, check encyclopedias, card catalog, reference librarian, and colleague in China studies). And notice how, as my purpose narrowed, I could begin to answer questions about my audience—who would want to know about my topic.

An interesting question is whether a different set of questions would produce a different focus. Probably. But there are three points to make here:

- *First,* the computer program has some of the urgency and immediacy of talking to a real person, and this starts me brainstorming. At least, I FEEL more like responding than when I stare at the grid.
- *Second,* I have some assurance that the spontaneity and randomness of the program doesn't prevent a systematic search. I have the grid to check with afterwards, once I've started, and I can check for completeness of coverage if I feel that I need further brainstorming.
- *Third,* I have more than enough material to continue my work with the paper. Instead of feeling uninspired and ignorant, I now realize that I have some starting place, some knowledge. Petuntze production, while still not a burning concern in my life, is nevertheless something that relates to my experience. And if I can relate to it, then I can probably get my audience to relate to it, too.

In contrast to my somewhat artificial example, contrast the following use of the Aristotelian program TOPOI by a student beginning work on a term project. She went in with no notion of what her paper would 'feel' like. She chose the topic 'translation by computers', and identified her purpose as an investigation of whether computer translation were possible. Here are some selections from her running of the program:

> DOES PUBLIC OPINION ABOUT TRANSLATION BY COMPUTERS DIFFER FROM PRIVATE OPINION?
> ? yes, many people probably believe computers could never translate.
> WHAT ARE THE GOOD CONSEQUENCES OF TRANSLATION BY COMPUTERS?

speed, objectivity, accuracy
WHAT COULD BE CONSIDERED A RESULT OF TRANSLATION BY COMPUTERS?
more literature from other countries being translated more often and more clearly
WHAT ARE SOME OF THE PREVIOUS MISTAKES ABOUT TRANSLATION BY COMPUTERS?
? explain
SIMPLY, WHAT HAS BEEN WRONG WITH THE WAY TRANSLATION BY COMPUTERS HAS BEEN HANDLED? MAYBE 'MISTAKE' IS TOO HARSH A TERM: 'MISTREATMENT' MAY BE BETTER FOR THIS TOPIC.
? i'll have to investigate?

(The student commented on the printout that this was a helpful question, identifying where she needed to do research: 'probably wouldn't have realized the importance' of this topic without the question.)

WHAT IS THE MOST LIKELY PLACE FOR TRANSLATION BY COMPUTERS TO EXIST?
? in publishing
THAT'S THE IDEA, PATTI. GIVE ME SOME MORE INFO NOW.
? by the authors
DIVIDE TRANSLATION BY COMPUTERS INTO THREE SUB-TOPICS
? can it be done, is it more efficient, and what are the problems

(The student identified this as a good suggestion. Would it have been helpful as the FIRST? Would it have been a better or worse approach if it did not suggest a specific number, like three? or if it suggested five sub-topics?)

WHAT SPECIAL EXPERIENCES MADE YOU SELECT TRANSLATION BY COMPUTERS AS YOUR TOPIC?
my literature in translation class. i would like to do similar research for both classes and i don't really think computers can translate concepts like man can

(This is an especially good question because it forces you to make a personal connection to the topic. This may suggest an angle into the topic that will be interesting to you, and therefore probably interesting to your reader.)

WHAT WOULD BE THE WORST THING THAT COULD HAPPEN TO TRANSLATION BY COMPUTERS?
? the translation would be stilted, conceptually inaccurate, and useless
WHAT WOULD BE THE BEST THING THAT COULD HAPPEN TO TRANSLATION BY COMPUTERS?
? that it was successful, bug-free, and promoted more translation
WHAT FACTS ARE YOU UNLIKELY TO KNOW ABOUT TRANSLATION BY COMPUTERS?
? explain!
I BET YOU ARE SAYING TO YOURSELF, 'HOW SHOULD I KNOW?' WELL, IF YOU ARE GOING TO WRITE A CONVINCING PAPER

ABOUT TRANSLATION BY COMPUTERS, YOU MUST FIND OUT AS EARLY AS POSSIBLE THOSE AREAS WHICH NEED TO BE RESEARCHED. RIGHT NOW, I'M ASKING YOU TO PREDICT WHERE YOU CAN FIND SOME MORE FACTS.
? programming difficulties, what has been done so far in the field
WHO WOULD YOU CONSIDER AN AUTHORITY ON TRANSLATION BY COMPUTERS?
? someone who's done it, tried, or knows about translation, or computers
BY 'AUTHORITY' I MEAN A SO-CALLED EXPERT. AS YOU WRITE THE PAPER, YOU MAY QUOTE THESE PEOPLE. GENERALLY, THEIR OPINIONS ARE RESPECTED—IF NOT BELIEVED.

The student commented, after the session was over, 'I made some things up in the beginning, but I learned *a lot* and am now interested in doing real research!'

CONVENTIONS OF THE DISCIPLINE

Sometimes a student will not want to be totally free to notice something new, but will want to follow an established procedure to find specific kinds of evidence. The heuristics or search procedures discussed earlier may not be very helpful, especially when writing for a more specialized audience on an assigned topic. The student may have trouble knowing what to say: What does the audience expect in the way of evidence? What is an acceptable form or presentation for arguing that evidence? Answers to these questions about content and form identify the CONVENTIONS of an audience.

And these conventions show how and what to observe. That is, conventions help people PERCEIVE what they have seen—to see it with particularity while also placing the object of our observation within a context.

The search procedures already discussed can help in general with this task of noticing and analyzing. But when writing should be guided by conventions, the writer who does not know the conventions faces special difficulties unless she can pick up the conventions quickly.

A computer program I've designed asks a series of questions conventional in a discipline, thereby helping the writer to 'perceive' what's been seen. As the questions occur again and again, the writer effortlessly picks up the conventions of evidence and learns to use them as guidelines in future observations. As the writer sees the ideas of others and comments on them, he or she realizes what kinds of evidence need to be argued and is able to refine his or her ideas in the give-and-take of discourse.

The computer program I've developed is called SEEN—the Seeing-Eye Elephant Network. The 'seeing-eye' part tutors a student to 'perceive' what he or she has 'seen'; here the student writes a 'notice' in response to questions that ask for evidence conventional to arguments in the discipline. The 'network' is the part of the program which allows students to see and write 'comments' on each others' work. (This helps develop critical ability in refining ideas.) The 'elephant' is the part of the program that records and remembers what the student has written (or revised) in a 'notice' or in a 'comment.' (This allows the student to learn how he or she has learned by tracing how ideas were developed.)

As in Burns's programs TAGI, BURKE, and TOPOI, the program cannot 'judge' the responses of the student—either in the tutorial or on the network.

But let's see how one student has actually used the program. In the version of SEEN used, the discipline was literary analysis, and the program was designed to help students develop a character analysis of some fictional person. A 20-year-old senior in biochemistry used SEEN as part of her world literature class. During a time scheduled for her convenience, she responded to the program's prompts, hypothesizing that Satan in *Paradise Lost* is 'tricky.' The tutorial then asked Kami (her pen-name) to provide various kinds of evidence (with the computer's prompts in capital letters):

> WHAT DOES SATAN DO THAT SHOWS SATAN IS TRICKY?
> 1) He enters the body of a serpent to disguise himself
> 2) He convinces Eve to eat from the tree of wisdom by telling her lies about it
> 3) He is able to convince Eve that he is a wise serpent and not her enemy.

The program then asked Kami for further evidence that Satan is tricky—because of (a) what he says, (b) how others react to him, (c) how he compares to others in a similar situation, and (d) what the third-person narrator (if any) says to him. (The user gets numerous chances to modify and edit her 'notice.') The program does not judge spelling or ideas, but it does, at this point, encourage self-criticism by asking the student to look at her evidence critically (with the computer prompts in all capital letters):

> OK, NOW TRY TO THINK OF ANY EXCEPTIONS OR CONTRADICTORY EXAMPLES. WHAT EVIDENCE SHOWS THAT SATAN IS NOT TRICKY?
> Adam and Eve know that there is someone out to get them
> AT THIS POINT DO YOU WANT TO
> 1 = CHANGE LIST ENTRY (& ERASE EXCEPTION JUST LISTED)
> 2 = EXPLAIN THE APPARENT CONTRADICTION
> 3 = ADD THE EXCEPTION WITHOUT COMMENT
> DO YOU WANT 1, 2 OR 3? *2* [carriage return]
> COMPLETE THE FOLLOWING STATEMENT:
> ADAM AND EVE KNOW THAT THERE IS SOMEONE OUT TO GET THEM BUT . . . they don't know what he will do or what he will look like.

When Kami finishes, she has the beginnings of an essay on Satan.

The following outlines the format of this analytical program, the current wording of the application, and selections from Kami's actual response:

General Format	Particular application	Student Response
Pick an X.	Name a fictional character X in a literary work	X = Satan in *Paradise Lost*
Create hypothesis:	Describe the character X by completing the following: X is	
X = Y	___Y___.	Satan is Y = tricky
Argue that X = Y —regarding type A evidence	Provide evidence to show that X is Y: What does Satan DO that shows Satan is tricky?	He enters the body of a serpent to disguise himself . . .
—regarding type B evidence	What does Satan SAY that shows Satan is tricky.	He tells Eve lies about the tree of wisdom to get her to eat from it . . .*
—regarding type C evidence	How do OTHERS react to Satan that shows Satan is tricky?	God had originally thrown Satan out of heaven because he didn't trust him
—regarding type D evidence	How does Satan COMPARE to others in a similar situation and how does this show Satan is tricky?	The other angels do not compare themselves to God & are not thrown out*
—regarding type E evidence	If there is a 3rd person narrator, what does he say that shows Satan is tricky?	He says that Satan chooses the subtlest of beasts for his embodiment
Consider conflicting evidence	What evidence shows that Satan is NOT tricky?	Adam and Eve know that there is someone out to get them

*Note that the program does not (and cannot) respond to inaccurate or unclear responses. That is a job for PEOPLE, who respond on the Network.

In light of this evidence, you can now revise your notice, explain the apparent contradiction or leave the exception without comment. The student 'explained' her contradiction by adding the following: 'But they don't know what he will do or what he will look like.'

After Kami finished the tutorial, her 'notice' was recorded in her individual computer file, and posted on the Network and signed with her chosen pen-name. This qualified her to (a) see any 'notice' on the Network, (b) add a comment (signed automatically with her pen-name) to any 'notice', or (c) see any comment.

On this particular occasion, after Kami wrote her notice, she got INDIRECT feedback by looking at a notice with a similar thesis:

> TELFON SAYS THAT SATAN IN PARADISE LOST IS CLEVER
> [BECAUSE OF WHAT HE] DOES: HE MANIPULATES EVE AND GETS

HER TO EAT FROM THE TREE
HE PRESENTED HIMSELF AS A SERPENT
[BECAUSE OF THE REACTIONS OF] OTHERS: EVE IS FOOLED MANY TIMES BY HIS CLEVERNESS
HOWEVER: HE CONTRADICTS HIMSELF SLIGHTLY WHEN HE TRIES TO GET EVE TO EAT FROM THE TREE

Furthermore, she opted to see a comment on Telfon's notice written by the instructor (known to the students as Snoopy):

SNOOPY: CAN YOU BE MORE SPECIFIC? FOR EXAMPLE, HOW ARE ARGUMENTS CONTRADICTORY? ALSO, IS HE PARALLEL TO EVE IN WANTING TO BE GOD-LIKE? HOW DOES THIS SIMILAR SITUATION REFLECT ON SATAN'S CHARACTER?

This comment gave direction not only to Telfon, the notice-writer, but also to readers of the comment, like Kami. Furthermore, she got support for her ideas from Telfon's work, since Telfon's thesis and evidence are similar to hers. But she also recognized a difference, and this pushed her to analyze and add the following comment on Telfon's notice: 'I agree, Satan is clever, but he must use lies to achieve what he wants.'

When Kami logged on again, she got direct feedback from students' comment on her notice:

HELEN: SATAN TELLS EVE THAT EVE WILL BECOME WISE AS HE HAS FROM EATING THE FRUIT. HE THEN TELLS EVE THAT GOD IS AFRAID OF HER BECOMING LIKE HIM.
ZAPION: TRICKY SEEMS TO BE KIND OF A SOFT WORD FOR SATAN. HOWEVER, IT'S ABSOLUTELY TRUE.

Here Helen pushes Kami's argument along by providing more concrete evidence, and Zapion supports Kami, but makes a criticism about her thesis, too.

Kami went on to write other notices, but her ideas about Satan, along with the comments that others wrote to her, were printed out for her use before the next essay exam. With this printout, she could 'trace' the development of her ideas and use her ideas (and the responses to them) as a starting place for an essay.

The Seeing-Eye Elephant prompts users to verbalize what they've noticed in their reading. Then the Network helps them refine ideas. Seeing other 'notices' and comments on them shows that not everyone has the same reaction to a character in literature. These responses show what needs to be explained and supported in an essay. Also, writing comments on other students' ideas helps sharpen critical ability. And reading comments on one's own work can help show ways to refine ideas.

The program provides a 'skeleton' for introducing conventions in a number of different disciplines. The individual prompts can be edited (by changing the PRINT statements). With the help of a colleague in Art History, Professor Charlotte Stokes, I've modified the Seeing-Eye Elephant Network for use in art appreciation. Here the tutorial asks the following core questions modified for an art application (with a sample student response):

General Format	Particular Application	Student Response
Pick an X.	Choose a work of art.	X = *The Swing* by Fragonard
Create hypothesis: X = Y	X is __Y__. What period or style of art does X illustrate?	The Swing is rococo
Argue that X = Y —regarding type A evidence	Provide evidence to show that X is Y: How does the artist's choice of subject matter show that The Swing is rococo?	love between the sexes; upper class people; sexual permissiveness; free & funloving people; frivolous subject; it is of a particular event
—regarding type B evidence	How does the use of color show that The Swing is rococo?	use of pastels to reinforce subject; pinks & light blues used; soft light
—regarding type C evidence	How does the artist's arrangement of forms show that The Swing is rococo?	human figures are relatively small; landscape surrounding people; man in foreground sneaking a view; unobtrusive pieces of classical sculpture; forms arranged to tell a story
—regarding type D evidence	How does the artist's exploitation of the medium show that The Swing is rococo?	to produce rich colors; to create a very detailed background; to create a work to be sold
—regarding type E evidence	If there are human beings represented, how does the artist's treatment of human forms show that The Swing is rococo?	dressed in contemporary fashions; dressed in aristocratic clothes; they are engaging in risque actions; the people are having fun; idealized poses
Consider conflicting evidence	What evidence shows that The Swing is NOT rococo?	None, Fragonard's style defines rococo

Just as computer programs can aid in memory search and analysis, so too computers can help in research—by linking them to information either too current or too difficult to be searchable through printed bibliographies. For example, a micro can be hooked up to other computers through a modem or acoustic coupler. Then the micro user can contract for use of a database information system through a telecommunications service such as The Source or Compuserve. For a fee, a user can dial up and get the latest Dow Jones information or Associated Press articles on a particular subject.

Furthermore, a number of bibliographic databases are available, not only in the sciences and social sciences, but also in the humanities. For interdisciplinary topics, especially those requiring searches by nonstandard key words, a computerized bibliographic search may be worth the cost.

ORGANIZATION

Computers are least useful, I feel, in arranging information for the audience and purpose intended. Some of this function is performed in the computer programs for invention. For example, one of the TOPOI questions asks the student to divide the topic into three different parts. And SEEN introduces a principle of organization: state a hypothesis and then support with specifics.

But I fear the reification of any organizing strategy—for example, the five-paragraph essay—within an inflexible computer program. Because form becomes a vehicle for content, because content can evolve in much nonformulaic writing, the best the computer can do is help writers discover form and arrangement or make it convenient for them to use notes.

For example, clustering could be accomplished by moving jottings into appropriate groupings. But it seems to me this is more easily accomplished with pencil and paper. Also, some word processing programs have an option to split the screen horizontally so that a writer could simultaneously see notes typed in at the beginning of a text as well as the current latest text. Again, I find pencil and paper more convenient, especially because the split screen halves the amount of text I can use as a prompt to writing of additional text.

WRITING

Word processing programs are useful in the actual writing down of texts primarily because they help writers 'turn off' internal editors. The best writing maxim I've ever heard comes from the poet William Stafford: 'There's no such thing as a writer's block; you just have to lower your standards.' Word processing programs help writers to lower their standards because they know it will then be so easy to raise them again. Word processing programs make insertions, deletions, replacements, and reordering ridiculously simple.

REVISION

Word processing programs, in and of themselves, aid in the process of revision because they allow the writer to try new ideas out easily and neatly, without necessarily losing the original. Furthermore, writers can concentrate more on the ideas when revising, since they do not physically change their operations in the course of revising. That is, they don't pick up a pen or pencil, scissors, and paste; they merely push different keys on the same keyboard they've been typing on. (However, it should be noted that some users never learn to compose or revise at the keyboard.) And since the final printing of the text will not cost the writer much trouble, more time is available for trying out reformulations.

Although word processing aids fluency and discovery of meaning, it may interfere with tight organizing. Speaking from my own experience, I find that I do less outlining beforehand (and stick to it less closely than I used to), so I need to do more careful checking for ordering within a piece of writing. For some writers, the best method is simply to have a draft printed out, work on that—with outlining, or making an issue tree—and then add the revisions to the text. However, for some kinds of writing, a good way to check for overall coherence and shape is to print the first sentences of each paragraph. With the word processing program AppleWriterII this is easily accomplished with one 'Load' command, directing that all sentences, from a carriage return to a period, should be loaded from a pre-existing file.

POLISHING

A number of programs exist which help writers check their prose for coherence, readability, and grammatical correctness. The program Sensible Speller checks for misspelling and allows a writer to add specialized terms to the spelling checker's list of words. Although the program cannot catch misspelling of homophones, writers can be alerted to check their document for any homophone they may have trouble with. The Find command can help them review each occasion when the word has been used.

Programs like Homer (written by Michael Cohen at UCLA) or Workbench (available through Bell Labs for Unix systems) help the writer check various aspects of style—sentence length and variability, use of prepositional phrases, *to be* verbs, passive voice, and certain nominalizations. Other programs, like Grammatik, check usage and suggest modifications.

A way instructors can help students to check for coherence is to do a modified CLOZE test. Using the Find and Replace commands on the word processor, the teacher can replace either key words or transitional words and phrases with blanks. When the 'blanked' version is printed out and tested on readers, the writer can observe the 'inevitability' of word choice (or lack thereof).

SUMMARY

As microcomputers come down in price, word processing programs improve in quality and availability, teachers will face a rare opportunity and challenge for using the instructional potential of computers in their writing classes. Whether used for invention, organizing, writing, revising, or polishing, computers using currently available programs can aid students in their development as writers.

PART III

DELAWARE SUMMER INSTITUTE IN COMPUTER-ASSISTED INSTRUCTION FOR FOREIGN LANGUAGES

EIGHTEEN

Overview of Goals, Methods, and Structure of the Institute

Gerald R. Culley
University of Delaware

Through a grant from the National Endowment for the Humanities, the Department of Languages and Literature and the Office of Computer-Based Instruction at the University of Delaware presented an institute for 30 secondary school foreign language teachers June 28–July 23, 1982.[1] Its purpose was threefold: to train the teachers in techniques of computer lesson design; to teach programming in BASIC on microcomputers; and to do panel reviews of the bulk of the foreign language programs now commercially available for use on microcomputers.

The program announcement was mailed to departments of foreign languages in the public schools and private schools of New York, New Jersey, Pennsylvania, Delaware, Maryland, Virginia, and the District of Columbia. One hundred fifty-three teachers applied, from whom 30 were selected. We wondered at first whether the attraction of 6 hours of graduate credit might have brought us some participants with only token interest in the subject matter; but that cloud of doubt was soon dissipated. Participants faced a very demanding schedule and responded magnificently to it. The spirit of cooperative effort among the 20 boarding participants and the 10 commuters could hardly have been better; and despite a very demanding schedule, only one person withdrew, and that for health reasons.

The commitment to review existing commercially-available microcomputer lessons required us to locate and obtain those lessons. Both activities turned out to be a challenge. The proliferation of software firms, many of them new, small, and ephemeral, has made it very hard just to learn what lessons are in fact available for purchase. Even after finding a listing for a particular program, we had no assurance of obtaining the disk; firms changed address, or name, without warning, and some were only brokers for other suppliers. We eventually did acquire the bulk of what is available, but it was much harder than we expected.

The staff for the institute was drawn from the Department of Languages and from the Office of Computer-Based Instruction, whose professional staff was the source

[1] The author wishes to acknowledge, and to express his appreciation for, a grant of $40,412 from the National Endowment for the Humanities; and for the $10,662 in cost-sharing which the University of Delaware provided. The institute, as described in this and the other papers from this session, was wholly funded by this grant.

of expertise on programming microcomputers and on designing and critiquing instructional computer lessons. The greater part of the day was devoted to classes and workshops. An individual participant would spend half the time in the microcomputer classroom for instruction in programming, and half the time in the study of lesson design techniques. The programming portion developed over the 4 weeks from elementary instruction to individual work on the participant's own instructional lesson. The other portion of the day requires a more chronological explanation.

In the first week, participants reviewed instructional lessons on the PLATO system. Materials were chosen for them which illustrated a range of instructional strategies and goals. The PLATO system was well-suited for this application because of the wide selection of sophisticated programs it can present. The participants were encouraged to make use of lessons that are instructor-editable, so as to familiarize themselves with the flexibility and power of such approaches. During that same week, staff members conducted three seminars in the techniques of lesson design.

The second week saw the beginnings of individual projects, with faculty members consulting with each participant on a design for an instructional lesson. Scripting of those lessons continued through the week, and critiques of the scripts were done at the end of the week.

At this time we also began panel reviews of the commercial lessons that had been acquired. Each review session was led by an expert in lesson design who ran the lessons and moderated discussion of it. Each participant attended at least five such review sessions, with responsibility for writing reviews for two of them. This arrangement guaranteed that a minimum of two written reviews would be generated for each lesson that was included.

The third and fourth weeks went rapidly as the participants worked at programming, revising, and debugging their individual lessons. While there was no requirement to complete these lessons by the end of the institute, many in fact did just that. Others made very substantial progress and were able to display, as we had hoped, some portions of their lessons on the final day of the institute. The products revealed a substantial variety of approaches, with drill and practice, tutorial, quiz, game, and stimulation formats all being represented.

What did we hope to accomplish with the institute? That is a question that has to be taken in two parts. For the teachers who participated, beyond the obvious goal of new skills in programming, we hoped to pass along an excitement about the possibilities of the microcomputer for language instruction, along with some sober awareness of the difficulties. The microcomputer is not a ditto machine; designing lessons is a demanding task with many aspects. Once made fully aware of this fact, we were confident that the teachers would know how to use it; whether in critiquing materials offered for sale in the field, or in continuing to work at lesson development themselves. Those of us who worked on the institute think that the goals were reached, but perhaps the judgment should be left to the participants to make. You will hear from three of them later in this program.

The other audience for which we hoped to accomplish something is the language teaching profession. If foreign language teachers generally can be alerted to the potential of computer-assisted instruction and to the standards of quality which computer lessons should meet, we will be well rewarded. We believe that the teachers who took part in the institute will be a part of this educational effort as they talk with colleagues and participate in workshops and inservice programs. It is exciting to note that several of them already report that they have been asked to organize just such activities in their respective areas. They have acquired a new area of expertise, and their own colleagues want to know about it.

Another part of the educational effort will be the volume of panel reviews which is now being edited. It should help teachers and administrators to select the best microcomputer lessons for use in their language classes. The terms of the grant from the NEH require us to publish that volume and make it available to interested persons without charge so long as the supply lasts.

NINETEEN

Developing 'Smart' Lessons

Gerald R. Culley
University of Delaware

Regardless of the state of affairs in research centers, it is clear that America discovered computers this year. The average man, long indifferent to, or intimidated by, the wonders of microcircuits, logic gates, and random access memory, came alive this year. It began in the surreal environment of the video arcade, where the air pulsed with bleeps, zaps, and wukka-wukkas. A commercial avalanche called Atari carried those same weird sounds into a million living rooms. Then, before we knew it, that average, nontechnical man was scanning the ads for Radio Shack and Computerland and mumbling under his breath about software and memory size. He had discovered computers, or, to be precise, microcomputers.

That new awareness will ultimately change our society in many ways. Among these will be a growing demand for the use of microcomputers in the schools; despite their financial woes, school districts will find money to buy the little machines. Programming classes, computer literacy, and computer-assisted instruction will become firmly established in the curriculum.

This much, I believe, can be predicted with confidence. The machines will soon be in the schools in much greater numbers than today. Language teachers will be invited to order diskettes to run in connection with their classes in French, Spanish, Latin, or German. What will they choose?

The experience of acquiring and reviewing microcomputer language lessons for this past summer's institute has left me concerned about this question. Many of the diskettes now on the market are worthless for instruction. Some are incoherently presented; others defy the basic principles of pedagogy; and many contain serious inaccuracies. Even the lessons that escape these deficiencies tend to be lifeless, boring drills. Students will find them little help, once the novelty wears off.

There is, however, another approach to computer instruction for foreign languages. It involves what I call 'smart' lessons. First, let me issue a disclaimer: I am not speaking here of artificial intelligence. AI applications to language instruction are possible and, I think, inevitable: but the microcomputers now in the public schools lack the memory and processing power to deal with such advanced and complex techniques, and so will any machines the schools are likely to acquire in the near future. What I am proposing is not artificial intelligence; but in some ways it may look like that to the student.

A 'smart' lesson is one that is in some sense capable of generating its own exercises and of understanding a student's typed responses. Neither of these is quite so difficult as it may seem at first, and there need not be any recourse to AI techniques. The basic requirement is a set of routines that can inflect the variable parts of speech in the target language. Given a set of such routines, a wide range of capability is opened up to the lesson designer.

Let me illustrate this from a series of Latin lessons now in use on the University's PLATO system. Although this is a large mainframe system, the materials are appropriate to illustrate my point; the university is now in the process of converting these lessons to BASIC for use on microcomputers, and, if everything goes as we hope, diskettes carrying this series of lessons will be available for use in the schools in about 18 months.

The first advantage of a 'smart' lesson is that it can generate an almost limitless number of exercise items from a very small database. Take the example of Cursus Honorum, a Latin verb lesson in game format. It presents a succession of verb challenges to the student, who works against a timer to type each one in turn. For example, the computer may display the principle parts of the verb *paro* and call for the third person plural, future active indicative. The student would havc to type *parabunt*. A conventional lesson would have to have all of the items in the challenge written into the code by the programmer, along with the correct answer, and every other exercise item would have to be done in the same way. To get any significant number of exercises would require a very large program. Cursus Honorum, however, has no answers stored in it at all, nor any list of grammatical challenges. It uses a small database of verbs: 100 verbs in all, with three stems for each, or 300 items. Each verb can be fully conjugated by the program to produce 281 forms, so the potential number of individual questions and answers is nearly 30,000. An added benefit comes in the flexibility this permits. Students may elect to practice only those items they want or need at a given session, turning on only the active voice, or limiting themselves to subjunctive forms. The computer will obediently present challenges to them from within the limits they have set, choosing specific items at random; and it will do this for as long as the users like. They may drop out of the game at any point and reset their parameters to include more conjugations in the pool from which their verbs are drawn, or to include another tense, varying the scope and skill level at will. In fact, this same lesson may be used all year long at the college level, or for two years in high school Latin classes. Its skill level can be adjusted to keep it challenging week after week. One lesson, then, does the work of many—a saving in soft ware costs that administrators will appreciate.

The next advantage of 'smart' lessons is their ability to accept content different from that supplied by the lesson designer. A lesson that can conjugate verbs will not care which verbs it has to work with. Cursus Honorum has an editing feature that permits instructors with no knowledge of programming techniques to insert verbs of their own choosing into the database. The process is a very simple and rapid one. Verbs are typed in groups—a set of first conjugation verbs, a set of second conjugation, and so on. Changes and corrections can be made at any time. Apart from being sure that they have their verbs in the right conjugations and take care to type the principal parts accurately, instructors need no special effort or knowledge. The computer will produce the correct verb forms as they are needed.

The third advantage of a 'smart' lesson is its ability to comment 'intelligently' on student errors. Consider here another Latin verb lesson, a diagnostic and remedial quiz called Verb Factory. It too uses the conjugating routine, as Cursus Honorum does, to produce the answer to a particular question; but it also uses that routine to analyze what the student has typed. There are four levels of diagnostics performed on an incorrect student response. First, the machine checks to see if the verb stem is correct. If so, it checks for the presence of the stem vowel and tense/mood sign. If the student calls for it, the third level of analysis is done: conjugate the verb fully and check each form against the one the student typed. If the typed form is in fact a form of the verb under consideration, the routine will find it and identify it. Finally, a fourth level is available for students who are baffled. That is a step by step grammatical analysis of the question, with the student being shown the answer one portion at a time, until he or she understands. Seen as a flow chart, this analytical process is rather forbidding. An example will be more helpful.

Let's say the English cue was *she was throwing;* the correct response would then be *iaciebat.* If the first attempt were something afield, the routine would look for the right answer, not find it, and then look for just the stem, *iac.* Not finding that, it would remark that the stem is wrong, and a new try would be needed. Perhaps the new attempt would be *iacit.* The machine would acknowledge the presence of the stem and, if desired, look further and find the tense/mood sign is wrong. Then suppose we get a third try: *iacebas.* This is better, but the routine will pick up a specific error there; failure to see that third conjugation *io* verbs have *ie,* not just *e,* before the *ba* of the imperfect tense. There are eight such specific common errors that can be caught in this way. If we have a very slow student, his or her next try may be only a little better: *iaciebas.* Now the first two elements are fine, but the personal ending is wrong; and he or she will be told so.

Sometimes, though, a student becomes convinced that he or she has the right answer and the computer just doesn't want to accept it. In that event, he or she presses a key for a verb scan—the third diagnostic level. The computer finds that his or her response was in fact the second person singular, imperfect tense. It will highlight *second* because that is the portion that is incorect.

There was one more level of diagnostics available. A completely puzzled student presses a key labelled HELP and is then led through a series of questions about the form he or she is trying to produce: what mood is it? what tense? and so on. When he or she correctly identifies tense and mood, the tense/mood sign is displayed and added to the stem that is already there on the screen. If the student needs more help, he or she continues the sequence. More leading questions elicit the person and number and the voice of the target word, at which point the personal ending is added to the form to complete it. This fourth level of diagnostics does not have to be pursued to the end, however. A student can stop at any point and apply his or her flash of insight to typing the correct answer.

Now, of course, no programmer could expect to code in so many commands and helps for any one question, even if he or she could anticipate them. These levels of help are available because the computer can analyze the typed form along grammatical lines, morpheme by morpheme, and react appropriately to what it finds. Within these very narrow limits, it 'understands' what the student typed.

There is another dividend from a 'smart' lesson: if it knows which kinds of errors a student is making, it can give individualized help by including more questions with the problem element in them. Review can be personally tailored for a student even as he or she sits at the terminal. For example, if a student running Cursus Honorum has missed a third person plural imperfect passive indicative of a third conjugation verb, the computer could bring back that particular form for him or her to do again; that is a common procedure in computer-assisted instruction. But since he or she saw that item so recently, he or she may just remember the question and the answer without yet understanding them. Better to do what a 'smart' lesson can do: show him or her another third person plural imperfect passive indicative of some different third conjugation verb. Then he or she will have to deal with the logical category, not the item; and real learning is much more likely to occur.

Yet one more advantage that derives from this approach can be noted in passing. A 'smart' lesson can collect data on student errors. These data will not be on just the specific errors themselves, but on the categories. In the most recent instance, the machine would record an error in the third person plural imperfect passive indicative, third conjugation. If students' errors cluster in particular grammatical categories, it will be obvious that more emphasis, or a different approach, is needed at that point. Thus a lesson of this kind can be used to improve the classroom treatment of the material as well, or, a little incestuously, to improve itself.

The range of applications to which these routines can be put is considerable; once the computer knows how to decline nouns, one can use that routine to drive many different formats. Here is a format that makes use of routines that inflect all of the variable parts of speech in Latin—nouns, pronouns, adjectives, and verbs. It is called Artifex Verborum 'Word Builder.' This puts the computer to work on one of the most traditional of exercises for language students: old-fashioned parsing of words in context. The student chooses a set of exercises from an index and is shown a Latin sentence. An arrow points to the first word, and below the sentence there are eight touch-sensitive boxes displayed, one labelled box for each part of speech. If the student touches the wrong one, the word *no* is flashed in that box. When he or she touches the correct one, more boxes appear below that first row. Their number and arrangement depend on the part of speech being treated. In the case of a verb, there are 17—one for each of the six tenses, plus three for person, two for number, and so on. The student touches boxes to parse the verb. Now, here, unlike in the first level of identification, the computer will accept any choice that is made. When the student has finished and is satisfied with his or her choices, he or she signals that fact to the computer, which then checks his or her work. If the word is properly parsed, that word is replotted in inverse mode on the screen, and he or she proceeds to the next word; but if it is not, the computer takes the grammatical elements the student provided, inflects the word according to those specifications, and displays the result just beneath the target form. In effect the student is told what a tutor might tell him or her: 'No, if this word were present tense, it would be *petit,* not *petet* as it is.'

Now, to provide this kind of feedback, the program obviously has to be able to produce millions of specific forms. The result, though, is that it is able to respond in a unique and precise way to errors, and offer much the same kind of help that a living tutor does.

You will recall that 'smart' lessons should be able to handle vocabulary other than what the lesson author first put into them. Here is an example of that capability. When instructors run Artifex Verborum, they can have the opportunity to change the exercises in it. The editing facility will display each sentence in turn for them. When they want to change something, they press the EDIT key, and can then edit any word or words in the sentence. The computer displays all that it knows about each word in turn. To take the same verb from the last illustration, *petet:* the computer will show that it is a verb; that its stem is *pete;* that it is third person singular, future active indicative, third conjugation, the verb of the main clause in its sentence. Any of these items can be changed at will. Suppose they want to change the verb to plural and make it imperfect tense. They touch the item labelled 'number', using the same touch-sensitive feature the students used, and that item is cleared so that they can input 'plural' there. When they do this, the computer immediately re-inflects the verb to incorporate that change; now it reads *petent.* Next the instructors touch 'tense', and the word 'future' is cleared so that they can input any of the six tenses at will. Once they have inserted 'imperfect' here, the verb form is inflected again to embody that choice: *petebant.*

You will note that all of this has been accomplished without any need for the instructors to write any computer code, or for that matter, even see any. And in the same way, the instructors could change the English meaning as stored, or add or delete sentences or entire exercises, change section headings, make in fact any modifications they might like. This is one of the other advantages of a 'smart' lesson: it can be made very easy to change. By entering one sentence in the format just described, the instructors provide the computer with raw material that it can process into hundreds of different inflected forms, each one to be produced only if a specific student makes a specific parsing error.

As we all know, research is being conducted in artificial intelligence systems at many facilities around the country. One day we will be able to incorporate these very sophisticated techniques into CAI, but it will be quite some time before there are machines in the public schools that can support such applications. Until then, we need not be limited to lockstep drill formats with no possible feedback for a student other than 'right' or 'no, try again'. It is possible to teach microcomputers how to recognize, within limits, student-typed input, and act on it. We can't yet have lessons that are truly intelligent, but we can have lessons that are 'smart.'

---

[1] This paper was made possible through a grant from the National Endowment for the Humanities. The author wishes to express his thanks to the Endowment for its support.

TWENTY

Do Micro-Computers Make Sense? Can I Use Them Without Getting Hurt? .... Or Is the Computer My Friend?

Richard C. Ten Eyck
High Point Regional High School
Sussex, NJ

Several years ago at an inservice day at our school, the speaker mentioned that, since we, as teachers, possessed Bachelor's degrees of some kind, we belonged to a relatively elite group of people. He then asked how many on the staff possessed degrees beyong the Bachelor's level. When a fairly substantial number raised their hands, he indicated that THOSE people belonged to an even SMALLER group of people in the country, or, in other words, they were abnormal.

Well, if those people on our staff who possessed Master's degrees are abnormal, one can barely imagine how those of us who possess such degrees AND teach foreign languages should be described. Maybe, since the entire country seems caught up in the computer craze, we can achieve a certain sense of acceptance by normal folks if we, too, jump on the computer bandwagon.

Seeking normalcy, this past July a group of us participated in the Summer Institute in Computer Based Education for Foreign Languages. The Organizers of the SICBE-FL created an atmosphere that we abnormal types pray will take place in our schools and classrooms. During the institute, I worked harder and learned more than I have in any formal program in my academic career. Not only that, but I enjoyed it. I enjoyed working until the early hours of the morning, learned to live with, if not love, the frustrations of a machine that simply could not understand my frequently feeble attempts to communicate my plans for the ultimate foreign language program, and even passed up nightly trips to the local oases.

This is more than a confession of an abnormal foreign language teacher, however. It is, in capsule form, a summary of the promise and problems in the use of computers for foreign language instruction. In short, I was hooked, I learned, I became frustrated and, as time went on, increasingly antisocial.

Let me go back a bit. It is my understanding that the National Endowment for the Humanities made this Institute possible in order to assess the viability of microcomputer use for the teaching of foreign languages. It seems only fair, then, that I should devote at least part of my presentation to that point: Does the use of computers make sense, and can they be used successfully in the teaching of foreign languages?

For those of you who would like to get on to thinking about other things, the answer to the first half of the question is a qualified 'yes.' The answer to the second half is . . . I don't know. Like most things, however, the answer isn't quite that simple, and a bit more time will yield some pertinent (I hope) observations.

The answer to the questions is closely related to the availability of good courseware or, as it was recently called, 'teachware.' Thus, an examination of the software problem may provide us with a part of the answer. One of the criteria which we were told to use in evaluating computer software during the institute is: Is it appropriate for computer use?

Do you want to drill the present tense endings? Would you like more time to devote to each student? Would you like each student to have individual and immediate feedback about the correctness of the answer? Well, computers were designed to repeat certain tasks endlessly. I guess computers are the answer, you say. But do you want the students to be able to hear the spoken language? Do you want them to be able to use the language conversationally? Do you want them to understand the transactional implications of language? Ah well, so much for computers! You see, the answer isn't quite so clear.

Another criteria used to evaluate software is: Does the computer do this better than any other (read cheaper) device I can use, including myself? I know of no other device that provides immediate, individualized, perhaps even corrective feedback to students in drill situations. On the other hand, I know of nothing better equipped to provide meaningful conversational experience than another human. In an era when we are finally recognizing the importance of learning languages as a tool for communication, we must be careful not to overemphasize repetitive drill programs just because they are easy to purchase or program.

Perhaps my very glib 'I don't know' wasn't quite fair. I do know. Computers CAN be used effectively in the teaching of foreign languages, provided we match the machine with the task to be accomplished.

If the use of one machine makes sense, does the use of more machines make more sense? My experience here at the University, and at home, indicates that the answer depends upon the resources available. Can I make use of one or two machines? You bet. Given the almost magical attraction that we, as a nation, have to computers and video games, most kids would even STUDY for the chance to use our microcomputers. This is a powerful bargaining tool. Two kids who need extra drill, one kid who needs a little extra to keep him or her interested, one or two who would like to go on to something different . . . can the machine do this better than I can? I think so. Could I use a lab full of machines? Now and then, if I could overcome the same problems that plagued me in the language lab, i.e., scheduling classes, mechanical breakdowns, poor quality tape programs, etc. Would I like to be the one who recommends the installation of a microcomputer lab for the instruction of foreign languages? Not at this time. Am I against the use of the microcomputer in foreign language instruction? I hope you don't believe that. There are some things I do in teaching German that can be better done with the computer than in any way I can think of.

This conclusion brings me to the second part of my presentation: How do I use the computer without getting hurt? I think most of us still view the computer in relatively simplistic terms. We assume that only programmers really communicate effectively with the machine, or that all we have to do is plug it in and watch it teach. Somewhere in between, there lies a whole world of computer use that the average teacher can find helpful.

I would like to dwell then on various levels of teacher involvement and the costs to the teacher for each level. After the presentation, I hope you'll have time to view one or more of the programs which were developed under our system.

It seems to me that there are a limited number of ways that teachers can become involved with computers:

1. Buying and using commercially prepared software. In order to use this software, we must be familiar with the machine which we are to use and the software which has been purchased. This level of involvement requires very little experience with computers. Such involvement does require from us enough knowledge of software design to be an intelligent consumer. A system for program evaluation should be developed and used. My limited experience tells me that, without some type of inservice training in program design and evaluation, we will probably purchase a substantial amount of useless software.

2. Using an authoring program. Such programs are designed for teachers with little or no previous background in computer programming. Using such programs, the teacher designs lessons by responding to prompts within the program. In many such programs, the prompts are in English. Examples of such programs are PILOT, AUTHOR, and CAIWARE, among others. I believe that for most teachers this is the most appropriate level of involvement. Given a good authoring program, the teacher can create lesson which incorporate tutorials, testing, graphics, lesson scheduling, and student record management. (If you are interested in such authoring programs, you might like to see the demonstration lessons created using CAIWARE-3D after these presentations are completed.)

3. Using student programmers to encode programs which are teacher designed. Such involvement provides an intermediate step between the use of the authoring program and encoding the program design yourself. We have found that our students are very interested in learning programming. They are not overly concerned with what they are programming as long as they have the opportunity to use the machines and gain experience. Difficulties involvement in this approach relate to the need to coordinate the time and activities for more than one person. Each of the programs that I am demonstrating today have been coded, at least partially, by students.

4. Designing and programming the lessons yourself. After the experience of the Institute, I am afraid that the average teacher simply does not have the time necessary to master BASIC (or other programming languages), design the lessons, and then write and debug the code for each lesson. This is not to say that some of us will not become adequate programmers, but, except in unusual circumstances, most of us might better spend our time learning good program design techniques and insuring that the programs written by others are worth using.

I suspect that any good nitpicker can find several other combinations of teacher involvement to further complicate the issue, but I think that the above categories give most of us a workable outline of the choices available to us. I have deliberately omitted, for example, the use of word processing, grade keeping, and record keeping programs. These represent a legitimate and helpful use of the machine, and I would hope you would explore them. They have made my life much easier, but they are far enough outside the scope of instruction for most teachers that I chose not to address their use here. (I would be glad, however, to discuss our use of word processors to help with the production of student materials in the demonstration segment of the symposium.)

In conclusion, I would like to speak a moment on the last section of my topic . . . Is the computer my friend? I hope that you realize that this is a critical question, perhaps the MOST critical question. By way of amplification, I would like to recount an interesting dynamic that occurred during the summer institute. After the initial discomfort of meeting new people was overcome, the evening meal became quite a social event. People laughed, carried on, and stretched the mealtime to an hour and often longer. Evenings were devoted to work; most of you won't imagine how much work.

As the institute progressed and each of us began work on the programming of our individual design masterworks, a change took place in the evening meal. The moods were no longer group moods, but rather individual reactions to the problems encountered with one's own programming experiences; people began to eat more quickly, talk less, and rush back to the 'Orchard' (the Apple computer lab). I even stopped thinking about late night thirst. Please don't misunderstand me . . . conviviality wasn't replaced with hostility, but the social aspect of the institute which had been so pleasant during the first 2 weeks was replaced with an increased dedication to task completion. Was this unpleasant? Not at all, at least not that we noticed.

In an era characterized by the lack of quality in human interaction and relationships, I don't believe that we wish to achieve the type of work accomplished during the institute if we cannot teach the importance of human relationships, and meaningful communication along with it. It is my hope that, by intelligently examining the uses of computers in the teaching of foreign languages, we can recognize the machine for the tremendous tool that it can be for us in our classrooms. Can I use the machine in my classroom? Most certainly! Will I get hurt? Not if I can match the use of the machine to the right task and my interests and abilities. Will the machine be my friend? . . . Do you really want it to be?

TWENTY-ONE

'It Makes You Want to Learn'

Helen St. Louis
Colton-Pierrepont Central School
Colton, New York

I'm pleased to have this opportunity to discuss computer-assisted instruction, because I believe that the computer has great potential for assisting our students in their learning. This opinion was reinforced not long ago when I was discussing a new computer lesson with some students. Imagine how gratified I was to hear one of them say, 'It makes you want to learn'. What more can a teacher ask, and what better justification for any teaching tool? With that in mind, I would like to share some of the ideas from and results of the University of Delaware Summer Institute in Computer-Based Instruction in Foreign Languages.

One year ago today, I had never set eyes on a computer. I would not have had any idea that I would be capable of writing a computer program. I thought that it involved a lot of math, which had always been one of my weak points. Today I am here to speak about a computer-assisted instruction (CAI) lesson that I designed and programmed and am using in my classes. Even though it took a lot of help to program the lesson, that is quite a jump in 1 year, which shows that the computer is not as frightening as many of us had thought.

Last winter, my school offered an inservice course about computers, and I signed up because computers are continually becoming more important to our society. In the beginning, I didn't have any idea of using the computers with the students. After the first class, however, I already had ideas for classroom possibilities. By the time I received the flier about an institute in computer-based instruction in the foreign languages, I was eager for more.

One of the objectives of the institute was to have each participant design and begin to program a lesson. To do that, we needed ideas. These were provided by class lectures and demonstrations, but particularly by viewing CAI lessons in use here at the University of Delaware on the PLATO mainframe computer.

The choice of a lesson subject brought up the controversy between simulation lessons and drill and practice. A lesson that simulates an actual situation—a conversation, for example—and forces the student to actively generate language, is a higher level activity than drill and practice, for both the student and the computer. It is, however, more difficult to program. While most of the participants agreed that simulation is excellent, many decided to do drill and practice lessons as our first attempts, both because of easier programming and because of the opinion that, if the students must do drill and practice sometime, why not do it on the computer?

Having decided to do a drill and practice lesson, I considered three areas in which the students need help and practice: vocabulary, object pronouns, and verbs. After some discussion with Dr. Jerry Culley, I decided on a verb drill because it would meet three criteria that I had set up: the lesson could be used for students at all levels, it could be used throughout the year, and at least a bare-bones lesson could be ready for use in September. My ambitious idea was that I would let the students choose what regular or irregular verbs they wanted to review and what tense/mood they wanted to study. After conferring with Dr. George Mulford and finding that a full-time programmer would require a year to complete that lesson, I cut back to just the present tense of the 20 irregular verbs presented in our text.

In addition to the simulation versus drill and practice controversy, another recurring topic of discussion at the institute was answer judging. It is not difficult to have the computer simply judge whether or not an answer is correct, even down to the spaces and punctuation. To give the student more information about a wrong answer is both more involved and more helpful to the student. This is particularly true in a lesson, where student mistakes result from confusion between two similar answers, as is often the case in a verb drill. It would be helpful to have the lesson tell the student if he or she had the wrong form of the right verb, or the right form of the wrong verb. For an example in English, if the student were asked for the *she* form of the verb *to be,* and said *she are,* he or she would be told that *are* is the form for *you.* If, on the other hand, he or she said *she has,* he or she would be told that *has* is the form for the verb *to have.* Since these were the kinds of often-repeated errors that I wanted to correct, when we got this part of the lesson to work, I felt that the lesson was essentially complete.

Many extras can be put in a basic lesson to make it more effective. I was able to add several before the end of the institute: allowing the students to choose which verbs to study, or to study all of those up to a certain chapter in the text; immediately repeating a question which had been answered incorrectly, and giving the correct answer if it were missed again; and making the entire conjugation available after a wrong answer, if the student chose to see it.

Near the end of the institute, we were working on another addition which was a third important concept often discussed: a review schedule for questions that were missed. It was reasoned that a student would better learn a difficult form which he or she had gotten wrong, if it were repeated several times, interspersed among new questions. I have not yet perfected this review schedule.

This brings us to what happened after the institute. The directors of the institute wanted to create enlightened consumers, and certainly succeeded in that. They also hoped that some of us would go on to design and some to program more lessons. I am sure that some of the participants will. Others, however, as well as myself, have probably found a problem in lack of local support and aid after returning home. The computer teacher at my school, for example, is helpful but busy, and some of the things that I want to do with my program are beyond the level of my skills. As more people, including our own students, become more proficient in programming, more help will be available.

My lesson has changed, however. Due to all the help available at the institute, a workable lesson was ready for the students this fall. Therefore, I was able to test it, observe the students, and get their reactions. This is one necessary step that we could not do at the institute. I enjoyed watching the students make the anticipated mistakes and have those mistakes explained to them. We also discovered some unanticipated advantages and disadvantages. Several changes resulted: adding one example from each group of regular verbs to the original list of only irregular verbs, past participles as another verb form, and a final review of all of the questions which had been answered incorrectly.

The lesson will be further improved by making the conjugation available at any time—not just after wrong answers—by showing a running tally and percentage of correct answers to give the student a better idea of how well he or she is doing, and by making the computer friendly (by calling the student by name, for example).

I observed that, many times, even though the student was guessing, he or she guessed the right answer. Right now, that question would be eliminated from the rotation because it was answered correctly, even though the student needs more review of it. The lesson will bc changed to give the student the option of leaving that question in the list, if he or she wants it repeated for further practice.

One weakness in the lesson is the fact that the student could answer questions correctly without knowing what any of the verbs mean. Eventually, the lesson will have a fill-in-the-blank sentence for each question, followed by a choice of three infinitives. The student will have to choose the correct infinitive and then put the correct form in the blank.

The ultimate ambition for this lesson is to add a third dimension and include, not just one tense, but the imperfect, future, and conditional. Because of stem changes and spelling similarities, these three are difficult and confusing.

The problem with a computer program seems to be that the programmer is never satisfied. There is always at least one more addition or improvement to make. That is one of the reasons why it is so challenging.

Before I conclude, I have two comments about CAI in general. The first involves the enlightened consumers to which I referred earlier. At the institute, we viewed all of the commercial foreign language lessons that the organizers were able to gather. To say that we were disappointed is an understatement. Only a couple of dozen lessons are available, and most, for one reason or another, are ineffective teaching tools. I see several possible steps to improve the materials available to us. First of all, we need education, not just on the computers themselves, but on what makes a good CAI lesson. This would improve the quality of the materials being produced by teachers and students in the schools, and help teachers make better choices of what to buy. Second, teachers and students who produce good lessons should get them published. If you could see some of the materials that we viewed last summer, you would see that no one needs to be shy about presenting his material. Thirdly, we need to let publishers know what we think of their lessons. And last of all, our journals need to publish critiques of new lessons as they become available.

The second comment is really a question. Should we buy poor materials now or wait for higher quality lessons? I said earlier that the computer is effective because of its motivation—that it makes the students want to learn. Novelty is the motivation now, even for poor lessons, so we might ask, 'Why not take advantage of it now?' But in a few years, when our students have been raised with computers and the novelty has started to wear off, we will need imaginative and challenging lessons to maintain that motivation. We need to start now to apply the same standards that we apply to other materials and teaching tools, or publishers will not be encouraged to improve the quality of their lessons. If I intend to buy only one of the French lessons which I saw this summer, it is because, in my opinion, a good ditto is better than a poor CAI lesson.

In summary, when we went home from the institute, we took with us a phenomenal amount of knowledge, and we had had a terrific time gaining it. Often, after classes, we would hurry back for a quick dinner and then return to the computer room to continue working into the evening. It was a challenge—like a giant puzzle. I mentioned earlier the student comment that the computer 'makes you want to learn'. Last summer I found out that it not only makes the students want to learn, it also makes the teachers want to learn.

TWENTY-TWO

The 1982 Summer Institute in Computer-Based Education for Foreign Languages: Branching Out

Danea A. Caskey
Baltimore County Public Schools

Last Spring, I told a faculty member at my school that I was planning to take a computer course. He said, 'What for? You're not going to teach math, are you?' When computers are mentioned, most teachers think of complicated calculations, class lists, and incredibly inaccurate bank account statements. In Baltimore County, the computer has been the property of the Math and Business Education teachers, Child Accounting, and the assistant principal in charge of scheduling and grade reporting. Only recently have more and more teachers from varying subject areas become interested in computers in the classroom.

I became convinced that there were other nonmath educators who were interested in finding out more about the ramifications of computer technology for education when I found in my mailbox a brochure that described an institute in computer-based education for foreign language teachers. It was an opportunity that I simply could not pass up.

When I found myself here at Delaware this past June, I was not completely certain of what to expect. I was not sure that I could or even should attempt to enter the computer domain that had been so long dominated by the mathematicians and those in the world of business. As I looked around that first day of the institute, I was comforted to notice that there were at least 30 other people who seemed to feel that secondary school teachers outside of the department of Mathematics or Business Education most definitely should be involved in bringing the technology to the classroom.

I would wager to say that none of us, not even Jerry Culley or George Mulford, was prepared for the magnitude of energy and excitement that was created as we became more and more confident about our ability to program, and even critique, the software of programmers a great deal more skillful than ourselves. The confidence most of us began to feel was a result of the fine instruction that we received at the hands of such people as Carl Gill and Pat Sine, our programming mentors; members of the Office of Computer-Based Instruction; and of course, Jerry Culley and George Mulford. The excitement and energy was the result of the enthusiastic and truly professional people who participated in the institute. When Jerry and

George planned the Summer Institute, it was because they felt that they had learned something about computer-based education by experiencing it first-hand in their own classrooms, and wanted to share it. That spirit of sharing was a characteristic of the institute also. We swapped programs or subroutines that we found particularly useful; we made contacts with software companies who were interested in foreign language materials; and many of us became even more excited about computers in the foreign language classroom when we could review all of the available software in the field and critique it with the assistance of design analysts. With all of these experiences behind us, many of us went back to our school districts inspired with ideas for implementing some kind of computer-based education in our schools, designing and even programming CAI (Computer-Assisted Instruction) materials for publication, or for securing financial support for increasing the availability of computers for teachers and eventually, for students. One of the fringe benefits of my Summer Institute experience was the new contacts I have made. When you walk around with a handful of floppy disks, you do look conspicuous. People began to ask questions. And when they did, I discovered that in my own school were several computer users who were applying the technology for classroom management only and had not had time nor opportunity to participate in the kind of experience the Summer Institute provided. In addition, I found that many other teachers were interested in learning about the various uses of the computer. The secretaries wanted to learn how to operate the computer that our principal had recently purchased to run our attendance program, and to use the word processor to help with correspondance. Our nurse wanted to find out what kinds of programs were available to help with her record-keeping. Faculty members who had taken a course years ago or were presently enrolled in a course that was unsatisfactory wanted a more personal approach to computing that might be custom-tailored to their particular needs. As a result, my principal and I are planning to offer an inservice course with computer literacy, word processing, and programming components. I mention the involvement of my principal in what I have been doing because the support of immediate superiors is extremely useful when you are trying to gain access to equipment and programs. Since July, I have spoken more often with my supervisor than I had in 10 years of teaching. Since he has also been bitten by the computer bug, he has been a valuable source of information and an invaluable source of support for bringing computer-based education to the foreign language students of Baltimore County. Presently, the Office of Foreign Languages in our county is offering the same introductory course that I took last year. As a result of my experiences at Delaware, I will be teaching the intermediate programming inservice course to be offered in the Spring to foreign language teachers. In order to prepare materials for that course and to experiment with various programs that might be useful to the teachers with whom I will be working, I have made it my business to find out who has a computer in our school and who would be willing to share it. One of the most recurrent problems for those not in the Departments of Mathematics or Business Education has been the unavailability of hardware. Many foreign language teachers have been known to say that merely being persistent in requesting access to computers in their schools is not enough. In many cases, department heads in Mathematics and Business Education tend to question the capabilities of anyone outside of their departments unless you can drop a few terms like RAM, ROM, or BOOT. Once you have gained their confidence, access to a computer can be as simple as committing yourself to countless after-school hours in the math lab. I have been lucky. My supervisor knew of my plans for the inservice course and my need for a computer. So, he managed to get one for me to use. In fact, I prepared my remarks today using a word processing program and that computer. Not such a great feat, you say? For someone who, 7 months ago, thought that a floppy disk was a back problem, it was, as George Mulford would put it, a 'nontrivial task.' Have I been sequestering myself at home every evening, working on projects for my local school inservice or for the foreign language inservice course? Definitely not! I made a few arrangements with the school librarian, checked with my principal, located a brief yet imaginative Apple (TM) tutorial suitable for students, and put together some commercially prepared software, namely *Spanish Hangman,*[1] and *The Linguist.*[2] I used 'The Translator' portion of *The Linguist* and programmed a word set that gave students practice in writing the present tense of stem-changing Spanish verbs, or writing the personal pronoun and infinitive for the verb form presented. When I mentioned to my Spanish II classes the possibility of using a computer in class, there was a great deal of interest. Some of them talked about computers they had seen or used. One even brought in some information on the new Atari (TM) 5200. For the first class session using the computer, we were scheduled to use the library. Since I had a class immediately before my Spanish class and I could not get to the library right away, I arranged with one of the librarians to start up the computer with some running messages for the class using the program *Marquee*. I must mention that the librarian was delighted to show what she knew about the computer. I anticipate that she will be an excellent candidate for the local school inservice. The messages that I left for my class were designed to show the friendly side of the computer. I wrote things such as 'Please take a seat', 'You will need a sheet of paper and a pen or pencil,' and 'I saw what you did!' The students' reactions were extremely encouraging. As we worked through the tutorial, I watched as students discovered that same excitement I had felt when the computer first called ME by name. The foreign language programs the students worked with were of the 'drill and practice' and 'game' types. They were fairly simple in design and need much improvement if they are to meet the criteria of good CAI lessons. And yet the students were fascinated with a machine that could speak a foreign language and communicate with them. How long they will be held by the novelty of this mode of instruction, and whether it is just the novelty that holds them, I do not know yet. I do know that I want to continue to design and program. I have already enrolled in an advanced programming course at my local community college. If the institute did nothing else, it taught us to do what we can with what we know. The ability to evaluate, select, and

---

[1] *Spanish Hangman,* diskette for Apple II. George Earl, San Antonio, TX, 1980.

[2] *The Linguist,* diskette for Apple II (48#K). Synergistic Software, Bellevue, WA, 1981.

effectively use commercially-prepared software was important for those of us who were not particularly brilliant programmers. Knowing just what constitutes good CAI materials was a worthwhile lesson. But also, the Institute served to whet our appetites even more. Jerry, George, and all of the others involved in the institute know how much more there is to learn. In the field of computer technology, the new and unheard-of quickly becomes commonplace. If the more conservative forces in education can stand on the sidelines and accuse us of moving too quickly into so rapidly changing a field, then those of us who are convinced of the value of computers in education must counter by saying that, if there is not presently available the kind of quality software good teaching requires, then it is up to us as teachers to learn all we can and provide that kind of software as new advancements come around the bend. I want to thank Dr. Culley and Dr. Mulford for giving me the opportunity to participate in such a worthwhile experience. I hope that I can in some way share with my students and fellow language teachers the best things that computer-based education has to offer.

Author Index

Italics indicate bibliographic citations

Subject Index